About the Author

James R. Lewis has contributed to the *New Age Almanac, Religious Leaders of America,* and *The Churches Speak* series and is author of *The Astrology Encyclopedia* as well as two forthcoming titles: *The Dream Encyclopedia* and *The Almanac of Magick, Neopagan Witchcraft, Goddess Religions, and Satanism.*

Professor Lewis is a world recognized authority on non-traditional religious movements, and is the editor of the only academic journal dedicated to alternative religions. He is currently chairman of the Department of Religious Studies at the World University of America.

ENCYCLOPEDIA OF

Afterlife Beliefs and Phenomena

ENCYCLOPEDIA OF

Afterlife Beliefs and Phenomena

James R. Lewis

Foreword by Raymond Moody

Gale Research Inc.

DETROIT WASHINGTON, D.C. LONDON

James R. Lewis
Gale Research Inc. Staff

Peg Bessette, Kelle Sisung Developmental Editors; **Christine Nasso,** Acquisitions Editor; **Lawrence W. Baker,** Managing Editor

Mary Beth Trimper, Production Director; **Evi Seoud,** Assistant Production Manager; **Shanna Philpott Heilveil,** Production Assistant

Cynthia Baldwin, Art Director; **Barbara J. Yarrow,** Graphic Services Supervisor; **Mary Krzewinski,** Cover Designer;
Willie F. Mathis, Camera Operator

Benita L. Spight, Data Entry Services Manager; **Gwendolyn S. Tucker,** Data Entry Coordinator; **Nancy K. Sheridan,** Data Entry Associate

Library of Congress Cataloging-in-Publication Data

Lewis, James R.
Encyclopedia of afterlife beliefs and phenomena / James R. Lewis.
p. cm.
Includes bibliographical references and index.
ISBN 0-8103-4879-9 (alk. paper) : $37.95
1. Future life--Encyclopedias. 2. Death--Encyclopedias.
3. Reincarnation--Encyclopedias. 4. Occultism--Encyclopedias.
5. Spiritualism--Encyclopedias. I Title.
BF1311.F8L48 1994
133.9'03--dc20 94-29172
CIP

This book is printed on acid-free paper that meets the minimum requirements of American National Standard for Information Sciences—Permanence Paper for Printed Library Materials, ANSI Z39.48-1984. ∞™

ISBN 0-8103-4879-9
Printed in the United States of America

Published simultaneously in the United Kingdom
by Gale Research International Limited
(An affiliated company of Gale Research Inc.)

ITP

The trademark ITP is used under license.
10 9 8 7 6 5 4 3 2 1

For my partner and wife Eve who originally
inspired this project, and without whose support
this book might never have been completed.

Highlights

The Encyclopedia of Afterlife Beliefs and Phenomena serves the student, researcher, and the interested individual seeking information on the popular, historical, and cultural aspects of death and the afterlife. Below is just a sampling of ***EABP's*** nearly 250 subjects:

- American Indian Messianic Religions
- Angels
- Hieronymus Bosch
- Channeling
- Conscious Dying
- Communication with the Dead
- Day of the Dead
- Eleusinian Mysteries
- Funeral Rites
- Ghost Hunting
- Heaven and Hell
- International Association for Near-Death Studies
- Elisabeth Kübler-Ross
- Mesopotamia
- Nirvana
- Orpheus
- Out-of-Body Experience
- Possession
- Reincarnation
- Resurrection
- Shamanism
- Snake Symbols
- Tombs
- Voodoo
- Walk-ins
- Yoga
- Zoroastrianism

The Encyclopedia of Afterlife Beliefs and Phenomena makes it easy to get the information you want through these valuable features:

- **Alphabetical Arrangement** of entries allows for ready access to information on topics of interest to you
- **Boldface Cross-References** within the text of each entry direct you to related entries
- **Sources** listed at the end of entries identify further reading
- **75 Photographs and Line Drawings** provide a vivid context for entries
- **Comprehensive Index** lists all important terms, people, places, organizations, and publications mentioned in the text
- **Related Organizations Appendix** lists pertinent associations

Contents

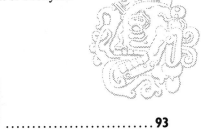

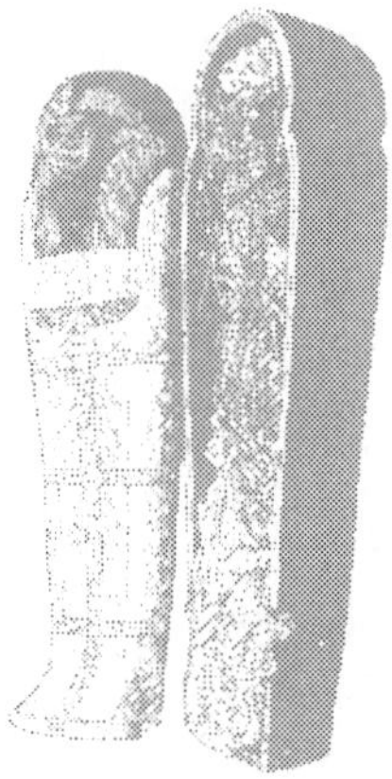

FOREWORD

Dr. Raymond A. Moody

Is there a life after death? It is notoriously difficult to form a simple response to this conundrum, and yet it is becoming an increasingly pressing issue. For now, baby boomers such as myself—a significant percentage of the population—are becoming acutely aware that death may happen someday to friends of our own age. It may already have happened to beloved parents or other loved ones. Suddenly we perceive an immediate need to think about issues that we long ago put far off into the future, but the future is now.

For years I have studiously avoided committing myself to a yes-or-no answer to the question: "Is there a life after death?" It was always convenient to accurately point out that science cannot decide the issue either way. But—much to my great horror and amusement—I am regarded as an *expert* on the topic of life after death. A scholarly publication such as the *Encyclopedia of Afterlife Beliefs and Phenomena,* however, seems just the right place to finally make a commitment, so here it is.

Yes, I concede that there *is* a life after death, but one cannot fully realize it until one achieves a certain kind of maturity, for one cannot attain the realization by applying ordinary rules of inference or through ordinary ways of learning. This knowledge is for neither the immature nor the young, except in rare cases. (My own sons, for example, both now in their twenties, have confided to me that they have realized it, too, even before I did. But, after all, they grew up sitting at the knees of good friends who had near-death experiences.)

Having seen, and talked at length with, my own grandmother several years after her death while I was wide awake, even extra-wide awake, and having realized that she is better than ever, super-alive, I can't get over the realization that there *is* life after death, even though my intellect still can't cope with it. One intellectual barrier is that "life after death" is a misnomer. The very language with which we attempt to discuss the issue needs drastic revision. In English the common forms of expression for the afterlife embody spatial or temporal metaphors. We say "the life after death," implying a time sequence, or "the beyond" or "the other side," implying a transition through space, or "the hereafter," combining temporal and spatial concepts. As I have traveled around the world, I have asked native speakers of many languages about this and they have told me that similar conventions exist in their languages. But ordinary language notions of the afterlife were formulated by our prehistoric forebears even before they were aware that the earth is round. What is more, persons who tell of their near-death experiences inform us that time and space as we know it was not even a factor in what they underwent. One woman told me, "You could say that my experience took place in one second or that it took ten thousand years, and it wouldn't make a bit of difference which way you say it." After talking with thousands of people who have had near-death experiences, and especially after my own reunion with my departed grandmother, I believe the time has come to update our semantics. Personally, I am more satisfied with a formulation based not on time and space but on modern information technology.

When I was a young child in the late 1940s my family and I listened to the radio. Disembodied voices brought us news from distant places. We were stirred by the sounds of music and—more importantly to me—we were entertained by Gene Autry, Edgar Bergen and Charlie McCarthy, and the Gangbusters.

In the early 1950s my grandparents bought a television set. Atlanta at that time had three channels—2, 5, and 11. Each morning at a few minutes before 7:00 the day's transmission would begin with a test pattern accompanied by a steady squeal, followed by the day's fare of soap operas, old Westerns, automobile and cigarette commercials, wrestling matches, and situation comedies. At 6:15 P.M., Douglas Edwards, speaking from behind a desk in New York City, would bring us the world and national news. If a major event had taken place that day in Europe, we were shown a still photograph of it; it was several days before moving picture film of the event would arrive by plane so that we could have a more realistic view.

All the action was in black and white, of course, and one had to remain on guard so as not to miss one's favorite program. If the set was on the blink, or one had conflicting obligations while *I Love Lucy* was airing one evening, the most one could hope for was that the show would be resurrected the following summer during the re-run season. Failing that, one had to turn to friends or relatives who saw the program to learn the details. The show itself had been lost forever—a kind of death.

In 1994, countless channels of full-color programming are available around the clock. Two of those channels do nothing but bring the news. When a major event transpires in Europe, we can see it instantaneously. We watch as the Berlin Wall falls and immediately participate in the event. A remote control device enables us to monitor several channels at once. And, whereas in 1955 if one missed an episode of *I Love Lucy* it was seemingly lost forever, almost 40 years later any episode of the show is available for viewing just in the time it takes to drive to the local video store and back.

Since I have witnessed and participated in this remarkable transformation within my own lifetime, I find in it a fitting metaphor for our understanding of what happens to us after death. If the life we are now leading is compared with the radio age, what has long been called the life after death can be compared with the contemporary age of electronic communication. And although the old time and space metaphors are called into question by descriptions of near-death experiences, even near-death visionaries talk as though their encounters involved the transmission, processing, and acquisition of information.

So I can say for sure that there is a life after death but that it is more like an information technology or a spiritual education and entertainment medium than anything else. For those who haven't yet gotten around to realizing that there is a life after death, who haven't had a near-death experience, who haven't visited with Grandpa after his death, or whatever, just relax; you'll find out. And right now there are probably more important things for you to worry about. So sit tight. And while you're waiting, read the *Encyclopedia of Afterlife Beliefs and Phenomena,* because the answers you seek may be somewhere in here.

Raymond Moody is currently a professor of psychology at West Georgia College. He is also the best-selling author of several books on near-death experiences (NDEs) and afterlife phenomena, including Life After Life *(1975), which became a best-seller in the United States and throughout the world, and his 1977 publication* Reflections on Life After Life.

Acknowledgments

I would like to thank the American Religions Collection in Santa Barbara, California for help with illustrations. Much thanks also to Gary L. Ward, Isotta Poggi, and Michela Zonta for their research assistance and significant contributions to some of the entries. At Gale Research/Visible Ink Press, I am grateful to Chris Nasso and Leah Knight for originally taking interest and acquiring this title, and to Developmental Editors Peg Bessette, Christa Brelin, and Kelle Sisung for seeing this title through to its fruition.

Introduction

It has been said that only two things are guaranteed in life, death and taxes. This item of proverbial wisdom is meant to be a wry commentary on the inevitability and undesirability of taxes. We might, however, invert the comparison and see what this proverb tells us about death in terms of what we know about taxes: Death, like taxes, is to be dreaded—absolutely no one enjoys paying taxes. Also, death, like paying taxes, is inescapable.

When Western society first accepted some version of traditional religion without question, death was not regarded quite so tragically. Death was *contemplated* more readily, and tended to be seen as the natural culmination of a full life. This was because society was generally more religious than it is today, and *some* notion of a continuation of life after death is an integral part of almost every religion.

Until recently, the idea of an afterlife was one of the constants of human thought. Even prehistoric sites contain graves in which one finds utensils, weapons, and other artifacts—indicating some sort of belief in a continuation of life beyond the dissolution of the physical body. Contemporary science has, however, called this universal belief into question. By demonstrating that the day-to-day operations of the human organism can be explained in terms of physics and chemistry, science has introduced doubts about the existence of a spiritual self or soul existing independently of the physical body.

FROM RELIGION TO SCIENCE AND BACK AGAIN: The notion of the continuity of human life is, however, a stubborn belief. While the authority of traditional religion may no longer be enough to assure us of life after death, this belief has been resurrected on the authority of the very institution that seemed to call it into question—science. In the nineteenth century, new forms of ''scientific religion'' emerged that claimed to establish religion, and especially afterlife beliefs, on a new scientific footing. Chief among these was Spiritualism, which was founded on the basis of communication with the so-called dead through mediums.

By the early twentieth century, exposés of fake mediums had called the Spiritualist enterprise into question, at least for the general public. More recently, the quest for a scientific basis for belief in life after death has shifted to an interest in near-death experiences (NDEs), referring to the seemingly supernatural experiences often undergone by individuals who have suffered apparent death and have been restored to life. The primary impetus for modern studies on NDEs was Dr. Raymond A. Moody's 1975 book *Life After Life,* which describes the results of more than 11 years of inquiry into near-death experiences. *Life After Life* was anecdotal, however, and Moody was careful to point out that it should not be regarded as a scientific study since the case history material presented was highly selective and the data was not subjected to any statistical analysis.

The first book to report an investigation of NDEs from a scientific point of view was *Life After Death,* published in 1980 by psychologist Kenneth Ring. Ring showed that NDEs were largely consistent over different conditions of near-death. Further, George Gallup's *Adventures in Immortality* reported the results of a national survey in which the incidence of NDEs was documented in about 5 percent of the American adult population, or eight million Americans. More generally, Gallup also found belief in life after death to be quite widespread; more than two-thirds of the nation holds some kind of belief in the afterlife. The poll further found that almost a quarter of Americans believe in reincarnation, and about the same percentage believe it is possible to communicate with the dead—a significant departure from tradition.

HISTORICAL SPREAD OF AFTERLIFE BELIEFS: When Persia became a mighty power and conquered much of the surrounding land, Zoroastrianism was spread across the world, exercising an influence on the doctrines of Judaism, Christianity, and Islam disproportionate to its size. Zoroastrianism is best known for its dualism. Its god of light is locked in a cosmic struggle with its god of darkness. Individual human beings are urged to align themselves with the forces of light and are judged according to the predominance of their good or evil deeds. After the final battle between good and evil (the ultimate source of the Judeo-Christian notions of the Apocalypse and Armageddon), there will be a general Judgment in which everyone will be put through an ordeal of fire; good individuals will have their dross burned away and evil people will be consumed. The souls of the blessed will be resurrected in physical bodies, which Ahura Mazda (the God of light in Zoroastrianism) will make both immortal and eternally youthful.

Many of the components of this vision of the end times—a final battle between good and evil, judgment of the wicked, resurrection of the dead, et cetera—were adopted by Jewish apocalyptic thinkers. From texts composed by these apocalypticists, such notions were adopted into Christianity and Islam. The Zoroastrian idea of resurrection was introduced into Christianity from apocalyptic Judaism. The idea of resurrection developed in tandem with an apocalyptic vision of history that entailed the end of the world as we know it, and which would result in the defeat of death and evil.

Early Christianity arose as a Jewish sect during the period of the apocalyptic thinkers. The first Christians strongly believed in the imminent second coming of Christ (within their lifetimes), which would be accompanied by the resurrection of the dead, a Final Judgment, and the end of this world. Bodily resurrection was thus the afterlife belief of the earliest Christians. While this idea of resurrection is Jewish in origin, belief in the immortality of the soul came from Greek culture.

By the time Christianity spread outside of Palestine and came into contact with Hellenistic culture, the ancient Greek views on death and the afterlife had been eclipsed by Oriental beliefs in the immortality of the soul and radical dualism between the body and soul. Greek Gnosticism, for example, was based on the principle that the human soul is a divine spark imprisoned in the body which, since taking embodiment, has forgotten its divine nature. By achieving *gnosis* (meaning, in this context, knowledge of its true identity), the soul can obtain salvation, liberating itself from its body-prison.

The New Testament—which is composed of about 27 books written in different historical contexts in different parts of the world by different people across a period of more than a hundred years—reflects the diversity of views on salvation and afterlife of everything from apocalyptic Judaism to Hellenistic religious culture. While Jewish apocalypticism envisioned salvation as union of soul and body at the resurrection, for the Gnostics salvation meant the exact opposite—the eternal separation of the two. Despite their contradictory emphases, the Jewish concept of resurrection and the gnostic idea of eternal life of the soul merged in the Christian notion of the afterlife in which the eternal soul is reunited with a transformed physical body at the end of time.

HEAVEN AND HELL: Heaven in the Old Testament was conceived of as the physical sky where God resided. From the period of the New Testament through the Middle Ages, heaven came to be viewed as a place open to all who were faithful, free from pain and sorrows, and as a blissful state in communion with the divine and the saints. Thomas Aquinas (1225–1274) in particular portrayed heaven as the place where one meets with and knows God.

The idea of hell was developed as a realm of pain in early Christianity, in opposition to the blissful state of heaven. The gospels' reference to ''Gehenna,'' viewed as a place of torment and punishment, was used to urge conversion in this life. In the Middle Ages, however, heaven and hell became part of popular piety through the graphic depiction of Dante Alighieri's *Divina Commedia* (*Divine Comedy*). Dante depicted heaven and hell as a series of multiple, concentric, spherical heavens and multi-layered, underground hells divided into levels in which good people and sinners were rewarded or punished according to the degree of their noble deeds or sins. Between the two realms, Dante also placed the multiple levels of the mountain of Purgatory (*purgatorium* which derives from Latin *purgare,* to cleanse), a place of temporary damnation for those who need to be purified before entering in eternal communion with God. Because certain religious practices for saving souls from purgatory were at the center of Martin Luther's argument with the Catholic Church, Protestantism adopted the notion of a simple dichotomy between heaven and hell.

SPIRITUALISM AND CONTEMPORARY AFTERLIFE BELIEFS: The contemporary period of afterlife belief began with 19th century Spiritualism. Spiritualism emphasizes survival after death, a belief Spiritualists claim is based upon scientific proof, and upon communication with the surviving personalities of deceased human beings by means of mediumship. The continuity of the personality after death is the central tenet of Spiritualism. According to Spiritualists, at death the soul—which is composed of a sort of subtle matter—withdraws itself and remains near the earth plane for a period of time. After this, it advances in knowledge and moral qualities and proceeds to higher planes, until it eventually reaches the sphere of pure spirit.

Departing markedly from tradition, Spiritualism rejects the notions of hell, eternal damnation, the last judgment, and the resurrection of the physical body. Communication with the dead through mediums is another central belief of Spiritualism. Spiritualism is regarded by its adherents as a religion based on a science, combining elements from other religions and creeds. Spiritualist Sir Arthur Conan Doyle, creator of the literary character Sherlock Holmes, wrote that "Spiritualism is a religion for those who find themselves outside all religions; while on the contrary it greatly strengthens the faith of those who already possess religious beliefs."

The belief in the possibility of communication with the spirit world has been held in most of the societies of which we have records. Spiritualism has many parallels and predecessors among so-called "primitive" people, and in the miracles of world religions. What is generally regarded as the origin of modern Spiritualism, however, is the incident that took place in America in 1848 when the sisters Maggie and Katie Fox started communicating with spirits through rappings in their house in Hydesville, New York. The Fox sisters discovered that if they clapped their hands, they received a response from a spirit who claimed to have been killed by a former occupant of the house. Their older sister Leah took charge of them, and eventually took them on tour, making money with their increasingly elaborate séances despite accusations of fraud. At the same time other mediums appeared, inspired by the success of the Fox sisters, and near the mid-1850s Spiritualism had achieved considerable popularity.

In response to fraud and other issues within the movement, the National Spiritualist Association of Churches (NSAC) was established in Chicago in 1893. In 1899 it adopted a "Declaration of Principles" with six articles; three other articles were added at a later time. Although a considerable number of people began to discover and practice mediumistic powers, the Spiritualist movement continued to come under attack. It was condemned by official religions and suffered negative publicity as a result of the many investigations of mediums that exposed frauds. After enjoying a resurgence of popularity during and after World War I, the heyday of mediumship was over by 1920, though interest in Spiritualism continued. The quest for scientific proof of life after death that manifested in Spiritualism eventually found a new avenue of expression in the study of near-death experiences.

Interest in reincarnation, while an integral part of many 19th century Western metaphysical religions, received new impetus from the East when immigration barriers into the United States were lowered in 1965. Reincarnation became almost an unquestioned tenet of belief in the West's metaphysical subculture, as well as its offspring, the new age movement. In the metaphysical subculture, reincarnation is regarded somewhat differently than in Asian religions. Whereas in a tradition like Buddhism, reincarnation tends to be viewed negatively, as a process that brought one back into the world to suffer, in the metaphysical subculture reincarnation is viewed as part of an extended learning process that one undergoes across many lifetimes. While earlier generations of people who dabbled in occult-metaphysical spirituality were often interested in learning about their past lifetimes in the hope of discovering that they were some famous or otherwise exalted personality, the new age emphasis on healing has lead the most recent generation of seekers to examine past lives for insights into current psychological problems. It is thus in the wake of the impact of the new age movement that the practice of past-lives therapy has been able to emerge as a serious therapy.

The larger metaphysical culture has also given birth to some unique conceptions about the nature of spiritual reality and the afterlife, such as the idea of soul mates, which is the notion that two individuals are "made for each other" and seek union with the other across the course of many lifetimes. The new age has also birthed the idea of the walk-in, which is an entity who occupies a body that has been vacated by its original soul. The walk-in situation is somewhat similar to possession, although in possession the original soul is merely overshadowed—rather than completely supplanted—by the possessing entity.

Other notions include extraterrestrial incarnations (lifetimes on other planets) and the idea of a plurality of existences, meaning that the same soul can *simultaneously* incarnate in different bodies, sometimes at great distances from each other, as when one claims to be in both a terrestrial and an extraterrestrial incarnation simultaneously. Also, one variant on the soul mate idea is that soul mates actually represent one soul in two bodies, which is a kind of double existence. In these notions one can perceive that, far from being "dead," reflections on the afterlife continue to inspire creative speculation, and are likely to be with us as long as human beings contemplate their own mortality.

ENCYCLOPEDIA OF

Afterlife Beliefs and Phenomena

A

Adventism

The distinctive doctrine of Adventism maintains that the Second Coming of Christ (the Advent) is imminent. Modern Adventism had its beginnings in the northeastern United States in the early nineteenth century with the preaching of William Miller (1782–1849), who, through a detailed study of the prophecies of Daniel and the Book of Revelation, predicted that March 21, 1844 (and, later, October 22, 1844), would be the day on which Christ would return. When these dates passed without event, many were disillusioned and drifted away.

The remaining Millerites coalesced into several religious bodies, the most important of which are the Seventh-Day Adventist church, the Advent Christian church, and the Church of God of the Abrahamic Faith. Besides the emphasis on Adventism, and such practices as baptism by immersion, Adventists are distinguished from many other Christians by the doctrine of conditional immortality. According to this tenet, only God has immortality, and mortals possess a nature inherently sinful and dying. There is no conscious entity that survives death, and the state after death is one of silence, inactivity, and complete unconsciousness, the grave being a place of darkness. All people, good and evil, remain in the grave from their death until the final **Resurrection,** which is believed to be a resurrection of the whole person.

Only corporeal resurrection can bring humankind out of the prison of the grave. Resurrection occurs at the Second Advent of Christ for the righteous, and a thousand years thereafter for the impenitent wicked. The immortalized righteous are then taken to heaven, the New Jerusalem, where they reign with Christ a thousand years, judging the world and fallen angels. During this time the earth is thought to be in a chaotic condition, to be a bottomless pit where Satan, the author of sin, is confined and finally destroyed.

At the end of this period, fire, which flows out of heaven from God to Gehenna, the lake of fire, devours and annihilates the wicked dead. The wicked, being raised only to undergo judgment and to meet everlasting punishment, become as though they had not been. Therefore, hell is not perceived as an unending torment, but, rather, as a final destruction of evil. It is also believed that a new heaven will stem from the ashes of the old earth, which will be purged from the curse of sin, and will be the place where the righteous shall dwell evermore.

Sources:

Damsteegt, P. Gerard. *Foundations of the Seventh-day Adventist Message and Mission.* Grand Rapids, MI: William B. Eerdmans, 1977.

Kastenbaum, Robert, and Beatrice Kastenbaum, eds. *Encyclopedia of Death.* Phoenix, AZ: Oryx Press, 1989.

Land, Gary, ed. *Adventism in America. A History.* Grand Rapids, MI: William B. Eerdmans, 1986.

AFRICA

In cultural analyses of Africa, it has become customary to subdivide the continent into northern Africa and the region south of the Sahara Desert. The Sahara is a traditional place of division, because for centuries the barriers of desert, forest, and sea prevented travelers and conquerers from moving southward. Afterlife beliefs in northern Africa are discussed in the entry on **Islam.**

Sub-Saharan Africa contains approximately 420 million people belonging to about two thousand ethnic groups in roughly 50 different countries. There is no single language, religion, culture, history, or political system that unites those who share sub-Saharan Africa, and thus it is difficult to make generalizations about their afterlife beliefs. There are, however, broad streams of social structure and practice that mark African life, and these can provide the basis of an overview of some African approaches to the afterlife.

AFRICA AND TRADITIONAL SOCIETIES: Africa is one of the few remaining large-scale regions where, despite a colonial history and the growing presence of such historical global religions as Islam and Christianity, indigenous religious beliefs and practices have maintained their place in the lives of a substantial portion of the population. One estimate has placed the number of Christian converts in tropical and southern Africa at 160 million and the number of Muslim converts at 130 million. This leaves approximately one-third of the sub-Saharan population in the indigenous category, with a small percentage relegated to "other." Conversion to either Islam or Christianity does not necessarily mean a sudden expunging of all former traditions and beliefs. A large percentage of Christian converts in Africa have assimilated indigenous beliefs and practices with Christian beliefs and practices, often with little practical change in orientation.

Traditional societies such as those in Africa do not depend upon written accounts or sacred texts for the transmittal of rituals and beliefs, but rely on elders or particular authoritative persons to pass on the worldviews from one generation to the next. The communities of belief so formed are small-scale, usually related to particular ethnic populations. Thus, within any one political region there may be represented dozens or even hundreds of different religious traditions, along with different linguistic and cultural histories. Traditional societies are oriented around either hunting-gathering or agriculture, and these two pursuits in turn influence the shape of their cultures, including religious beliefs.

Anthropologists have noted that agricultural societies tend to have ancestor cults with a fairly developed concept of an afterlife, and hunting- gathering societies tend not to have ancestor cults, nor do they give much recognition to afterlife beliefs. Although the beliefs and practices of traditional societies are little discussed in contemporary (and relatively recent) industrial/ technological societies, it is instructive to remember that more than 99 percent of human cultural history has been lived within the context of such small-scale, traditional groupings.

THE HADZA: The Hadza of northern Tanzania provide an example of a hunting-and-gathering population. The Hadza take death as a matter of course and have almost no concept of an afterlife:

> There is no period of mourning involving a second phase of rites, and the deceased's possessions are immediately shared without ceremony. . . . Death is thought to have neither social nor supernatural consequences for the living. . . . The social and spiritual existence of the person ends with the burial of the corpse. (Bond 1992, 6)

The Hadza do remember the recently deceased in their monthly *epeme* dance, performed to promote well-being and good hunting. The dance is not an attempt to communicate with the dead, nor is it an effort to appease or ask for favors. In this monthly ritual, the dancer is thought to become epeme (a sacred being), with the power to influence events.

ANCESTOR CULTS: It is important to recognize the existence of populations like the Hadza that have no ancestor cults and little in the way of afterlife beliefs. Much of the literature on African religions, however, focuses on those populations that pay more attention to the afterlife, particularly through **ancestor worship** or, more properly, ancestor cults. *Ancestor cult* is the preferred term because ancestors are not considered gods and are therefore not worshiped in that sense. Ancestors are simply deceased human beings. An exception to this general rule may be noted in the case of the high god or creator god in at least one cosmology—that of the Boshongo.

The Boshongo, a central Bantu tribe, describe the creation of the world and humans as the act of the deity Bumba, who is also considered an ancestor:

> When at last the work of creation was finished, Bumba walked through the peaceful villages and said to the people, "Behold these wonders. They belong to you." Thus from Bumba, the Creator, the First Ancestor, came forth all the wonders that we see and hold and use, and all the brotherhood of

> beasts and man. (From Maria Leach, *The Beginning,* as quoted in Eliade 1976, 92)

As mentioned, however, *ancestor cult,* referring to a recurring set of devotional rituals, is generally a more accurate term for describing African religions with strong notions of the afterlife than is *ancestor worship.* Neither are ancestor cults the same as cults of the dead. Only certain of the dead occupying certain genealogical positions in relation to the kin group (extended family), such as founders, elders, chiefs, or kings, can be recognized as powerful ancestors, just as only certain of the living elders of the kin group have the authority to communicate with the ancestors and interpret responses.

Deceased persons who are not privileged to become ancestors remain as mere ghosts or shadows. Such spirits are honored at grave sites and given ritual attention at family shrines, but their influence is slight and passing. After a time, their name and memory fade into final rest. Bantu-speaking peoples make a distinction between ancestors who are a real force in the community, called *vidye,* and the ordinary dead, called *fu.* Powerful ancestors do not fade away but are invoked generation after generation.

Some African groups speak of **reincarnation,** which can occur only in a child of the same sex and lineage as the deceased. A claimed occurrence of reincarnation means that the memory of the deceased is still current among the living. Reincarnation is yet another way in which an ancestor may contribute genetically and spiritually to the living community. Interestingly, its occurrence does not mean that the reincarnated being is not at the same time living in the beyond. For the deceased to be at the same time a revered ancestor and a living member of the community is a concept that is difficult for Westerners to grasp. This belief requires that a person's life force be seen as having multiple elements or levels, depending on the time, place, or needs of the community.

So widespread is the existence of African ancestor cults that African kin groups are often described as "communities of both the living and the dead." Ancestor cults have been considered the primary feature of religious life among various African tribes, especially in eastern and southern Africa. Ancestral spirits are regarded as the major maintenance and control factors in the continuity of proper family and village life. They are consulted, through the proper channels, on most issues of community life, and their approval is most important. The ancestors serve as a moral force, maintaining a stable society despite the instabilities caused by death. They are oriented toward this life and not to some otherworldly life.

COMMUNICATION WITH ANCESTORS: Because knowing the will of the ancestors is so important, there are various means of communication between them and living relatives. The latter try to keep on good terms with the ancestors through regular prayers and sacrifices. If someone needs ancestral advice on a particular problem, lots may be thrown and certain elders will interpret the result as the message of the ancestor. A diviner may be sought out to ascertain the will of the ancestors in a given situation. If an ancestor needs to contact someone, there are several means available. The ancestor may appear in a dream, the meaning of which might be immediately clear or might require a diviner's interpretation. An ancestor may temporarily take over the consciousness of an individual to get a message across; the person so contacted might be the person to whom the message is directed or might be a professional medium.

Communication may also occur through symbolic evocation, as through the use of masks. Wooden masks representing ancestors, animals, or other powers are famous, not only as an important part of African religious life but also as some of the most striking and important contributions Africa has made to the artistic world. Sometimes in ceremonies figures wearing these masks appear and offer words of counsel or warning to relatives of the represented ancestors. Depending on the situation, the masks might depict a natural-looking face, serene or angry, or the depiction might be abstract. Masks representing ancestors are also important in initiation ceremonies for young boys and girls, who receive at that time important information about tribal customs and the ancestors. In some tribes the male children are circumcised by a man wearing a mask to represent the ancestors. Carved images, whether on masks or on ancestor shrines, serve as powerful tools for conveying the characteristics of the ancestors and making the ancestors "psychologically present."

Ancestors may also act directly in someone's life. If they are pleased, they might grant favors ranging from a healthy birth to good weather. If displeased, ancestral spirits are usually believed to be capable of leading a person or an entire tribe to misfortune, illness, and even death. Departed spirits are believed even to be able to read minds, tell the future, or grant or withhold fertility to the soil or to people. Communication with the ancestors is always something of a risky business, however, because of misinterpretations and the sense that ancestors are not always predictable and are even somewhat capricious. These characteristics cause petitioners to relate to ancestors with more fear than consolation, and attention to the ancestors usually supersedes any attention paid to deities. Since lineage or descent defines most of what is important in these traditional societies, and ancestors are the revered heads of the clan in addition to having supernatural powers, they are naturally the focus for the most cherished hopes and nameless terrors of clan members.

Among the Tallensi the story is told (Hoopfe 1979, 59) of a young man named Pu-eng-yii who moved in with a rival family in search of greater fortunes than he thought he could achieve with his birth family. These actions offended his ancestors, and eventually Pu-eng-yii suffered a severe leg injury in a car accident. He consulted a diviner to ascertain what was going on and was told that his ancestors were actually trying to kill him. Following the diviner's instructions, Pu-eng-yii returned to his family and made full restitution to his ancestors in hopes of avoiding the penalty of death. This story illustrates not only the ancestors' sometime unexpected ways of acting and communicating but also the way in which ancestors share with the deities responsibility for shaping the proper path of persons and villages. If they bring misfortune to a person or a community, it is supposed to be for a constructive purpose, that is, punishment aimed at correcting some improper behavior.

FUNERAL RITES AND BEYOND: Various rituals of sacrifice have evolved among African communities of faith and may be directed to either deities or ancestors. Usually the sacrifice consists of a display of small bits of food or the pouring of a libation. At certain more important occasions it consists of a blood sacrifice of some animal.

Beyond the ritual sacrifices, however, the funeral rites are the single most important service that the living can offer the dead, as improper observance of the rites can supposedly disrupt the settlement of the spirits into the ancestral home, bringing dishonor and possibly catastrophe to the families involved. In some cases, women fear that their husband's ghost will return and cause their wombs to become infertile. Some societies bury the dead with weapons, personal belongings, food, money, and other items to assist in the journey from this world to the next. Often the corpse is ritually treated with a view toward starting its new life. The body is treated carefully, so as not to bruise it or change its appearance. A fine white clay called kaolin may be applied to the body as symbolic of rebirth and life. Through these rites the spirit of the deceased is carried to its new position in the life beyond and the balance of the surviving society is restored.

Funeral rites do not generally include any references to an afterlife system of reward and punishment. In most African societies with ancestor cults, the issue of whether the deceased was a good or bad person does not arise, because it does not matter in the afterlife: "What matters in ancestors is their jural status. . . . [T]he personality and character, the virtues or vices, success or failures, popularity or unpopularity, of a person during his lifetime make no difference to his attainment of ancestorhood" (Meyer Fortes, quoted in Brain, 1979, 395). In other words, an ancestral afterlife is not typically one in which individual personality plays any role. The role of an ancestor is an impersonal one that depends almost entirely upon descent and social function.

Thus, immortality is considered not so much an individual possession, as something that is possible only through the continuity of the community. If there is reward and punishment for ancestors, perhaps it is based upon the actions of the living relatives rather than on the previous life of the ancestor. The more relatives misbehave or fail to observe the proper rituals, the more the ancestors are troubled and have to take action. There is commonly believed to be an immortal part of a person, which at death is what becomes a ghost, an ancestor, and/or a reincarnated being. In some societies the teaching is that whenever a birth occurs, the relevant ancestor invests the infant with a portion of his own life force. Here again is reinforced the idea that immortality is something placed at the service of the whole people.

Exactly where the ancestors are located is a matter of some ambiguity and there is a great deal of variation among the different communities of belief. Sometimes the ancestor is believed to be hovering near his or her village or grave, or the hut of the closest relative, or a former treasured object; sometimes the ancestor is believed to be

remember you all, to sacrifice to you all who went before, may you all sleep'' (quoted in Brain 1979, 400).

The Dinka of the southern Sudan are a large tribe of about four million people who are variously hunter- gatherers and crop growers. They believe that every person has a *tiep* (a shadow, ghost, or spirit) that leaves the body at death and remains near the place of burial. Surviving relatives offer sacrifices to the tiep (ancestors) to maintain their goodwill, as tiep are believed to be able to influence events in daily life. The tiep are not the only forces affecting the fortunes of the people, however, as there are numerous divinities believed to need continued attention and gifts to ensure such things as a good hunt or good health. The status and power of the tiep are not the same as those forces with superhuman origins (deities), and the influence of a tiep declines with each succeeding generation, until finally they are ignored and forgotten.

The Yoruba are a highly urbanized tribal grouping several times larger than the Dinka and are centered around southwestern Nigeria and neighboring areas. The Yoruba religion is centered upon worship of any one of many *orisha* (powers or divinities), particularly the orisha worshiped by one's father. Each person is believed to have a guardian soul, which is assigned a fixed destiny and life span by the supreme orisha, Olorun. Unlike most African populations, the Yoruba believe in an afterlife structure that depends on the level of goodness of a person's life. If Olorun believes that the person has led a good life, he may grant reincarnation; if not, he may send the soul to a place of punishment.

The LoDagaa people of Ghana provide another instance of tribal belief in moral judgment in the afterlife. According to their religion, the deceased journeys toward the land of the ancestors, but before reaching that destination must first cross a river. There is a ferryman who must be paid, but if the deceased has led a good life, the crossing will be easy. If the person died owing any money, the river cannot be crossed until the creditor shows up and payment can be completed. If the person has led an evil life, a swim of three years' length is the only means of crossing the river. Once in the land of the ancestors, there may be still other trials to overcome, depending upon the quality of the life lived on earth. It is said that those who must suffer for their evil deeds question the great God:

> ''Why do you make us suffer? . . .'' God replies, ''Because you sinned on earth.'' And they ask, ''Who created us?'' To which God replies, ''I did.'' And they ask, ''If you created us, did we know evil when we came or did you give it to us?'' God replies, ''I gave it to you.'' Then the people ask God, ''Why was it that you knew it was evil and gave it to us?'' God replies, ''Stop, let me think and find the answer'' (Benjamin Ray, *African Religions;* quoted in Hopfe 1979, 64–65).

Funeral rites for many African populations are not an occasion for saying good-bye but serve as a rite of passage from one kind of social condition to another, more exalted one. The ordinary dead become shadows or ghosts whose existence is relatively short and uneventful. The "special" dead become ancestors with the power and influence to continue to lead the clan. Their existence and abilities are extended beyond those of the ordinary dead because of the will of the living. The ancestors survive because the relatives remember them and call upon them. Sometimes reincarnation is a means of calling upon them. There is generally no sense of a heavenly paradise that might compete with the relatives for the attention of the deceased. The alternative to maintaining a role in the community is a nameless sleep.

The existence of ancestor cults depends upon a society with certain features that include a reverence for the past as containing the ideal world for the living. Tradition is understood as vital for the proper ordering of lives. Ancestor cults also depend at least partly on the notion, common to traditional societies, that age tends to generate respect. Ancestors gain an exalted status, not only because they now occupy the world of the spirits but also because they carry age and the accomplishments that come with age to its farthest limits. They are prototypically "the ones who have gone before," and thus the ones to be treated with awe. They are the ones who founded the clan, conquered territories, established rules and regulations, told the stories, and created the history. For many Africans, ancestor cults are a means of recognizing the authority of the elders. The contrary Western tendency to denigrate those of advancing years is one of many points of contention that arise in the continuing struggle between indigenous and Western cultures.

Sources:

Bond, George C. "Living with Spirits: Death and Afterlife in African Religions." In Hiroshi Obayashi, ed. *Death and Afterlife: Perspective of World Religions.* Westport, CT: Greenwood Press, 1992.

Brain, James L. "Ancestors as Elders in Africa—Further Thoughts." In William A. Less and Evon Z. Vogt, eds. *Reader in Comparative Religion.* 4th ed. New York: Harper and Row, 1979.

Eliade, Mircea. *From Primitives to Zen.* San Francisco: Harper & Row, 1967.

Hopfe, Lewis M. *Religions of the World.* 2d ed. Encino, CA: Glencoe Publishing, 1979.

"Immortality." In Mircea Eliade, ed. *The Encyclopedia of Religion.* 16 vols. New York: Macmillan, 1987.

Nigosian, S. A. *World Faiths.* New York: St. Martin's Press, 1990.

Parrinder, Geoffrey, ed. *World Religions: From Ancient History to the Present.* New York: Facts on File, 1971.

Smart, Ninian. *The Religious Experience of Mankind.* 3d ed. New York: Charles Scribner's Sons, 1984.

Smaart, Ninian, and Richard D. Hecht, eds. *Sacred Texts of the World: A Universal Anthology.* New York: Crossroad Publishing, 1982.

AGASHA TEMPLE OF WISDOM

The Agasha Temple of Wisdom is a **Spiritualist** body founded in 1943 by Richard Zenor, **medium** for a spirit who identified himself as the "master teacher Agasha." Zenor and the church achieved prominence when it was featured in James Crenshaw's popular book *Telephone Between Two Worlds* (1950). After Zenor died in 1978, Geary Salvat was chosen to continue his ministry. In the 1980s, Agasha's teachings were compiled into a book series written by church member William Eisen.

While the church continues the Spiritualist tradition of communicating with the dead, the principal focus of the Agasha Temple of Wisdom is on receiving and studying teachings from master teachers. These teachings are embodied in certain universal spiritual laws, such as the moral law of cause and effect ("as you sow, so shall you reap") and the Golden Rule. The notion of "master teachers" is not unique to Agasha, but rather flows directly out of Spiritualism. The basic idea is that certain souls who have "mastered" spiritual wisdom remain in a disembodied state and communicate to ordinary human beings through mediums. Similar ideas are found in the practice of **channeling.**

Sources:

Crenshaw, James. *Telephone Between Two Worlds.* Marina del Rey, CA: DeVorss, 1950.
Eisen, William. *Agasha, Master of Wisdom.* Marina del Rey, CA: DeVorss, 1977.

AIDS

The sudden eruption of the disease known as acquired immune deficiency syndrome (AIDS) in 1981 resulted in an exaggerated and fearful response from both the public and the media. It has reached epidemic proportions throughout the world since then, and no cure is available yet. The disease is fatal, and its fast spread is difficult to control. Preventing its transmission is the only method to control it, and can be accomplished by avoiding high-risk behaviors.

AIDS produces devastating physical and psychological effects on its victims, as well as such social problems as discrimination in jobs, housing, and insurance coverage. It has been the subject of special polls, extensive research, and prevention initiatives by the media, the government, and the scientific community, even though some conservatives have opposed AIDS education. AIDS is considered by some to be the product of a dirty life or punishment by God of those who reject his laws.

The threat of AIDS affects not only people's sense of reality but also their fantasies. Its fatal nature leads to a catastrophic vision of death, and the predominantly sexual mode of transmission of the virus produces the horrific image of death through sex. The disease's transmission via blood evokes powerful images associated with fantasies of threatening vampires. AIDS is also regarded as a kind of modern Black Death.

AIDS has been instrumental in forcibly bringing awareness of death back into the consciousness of many people. It has thus served indirectly to focus attention on the question of life after death. This new interest in the afterlife is reflected in such phenomena as the increasing popularity of books and films in which **reincarnation** plays a central role and the tremendous attention that has been paid to the **near-death experience.**

Sources:

Kastenbaum, Robert, and Beatrice Kastenbaum. *Encyclopedia of Death.* New York: Avon, 1988.

Akashic Records

The theosophical concept of akashic records refers to the records of all world events and personal experiences—of all the thoughts and deeds that have ever taken place on the earth. These events are transcribed in the form of complex images composed of pictures, sounds, and other sensory phenomena upon the ''matter'' of the astral plane (called the akasha) and may be ''read'' only when the reader is in a special altered (one might even say mystical) state of consciousness. In such a frame of mind, one is able to tap the akashic records and receive direct information about past ages. Certain theosophical descriptions of Atlantis, for example, are supposedly received via this technique. Also, some psychics who do past-life readings claim to receive their information from the akashic records. The Lipika are said to be the spiritual beings responsible for inscribing the records of past ages on the akasha.

Akasha is derived from a Sanskrit word meaning luminous and is taken to refer to essence or space. It is conceived of as an all-pervading medium similar to the ether of nineteenth-century physics, which was thought to be the medium for both light and sound vibrations. Akasha is the first of the five Hindu elements or principles of nature; the other elements are created out of this quintessence. These subtle principles, called Tattvas, are associated with the five senses of human beings and with the basic elements of matter: earth (prithivi), water (apas), fire (tejas), and air (vayu).

Helena Blavatsky, founder of the Theosophical Society, referred to the akasha as ''a radiant, cool, diathermous plastic matter, creative in its physical nature.'' In medieval occultism, the akasha, from which akashic records or chronicles derive, was sometimes called the luminous waters or the mercurial waters, and in modern occultism it is sometimes called the akashic tableau or the cosmic memory.

Sources:

Bletzer, June G. *The Donning International Encyclopedic Psychic Dictionary.* Norfolk, VA: Donning, 1986.
Shepard, Leslie A., ed. *Encyclopedia of Occultism & Parapsychology.* Detroit, MI: Gale Research, 1991.

Alchemy

Alchemy is the ancient art of transmuting base metals into gold and silver through long and complicated chemical processes. According to the Aristotelian theory of the composition of matter, which had a significant influence on the practice of alchemy, all materials found in nature are composed of different ratios of four basic elements: water, earth, fire, and air. This concept was modified by the Arab alchemists, who postulated that all metals are composed of two intermediate elements, sulfur and mercury, and who adopted the Chinese concept of a philosophers' stone, which was supposed to have in itself the power to perfect raw materials and turn them into gold, as well as act as an elixir of life.

Although it was probably in Byzantium during the fourth century that it achieved embryonic form, there is little doubt that alchemy arose about 100 A.D. in Alexandria, Egypt, from the fusion of Greek and Oriental cultures. The aim of the early Egyptian alchemists was to separate gold and silver from the native matrix in order to obtain a black powder that was mystically identified with the underworld god Osiris and credited with magical properties.

At about the same time alchemical science appeared in China, where it was associated with Taoist philosophy and had the purpose of transmuting base metals into gold, which was thought to have the ability to cure diseases and prolong life indefinitely. Besides considering gold to be the symbol of immortality and attributing sacredness to it, alchemists often regarded it as a vehicle for bringing humankind into rapport with the supermundane spheres.

It has been suggested that the principal object of alchemy was not the transmutation of metals but the spiritual regeneration of humankind. According to this vision, the human soul, which is enchained in matter, can be purified and exalted through spiritual processes related to those of the chemical processes of alchemy. Alchemy is thought to free parts of the cosmos from temporal existence and conduct them to perfection, which for metal is gold and for man is longevity, immortality, and finally redemption.

Alchemy has always been connected to the esoteric or mystical traditions of the cultures in which it flourished, and this mystical component gained importance from the Renaissance onward. There is also a link between alchemy and Gnosticism and Hermetism as well as Christian mysticism.

Sources:

Eliade, Mircea. *The Forge and the Crucible.* New York: Harper & Brothers, 1962.

Eliade, Mircea, ed. *The Encyclopedia of Religion.* 16 vols. New York: Macmillan, 1987.

Shumaker, Wayne. *The Occult Sciences in the Renaissance. A Study in Intellectual Patterns.* Berkeley: University of California Press, 1972.

ALL SOUL'S DAY *See:* DAY OF THE DEAD

American Indian Messianic Religions

The religious life of a traditional culture is built around the most pressing concerns of the group, such as its economic activities. Thus, a hunting society, to take a prominent example, usually develops hunting myths and rituals. After traditional American Indian hunting practices were destroyed or radically altered by Euroamerican invaders, this aspect of their religion lost relevancy. In response to this state of affairs, new native American religions arose that, among other things, addressed the changed economic situation, providing divine sanctions for a new life-style.

A GHOST DANCER WHO HAS PASSED OUT, AND WHO IS PRESUMABLY COMMUNICATING WITH DEPARTED RELATIVES AND FRIENDS. (FROM JAMES MOONEY, *THE GHOST-DANCE RELIGION AND WOUNDED KNEE.* [1896]) COURTESY OF THE ARC.

Characteristically, these new religious ideas or movements began with the religious experience of a single individual—a ''prophet'' for lack of a better term. Although there was a fair amount of variability among the religious visions of different American Indian prophets, the central tendency was to speak to those aspects of the new environment—including the presence of EuroAmericans—that traditional religions did not address.

Many of the prophets introduced the twin notions of **heaven** (reward for the good) and **hell** (punishment for the evil) into their respective cultures. Others, such as the ghost dancers, received messages from the departed and promised that the dead would return to life. A good example of the first type of teaching can be found in the visions of Tenskwatawa.

Tenskwatawa (literally ''open door'') was the Shawnee prophet who, together with his brother Tecumseh, forged a pan-Indian alliance opposed to Euroamerican intrusions in the years leading up to the War of 1812. In early 1805 he was a less-than-successful medicine man for a group of Shawnee living in eastern Indiana. In the wake of military defeat and an unfavorable treaty that had been imposed a decade earlier, many of the midwestern tribes slid into a state of social and cultural demoralization. Tenskwatawa, a boastful alcoholic, fully embodied this demoralized state. In the wake of an epidemic, he fell into a coma-like state that the Shawnee interpreted as death. However, before the funeral arrangements could be completed, he revived, to the amazement of his fellow tribesmen. Considerably more amazing were the revelations he had received during his deathlike trance.

Tenskwatawa had had an **out-of-body experience** in which he had been permitted to view heaven, ''a rich, fertile country, abounding in game, fish, pleasant hunting grounds and fine corn fields.'' But he had also witnessed sinful Shawnee spirits being tortured in hell according to the degree of their wickedness, with drunkards being forced to swallow molten lead. Overwhelmed by the power of his vision, Tenskwatawa abandoned his old ways. More revelations followed in the succeeding months— revelations that eventually added up to a coherent new vision of religion and society.

Although the ideas in the new revelation departed from tradition on many points (e.g., new songs and dances were introduced), their central thrust was a nativistic exhortation to abandon Euroamerican ways for the life-style of earlier generations. Tenskwatawa successfully extended his religion to other tribes, particularly the Kickapoos, Winnebagos, Sacs, and Miamis. New rituals that reflected the Shawnee's contact with Catholicism were evolved to formalize conversions.

With certain variations, the pattern of Tenskwatawa's experiences and the transformation of tradition that occurred as a result of the new revelation are characteristic of most nineteenth-century native American religions for which records have survived. Often, though not always, they incorporated elements of Christianity. Typically, innovations were brought about as a result of new revelations to a single prophet. The prophet was often a dissolute individual who fully embodied the demoralized state of his people. He also frequently had followed the vocation of **shaman** and/or healer prior to receiving his new vision of society and religion. To understand these movements better, it is useful to compare the most famous of them, the Ghost Dance of 1890, with Tenskwatawa's.

The Ghost Dance of 1890 was the most widespread native American millenarian movement of the nineteenth century. The year 1890 is added to its name to distinguish it from the Ghost Dance of 1870, a movement that was in many ways the prototype of the Ghost Dance of 1890. Both began among the Paiute of northern Nevada and spread to other tribes—the earlier to western tribal groups, and the later to eastern tribes— and scholars have noted that the basic structure of the ghost dance was taken from the traditional Paiute round dance.

The prophet of the Ghost Dance of 1890 was known as Wovoka (also called Jack Wilson, not to be confused with the peyote prophet, John Wilson). Like many earlier prophets, Wovoka was a healer and shaman who experienced his initial revelation when he seemed to fall down dead and receive a message in a disembodied state. Similarly to Tenskwatawa's experiences, God instructed him to propagate strongly ethical teachings. Additionally, Wovoka received a revelation of a **millennium** in which the earth would be renewed, the spirits of the dead return, and death and misery end. The millennium would be preceded by a general catastrophe that would destroy Euroamericans and their material culture. Specifically, righteous native Americans would be lifted off the planet, and a new earth rolled down across the surface, burying Euroamericans and unrighteous Indians. Consequently, native Americans were instructed to keep the peace and wait.

Beyond remaining at peace and following Wovoka's ethical injunctions, American Indians were periodically to perform what Euroamericans came to call the ghost dance. In this dance, men and women painted their bodies to indicate the revelations they had received and danced in concentric circles. The arms of each dancer rested on the shoulders of both neighbors, so that the vibrant rhythm of the dance swayed the worshipers as if they were a single body. The mood created by the dance, which was usually performed at night, was conducive to collective exaltation and trance. Wovoka's original instructions were to practice the dance for five days at a time. Eventually, some participants fell down into a trance during which they received revelations, usually from departed relatives. Performing the dance would hasten the advent of the new age.

Wovoka's revelation spoke powerfully to his contemporaries, and the dance was taken up by a wide variety of different tribes, such as the Shoshoni, Arapaho, Crow, Cheyenne, Pawnee, Kiowa, Comanche, and Sioux. As one might anticipate, relatively stable tribal groups that had adjusted successfully to changed conditions were least inclined to accept the new teaching. The widespread excitement generated by Wovoka's vision declined rapidly in the wake of the Wounded Knee Massacre (December 29, 1890), when U.S. troops—mistakenly believing that the new religion was a facade for a violent uprising—massacred a group of peaceful Sioux ghost dancers.

Quite independently of the prophet and the larger movement, however, the ghost dance continued to be practiced. For example, as late as the 1950s, the dance was still being performed by the Shoshoni in something like its original form. Perhaps the most important adaptive responses were in tribal groups that partially adopted the ghost dance as a medium for reviving selected aspects of their traditional religion, such as among the Pawnee, who began to practice an abandoned sacred hand game under the influence of the ghost dance.

Many of the native American prophet religions of the nineteenth century have survived into the late twentieth century. Particularly notable are Handsome Lake's religious movement, John Slocum's Indian Shaker church, and the Native American church.

Sources:

Edmunds, R. David. *The Shawnee Prophet.* Lincoln: University of Nebraska Press, 1983.
Eliade, Mircea. *Shamanism: Archaic Techniques of Ecstasy.* Princtone: Princeton University Press, 1964.
Kehoe, Alice Beck. *The Ghost Dance: Ethnohistory and Revitalization.* New York: Holt, Rinehart and Winston, 1989.
Mooney, James. *The Ghost-Dance Religion and the Sioux Outbreak of 1890.* 1896. Reprint, Chicago: University of Chicago Press, 1965.
Trafzer, Clifford E., ed. *American Indian Prophets.* Newcastle, CA: Sierra Oaks, 1986.

ANATTA

Anatta is the Pali (language of the earliest Buddhist scriptures) term for the Buddhist doctrine asserting that individuals do not possess eternal souls. The corresponding Sanskrit term is *anatman.* Instead of an eternal soul, individuals consist of a "bundle" of habits, memories, sensations, desires, and so forth, which together delude one into thinking that he or she consists of a stable, lasting self. Despite its transitory nature, this false self hangs together as a unit, and even reincarnates in body after body. This process of ongoing death and rebirth is referred to as *samsara.* In Hinduism, Buddhism, and other Indian religions, life in a corporeal body is viewed negatively, as the source of all suffering; hence, the goal of these religions is to release one from the samsaric process. In Buddhism, this means abandoning the false sense of self so that the bundle of memories and impulses disintegrates, leaving nothing to reincarnate and hence nothing to experience pain.

Sources:

Rahula, Walpola. *What the Buddha Taught.* 2d ed. New York: Evergreen, 1974.
Zimmer, Heinrich. *Philosophies of India.* New York: Bollingen, 1951.

ANCESTOR WORSHIP

Ancestor worship concerns religious beliefs and rituals associated with departed relatives. It is a religious practice found throughout the world, although it achieves its

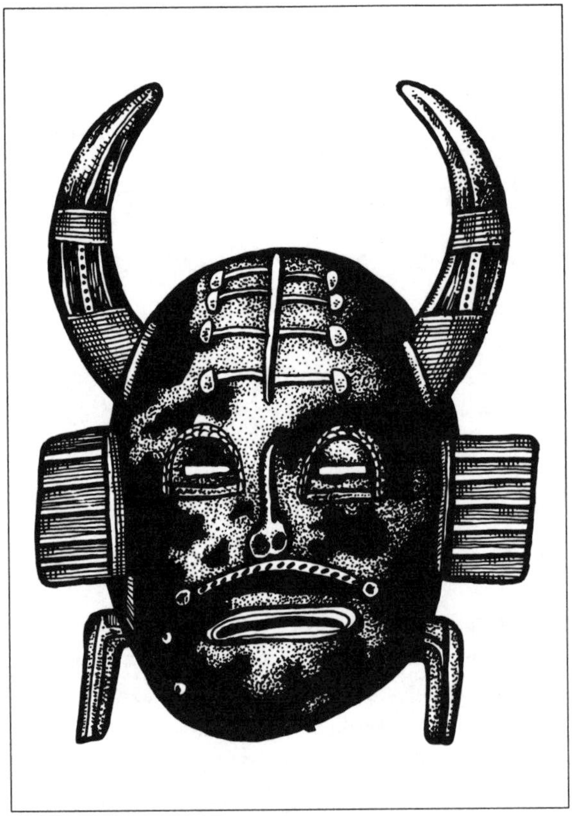

ANCESTOR MASK, WESTERN SUDAN.

fullest development in the Far East. Ancestor worship is characteristic of certain African tribes, Shinto (Japan), Confucianism (China), and some strands of Buddhism.

Although *ancestor worship* has been the accepted designation utilized by anthropologists and other students of religion, the connotations of *worship* make the term somewhat misleading. While some cultures tend to raise the departed to godlike stature, others simply set aside times to remember and honor the dead. (Would we regard the American observance of Memorial Day as ancestor worship?)

The exact nature of ancestor worship in any given culture naturally depends upon that society's concept of the afterlife. In some instances, one provides offerings to the dead in order to help make their residence in the beyond more comfortable. In other cultures, one performs ceremonies for the dead out of fear of their displeasure. In yet other societies, honoring the ancestors is simply a way of honoring one's tradition.

Of particular interest are cultures in which the departed relatives are thought to take an active interest in the affairs of the living. The deceased ancestors can provide information that will help their descendants live a better life, or even intercede on their behalf with divine forces. In these societies, ancestor worship may consist of requesting the departed to help the living with a particular problem, much as one would make requests of a parent or grandparent. In these cases, it is easy to see where the usual meaning of the term *worship* renders its application to such practices problematic.

Sources:

Eliade, Mircea. *Encyclopedia of Religion.* New York: Macmillan, 1987.
———. *A History of Religious Ideas.* 3 vols. Chicago: University of Chicago Press, 1978.

ANGEL OF DEATH

The Angel of Death, a notion that was particularly developed in rabbinical **Judaism,** was the being who extracted one's soul from the body at the moment of death. Whereas the biblical emissaries of death were clearly under the direct command of God (see, for example, Exodus 12:23, Isaiah 37:36), in postbiblical literature such forces began to act on their own initiative. By the time of the Talmud, the Angel of Death was identified with Satan, and the notion of an evil Angel of Death was reflected in many folk tales and in many folk practices associated with death, burial, and mourning.

In Talmudic legend, Joshua ben Levi was pictured as outsmarting the Angel of Death. He refused to give the angel back his sword until God intervened. This legend formed the basis of Longfellow's "The Legend of Rabbi Ben Levi," originally published in *Tales of a Wayside Inn* (1863).

Sources:

Eliade, Mircea, ed. *The Encyclopedia of Religion.* 16 vols. New York: Macmillan, 1987.
Wigoder, Geoffrey. *The Encyclopedia of Judaism.* New York: Macmillan, 1989.

ANGELS

Angels (from the Greek *angelos,* messengers) are intermediary spiritual beings between God and humanity. They are found predominantly in the Western monothe-

DEATH AND THE GRAVEDIGGER BY BELGIAN PAINTER CARLOS SCHWABE (1866–1926).

istic religions where God is conceived of as being so elevated that he does not intervene directly in the world. Angels are often pictured as delivering messages to mortals or carrying out God's will in other ways. Many traditions contain notions of

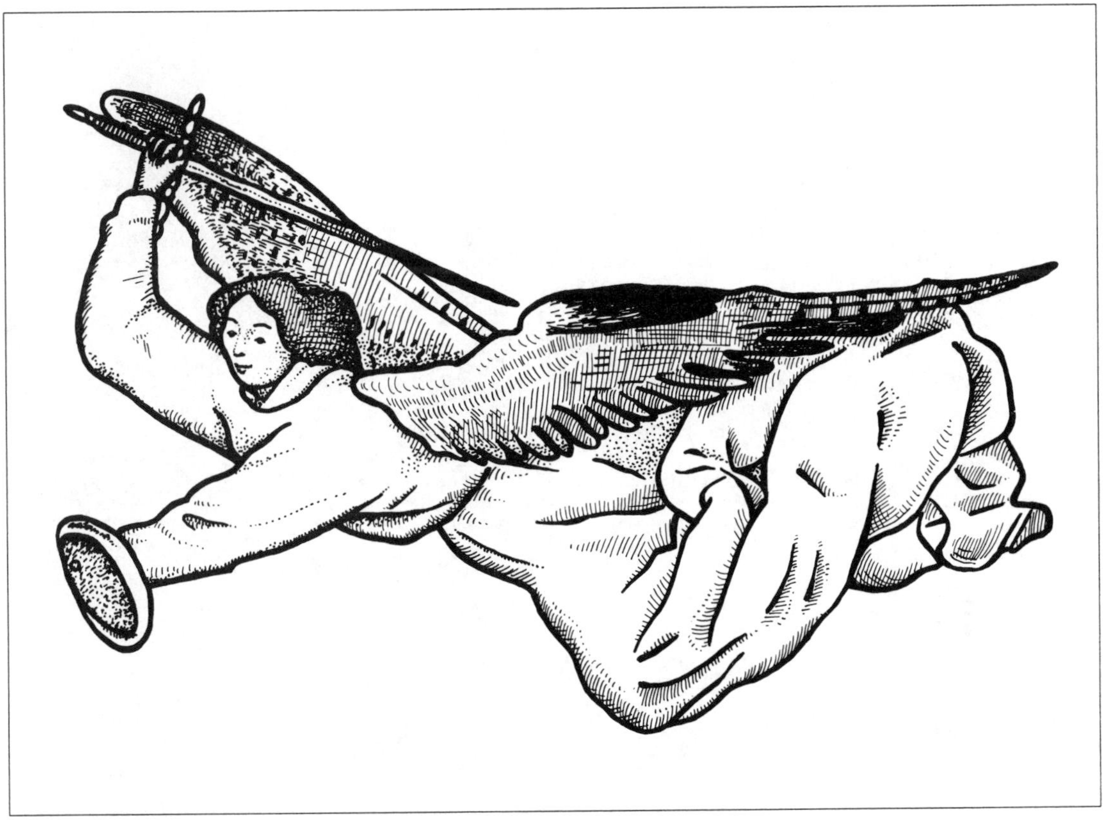

ANGEL FROM *THE FALL OF THE REBEL ANGELS* BY PETER BRUEGHEL THE YOUNGER, CA. 1600.

guardian angels assigned to watch over and protect individuals. In Western religions, angels refer exclusively to good beings. They are opposed by evil spirits (devils or demons), who are sometimes "fallen angels"—angels who revolted against God and were tossed out of heaven.

Angels are traditionally pictured as cohabiting heaven with deceased human beings. In early Christianity, stern, righteous angels tormented sinners and unbelievers for an eternity. It was only later that fallen angels acquired employment tormenting the souls of the damned. As popular notion removed the righteous angels from hell, Satan, ruler of all other fallen angels, became the king of the underworld.

Today, it is not uncommon to find confusion between angels and deceased human beings. As a significant contributor to popular ideas about spirits, **Spiritualism** has often pictured the individual as surrounded by helping spirits—spirits who at one time were all incarnated in human bodies. Thus, it has not been uncommon to equate guardian angels with the spirits of departed individuals. Popular movies have even portrayed deceased people as having wings—an attribute formerly reserved for

BOTTICINI'S *TOBIAS AND THE ANGELS* (15TH CENTURY).

angels—and even as becoming angels. These portrayals fly in the face of the traditional understanding of angels as constituting a separate order of creation.

Sources:

Eliade, Mircea, ed. *The Encyclopedia of Religion.* 16 vols. New York: Macmillan, 1987.
Guiley, Rosemary Ellen. *The Encyclopedia of Ghosts and Spirits.* New York: Facts on File, 1992.
Turner, Alice K. *The History of Hell.* New York: Harcourt Brace, 1993.

Animal Reincarnation

Belief in **reincarnation**—the concept that the soul is reembodied one lifetime after another—is usually limited to the transmigration of the souls of human beings. There is a widespread belief, however, in metempsychosis—the passing of the soul at death into another body either human or animal. In particular, certain strands of **Hinduism** preach the idea that people who lead morally degraded lives can return as animals (as a form of punishment).

Also, certain strands of the occult–metaphysical tradition, such as theosophy, view the ''souls'' of almost everything—from rocks to plants to animals—as being involved in the reincarnation progress. The overarching idea behind this comprehensive vision is that of spiritual ''evolution'' from simpler forms of life to more complex types. Hence, a mineral soul will eventually become a plant soul, a plant soul an animal soul, and an animal soul a human soul.

Sources:

Eliade, Mircea, ed. *Encyclopedia of Religion.* New York: Macmillan, 1987.

Eliade, Mircea. *Shamanism: Archaic Techniques of Ecstasy.* Princeton, NJ: Princeton University Press, 1964.

Turner, Alice K. *The History of Hell.* New York: Harcourt Brace, 1993.

APOCALYPSE

Apocalypse, a Greek word for ''revelation,'' originally referred to a literary genre in which mysterious revelations were given or explained by a supernatural figure, such as an angel. Apocalyptic literature generally includes an account of an **eschatological** scenario that includes a **Last Judgment** of the living and the dead. Because apocalyptic literature invariably included an account of cosmic cataclysm, the term *apocalypse* came to refer to complete destruction.

The first work to be formally called an apocalypse is the Apocalypse of John, more familiarly known as the Book of Revelation, which is well known for its plagues, wars, and other indicators of violence and destruction. Although the name comes from a Christian composition, the genre is much older, with Jewish apocalyptic literature appearing by at least the third century B.C. The earliest apocalyptic work was probably **Zoroastrian.**

Early Jewish apocalypes can be roughly divided into two principal groups. The first subgenre is what might be called historical apocalypses. These compositions, the most familiar of which is the Book of Daniel (the only apocalypse to be incorporated into the canonical Scriptures), were extended prophecies presented in the form of allegorical visions (the Book of Revelation is clearly in this tradition). The other subgenre was constituted by narratives of otherworldly journeys, focusing especially on ascent through a series of heavens, and culminating in a vision of the throne of God.

In the contemporary period, the near approach of the year 2000 on the Western calendar has led to a heightened interest in popular belief about the possible end of the world, and most portrayals of the end-time are apocalyptic. Although over the last several centuries there has been a steady flow of predictions that the world is coming to an end, their number has slowly increased as the end of the second Christian millennium approaches.

Much apocalyptic thought is tied to the Christian New Testament idea of a millennium, the predicted period of a thousand years during which Satan would be chained and not allowed to pursue his evil work on earth. The arrival of the

THE OPENING OF THE SIXTH SEAL.

millennium has been a major theme in American Christian thought, the principal debate being whether the millennium would be brought in by a sudden act of God in the near future (premillennialism), emerge gradually as society became more Christian (postmillennialism), or not occur at all as a literal historical period.

All of the predictions of an apocalyptic end of the world to date share one important characteristic: They have been wrong. Prophets have become objects of comic delight, and thus the general media (quite apart from the tabloids) have tended to treat news of new predictions as an opportunity for entertainment.

Apocalypticism appears in every era and every culture, but has become a uniquely vital theme in American religious life, especially since the rise of the Millerite movement in the 1830s. The failure of William Miller's predictions in the 1840s led directly to the Bible Students Movement, built around the predictions of Charles Taze Russell, which in turn were succeeded by the prophetic proclamation of the Jehovah's Witnesses. Within the emerging fundamentalist movement of the late nineteenth century, prophecy conferences provided hope for the eventual triumph of beleaguered evangelicals locked in a losing confrontation with modernists for control of American Protestant churches. As evangelicalism prospered in the twentieth century, it produced literally thousands of books advocating an expectancy of the near end of the world as we know it.

Sources:

Cohn, Norman. *Cosmos, Chaos and the World to Come: The AncientRoots ofApocalyptic Faith.* New Haven: Yale University Press, 1993.
Eliade, Mircea, ed. *Encyclopedia of Religion.* 16 vols. New York: Macmillan, 1987.
Turner, Alice K. *The History of Hell.* New York: Harcourt Brace, 1993.

APOTHEOSIS

Apotheosis (from Greek *apo,* from, and *theos,* god) is the official act of deification of a human being for some heroic act. In ancient times people who had been successful militarily or politically were sometimes deified even while still alive.

Rulers in the ancient world were often honored as divinities, either during life or after death. The Egyptian pharaohs, in particular, were believed to be divine because of their membership in the royal ruling family. The sanctioning of divinity because of genealogical origin was also found in ancient Greece, where some heroes and benefactors were believed to be descendants of divine beings. Alexander the Great (356–323 B.C.) was also consecrated by his successors and deified upon his death.

The phenomenon of deification was practiced most fully, however, during the Roman Imperial Age. All the Roman emperors after Augustus (63 B.C.–14 A.D.) were consecrated and deified upon their death. This ritual involved constructing a four-tiered pyre made of combustible planks and decorated with colorful precious fabrics, golden ornaments, and garlands. The succeeding emperor first lit the sacred fire on the pyre, where the corpse, covered with fragrant spices and fruits, was displayed. An eagle, believed to carry the soul of the deceased to heaven, was then set free. This ceremonial consecration was part of the cult of the emperor in pre-Christian Rome. With the adoption of Christianity, this ritual became incompatible with belief in the exclusively divine nature of Jesus. Upon his death, Constantine, the first Christian emperor, was depicted riding a chariot directed toward heaven, from whence God's hand was extended to him, symbolizing the unbroken traditional belief of the soul's journey to heaven but acknowledging the rulership of the new, non-Olympian, God.

Sources:

Eliade, Mircea, ed. *The Encyclopedia of Religion.* 16 vols. New York: Macmillan, 1987.
Smart, Ninian. *The Religious Experience of Mankind.* 3d ed. New York: Charles Scribner's Sons, 1984.

APPARITION

The term *apparition* usually refers to immaterial appearances of people, also called ghosts, animals, objects, or spirits. Despite much skepticism, reports of apparitions have always had a particular importance in folk belief and in the history of religion.

Apparitions, which usually appear to only a select few, involve noises, unusual smells, extreme cold, and the displacement of objects. Visual images, tactile sensations, and voices may also be observed. Apparitions move through solid matter, appear and disappear abruptly, may cast shadows and be reflected in mirrors, seem corporeal or luminous and transparent, and may be lifelike or have limited movement.

Invariably clothed, apparitions usually manifest for a particular reason—to communicate a crisis or death, provide warning, comfort the grieving, convey needed information—and appear in places where emotional events have occurred. Studies reveal few differences between apparitions of living persons and of the dead. Sometimes apparitions are collective, occurring simultaneously to multiple witnesses, and sometimes are reciprocal, when both agent and percipient—who are separated by distance—experience each other simultaneously. Other types of apparitions include deathbed apparitions, which usually involve images of divine or religious beings as well as dead loved ones, and apparitions suggestive of reincarnation, such as "announcing dreams," in which the deceased appears in a dream to a member of the family into which he or she will be born.

Numerous theories have been offered to explain apparitions, from the assertion that they are mental hallucinations to the notion of telepathy from the dead to the living. Other theories posit that apparitions are astral or ethereal bodies, an amalgam of personality patterns, recording or imprints of vibrations, projections of the human unconscious or will and concentration, true spirits of the dead, and localized phenomena with their own physicality, directed by an intelligence or personality. One of the most elaborate theories is that of "idea-patterns" contained in G. N. M. Tyrell's *Apparitions* (1943), in which apparitions are believed to be hallucinations on the part of a percipient based on information received from the agent.

Science still has little knowledge about the nature of apparitions, even though there have been systematic studies since the late nineteenth century, inaugurated by the British Society for Psychical Research. Among its most important works are the research studies reported in *Phantasm of the Living* (1886) and the 1889 Census of Hallucinations, about apparitions of both the living and the dead. Similar censuses were taken in France, Germany, and the United States.

Sources:

Cavendish, Richard. *The Encyclopedia of the Unexplained.* New York: McGraw-Hill, 1967.
Green, Celia, and Charles McCreery. *Apparitions.* London: Hamish Hamilton, 1975.
Gurney, Edmund, F. W. H. Myers, and Frank Podmore. *Phantasms of the Living.* 1886. Reprint, London: Kegan Paul, Trench, Trubner & Co., 1918.
Myers, Frederic W. H. *Human Personality and Its Survival of Bodily Death.* Vols. 1 and 2. 1903. New ed. New York: Longmans, Green & Co., 1954.
Stevenson, Ian. "The Contribution of Apparitions to the Evidence for Survival." *The Journal of the American Society for Psychical Research* 76, no. 4 (October 1982): 341–56.
Tyrrell, G. N. M. *Apparitions.* 1943. Rev. ed. London: The Society for Psychical Research, 1973.

Aquarian Fellowship Church

The Aquarian Fellowship Church is a defunct **Spiritualist** body founded in 1969 by Robert A. Ferguson. Ferguson had been president of the **Universal Church of the Master (UCM),** one of the more important Spiritualist organizations which also absorbed certain influences from **New Thought.** He left UCM partially because he felt inspired to do so as a result of information received in dreams, and partially because he disagreed with the doctrine of **reincarnation,** a notion accepted and taught by UCM.

The Aquarian Fellowship Church based its teachings on the Bible, on Ferguson's own writings, and on the writings of **Andrew Jackson Davis,** a speculative metaphysician who, although never a member of the Spiritualist church, was adopted as the official theorist of nineteenth-century Spiritualists. Ferguson started a program for reprinting Davis's books. The thrust of Aquarian Fellowship services was the same as that of classical Spiritualism, namely communication with the so-called dead.

Sources:

Ferguson, Robert A. *Universal Mind.* West Nyack, NY: Parker Publishing, 1979.
Melton, J. Gordon. *Encyclopedia of American Religions.* 4th ed. Detroit, MI: Gale Research, 1993.

Aquarian Foundation

Rev. Keith Milton Rhinehart, a Spiritualist minister, founded the Aquarian Foundation in 1955 as a blending of Spiritualist, theosophical, and Eastern ideas. After existing for years as a lone congregation in Seattle, Washington, the foundation gained more and more visibility in the 1960s through regular "materialization" séances and Rhinehart's claims to be in contact with the same spiritual masters supposedly contacted by **Helena Blavatsky,** founder of the Theosophical Society. In the 1970s the foundation gained other congregations across the United States and in several other countries.

Unlike the Spiritualist groups of the nineteenth century, the Aquarian Foundation does not focus on contacting deceased friends and loved ones, but rather on contacting the Masters of the Great White Brotherhood of Cosmic Light. This is the same brotherhood as discussed in the Theosophical Society, and the teachings are similar. The "masters" are considered to be highly evolved beings who are aiding humanity's development; they make their teachings known through certain selected mediums such as Rhinehart.

Rhinehart claims regular contact not only with the standard theosophical list of masters but also with other "ascended" beings, including Mahatma Gandhi, the angel Moroni (from Mormon teachings), UFO entities Ashtar and Clarion, and others. The teachings gathered from all these sources center on the ideas of reincarnation, karma, the law of cause and effect, and mastery of one's personal existence, even mastery of death itself. The Aquarian Foundation believes that the soul does not die, but continues to evolve and learn.

Sources:

Melton, J. Gordon. *Encyclopedia of American Religions.* 4th ed. Detroit, MI: Gale Research, 1993.
Rhinehart, Keith Milton. *Soul Mates and Twin Rays.* Seattle, WA: Aquarian Foundation, 1972.

AQUINAS, THOMAS

The Catholic theologian and philosopher St. Thomas Aquinas (ca. 1224–1274) was born in Roccasecca, Italy. Educated by the Benedectines of Monte Cassino, he took a Master in Arts at the University of Naples before entering the Order of Dominicans in 1244. In 1252 he was sent to the University of Paris for advanced study in theology and taught until 1259, when he went back to Italy to spend about 10 years at various Dominican monasteries, lecturing on theology and philosophy. After spending four years in Paris, he returned to Naples, where he taught for more than a year at the university and where he preached a notable series of sermons. Illness forced him to interrupt his teaching, and later on to interrupt a trip to Lyons, where he was supposed to attend a church council in 1274, the year of his death.

Thomas Aquinas's eclectic philosophy can be characterized as a rethinking of Aristotelianism, with the significant addition of Christianity and of the philosophies of his predecessors. His philosophy was expressed in his writings, which he produced during his 20 years as an active teacher. Besides a variety of recorded disputations and commentaries (*On Being and Essence, De Anima, On Physics, On Interpretation, Posterior Analytics, Ethics, Metaphysics, Politics,* and the unfinished expositions of Aristotle's *De Caelo, De Generatione,* and *Metheora*), his works primarily consist of theological and philosophical treatises written in Latin. These include the short treatise *Principles of Nature,* in which he discusses several philosophical subjects, from the distinction between essence and existence to the Aristotelian dependence of abstract, universal categories on individual material things; four books in which he argues against nonbelievers and heretics; *Against the Errors of the Greeks,* in which he expresses his opinion about the doctrinal points disputed by Greek and Latin

Christians; and the unfinished three-part treatise on sacred doctrine that contains the principles of theology.

The element providing his theology with conceptual unity consists of the Dionysian circle, implying the going forth of all things from God and the return of all things to God. Part 1 includes questions and treatises about creation, the angels, the human being, and divine government. The two divisions of the second part are about virtues, vices, law, and grace, and the questions contained in the third part consider Christ and his sacraments as indispensable means to salvation.

According to Thomas Aquinas, salvation is possible through scriptural knowledge, awareness of certain truths which exceed human reason and can be accepted only on faith. Human beings cannot directly know God's essence, which transcends all species and genera. God's existence can be proved in five ways employing the principle of causality and empirical knowledge of the physical world, such as the argument from nature of efficient cause (i.e., We perceive that everything is caused by something else, which was in turn the result of yet another prior cause. Human reason insists that there must be a first, original cause of everything. This first cause we call God). All of these arguments imply the principle that reason needs a final stopping point in any chain of explanation, one that must be outside the series itself and be of a different nature—that is, the nature of God.

Thomas Aquinas maintains that God's simultaneous presence occurs in all things as the source of their being, power, and operation. God's essence, defined as an immutable pure act, cannot be fully understood by the created intellect, unless God makes himself intelligible to it through his grace, a foretaste of eternal life in heaven that is achieved by good works and exercise of all the virtues. Those who possess the more divine grace will be able to see God the more perfectly, and they will be the more beatified (blessed).

Aquinas asserts that God cannot be seen in his essence by a mere human being, and the goals of beatific vision and ultimate happiness, which have an eternal nature and cannot be lost once attained, can be achieved only by separation from mortal life. Humanity reaches immortal life through resurrection, when the soul is rejoined to the body. Death, even that of the people alive at the end of the world, is a necessary circumstance in the process whereby human beings become immortal. All people are directed to one last fixed end, and after death both intellect and will of all the dead, whether they are in hell, purgatory, or in heaven, whether before or after resurrection, become immutable and are brought to eternity.

According to Aquinas, the localities of life after death are Limbus Patrum (limbo of the fathers), where the good who died before Christ went; Limbus Infantum (limbo of the infants), where the children who died unbaptized go; Purgatory, the place where all sinners stay until they are purified or redeemed by the Church, or until Judgment Day; Hell, or Gehenna, where the wicked are condemned; and finally Heaven, where the good are admitted. At the Day of Judgment, all souls will reassume their bodies. The intermediate states will then be destroyed, and when the last sentence is pronounced, the condemned will depart for hell and the good will go to heaven forever. Before the Judgment Day the souls in purgatory can be redeemed and transferred to heaven through the prayers of the living and the transfer of good works to their account.

Sources:

Alger, William Rounseville. *The Destiny of the Soul. A Critical History of the Doctrine of a Future Life.* New York: Greenwood Press, 1968.

Edward, Paul, ed. *The Encyclopedia of Philosophy.* New York: Macmillan, 1967.

Magill, Frank N., ed. *Masterpieces of World Philosophy.* New York: HarperCollins, 1990.

Tugwell, Simon. *Human Immortality and the Redemption of Death.* London: Darton, Longman and Todd, 1990.

ARCHITECTURE

A society's concept of the afterlife sometimes influences its architecture, especially the architecture of its temples. The realm of the gods as well as the postmortem abode of souls is often imagined as being somewhere in the sky, so temples tended to be built emphasizing the dimension of height (e.g., the ancient Babylonian ziggurat) or the dome of heaven (e.g., the domes of mosques). Traditionally, Christians have viewed heaven as being in the sky, so the roofs and spires of Christian churches often reach upward. The cathedrals of the Gothic period, in particular, seem to have the lines of spaceships, as if the whole building is about to take off from the earth and travel to heaven.

This consideration throws light on possible afterlife belief influences of such structures as the pyramids of **Mesopotamia** and Mesoamerica. This does not, however, explain the pyramids of Egypt, which, despite their great height, were built as tombs rather than to bring one closer to the sky? Egyptian pyramids are at least partially explainable in terms of the universal pattern of the ''cosmic mountain.'' As have the majority of human societies, the ancient Egyptians tended to see the cosmos as consisting of three principal realms—this world, the upper world, and the underworld. This structure is held together and supported at the center of the three worlds (the *axis mundi)* by a cosmic tree or mountain. The passageway between the worlds also tends to be located at this juncture of the three realms. A pyramid is, in a sense, an artificial mountain, and thus a model of the center of the cosmos. By building one's tomb in the shape of a mountain, one symbolically locates oneself at or near a passageway between the worlds, thus allowing easier transit to the afterlife.

Sources:

Eliade, Mircea, ed. *The Encyclopedia of Religion.* 16 vols. New York: Macmillan, 1987.

Mann, A. T. *Sacred Architecture.* Rockport, MA: Element Books, 1993.

ASCENSION

Stories of divine, heroic, and human journeys to a heaven where gods reside have been told since the beginning of recorded history. Ecstatic (trance) techniques

BABYLON AT THE TIME OF NEBUCHADREZZAR II. THE GREAT ZIGGURAT STANDS AT THE LEFT. COURTESY OF THE ARC.

enabling such an ascent have been practiced throughout the world by shamans, healers, medicine men, and so forth, on behalf of their community. Western notions of ascension to heaven developed principally from the religious traditions of Mesopotamia and Greece.

In ancient Egypt, the Pyramid texts document the belief in the pharaoh's ascension to heaven upon his death. It was his destiny to be transformed into **Osiris,** king of the dead, through a series of magic formulas. The pharaoh was believed to ascend either by a ladder made by the solar divinity Ra, or by transforming himself into a bird. Once the pharaoh reached the afterlife, a series of magic practices followed, converting him into a spirit or a star.

Several famous Greek mystics of the pre-Christian era (such as Aristeas, Epimenides, and Hermotimos) supposedly knew how to fly in a state of trance. Such a state implies the concept of separation of body and soul, which in Platonic thought was related in the tale of Er. Er, wounded in a battle, was believed to be dead. But after 12 days he returned to life and gave a detailed account of the afterlife. Through Plato the idea of a human being reaching heavenly states was passed on to Hellenism. The Hellenistic period was actually dominated by human efforts to obtain liberation from

THE ASCENSION OF CHRIST.

the world by escaping through the heavenly spheres. Various mystery religions spread into the Greco-Roman world and contributed to the development of ecstatic traditions, such as the mysteries of Isis and Mithra.

With Hellenism, the ancient idea of **Hades** as a shadowy place was eclipsed by the more sophisticated image of a celestial afterlife that could be achieved through a certain type of knowledge, *gnosis.* The Gnostics believed that salvation could be obtained through knowledge of certain practices and of the true principles that govern reality. The soul of a Gnostic could pass through the seven spheres and ultimately reach the *pleroma*—the fullness, the godhead. Another concept to developed within Gnosticism was the *antimimon pneuma* (counterfeit spirit), which became important in the Hermetic tradition. This concept posited the existence of an intermediary spirit between the soul and the body that causes the soul to **reincarnate** and follows it in all of its reincarnations. The soul was believed to come into incarnation by descending through the planetary spheres, thus acquiring in the process the characteristics attributed to planets by astrology. In the reverse process of disembodiment, the soul was believed to ascend the planetary spheres, thus abandoning the characteristics of those planets (the astrological patterns) to the planets themselves.

In the Judeo-Christian tradition, the heavenly journey of the soul is confined mostly to apocalyptic literature, such as the Apocalypse of Abraham, the Vision of Isaiah, and the Apocalypse of Paul. Typically, the cosmos is pictured as having seven heavens (which are not identified with the seven planets of the Hellenistic tradition). In Islam, following the pattern of Judeo-Christian tradition, the prophet Mohammed ascended to the ultimate heaven (the *Mi'raj*) via seven intermediate ones (again not identified with the planetary spheres). Medieval Christian literature contains apocalyptic works that relate the ascension to heaven of saints (such as the Purgatory of St. Patrick) and historical characters (such as the *Vision of Alberic.)* In the thirteenth century, **Dante** Alighieri's *Paradise,* the third part of *The Divine Comedy,* presented Dante's journey through the heavenly spheres (which Dante identified with the planets as well), thus combining elements drawn from Hellenistic-Hermetic-Neoplatonic thought and the Judeo-Christian-Muslim tradition.

Sources:

Eliade, Mircea, ed. *The Encyclopedia of Religion.* 16 vols. New York: Macmillan, 1987.
McDannell, Colleen, and Bernhard Lang. *Heaven: A History.* 1988. Reprint, New York: Vintage, 1990.
Turner, Alice K. *The History of Hell.* New York: Harcourt Brace, 1993.

ASSOCIATION FOR PAST-LIFE RESEARCH AND THERAPIES

The Association for Past-Life Research and Therapies (APRT) is an association concerned with research into **reincarnation** and with the advancement of methods for accessing past lives as part of therapy. Composed primarily of mental health professionals and others interested in the advancement of **past-life therapy,** the APRT has been less concerned with general reincarnation research than with matters directly relevant to therapeutic intervention. Most of the association's research has arisen directly out of clinical settings. Since 1986, APRT has published such research in its *Journal of Regression Therapy.*

APRT had its beginnings in a conference held at the University of California, Irvine, on May 14, 1980. The conference, organized by Ronald Jue, focused on reincarnation and past-life therapy. Speakers included such well-known figures as Gina Cerminara, Edith Fiore, and Morris Netherton. During the conference, a group of interested participants organized a committee that was assigned the task of creating a past-life therapy association. This new organization, the Association for Past-Life Research and Therapies, formally came into being later that year at a conference held in Anaheim, California.

Along with other concerns, the APRT has struggled with the question of who should practice past-life therapy. Particularly at the beginning, the association's membership was diverse, ranging from uncredentialed psychics whose principal focus was past-life *readings* (rather than *therapy)* to fully licensed psychologists. In an effort to gain professional status, the APRT has sponsored training seminars and set progressively more rigorous requirements.

Sources:

Lucas, Winafred Blake. *Regression Therapy: A Handbook for Professionals. 2 vols.* Crest Park, CA: Deep Forest Press, 1993.

ASTRAL PROJECTION

The term *astral projection,* also known as etheric projection or out-of-body traveling, refers to the ability to travel outside the physical body. The astral body is said to be an exact replica of the physical body but more subtle. It is the body that one is said to inhabit after death. It is further said that the astral body can detach from the physical body at will, or under certain special circumstances. It can also spontaneously leave the physical body during sleep, trance, or coma, under the influence of anesthetics or drugs, or as the result of accidents. The astral body is said to be composed of subtle elements, etheric in nature, that correspond to what the Yogis consider the vital centers of the physical body, more connected with the life force than with matter. The astral body is the vehicle of consciousness and the instrument of passions, desires, and feelings, which are conveyed to the physical body through this invisible, intangible medium. When it separates from the denser, physical body, it takes with it the capacity for feeling.

The concept of bilocation is associated with the concept of astral projection. Bilocation means the ability to be in two places at the same time, and since a person cannot be in both places at once, an explanation could be that the physical body is in one place, while the astral body is in another. The astral body of a dying person is often projected to the presence of loved ones a few moments before physical death, and this phenomenon is said to arise from the strong desire of the dying person to see and be seen. There are many reports of this phenomenon, and some have claimed it is possible to project this body at will during subjective experimentation, but the existence of such a body has not been proved to the satisfaction of mainstream science.

Many everyday experiences of astral projection have been reported. The British scientist Robert Crookall, has studied hundreds of cases in which people left the physical body during their lifetime and reentered it after traveling unseen in the astral body. Sylvan Muldoon and Hereward Carrington, in their famous books *The Phenomena of Astral Projection* and *The Projection of the Astral Body,* maintain that there are three kinds of projection: conscious projection, in which the subject is awake; partially conscious projection; and unconscious projection. Unconscious projection has two distinct forms: immotive astral projection, which is an unconscious astral catalepsy occurring while a person is sitting or standing, and motive astral projection, which occurs while the subject is lying down. Muldoon and Carrington also report some techniques for experiencing astral projection at will. The methods are based on a simple, strong desire to project one's own astral body.

Sources:

Muldoon, Sylvan J., and Hereward Carrington. *The Phenomena of Astral Projection.* London: Rider & Company, 1969.

———. *The Projection of the Astral Body.* New York: Samuel Weiser, 1970.

Shepard, Leslie A., ed. *Encyclopedia of Occultism & Parapsychology.* Detroit, MI: Gale Research, 1991.

ASTROLOGY AND REINCARNATION

Astrology literally means the study (or science) of the stars. Most people are familiar with only a tiny portion of this vast subject, namely, the 12 signs of the *zodiac* (''circle of animals'') as they relate to the personality of individuals and to the use of astrology for divinatory purposes. The zodiac is the belt constituted by the 12 signs—Aries, Taurus, Gemini, Cancer, Leo, Virgo, Libra, Scorpio, Sagittarius, Capricorn, Aquarius, and Pisces.

The notion of the zodiac is very ancient, with roots in the early cited cultures of Mesopotamia. The first 12-sign zodiacs were named after the gods of these cultures. The Greeks adopted astrology from the Babylonians, and the Romans in turn adopted astrology from the Greeks. These peoples renamed the signs of the Mesopotamian zodiac in terms of their own mythologies, which is why the familiar zodiac of the contemporary West bears names out of Mediterranean mythology.

Zodiacal symbolism is pervasive. The popularity of Sun sign astrology (the kind found in the daily newspaper) has kept these ancient symbols alive in modern society, so that even such prominent artifacts as automobiles have been named after some of the signs (e.g., the Taurus and the Scorpio).

Derided as medieval superstition, astrology nevertheless continues to exercise a fascination over the human mind. Furthermore, polls indicate that its popularity is growing rather than waning. Currently, astrology's greatest strength is in the metaphysical community, a loose-knit subculture. The most distinctive institution of this subculture is the metaphysical bookstore, and its most visible manifestation has been the so-called New Age movement. The most widespread aspect of the modern renewal of interest in things occult has been the growth of interest in astrology.

Although astrology and **reincarnation** are not necessarily connected, their proximity in the metaphysical subculture has led to the wholesale adoption of reincarnationist thought by astrologers. The notions of reincarnation and karma together explain why some people are born into lucky circumstances and others into unfortunate conditions. For astrologers concerned with the issue of why some people come into this life with hardship written large across their horoscopes and other people seem to be born under a lucky star, reincarnation and **karma** prove important explanatory tools. Reincarnation also provides a framework for explaining why a person has certain personality traits—they are carryovers from ''past lifetimes.''

THE CONSTELLATIONS AND THE STARS.

Sources:

Lewis, James R. *The Astrology Encyclopedia.* Detroit, MI: Gale Research, 1994.

Melton, J. Gordon. "The Revival of Astrology in the United States." In Rodney Stark, ed., *Religious Movements: Genesis, Exodus, and Numbers.* New York: Paragon, 1985.

Tiryakian, Edward, ed. *On the Margin of the Visible.* New York: John Wiley and Sons, 1974.

ATMAN

Atman is a **Hindu** word for "the essence of the individual." An ancient Sanskrit term, it appears to have originally referred to the breath. (As the invisible part of the person that stopped once life had departed, the breath was often associated with—and sometimes even identified with—the soul in many different world cultures.) Although often translated as "soul" or "self," *atman* refers to the deeper self that remains unchanged during the cycle of reincarnation. Heinrich Zimmer, the great German Indologist, explains it this way:

> Everything that we normally know and express about ourselves belongs to

> the sphere of change, the sphere of time and space, but this Self *(atman)* is forever changeless, beyond time, beyond space and the veiling net of causality, beyond measure, beyond the dominion of the eye. (1951, 3)

The changing part of the self that carries distinct personality traits from one lifetime to the next is termed the *jiva.* From the standpoint of classical Hinduism, the atman is eternal whereas the jiva is not. After the classical period, however, *atman* was sometimes used interchangeably with *jiva,* so one has to pay attention to the context in more recent texts to determine the exact referent.

Sources:

Feuerstein, Georg. *Encyclopedic Dictionary of Yoga.* New York: Paragon House, 1990.
Zimmer, Heinrich. *Philosophies of India.* New York: Bollingen, 1951.

AURA

An aura is a field or body of subtle (nonphysical or quasiphysical) energy that envelops living entities. Sometimes conceived of as emanating from nonliving minerals, auras are undetectable by human sight but can be seen by people with the gift of clairvoyance, or ''psychic sight.'' Individuals with such gifts describe the aura as a colorful field that may have rays, streamers, and other distinct phenomena associated with it. The size, brightness, colors, and so forth indicate different things about the individual's emotional and physical state. Clairvoyant healers assert that illness begins as a disturbance in the aura, and that it take months or sometimes even years before a physical illness manifests.

Because they can be seen only by clairvoyants, auras are not, as might be expected, the subject of mainstream scientific research. Although living tissue does emit a magnetic field, termed a biofield, this field seems much too weak to be the same as the aura described in occult literature. A popular quasi-scientific theory postulates that the aura is a form of light vibrating at frequencies that normal vision cannot perceive.

The basic idea of an envelope of subtle, vital energy emanating from the body and other forms of life has been widely accepted in many cultures and times. Artwork and written records indicate such a belief in ancient India, Egypt, Rome, and Greece. The great sixteenth-century alchemist and occultist Paracelsus was one of the earliest Westerners to write at length on this envelope of energy, which he referred to as a ''fiery globe.'' In the late eighteenth century, Franz Anton Mesmer explained hypnotism via his notion ''animal magnetism,'' an electromagnetic energy that could be transmitted from one person to another in healing situations. In the mid-nineteenth century, Baron Karl von Reichenbach described a similar energy, which he termed odic force.

In the second decade of the current century, Dr. Walter J. Kilner, an electrotherapist at St. Thomas's Hospital in London, invented an apparatus for seeing what appeared to be a human aura. This device contained dicyanin, a coal-tar dye that allowed one to see ultraviolet light. Kilner asserted that the state of the aura indicated the state of one's physical health, and in 1919 he claimed to have developed a way of using the aura to diagnose illness. Kilner also claimed that weaker auras tended to draw off the energy from more vigorous auras with which they came into contact. His early research was published in 1911 in *The Human Aura.* Despite the criticism with which the book was greeted, Kilner continued his research until World War I interrupted it. When a revised edition of *The Human Aura* appeared in 1920, it was greeted more sympathetically. Kilner died soon afterward, on June 23, 1920. A more recent procedure for sensing the aura, developed in 1939 by a Russian electrician, Semyon Davidovich Kirlian, produces photographs of the energy field.

Many religious traditions, as well as traditional occultism, view the aura as emanating from a subtle, nonphysical "body." This subtle body may be one of several secondary bodies in which the soul is "clothed." These subtle bodies constitute intermediary levels between the physical body and the soul proper. Because they are nonphysical, they survive the death of the physical body. Some traditional cultures have gone so far as to map out the anatomy of some of the subtle bodies. The best-known example of these is the Chinese culture—with its acupuncture.

Another tradition with a complex understanding of the subtle body is the Hindu yoga tradition, in which the subtle body is referred to as the **linga sharira.** Differing strands of the Western occult tradition postulate different sets of bodies. The most common are (1.) etheric, or vital energy body, (2.) astral or emotional body, (3.) mental body, (4.) causal body (containing the seeds of all of one's **karma**), and (5.) spiritual body.

Sources:

Bagnall, Oscar. *The Properties of the Human Aura.* Rev. ed. New York: University Books, 1970. (Originally published 1937.)

Becker, Robert O., and Gary Selden. *The Body Electric: Electromagnetism and the Foundation of Life.* New York: William Morrow, 1985.

Feuerstein, Georg. *Encyclopedic Dictionary of Yoga.* New York: Paragon House, 1990.

Kilner, Walter J. *The Human Aura.* Rev. ed. New Hyde Park, NY: University Books, 1964. (Originally published 1920.)

Ostrander, Sheila, and Lynn Schroeder. *Psychic Discoveries Behind the Iron Curtain.* Englewood Cliffs, NJ: Prentice-Hall, 1970.

Australia (Aboriginal)

Traditional Australian societies share the notion that human beings and society were created in a distant time period referred to as the Dreaming or the Dream Time (considered sacred time). Simultaneously, the Dreaming refers to the realm of the spiritual, which is coextensive with the time of origins (creation). As the name

AZTEC GOD OF DEATH.

The Aztec left behind records of a far more elaborate conceptualization of the afterlife than the other societies of Mesoamerica, which is largely the result of their greater interest in death. The greater interest in death, in turn, seems to have been the result of the centrality of sacrifice—including human sacrifice—in Aztecan religion.

The Aztec postulated four different realms, corresponding to the four directions, to which the soul could go following death. Warriors who died in battle, sacrificial victims, and tradesmen who died during their journeys were cremated, went to the eastern paradise, and become companions of the sun. Women who died in childbirth also become companions of the sun, although they went to the west.

People who died by lightning, drowning, and marsh fevers (all having to do with water or rain) were buried and went to Tlaloc's southern paradise. This realm was said to be free of sorrow and the souls there enjoyed a luxurious tropical garden. Although there was apparently no notion of an afterlife retribution, Mictlán, the northern land of the dead and the ultimate destiny of the majority of people, was distinctly unpleasant. The deceased took four years to traverse nine intervening subterranean realms containing mountains, ferocious beasts, and chilling winds. All the dead were buried with amulets and cremated dogs to help them during their journey.

Sources:

Eliade, Mircea, ed. *The Encyclopedia of Religion.* 16 vols. New York: Macmillan, 1987.

Hultkrantz, Ake. *The Religions of the American Indians.* 1967. Reprint, Berkeley: University of California Press, 1979.

León-Portilla, Miguel. "Those Made Worthy by Divine Sacrifice: The Faith of Ancient Mexico." In Gary H. Gossen, ed., *South and Meso-American Native Spirituality.* New York: Crossroad, 1993.

B

BAHA'I

The Baha'i faith has its roots in Islamic culture. It was established in 1844 in Persia, from where it spread throughout the world. Baha'i is based on the writings of the founder, Baha'u'llah, and espouses the essential unity of all world religions. According to this faith, God expresses himself through a succession of Divine Teachers, the Manifestations, the most recent of which is represented by Baha'u'llah, who claims that during the present historical period human spiritual destiny will be fulfilled.

Baha'i adherents believe that the physical world is a reflection of the world of the spirit and, likewise, the fundamental reality of each individual is the soul, whose education represents the main purpose of physical creation itself. Spiritual progress, which is equally available to all, and this process of development continue after the dissociation of the soul from the physical body at death, and it occurs in the presence of God in an eternal and more expansive stage of spiritual education.

Therefore, death is regarded as a time of happy release and achievement, even though one is not automatically ensured of success, because each individual is believed to enter the next world in essentially the same condition in which he or she departs this life, which condition is evaluated in a sort of judgment at the point of transition to the afterlife.

The progress of each soul depends on its own efforts, and its salvation is regarded as a motion toward endless possibilities, the soul being capable of infinite development. Also, there is no regression in the afterlife, only progress.

Sources:

Johnson, Christopher Jay, and Marsha G. McGee. *Encounters with Eternity: Religious Views of Death and Life After-Death.* New York: Philosophical Library, 1986.

Kastenbaum, Robert, and Beatrice Kastenbaum, eds. *Encyclopedia of Death.* Phoenix, AZ: Oryx Press, 1989.

BALFOUR, ARTHUR J.

Arthur J. Balfour (1848–1930), also known as the first Earl of Balfour, was very interested in psychical research and the question of survival after death, as was his brother Gerald W. Balfour and his sister, the wife of **Henry Sidgwick.** Born at Whittinghame, East Lothian, Scotland, he studied law and philosophy at Eton and Trinity College, Cambridge University. After serving in the British Parliament from 1874 to 1885, Balfour became prime minister in 1902, first lord of the admiralty in 1915 (succeeding Winston Churchill), and foreign secretary in 1916. In 1894 he became president of the **Society for Psychical Research,** occupying a position which had previously been held by his brother.

Balfour held many séances with Mrs. Willett, a medium who, in one series of communications received by **automatic writing** and referred to as the Palm Sunday case, mentioned Mary Lyttelton, who had died shortly before her engagement to Arthur Balfour was to have been announced. The Palm Sunday case was considered one of the most striking evidences of survival after death utilizing the method of **cross-correspondences.** Balfour never married and died 55 years after the death of his beloved Mary, whose ghostly presence in Balfour's house was occasionally perceived by Mrs. Willett.

Sources:

Cavendish, Richard, ed. *Encyclopedia of the Unexplained. Magic, Occultism and Parapsychology.* London: Arkana Penguin Books, 1989.

Shepard, Leslie A., ed. *Encyclopedia of Occultism & Parapsychology.* Detroit, MI: Gale Research, 1991.

BAPTISTS

The majority of Baptists adhere to the basic concepts about death included in the Bible and expressed in classical Christianity and conservative Protestant thought. Death is considered an intrusion into God's will about human beings, and is the result of sin, which, since Adam, all people encounter in their lives. Nevertheless, death is defeated by life because of the Creator's final word for humankind, involving the resurrection of Jesus Christ. Only those persons and rebellious angels who reject God will not achieve cosmic redemption from the ravages of human wrongdoing, after which all things will be restored as they were intended to be.

The individual's relationship with Christ is considered crucial to the person's destiny, which depends on the total acceptance or rejection of what the Gospel of Jesus Christ embodies. By accepting the good news of God contained in the Gospel, people will be saved; that is, they will live in God's presence after death.

On the other hand, unbelief and wickedness will be punished by God, and those who deny Jesus Christ will be addressed to hell, a place of darkness and fire, where nobody can see God. Reincarnation, transmigration of souls, and universalism, which postulates that all persons must be saved, are generally denied by Baptists.

Sources:

Johnson, Christopher Jay, and Marsha G. McGee. *Encounters with Eternity: Religious Views of Death and Life After-Death.* New York: Philosophical Library, 1986.

Kastenbaum, Robert, and Kastenbaum, Beatrice, eds. *Encyclopedia of Death.* Phoenix: Oryx Press, 1989.

BHAGAVAD GITA

The scriptures of **Hinduism** are a complex, multilayered body of literature, difficult to describe or characterize in a short space. The oldest layer of this tradition, which is constituted by the Vedas (something of a Hindu Old Testament), goes back thousands of years before the Christian era. One of the most significant and popular Hindu texts is the *Bhagavad Gita* (the Lord's Song), a short work that was inserted into the *Mahabharata,* the world's longest epic, sometime between 200 B.C. and 200 A.D. The *Bhagavad Gita* contains one of the most important discussions of the immortality of the soul—and the consequences of such immortality for action in this world—in all of world literature.

The central narrative of the *Mahabharata* is about a civil war, and the events surrounding the culminating battle, in an ancient Indian kingdom. Before the great battle is about to begin, Arjuna, the leading protagonist, asks his chariot driver, who is Krishna, to drive his chariot out between the two armies. Krishna is a complex figure whom many Hindus regard as god himself. The text of the *Bhagavad Gita* contains a conversation between Arjuna and Krishna. From his vantage point on the field between the two armies, Arjuna sees all of his closest friends and relatives in both armies and loses the willingness to fight:

> Arjuna saw in both armies fathers, grandfathers, sons, grandsons; fathers of wives, uncles, masters; brothers, companions and friends. When Arjuna thus saw his kinsmen face to face in both lines of battle, he was overcome by grief and despair. . . . (1:26–28)

Arjuna realizes that many of the people dearest to him are about to lay down their lives. After unburdening his heart to Krishna about these matters, Arjuna firmly asserts, "I will not fight."

Krishna smiles and then responds to his friend with an extended discourse on the nature of life and reality. With respect to the soul and death, Krishna reminds Arjuna of certain "truths" of classical Hinduism: The real human being, as opposed to our false sense of self, is the soul, not the body. The soul, which reincarnates in different, successive bodies, is eternal and basically changeless. Because we are all eternal souls, who can ever really "die"? And for that matter, who can ever really "kill"?

> If any man thinks he slays, and if another thinks he is slain, neither knows the ways of truth. The Eternal in man cannot kill; the Eternal in man cannot die. (2:19)

Krishna also reminds Arjuna that, as someone born into the warrior class, it is his duty to fight, particularly in a righteous war such as the one at hand. Arjuna is encouraged to perform this worldly duty without attachment, keeping his mind fixed on eternal rather than on earthly matters. If he can adhere to the eternal perspective, acting only as his social duty dictates, then he can kill without sin:

> He who is free from the chains of selfishness, and whose mind is free from any ill-will, even if he kills all these warriors he kills them not and he is free. (18:17)

Krishna further asserts that, in his role as supreme deity of the universe, he is about to take the lives of Arjuna's enemies. Thus, if Arjuna takes up the fight, he will merely be the instrument of God's will. After these and many other philosophical points are made, Arjuna agrees to engage in battle.

These passages, which may strike the reader as having radical and even dangerous implications, are not often emphasized in studies of the *Bhagavad Gita,* which contains many profound and deeply moving reflections that have nothing to do with killing, and a significant number of the book's admirers have tended to de-emphasize its discussion of the ethics of combat and encouragement of righteous war. Mahatma Gandhi, for example, asserted that war in the *Bhagavad Gita* was meant to be taken symbolically, as an allegory for the struggle of the soul. This interpretation, however, does not stand up to a close reading of the text, which, although it does discuss the struggle of the soul, also clearly advocates a path of detached action that may include mortal combat.

Sources:

Feuerstein, Georg. *Encyclopedic Dictionary of Yoga.* New York: Paragon House, 1990.
Mascaro, Juan, trans. *Bhagavad Gita.* Baltimore, MD: Penguin, 1970.

BIBLE

Although the term Bible may be used to refer to the sacred writings of a variety of different religions, it is usually reserved for either the Hebrew Scriptures—designated within Christianity as the Old Testament—or for the **Christian** Scriptures, which consist of the Hebrew Scriptures plus the New Testament. The Christian tradition regards the Hebrew Scriptures as composing the larger part of its own Scriptures. This is a peculiar tenet because, on many points, Old Testament notions contrast markedly with New Testament teachings. Nowhere is this more striking than in the area of afterlife ideas.

Whereas Christianity emphasizes the importance of the afterlife, the ancient Hebrews emphasized the present life. As in the case of both the ancient Greeks and

Mesopotamians, the Hebrews rarely dwelled on the afterlife. Also like the Greek Hades, and again in sharp contrast to Christianity, the Hebrews made no distinction between the treatment of the just and the unjust after death. Instead, rewards and punishments were meted out in the present life.

The ancient Hebrews, as did many of the other traditional peoples of the world, imagined the universe as a three-tiered cosmos of heaven, earth, and underworld. Heaven was reserved for god and the angels; living human beings occupied the middle world; and the spirits of the dead resided beneath the earth in **She'ol.** As in other cultures, the conceptualization of the realm of the dead as being located beneath the earth's surface probably derives from the custom of burying the dead underground. Again similar to the Mesopotamian underworld, She'ol was not much more than a gloomy pit where the spirits of the dead exist as pale shadows of their earthly selves.

With the exception of the comparatively late **apocalyptic** Book of Daniel, the only stories in Hebrew Scriptures that refer to afterlife notions are the story of Elijah's bodily ascent to heaven, which was not taken to indicate that all righteous human beings would eventually reside in the sky, and the story of the so-called Witch of Endor. King Saul had banished, under threat of death, "all who trafficked with ghosts and spirits" (I Samuel 28:3). However, faced with a superior army and feeling himself in a desperate situation, Saul, in disguise, consults a woman whom today we would refer to as a **medium.** This woman, who lives at Endor, summons the spirit of the prophet Samuel from She'ol. When he arrives, he asks Saul, "Why have you disturbed me and brought me up?" (I Samuel 28:15). By making a directional reference ("brought me *up*"), the clear implication is that She'ol is underneath the surface of the earth.

Samuel tells Saul that he should never have turned away from God, that he is on the verge of defeat, and, furthermore, that "tomorrow you and your sons will be with me" (I Samuel 28:19)—that is, they will be dead. By asserting that Saul's soul will soon be residing in the same resting place, the clear implication is that moral distinctions do not influence one's afterlife fate—the spirits of the good (e.g., Samuel) and those of morally bad people (e.g., Saul) both end up in the same place, presumably under much the same conditions.

For the most part, the God of the Old Testament is a "this worldly" god who rewards the righteous and punishes the wicked in this life. However, reflection on the inequalities of this life, and on the apparent failure of Yahweh to make good on his covenant promises, led serious religious thinkers to consider the option of **resurrection.** The resurrection of ordinary human beings seems to have originated in the Persian (Iranian) religion **Zoroastrianism.** As a result of several centuries of Persian control of what is today the Middle East, Jews were brought into contact with Zoroastrian religious ideas and the notion of resurrection. Zoroaster combined resurrection with the idea of a final judgment, in which the entire human race would be resurrected and individuals rewarded or punished. This clearly appealed to Jewish religious thinkers of the time as an adequate way of coming to grips with the injustices that were so apparent in this life.

There are few references to resurrection in biblical Judaism. The oldest explicit mention of the belief in resurrection is in the second century B.C., where it is viewed as the revival of bodies—to a fate of eternal bliss for the righteous and to eternal shame for the sinners. At the end of the first century B.C., resurrection is often mentioned as the restoration, and sometimes the transfiguration, of the body, and in different sources is conceived of as a renewal of righteous people in a new earth, or as their transformation into angelic forms, or as the reunification of their body and soul. In postbiblical Judaism, the belief in resurrection was completely accepted as reunion of body and soul, using images drawn from nature, such as bodies sprouting forth from the earth.

Christianity borrowed the idea of resurrection from the Jewish tradition, and that belief is expressed in the New Testament. To the extent that the Gospels are adequate guides, Jesus clearly assumed the doctrine of resurrection, as when the **Sadducees** asked him about the postresurrection fate of a woman who married another man after her first husband had died (Mark 12:18–27). Jesus also provided concrete evidence for resurrection when he raised Lazarus from the dead, as well as when he was resurrected.

However, in the course of propagating its doctrines to the non-Hebrew world, Christianity was confronted with popular afterlife ideas that were not part of its original creed. Whereas the Hebrews viewed the body as being an intimate and essential part of the human being, the Hellenistic notion—a notion that prevailed throughout the Mediterranean world—was that the essential human being was an immortal soul trapped inside a physical body. Upon death, the body was abandoned and the soul continued to exist as an independent entity. In the Gospel of John, Jesus seems to accept this Greek view when he promises believers that he will come to them in the hour of their death and take them to heaven (John 14:2–3).

Christianity had to reconcile these two very different notions of the afterlife. As a consequence, we get a scenario in which, immediately after death, sinners go to hell and the saved go to heaven. However, at the end of time the souls of the dead leave heaven and hell, are reunited with physical bodies, and face Judgment Day on the earth—even though, by virtue of their former residence in either heaven or hell, they have already been judged. The unnecessary redundancy resulting from the awkward attempt to reconcile two different schemes of survival after death should be quite evident, and most modern-day Christians embrace the Greek view of an immortal soul that goes directly to heaven or hell following death.

Sources:

Eliade, Mircea. *Encyclopedia of Religion.* 16 vols. New York: Macmillan, 1987.

Keck, Leander E. "Death and Afterlife in the New Testament." In Hiroshi Obayashi, ed., *Death and Afterlife: Perspectives of World Religions.* Westport, CT: Greenwood Press, 1992.

MacGregor, Geddes. *Images of Afterlife: Beliefs from Antiquity to Modern Times.* New York: Paragon House, 1992.

BAI, OR SOUL-BIRD, FROM A WALL PAINTING, 13TH CENTURY B.C.

Mendenhall, George E. "From Witchcraft to Justice: Death and Afterlife in the Old Testament." In Hiroshi Obayashi, ed., *Death and Afterlife: Perspectives of World Religions.* Westport, CT: Greenwood Press, 1992.

Birds

In mythology, birds are often used as symbols for the souls of the dead and as carriers of the souls to the otherworld. They are also portrayed as death omens, and sometimes as messengers to the gods. As dream symbols, birds may represent angels, supernatural aid, and spirits.

In Western folklore, a bird that flies into one's home is taken to be a harbinger of some important news, often death. Swallows and jackdaws that come down chimneys are taken to be omens of death, as are birds who flap their wings along windows and those who fly into windows and die upon impact. Blackbirds are also taken to presage death, particularly if they gather near a house, as are owls, especially when they hoot near a dwelling.

Traditional societies across the globe have viewed birds as bearers of the departed to the otherworld. This belief results in such practices as interring the deceased in a coffin shaped like a bird so that the soul will be carried to the afterworld, a custom of certain Pacific island societies. In some West African societies, it is the practice to bind a bird to a corpse for the same purpose.

In Greek and Roman mythology, birds were often messengers between the gods and humanity. The Egyptians pictured the soul as a human-headed bird, and the souls of the pharaoh and the god Horus as hawks. The Aztecs believed that the dead were reborn as birds.

Why birds should have been taken to represent the spirit is not difficult to understand. The atmosphere is a comparatively subtle medium, an invisible but nevertheless tangible presence, much like the spirit world. To members of traditional societies, birds must have appeared to be marvelous creatures—animals who could shake themselves loose from the earth and float aloft in the invisible medium of the air. When one views birds in this manner, it is but a short step from seeing them as travelers of the air to seeing them as travelers of the spirit realm.

Sources:

Cirlot, J. E. *A Dictionary of Symbols.* New York: Philosophical Library, 1971.

Jung, Carl G., ed. *Man and His Symbols.* New York: Anchor Press/Doubleday, 1988.

Leach, Maria, and Jerome Fried, eds. *Funk & Wagnalls Standard Dictionary of Folklore, Mythology, and Legend.* San Francisco: Harper & Row, 1979.

BLAVATSKY, HELENA PETROVNA

Helena Petrovna Blavatsky (1831–1891), born in Dnepropetrovsk, Russia, was the cofounder and moving force behind Theosophy. Her early fame was partially based on reports of supernormal phenomena that occurred in her presence. These phenomena, which she attributed to her ability to manipulate superphysical forces, sometimes aroused hostility, including that of the **Society for Psychical Research,** which tried to discredit her and accused her of being an impostor.

After many years of world travel she moved to the United States, where with the American **Spiritualist** Henry Steel Olcott she established the Theosophical Society in New York City on November 17, 1875. The goals of the society were to counter scientific materialism and agnosticism, promote research on the secret laws of nature, and study and make known the ancient religions, philosophies, and sciences. *The Theosophist,* the journal of the society, was dedicated to uniting Eastern spirituality with Western advances in thought and science.

Blavatsky spent years traveling alone in Europe, the Americas, Egypt, India, and Tibet, where she met the personage she maintained was the master who had chosen her to reveal ancient wisdom to mankind and who had long appeared in her dreams.

HELENA PETROVNA BLAVATSKY AND AMERICAN CO-FOUNDER OF THE THEOSOPHICAL SOCIETY, HENRY STEELE OLCOTT. COURTESY OF THE ARC.

Her reputation as an occultist was established with the publication of *Isis Unveiled,* a survey of the literature of magic, witchcraft, alchemy, Eastern thought, and Western science. The principal aim of this work was to redeem magic from the disapproval it had gained with the rise of science in the seventeenth century and to postulate the notion of a secret science known to the ancients and transmitted down the ages to those ready to receive it through a secret brotherhood of adepts.

The international center of the Theosophical Society was founded in 1882 in Madras, India, where Blavatsky's philosophy was greatly influenced by Indian esoteric doctrines and Buddhism. After returning to Europe, she wrote her masterpiece, *The Secret Doctrine* (1888), which she claimed to have produced in a supernormal condition. During the last years of her life she founded the journal *Lucifer* and wrote *The Voice of the Silence* and *The Key to Theosophy,* both in 1889.

In the latter, she delineated the fundamental teachings of Theosophy, and a considerable part of the work is dedicated to the states of humankind after death. In accordance with theosophical principles, she rejected the idea of a new soul created for every newly born human being. The individual person is considered the vehicle of an *ego,* which represents an emanation of the one universal infinite *Ego* (the manifested divine principle). Blavatsky asserted that to achieve immortality one must ascend toward that spirit of the universal ego, which never descends directly into the living human being, but rather showers its radiance on the inner person. Once an ego achieves immortal life as spirit, it will remain the same inner self throughout all rebirths on earth.

Blavatsky did not accept the notions of paradise, hell, or eternal rewards and eternal punishments, because she believed that crimes and sins committed on a plane of objectivity (in this world) cannot receive punishment in a world of pure subjectivity (the other world). Instead, she postulated a postmortem state or transitory mental condition that represents the interval between two incarnations, and is similar to a vivid dream. She also accepted the moral law of cause and effect, or **karma,** which manifests itself through a natural concatenation of causes and their unavoidable results.

Sources:

Blavatsky, Helena P. *The Key to Theosophy.* Los Angeles: The Theosophy Company, 1973.

Cavendish, Richard, ed. *Man, Myth & Magic: The Illustrated Encyclopedia of Mythology, Religion and the Unknown.* New York: Marshall Cavendish, 1983.

Eliade, Mircea, ed. *The Encyclopedia of Religion.* 16 vols. New York: Macmillan, 1987.

BOAT SYMBOLS

The passage from this world to the next is infrequently viewed as a quick transition that occurs immediately after death. Instead, most traditional cultures conceive of the soul as undertaking a postmortem journey to the afterlife. This trip can be represented in many ways. Often the departed soul crosses a **river,** either across a **bridge** or in a boat. The most well-known boat is that of Greek figure **Charon,** who ferries the souls of the dead across the river Styx to **Hades.**

The notion of ships that carry the souls of the dead to the otherworld is very ancient. Drawings of boats on the walls of graves date back to the neolithic period. As one might anticipate, the image of ships carrying the departed to the afterlife was especially prevalent in seagoing cultures. In the southern Asian (particularly the **Hindu** and **Buddhist)** traditions the symbol of stream-crossing is carried over to the process of seeking liberation from the cycle of death and rebirth (**reincarnation**). In Buddhism, the image is used often. The *yana* that one finds appended to such important Buddhist denominations as the Mahayana means vehicle or boat. The great Indologist Heinrich Zimmer discussed Buddha's doctrine as a "ferryboat" in his *Philosophies of India.*

Sources:

Biedermann, Hans. *Dictionary of Symbolism: Cultural Icons and the Meanings Behind Them.* New York: Meridian, 1994.

Zimmer, Heinrich. *Philosophies of India.* New York: Bollingen, 1951.

BOSCH, HIERONYMUS

As a result of the complicated messages of his art, Hieronymus Bosch (ca. 1450–ca. 1516) has often been described as a worshiper of Satan, as well as a devout Catholic, a psychotic madman, a naive humorist, and a religious fanatic. Even though little is known about his life, it is presumed that the popular, moralizing literature and other beliefs of his time influenced Bosch's symbolism.

The paintings of the Flemish artist reflect his obsession with man's sin and damnation. The world portrayed by the artist is populated by a multitude of symbols from astrology, sorcery and alchemy, and strange forms that are often composed of dislocated elements of real beings. Each detail of his paintings contains an allusion to a symbolic significance within the whole, which can be considered a kind of allegory illustrating the opposite guises of Christian life: sin and attachment to earthly pleasures on one hand, and the force of righteousness and faith against evil on the other. Bosch's themes, however, reveal his pessimism about man's redemption after life, and hell is usually portrayed as a common condition of the world in which man lives.

The great themes of Bosch's work, such as the snares of the Devil and the soul's perpetual exposure to the wiles of evil, already appear in the paintings attributed to his early period, which include the *Crucifixion,* containing the theme later developed in the painter's scenes from the Passion; the *Seven Deadly Sins,* in which the circle symbolizes the world and the three concentric circles with the seven sins represent the divine eye with Christ as the pupil; and the *Conjurer,* an image of the credulity that leads to heresy, with the first known portrayal of tarot cards and astrology. The famous great triptychs, the *Hay Wain,* the *Garden of Delights,* and *The Temptation of St. Anthony* belong to the period 1485–1505.

In the *Hay Wain,* Bosch illustrates an old Flemish proverb: "The world is a mountain of hay; each one grabs what he can." The demon, who assumes human, animal, and vegetable forms, gives a fictitious value to the goods and pleasures of life on earth and leads the procession of humanity from the garden of heaven, situated on the left wing, toward hell, on the right wing.

The visions of Eden and hell are also the theme of the *Last Judgment,* of four panels in the Doges's Palace in Venice (*The Fall of the Damned, Hell, Paradise,* and

◀ *THE LAST JUDGMENT* BY HIERONYMUS BOSCH.

the *Ascent into the Empyrean,* which is rendered as a great cylinder seen in perspective in a blue light), and of *The Garden of Earthly Delights.* The closed wings of the famous triptych represent the world on the third day of creation, a transparent sphere that shows, at the center, the dry land covered with vegetation, separating from the waters. The left wing shows the earthly paradise, the central panel is the garden of worldly delight itself, and the right panel represents the frightening images of hell, where devils torment the damned with their former pleasures.

The full maturity of the artist is revealed in *The Temptation of St. Anthony,* which represents the mystical theme of contemplation struggling against temptation. A world of fire is portrayed, with spectral visions and nightmare beings. A complex system of signs and symbols characterizes the work, rendering the medieval concept of the Devil's omnipresence in human life. The allusion to demonology in Bosch's art reflects the common wisdom of his time, when belief in the Devil was fundamental to proper religious devotion.

Sources:

Beagle, Peter S. *The Garden of Earthly Delights,* London: Pan Books, 1982.

Cavendish, Richard, ed. *Man, Myth & Magic: The Illustrated Encyclopedia of Mythology, Religion and the Unknown.* New York: Marshall Cavendish, 1983.

Encyclopedia of World Art. London: McGraw-Hill , 1960.
Linfert, Carl, *Hieronymus Bosch.* New York: Harry N. Abrams, 1989.

Bridge Symbols

In most of the world's religions, the transition from this world to the otherworld is not thought of as a smooth, immediate step that one takes immediately upon death. Rather, after death one must frequently undertake a journey (or at least a short trip) to the otherworld. In many traditions, this transition is symbolized by ferrying across a river on a boat, in others it is symbolized by crossing a bridge.

The most well-known afterlife bridge is the Chinvat Bridge. The Zoroastrians were deeply concerned with morality, and as a consequence pictured the afterlife as a place where one was judged with respect to the good or evil of one's deed. On the way to judgment, the soul walks onto the Chinvat Bridge. In the middle of the bridge, according to the Pahlevi (Pahlevi is the ancient language of Persia) text the *Bundahishn,*

> There is a sharp edge which stands like a sword; and Hell is below the Bridge. Then the soul is carried to where stands a sword. If the soul is righteous, the sword presents its broad side. If the soul be wicked, that sword continues to stand edgewise, and does not give passage. With three steps which the soul takes forward—which are the evil thoughts, words, and deeds that it has performed—it is cut down from the head of the Bridge, and falls headlong to Hell. (pp. 92-93)

In latter texts, a person's deeds greet him on the bridge in personified form—a beautiful maiden for a good person; an ugly hag for a bad person—who either leads the soul to paradise or embraces the soul and falls into hell, according to whether the person has been good or evil.

In Islam one finds a similar image; the bridge to heaven is as narrow as a sword, and only one who is free from sin can navigate it without falling off. In some Native American tales, a narrow wooden beam serves the same purpose. And in ancient China, the transition to the otherworld was sometimes envisioned as a narrow bridge over a river of pus and blood, into which sinners fell.

Sources:

Biedermann, Hans. *Dictionary of Symbolism: Cultural Icons and the Meanings Behind Them.* New York: Meridian, 1994.
Pavry, Jal Dastur Cursetji *The Zoroastrian Doctrine of a Future Life.* New York: Columbia University Press, 1926.

Buddhism

The story is told about Kisa Gotami, who was so distraught over the death of her only child that she continued to carry the body of the boy around with her, seeking

SOULS CROSSING THE BRIDGE TO THE OTHERWORLD. FRESCO IN THE CHURCH OF SANTA MARIA, LORETTO APRUTINO, ITALY, 13TH CENTURY.

medicine that would miraculously revive him. On the advice of an elderly man, she sought out the Buddha in hopes that he could bring back her son from the dead. Rather than telling her point blank that her quest was in vain, the Buddha instructed her to go into town and bring back a mustard seed from a household in which no death had yet occurred.

She went door to door without success, often evoking pained responses from the townspeople as they recalled the deaths of loved ones. Eventually the sad truth dawned on her: Death and the accompanying emptiness it leaves in the hearts of surviving loved ones is a universal condition of humanity. With this harsh realization, she finally abandoned hope of reviving her child, renounced worldly life, and joined the Buddhist order. She eventually became an *arhat,* a fully realized Buddhist saint. Kisa Gotami's tale is an appropriate point of reference for understanding Buddhism's view of death, rebirth, and liberation from the cycle of repeated life and death.

Buddhism is a major world religion that was founded by Gautama Buddha in the Indian subcontinent around 600 B.C. As did many other religious leaders, Buddha saw

MARA, THE BUDDHIST TEMPTER AND ARCH FIEND.

himself as being more of a reformer than an innovator, and early Buddhism is clearly in the same religious "family" as Buddhism's parent religious tradition, Hinduism. However, to be considered within the Hindu fold, one must nominally acknowledge the authority of the four Vedas, Hinduism's most ancient religious texts. Buddha rejected the authority of the Vedas, and hence, despite its close relationship with Hinduism, Buddhism is technically non-Hindu. Interestingly, Buddhism almost completely disappeared from the land of its birth, but it was transplanted and bore fruit in other parts of Asia, to the north, south, and east of India.

For many years, Buddha studied under spiritual teachers in the Upanishadic tradition. The religious texts collectively referred to as the Upanishads articulate a worldview centered around release or liberation (***moksha***) from the cycle of death and rebirth (**reincarnation**). The Upanishads also postulated an eternal, changeless core of the self that was referred to as the ***Atman***. This soul or deep self was viewed as being identical with the unchanging godhead, referred to as Brahman (the unitary ground of being that transcends particular gods and goddesses). Untouched by the variations of time and circumstance, the Atman was nevertheless entrapped in the world of *samsara* (the world we experience in our everyday lives). This continually

CITIPATI, BRONZE FIGURINE, TIBET, 19TH CENTURY.

changing, unstable world contrasts with the spiritual realm of Atman/Brahma, which is stable and unchanging. ***Samsara*** also refers to the process of reincarnation, through which we are "trapped" in this world.

What keeps us trapped in the samsaric cycle is the law of **karma.** Karma operates impersonally, like a natural law, ensuring that every good or bad deed eventually returns to the individual in the form of reward or punishment commensurate with the original deed. It is the necessity of "reaping one's karma" that compels human beings to reincarnate in successive lifetimes. In other words, if one dies before reaping the effects of one's actions (as most people do), the karmic process demands that the person come back in a future life. Coming back in another life also allows karmic forces to reward or punish people through the circumstances into which they are born. For example, an individual who was generous in one lifetime might be reborn as a wealthy person in the next incarnation. *Moksha* is the traditional Hindu term for release or liberation from the endless chain of deaths and rebirths. According to the Upanishadic view, what happens at the point of moksha is that the individual Atman merges into the cosmic Brahman, much like a drop of water, which, when dropped into the ocean, loses its individuality and becomes one with the sea.

Buddha accepted the basic Hindu doctrines of reincarnation and karma, as well as the notion, common to most southern Asian religions, that the ultimate goal of the religious life is to escape the cycle of death and rebirth (samsara). Buddha asserted that what keeps us bound to the death/rebirth process is desire, desire in the sense of wanting or craving anything in the world of samsara. Hence, the goal of getting off the ferris wheel of reincarnation necessarily involves freeing oneself from desire. *Nibbana*—or, in later Buddhism, ***nirvana***—is the Buddhist equivalent of moksha. *Nirvana* literally means extinction, and it refers to the extinction of all craving, an extinction that allows one to break out of samsara.

Where Buddha departed most radically from Upanishadic Hinduism was in his doctrine of ***anatta,*** the notion that individuals do not possess eternal souls. Instead of eternal souls, individuals consist of a "bundle" of habits, memories, sensations, desires, and so forth, which together delude one into thinking that he or she consists of a stable, lasting self. Despite its transitory nature, this false self hangs together as a unit, and even reincarnates in body after body. In Buddhism as well as in Hinduism, life in a corporeal body is viewed negatively, as the source of all suffering. Hence, the goal is to obtain release from the samsaric process. In Buddhism, this means abandoning the false sense of self so that the bundle of memories and impulses disintegrates, leaving nothing to reincarnate and hence nothing to experience pain.

From the perspective of present-day, world-affirming Western society, the Buddhist vision cannot but appear distinctly unappealing: Not only is this life portrayed as unattractive, the prospect of nirvana, in which one dissolves into nothingness, seems even less desirable. A modern-day Buddha might respond, however, that our reaction to being confronted with the dark side of life merely shows how insulated we are from the pain and suffering that is so fundamental to human existence. In the contemporary Western world, we shut up our elderly and deformed citizens in institutions where we do not have to view them. This stands in marked contrast to the third world, in which it is not uncommon to be forced to see the ravages of disease and mortality on a daily basis.

Our situation is, in fact, much like that of the young Gautama in the story of the Four Signs. According to Buddhist tradition, an astrologer who examined the future Buddha's horoscope immediately after birth asserted that the young prince would eventually become either a world ruler (meaning he would become king of all of India) or a world teacher (in the sense of a religious teacher). The direction—religious or political—the young man would pursue would depend on whether or not he reflected seriously on the suffering and transitoriness of humanity. Gautama's father, the king of a small state in what is today southern Nepal, was a worldly man who naturally wanted his son to become a world ruler. As a consequence, he made sure to surround the young man with continual merrymaking, and forbade anyone who was elderly or sick to be in the prince's presence.

All went according to plan until about age 30, when Gautama decided to travel outside his palace without first informing his parents. On the first day he happened to see a severely sick person. Upon asking his chariot driver about the man's unusual condition, his servant replied that all people were subject to disease. This troubled the future Buddha. On the second day he happened to see an exceedingly old man. Upon again inquiring of the chariot driver (who, legend has it, was a god in disguise), he discovered that everyone was subject to the aging process. On the third day he saw a corpse, and became *really* troubled after he was informed that every person eventually met death. Finally, on the fourth day, he saw a *sadhu*—a Hindu holy man who had renounced the world to seek moksha—and resolved that he would also renounce the world and seek liberation. Gautama then left home, and years later achieved the goal of release.

But, one might respond, why not just try to live life, despite its many flaws, as best one can, avoiding pain and seeking pleasure? Because, Buddha would respond, although we might be able to exercise a certain amount of control over this incarnation, we cannot foresee the circumstances in which our karma would compel us to incarnate in future lives, which might be, for example, as a starving child in a war-torn area of the third world. Also, the Buddha would point out, if we closely examine our life, we can see that even the things that seem to bring us our greatest enjoyments also bring us the greatest pain. This aspect of Buddhist thought was embodied in that part of Buddha's system referred to as the Three Marks of Being, which are as follows.

First, Buddha points out, we have to contend with the experiences everyone recognizes as painful—illness, accidents, disappointments, and so forth. Second, the world is in a continual state of change, so even the things we experience as pleasurable do not last, and ultimately lead to pain. (Romantic relationships, for example, initially bring us great happiness, but usually end in greater suffering.) And third, because we ourselves are in a continual process of change (because of the ever-changing ***skandhas***), we ultimately lose everything we have gained, particularly in the transition we call death.

Buddha, as should be clear by this point, was less inclined to speculative metaphysics than to practical psychology. Someone once asked him about the nature of ultimate reality, and Buddha responded that the question was insignificant. He compared human existence to someone who has been shot by an arrow, and declared that metaphysical questions are like the wounded person asking what type of wood the arrow was made from, the kind of bird the feathers came from, and the name and occupation of the person who shot the arrow. If one insisted on knowing the answers to all of these queries before having the arrow extracted, one would surely die. Buddha concluded this discourse by saying that what concerned him was extracting arrows and healing wounds; everything else was unimportant. For similar reasons, he refused to speculate on the nature of the afterlife state of one who had experienced nirvana. The practical, no-nonsense approach of the Buddha is particularly evident in the Four Noble Truths, which constitute the core of his teaching.

1. *Life is suffering.* The word Buddha originally used for suffering was *dukkha,* which means out of joint. Dukkha is a comprehensive term covering everything from physical pain to vague psychological dissatisfactions.
2. *The cause of suffering is desire.* The word for desire here is *tanha* (literally, "thirst"), which refers to any craving, from sexual desire to even mild desires to help humanity.
3. *To eliminate suffering, one must eliminate desire.* This is a logical corollary to the second Noble Truth.
4. *To eliminate desire, one must follow the eightfold path.* Buddha outlined the process of overcoming one's cravings under eight principal headings, which covered everything from proper meditation procedure to following a proper career that did not interfere with the goal of reaching nirvana.

As befits Buddha's practical emphasis, these four points present a one-to-one correspondence with medical practice. In other words, the first Noble Truth corresponds with symptoms, the second with diagnosis, the third with prognosis, and the fourth with prescription.

Although Buddha himself was profoundly antispeculative and antimetaphysical, many of his later followers were not. Particularly after Buddhism split into Theravada (southern Buddhism, found today in Sri Lanka and Southeast Asia) and Mahayana (northern Buddhism, found today in Korea, Japan, and Taiwan), metaphysical speculation flowered in Mahayana Buddhism. Various forms of devotional Buddhism also developed within the Mahayana fold. Devotional Buddhism focused on different *bodhisattvas* (enlightened souls who delayed the final stages of their nirvana so that they could stay around and help ordinary mortals), which, like the great gods and goddesses of later Hinduism, could help their devotees. The notion of heaven worlds was also developed in these forms of Buddhism. Earnest devotees would be transported to such a world after death, and there could continue the quest for enlightenment, less hindered by the demands of this world.

In these developments it is clear that popular theism has reemerged in the worship of godlike bodhisattvas. The development of heaven realms is also interesting. Although devotees continue to express an ideology of regarding such realms as temporary way stations on the journey to nirvana, de facto such realms occupy the foreground in devotees' contemplation of the afterlife, and nirvana is pushed to the background. Pure-land Buddhism is perhaps the most widely known form of popular Buddhism. When a Pure-land Buddhist is on the edge of death, a scroll depicting the Pure-land is unrolled and placed in the dying person's field of vision so that it will be easier to make it to the Pure-land after death.

Along with heaven realms, Buddhism also developed notions of hell realms in which exceptionally sinful individuals were punished. In earlier stages of the Buddhist tradition the impersonal force of karma carried out punishment for evil deeds through the circumstances in which one was reborn and through the unfortunate events one experienced while incarnated in a body. As with their emergence in later Hinduism, in Buddhism hell worlds originated to supplement—rather than supplant—earlier notions of karmic punishment. Unlike Western hells, however, Buddhist hell worlds are not final dwelling places. They are more like **purgatories** in which sinful souls experience suffering for a limited term. After that term is over, even the most evil person is turned out of hell to once again participate in the cycle of reincarnation.

Speculation regarding heaven and hell realms, particularly as they relate to afterlife states, receives its fullest development in Tibetan Buddhism, the most prominent school of Tantric Buddhism. Tantric Buddhism sometimes is viewed as a form of Mahayana Buddhism; at others, as a third form of Buddhism. However it is classified, Tantric Buddhism is characterized by an elaborately developed mythology and exotic spiritual practices.

Wherever Buddhism was carried, it tended to merge with the indigenous religion, or at least pick up elements of it. A notion found in many different cultures is that the transition between death and afterlife is a problematic one in which the newly departed soul can lose its way to the otherworld. These spirits tend to linger around their relatives, causing various problems for the living. In such societies, shamans (religious personages who use magic to cure the sick, divine the hidden, and control events) are regularly called upon to serve as **psychopomps**—guides of the departed who project their spirit into the otherworld in order to lead lost souls to the realm of the dead. This complex of ideas is often found in shamanistic societies such as Tibet, whose indigenous Bön religion was, or included, a rather elaborate form of **shamanism.** This pattern, which in its original form has little to do with the practical Buddhist goal of achieving release from the cycle of death and rebirth, became the foundation for a rather exotic spiritual practice utilizing the dying process to reach liberation.

Nowhere is the art of dying more sophisticated than in the culture of Tibet. In fact, over the centuries the practice of ***conscious dying*** was developed by Tibetan Buddhists into a meditative spiritual discipline (a form of yoga) designed to guide the departed on their afterlife journey, enabling them to anticipate the various experiences they would encounter. The Tibetan handbook on dying, afterlife, and rebirth, the Bardo Thödol, is quite ancient. Its authorship is attributed to Padmasambhava, the famous Indian Tantric master of the eighth century, and it has likely evolved over the course of the centuries. The purpose of the Tibetan yoga of death is to discipline the consciousness so that the individual can accurately perceive and understand the nature of her postmortem experiences. Following death, according to Tibetan tradition, the spirit of the departed goes through a process lasting 49 days that is divided into three stages. At the conclusion of the Bardo, the person either enters nirvana or returns to earth for rebirth.

It is imperative that the dying individual remain fully aware for as long as possible, because the thoughts one has while passing over into death heavily influence the nature of both after-death experience and, if one fails to achieve nirvana, the state of one's next incarnation. The dying person is placed on her right side, in a yogic pose termed the lion posture. The neck arteries are pressed to prevent loss of consciousness.

The person is also guided by an attending guru or lama, who advises on what to anticipate.

Stage one of the Bardo begins at death and extends from half a day to four days. This is the period of time necessary for the departed to realize that she has dropped the body. Once the person dies, the face is covered with a white cloth, the body is not permitted to be touched, and the windows and doors are covered. The "extractor of consciousness-principle" lama positions himself at the body's head and begins a chant that gives the departed directions to the Bodhisattva Amitabha's Western Paradise. (Depending on the state of one's karma, the ability to follow directions allows the deceased to avoid the ordeal of the Bardo's second period.) The lama studies the crown of the head and determines whether the individual has left the body through the *aperture of Brahma* (there are several potential exit points, some less auspicious than others).

If a lama astrologer is present, he erects a horoscope for the death moment. The information gained from reading this chart allows him to decide how to dispose of the body, as well as the appropriate funeral rites. At the conclusion of stage one, the body is seated in one corner of the room in which death took place. Relatives are summoned for a two-day funeral feast during which the corpse is offered the essence of all the food and drink present.

Afterward, the corpse is disposed of, and a wooden model of the body is covered in the departed's clothes. For the rest of the Bardo, this effigy is in the presence of lamas who chant different liturgies at particular periods of time. After the 49 days are up, the wooden model is decorated, taken apart, and the individual's spirit warned not to haunt the living. The body, meanwhile, is cremated or otherwise sent back to the elements of the earth.

These are the outer practices. The consciousness of the departed has an ecstatic experience of the primary "clear light" at the death moment. Everyone gets at least a fleeting glimpse of the light. The more spiritually developed see it longer, and are able to go beyond it to a higher level of reality. The average person, however, drops into the lesser state of the secondary "clear light."

In stage two, the departed encounters the hallucinations resulting from the karma created during life. Unless highly developed, the individual will feel that she is still in the body. The departed then encounters various apparitions, the "peaceful" and "wrathful" deities, that are actually personifications of human feelings and that, to successfully achieve nirvana, the deceased must encounter unflinchingly. Only the most evolved individuals can skip the Bardo experience altogether and transit directly into a paradise realm.

Sources:

Benard, Elisabeth. "The Tibetan Tantric View of Death and Afterlife." In Hiroshi Obayashi, ed., *Death and Afterlife: Perspectives of World Religions.* Westport, CT: Greenwood Press, 1992.

Bromage, Bernard. *Tibetan Yoga.* Wellingborough, Northamptonshire, England: Aquarian Press, 1979. (Originally published 1952.)

Conze, Edward. *Buddhist Thought in India.* 1962. Reprint. Ann Arbor: University of Michigan Press, 1967.

Evans-Wentz, W. Y., ed. *The Tibetan Book of the Dead.* 3d ed. London: Oxford University Press, 1960.

MacGregor, Geddes. *Images of Afterlife: Beliefs from Antiquity to Modern Times.* New York: Paragon House, 1992.
Rahula, Walpola. *What the Buddha Taught.* 2d ed., rev. and enl. New York: Evergreen, 1974.
Reynolds, Frank E. "Death as Threat, Death as Achievement: Buddhist Perspectives with Particular Reference to the Theravada Tradition." In Hiroshi Obayashi, ed., *Death and Afterlife: Perspectives of World Religions.* Westport, CT: Greenwood Press, 1992.
Zimmer, Heinrich. *Philosophies of India.* Rev. ed. New York: Macmillan, 1987.

BURIAL

Burial refers to the widespread custom of disposing of corpses by interring them in the ground, as well as through, by extension, such related practices as "burying" them in aboveground structures like mausoleums. Burial seems to be a fairly self-evident way of disposing of the corpses of loved ones. Archaeological discoveries that prehistoric cultures often buried their dead with possessions provide evidence that such peoples anticipated that the deceased would be able to utilize these artifacts in some form of postmortem existence.

The idea that the dead must be properly buried in order to make a smooth transition to the afterlife is also quite widespread, in the ancient world as well as in contemporary tribal societies. **Virgil,** for example, placed souls who had not been properly buried in a **Limbo** realm where they had to wait a hundred years before being admitted to the Land of the Dead.

Many of the world's religious traditions visualize the universe as a three-tiered cosmos of heaven, earth, and underworld. Heaven is often reserved for gods, living human beings occupy the middle world, and the spirits of the dead frequently reside beneath the earth. Conceptualizing the realm of the dead as being located beneath the earth's surface probably derives from the custom of burying the dead underground.

Sources:

Eliade, Mircea, ed. *Encyclopedia of Religion.* 16 vols. New York: Macmillan, 1987.
Kastenbaum, Robert, and Beatric Kastenbaum. Reprint. *Encyclopedia of Death.* New York: Avon, 1993.

C

CATHARS

Derived from the Greek word *katharos,* meaning pure, Cathars (or Cathari) was the name given by the Church to members of a dualistic heresy of **Gnostic** origin in the twelfth century. Catharism arose in the eastern Mediterranean region during the Middle Ages and spread slowly westward. Among its most important adherents were the Albigensians of southern France, who were militarily destroyed in the early 1200s by the only successful medieval Crusade, which began in 1209.

Cathars were distinguished from other medieval heretic groups for rejecting such basic Christian beliefs as the doctrine of incarnation, Christ's two natures, the Virgin Birth, and bodily resurrection. They also repudiated the Church hierarchy and sacraments, particularly baptism by water and matrimony, and followed an ascetic life-style that included celibacy, vegetarianism, and even ritual suicide. Most Cathars accepted only the New Testament, which they read in its Catholic version.

The Cathars believed the universe consists of two coexisting spheres: the kingdom of the good god, who is spiritual and suprasensible and who created the invisible heaven, its spirits, and the four elements; and the kingdom of the evil god, Satan, who created the material world and who, being unable to make the human soul, captured it from heaven and imprisoned it in the material body. Thus, the fundamental aim of their religious practice was to release the soul from the body by freeing it from Satan's power and helping it to return to its original place in heaven.

In marked contrast with orthodox Christian belief, bodily resurrection was not viewed as part of the scheme of redemption. Rather, only the destruction of the body and of all Satan's visible creation—which is hell—was adequate to ensure salvation of the soul and its ascent to heaven. The only way to do so was to receive the Cathars' unique sacrament, the *consolamentum,* which was administered by the laying on of hands.

Individuals could come to recognize evil through a series of reincarnations, and could eventually free their souls from Satan and thereby become perfect. According to Catharism, at the end of time all souls will be saved or damned, even though there were some differences between the doctrine of the absolute dualists and that of the mitigate dualists. For the former group, free will played no part in salvation, and in the end the material world would fall apart after all souls had departed. For the latter, Satan would be captured, and the proper order of all things would be reestablished.

Sources:

Brenon, Anne. *Le Vrai Visage du Catharisme.* Portet-sur-Garonne, France: Editions Loubatières, 1988.
Clifton, Chas S. *Encyclopedia of Heresies and Heretics.* Santa Barbara, CA: ABC-CLIO, 1992.
Eliade, Mircea, ed. *The Encyclopedia of Religion.* 16 vols. New York: Macmillan, 1987.
New Catholic Encyclopedia. New York: Mc Graw-Hill, 1967.

CAYCE, EDGAR

Edgar Cayce (1877–1945), was an early twentieth century "psychic," best known for his pronouncements on health and reincarnation. He was born near Hopkinsville, Kentucky, the son of Leslie B. Cayce, a businessman and tobacco farmer, and Carrie Elizabeth Cayce. Cayce was raised in the Christian Church (Disciples of Christ) and eventually taught Sunday school. He dropped out of school to became a photographer's apprentice and later made his living as a photographer. Married to Gertrude Evans in 1903, he fathered two sons.

Cayce developed a case of severe laryngitis in 1900. During this health crisis, according to some accounts, an acquaintance hypnotized Cayce (in other accounts, the trance was self-induced). During the trance, Cayce diagnosed his health problem and prescribed a cure. At some point soon after this experience, he began to perform the same trance prescriptions for others, and his reputation gradually grew.

In 1909, Cayce met an ill homeopathic physician, Dr. Wesley Ketchum, who requested that Cayce give him a reading. Ketchum was cured, and he publicized his story and the story of other Cayce cures widely. Some of Ketchum's remarks about Cayce were quoted in a sensational article that appeared in the *New York Times* in September 1910. After this exposure, Cayce, now widely known as the Sleeping Prophet, was sought after by thousands of ailing people. His prescriptions varied from psychic treatments to home remedies, to referrals to a particular medical doctor. In time, he performed "distance reading," prescribing cures to people who wrote letters requesting medical assistance.

A turning point in Cayce's readings began in 1923 when he met Arthur Lammers, a wealthy printer and student of theosophy and Eastern religions. One of Lammers's central articles of faith was belief in reincarnation, and Cayce mentioned Lammers's past lives in one of a series of private readings. Cayce subsequently began to explore the past lives of his other clients, including previous lives in such exotic lands as Atlantis. He soon added past-life readings to his health readings. Not long after his sessions with Lammers, he closed his photography studio and moved to Ohio, where Lammers lived.

After Lammers suffered some financial reverses, Morton Blumenthal—a New York stockbroker—offered to finance a teaching and information center dedicated to the East Coast, and a hospital built there. Cayce then moved to Virginia Beach, Virginia, where he resided for the balance of his life. The hospital opened in 1928 and Atlantic University in 1930. In 1931, however, Blumenthal's business failed, a casualty of the Great Depression. Without Blumenthal, both the hospital and the university had to be shut down.

In spite of these setbacks, Cayce's readings were still his principal asset. Following the closings, the Cayce family and some supporters set up the Association for Research and Enlightenment (ARE) as a vehicle for Cayce's work. Also, the Edgar Cayce Foundation was established to preserve the Cayce papers. Cayce gave readings for the rest of his life, until shortly before his death.

Because stenographic records of readings were kept for most of his life, a tremendous body of material was accumulated. These records now reside in the Association for Research and Enlightenment library in Virginia Beach, where they have served as a source for research and speculation. It was the careful preservation of these readings that enabled Cayce to become so famous. After his death, his son Hugh Lynn Cayce became head of both the Edgar Cayce Foundation and the ARE. He developed an aggressive program of publishing, mining the collection of his father's readings at the ARE library as the basis for a series of books on popular metaphysical topics, including a paperback series he edited that included *Edgar Cayce on Atlantis* (1968) and *Edgar Cayce on Prophecy* (1968). In the late 1960s and early 1970s, Cayce books were so widely read that they could be found on the paperback book racks in drugstores and grocery stores across North America. Some of these titles are still in print. By the early 1970s, Cayce had achieved a level of fame that he had not experienced during his lifetime.

More than any other single factor, the promotion of the Cayce material popularized the notion of past-life readings among the general public. His books also fed the widespread interest about reincarnation and helped spread belief in it.

Cayce's reincarnation material exhibits some rather peculiar patterns, however. In the first place, the settings for the largest number of past lives in his writings are Atlantis, ancient Egypt, and colonial/ revolutionary America. Other periods and other significant civilizations are rarely mentioned. In the second place, when the social status of an individual is given, it is usually for royalty or some significant historical figure such as Patrick Henry. This pattern runs contrary to the experience of most contemporary past-life therapists, whose patients were normally unknown individuals in previous incarnations, coming from a wide variety of different cultures and time periods. The peculiarities of the Cayce corpus are such as to make even believers in reincarnation hesitant about the accuracy of the ARE material.

Sources:

Cayce, Edgar. *What I Believe*. Virginia Beach, VA: Edgar Cayce Publishing, 1946.

Cayce, Hugh Lynn. *Venture Inward.* New York: Harper & Row, 1964. Reprint. New York: Paperback Library, 1966.

Lewis, James R. "Edgar Cayce." In the *American National Biography.* New York: Oxford University Press, forthcoming.

Melton, J. Gordon. *Biographical Dictionary of American Cults and Sect Leaders.* New York: Garland, 1986.

Sugrue, Thomas. *There is a River.* New York: Henry Holt, 1945.

CERBERUS

In Greek mythology, Cerberus was a the guardian or ''watchdog'' of the underworld, **Hades.** The offspring of Typhon and Echidna (who also parented the Hydra and the Chimaera), he was described as having three heads (Hesiod attributes him with 50 heads), a snake's tail, and a row of snake heads sprouting from his neck. He greeted the newly dead with eagerness, but ate anyone who tried to escape. Cerberus was said to have been charmed by **Orpheus,** who was the only mortal he willingly let enter Hades. In another story he was defeated in a struggle with Hercules, who forced him to come with him to the upper world (this was the twelfth labor of Hercules). It was said that anyone who chanced to look at Cerberus turned to stone, and also that upon falling to the ground the animal's spittle gave birth to the poisonous aconite plant.

Both Cerberus and **Charon,** the ferryman of the underworld, were threshold guardians, a type of mythological figure that is widespread in world culture. Threshold guardians allowed only those who were appropriately qualified to pass from one realm to the other. Thus, Cerberus allowed only the dead to pass into Hades, and he prevented the departed from returning to the realm of the living.

The closest figure we have in popular Western culture to a threshold guardian of the otherworld is Saint Peter, the gateman of heaven. In innumerable jokes, some more tasteful than others, Saint Peter either gives the departed a tour of heaven or else meets them at the gate, requiring that they solve a riddle or answer a question before he will allow them to pass. Asking the deceased to answer a question properly before they pass is a standard mode of operation of threshold guardians in many different cultures, and Saint Peter jokes are a reflection—however distorted—of this pattern.

Sources:

Grant, Michael and John Hazel. *Who's Who in Classical Mythology.* New York: Oxford University Press, 1993.

Tripp, Edward. *The Meridian Handbook of Classical Mythology.* New York: New American Library, 1970.

CHANNELING

Channeling is a more recent term for what **Spiritualists** traditionally termed *mediumship*—an event or process in which a person called a channel is able to transmit information from a source, most often an incorporeal spirit. The term *channeling* was popularized in UFO circles as the name for psychic communications from ''space brothers'' and was only later applied to New Age mediums. Although some channels retain full consciousness during their transmissions, most of the prominent New Age channels are what Spiritualists refer to as trance mediums—mediums who lose consciousness as a spirit takes over the channel's body and communicates through it. These spirits frequently claim to be spiritually advanced souls, and their communications consist of metaphysical teachings. This teaching function contrasts with the communications of traditional, nineteenth-century mediums, who were more concerned with transmitting messages from departed relatives and with demonstrating the reality of life after death.

As vehicles for communications with the otherworld, channels are merely the most recent manifestation of a phenomenon that can be traced back at least as far as prehistoric shamanism. Ancient shamans mediated the relationship between their communities and the otherworld, often transmitting messages from the deceased. Modern channels also sometimes view themselves as following in the tradition of ancient prophets, transmitting messages from more elevated sources. Unlike the prophets, however, New Age channels rarely claim to be delivering messages directly from God, nor do they usually rail against the sins of society as did the Hebrew prophets. Most often their communications consist of some form of New Age philosophy, which they explain to their listeners. With respect to this teaching function, contemporary channels can be placed in the tradition of Western theosophy. Although neither movement would claim them, New Age channels can be looked at as representing a blend of Spiritualism and theosophy.

Important precursors to modern channeling were Edgar Cayce, Jane Roberts, and Ruth Montgomery. Cayce was a trance medium who died in 1945 but—through the promotional activities of his son—achieved the peak of his fame in the 1960s. He began his psychic career giving health readings and only later began "channeling" information about past lifetimes. Upon occasion, he would relay messages from departed relatives.

In the early 1970s a series of books by Jane Roberts were published that she claimed contained information from Seth, a discarnate spirit entity. A number of the Seth books, which contained metaphysical information related to New Age philosophy, became best-sellers.

Ruth Montgomery was a newspaper reporter who became a popular New Age author after she became interested in psychic phenomena. In her writings, Montgomery described her meetings with the Guides (spirits from the otherworld) and the practice of automatic writing—a form of mediumship in which spirit entities write (or, in Montgomery's case, type) messages through the medium. Her contact with the Guides was focused on reception of information about the other realm, reincarnation, and a variety of occult topics that appeared in a series of popular books.

At the time New Age issues became a popular topic in 1987, the most publicized channel was J. Z. Knight. She made frequent media appearances, even channeling for TV audiences, before the general public's interest in New Age waned. Knight channeled an entity named Ramtha, who claimed to be the spirit of an ancient Atlantean warlord. When channeling Ramtha, Knight appeared to take on a more masculine demeanor and spoke in an indecipherable accent that many less famous channels imitated. Ramtha taught a variation on New Age philosophy built around standard metaphysical teachings. Channeling began a gradual but steady decline in popularity following the media blitz of the late 1980s.

The entities speaking through New Age channels have sometimes described themselves in standard Spiritualist terminology as ''spirit guides,'' while others, relying on theosophical language, have claimed to be ''ascended masters.'' Others claim to be spirits of a wide variety of historical personalities, nature spirits, angels, gods, goddesses, extraterrestrials, or even the spirits of discarnate animals. Yet others tune in to higher levels of their own consciousness (e.g., their ''higher self'') or to the cosmic library, sometimes referred to as the **Akashic records.**

Some popular New Age publications have been produced by ''automatic'' or ''inspired'' writing, including books by Ken Carey and Ruth Shick Montgomery. Other than Montgomery's books, the most well-known ''channeled'' book is probably *A Course in Miracles,* which is claimed to be the New Age teachings of the historical Jesus. Some channelers are primarily psychics who give private readings to individual clients. Others conduct workshops and lectures for large groups and have become quite well known in New Age circles, for example, Jach Pursel (Lazarus) and Penny Torres (Mafu).

Many people have learned to channel, and numerous publications, tapes, and videos contain channeled material. Despite the number of people involved in this phenomenon, the range of ideas presented by New Age channels is rather limited. For critics, this is a sign that the teachings are derivative, being picked up—consciously or unconsciously—by the channel from the ideas present in the surrounding New Age subculture. For believers, the convergence of viewpoint of diverse channels indicates that they are all drawing upon the same universal truths.

Beyond such metaphysical basics as reincarnation, karma, and the ''evolution'' of the soul through a series of embodiments, the central teaching propagated by most New Age channels is the notion that the world as we experience it is completely the product of our own minds. This notion is combined with the doctrine of karma (the moral law of cause and effect) in the teaching that not only are we responsible for everything we experience but we ultimately attract everything we experience, whether we are conscious of these acts of will or not. Thus, if one is mugged, for example, this teaching would suggest that one somehow, at some level, wanted to be mugged. These notions appear unattractive until their corollary is examined, which is that by changing one's mind one can completely transform one's life. If one is poor, for instance, one can decide that one instead wants abundance, and the simple act of changing one's attitude will attract wealth—or so this teaching would dictate. Because so many of the entities that speak through the channels identify themselves as the souls of departed persons, channeling is difficult to accept for those who do not believe in life after death. However, unlike Spiritualist mediums, their nineteenth-century counterparts, the great majority of New Age channels are disinterested in proving to skeptics that consciousness survives the transition we call death. The existence of an afterlife is simply assumed. In the late twentieth century, the debate over the reality of life after death has shifted from the investigation of mediumship/channeling to the investigation of **near death** experiences.

Sources:

Klimo, Jon. *Channeling.* Los Angeles: Jeremy P. Tarcher, 1987.
Roberts, Jane. *The Seth Material.* Englewood Cliffs, NJ: Prentice-Hall, 1970.
Ryerson, Kevin, and Stephanie Harolde. *Spirit Communication: The Soul's Path.* New York: Bantam Books, 1989.
Wilson, Colin. *Afterlife.* London: Harrap, 1985.

CHARACTER

Character is one's personality—the manners, thoughts, and habits of responding to the world that define one as a distinct individual. It has been debated whether one's personality continues into the afterlife or instead becomes an impersonal spiritual entity whose character would be unrecognizable to surviving friends and family members. In certain traditional religions, for instance, the dead become ''depersonalized'' as they are absorbed into a generic body of ancestors. In general, the response of Western religions has been that the personality of the postmortem individual retains intact, albeit modified by the person's transformed state.

In Eastern religions such as **Hinduism** and **Buddhism,** the response is more complex. In the cycle of **reincarnation,** individuals are envisioned as beginning each new life where they left off in the preceding incarnation. As part and parcel of this ''passing of the torch,'' the character of someone beginning a new lifetime resembles the person's prior personality. The continuity of the personality is carried by one's **samskaras,** the subconscious habit patterns that result from one's experiences in the world. The ultimate goal is release from the cycle of death and rebirth. At the point of this release (referred to as **moksha** in Hinduism and **nirvana** in Buddhism), the **soul** ceases to be a distinct individual with a distinct individual character.

Sources:

Bletzer, June G. *The Donning International Encyclopedic Psychic Dictionary.* Norfolk, VA: Donning, 1986.
Zimmer, Heinrich. *Philosophies of India.* New York: Bollingen, 1951.

CHARON

Charon is the ferryman in Greek mythology responsible for transporting the spirits of the deceased across the river Styx and into the realm of the dead, **Hades.** The offspring of Nyx (night) and Erebus (darkness), he was portrayed as a squalid, grumpy old man with a bad temper. He required payment of one obol before he would transport the soul to the other side, and the ancient Greeks accordingly buried their dead with an obol coin in their mouths so that they would be able to pay Charon's fare.

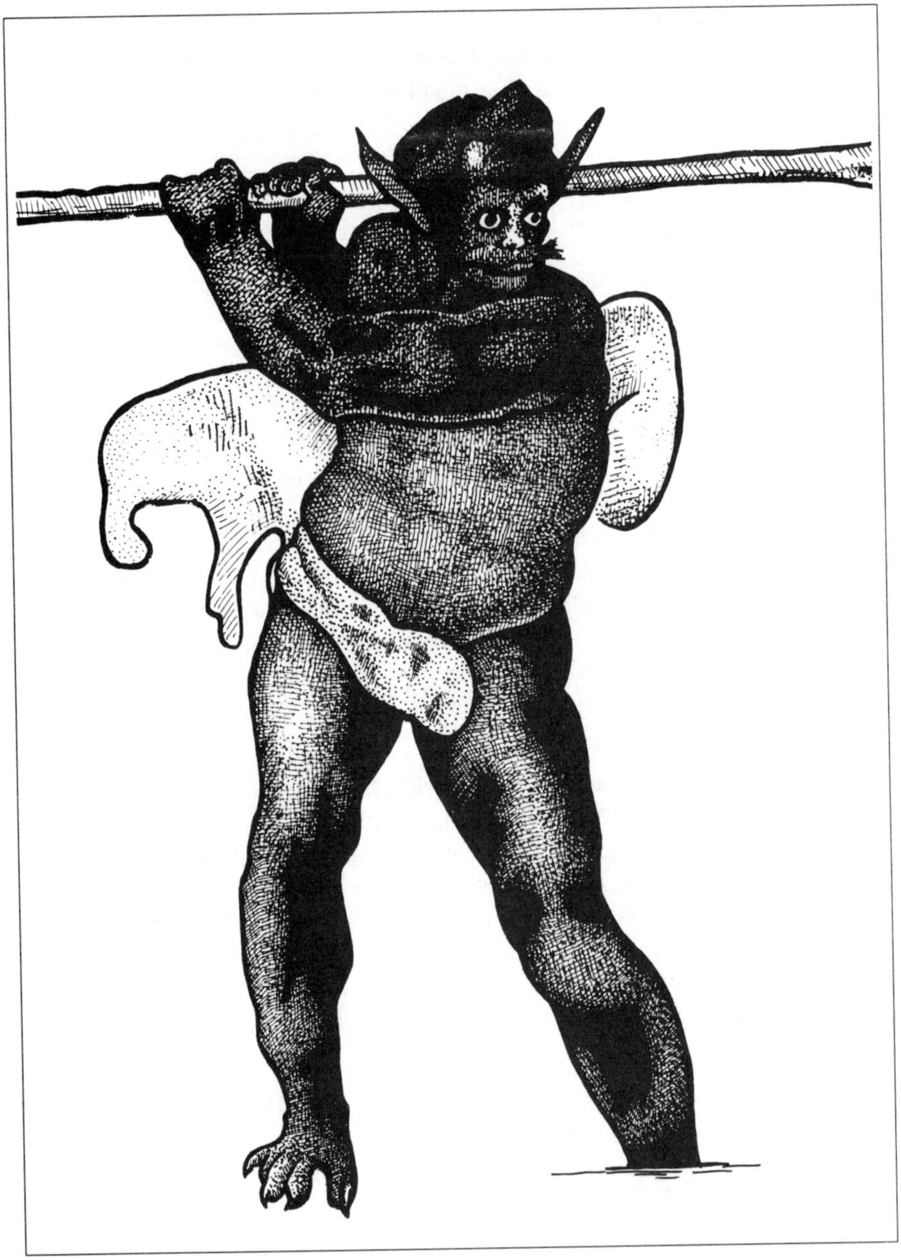

CHARON, FERRYMAN TO THE REALM OF THE DEAD, FROM *THE LAST JUDGMENT* BY MICHELANGELO, SISTINE CHAPEL.

In many cultures worldwide, one comes across the notion that the souls of the deceased do not, after leaving their bodies, immediately find themselves in heaven or hell. Rather, they must make a transition to the next realm. This transition is often symbolized by **birds** that take the soul to heaven, by a **bridge** that the departed must cross, or by a journey through a tunnel or across a body of water.

In many traditional societies, the deceased are often thought to linger around the living, either because they have not fully resolved some matter with their families or because they are unable to find their way to the realm of the dead. In these societies, a religious functionary, such as a priest or a **shaman,** performs the role of **psychopomp**—one who guides the dead to the otherworld.

Charon, although neither a shaman nor a psychopomp, exhibits certain characteristics of both. A resident of the otherworld, he is a kind of psychopomp who guides souls to the realm of the dead. Like many traditional shamans, he is an eccentric character who requires payment before he will perform his task. Charon is also a type of threshold guardian, a universal figure who allows some but not all to cross over into the other realm. Perhaps because he contains reflections of many different archetypes, Charon has been a popular figure in Western literature.

Sources:

Grant, Michael, and John Hazel. *Who's Who in Classical Mythology.* New York: Oxford University Press, 1993.

Tripp, Edward. *The Meridian Handbook of Classical Mythology.* New York: New American Library, 1970.

CHINA

The Chinese idea of the afterlife represents a combination of different spiritual traditions that were integrated into a few pivotal principles: ensuring one's health (and longevity), showing compassion (ethical and moral responsibilities), and giving devotion and support to the ancestors (**ancestor worship**). During the time of the Shan royal dynasty (late second-century B.C.), ancestors were consulted to interpret signs and to foresee the future. They were treated as if they led an existence in their tombs, which were furnished and decorated for living beings parallel to their premortem life.

A later tradition developed the belief that the royal family and aristocrats had two complementary souls that separated at death. Upon one's death, the *hun* soul, of the yang (masculine, solar, positive) type, was believed to move outward into the universe and was invited ultimately to inhabit a tablet that could be commemorated as the spirit of the ancestor. The other soul, *p'o,* of the yin (feminine, lunar, negative) type, was believed to follow the body under the earth, into a kingdom known as Yellow Springs. Resembling the ancient Greek **Hades,** this netherworld absorbed the souls, believed to be yellow in color. Various funerary rites were performed for the soul that followed the body (s'o), which if maltreated could mutate into a ghost or some other negative force.

Early Chinese efforts to achieve physical immortality, especially within the philosophical milieu, stemmed from the belief that death meant the dispersion of vital forces (the *chi*)—in contrast with the Western idea of death as separation of matter from spirit. From the same perspective, life was viewed by Chinese philosophers as the coming together of vital forces, and the alternating of life and death were considered parts of the same process of metamorphosis and transformation of nature, of which human beings were also a part. The effort to prolong one's life through body and mind techniques (such as fasting and certain martial arts) and diets (such as macrobiotics) has always been an important issue for Chinese people, along with living in good health. Thus, much of the Chinese interest in religion was as a practice that could ensure physical and mental well-being. Since the second millennium, belief in the physical immortality of special individuals, mythologized in the shape of **birds,** was believed to occur when practicing the techniques developed within the Taoist tradition.

During the third century B.C., the mythical Queen Mother of the West (Hsi Wang Mu), who played an important role in funerary rites, became known as the donor of the drug of immortality. Those who had been given the drug were believed to ascend directly to heaven, leaving behind their body. The belief that death privileges pertained only to the nobles began to be questioned in the first century B.C., and the lower classes began to believe in the existence of immortality elixirs that ensured the immortality of one's entire family.

Besides physical immortality, it was important to ensure the preservation of the body as the adobe of the p'o (the soul that remains with the body upon death). Ancestor worship developed out of the practices surrounding the p'o. Upon one's death, during the funerary rites, and even in the grave, there was a set of rules followed to protect the body that were designed to ensure that the p'o could not leave the body or that negative forces could not enter into it. Determining the physical orientation of the coffin was also an important part of the funerary rite, as it could have positive or negative influence on the family of the person who died. If an inauspicious event occurred within a family, it was ascribed to the wrong orientation of the coffin, which was then accordingly changed.

The preservation of the body was the principal goal of a Buddhist practice known as meat bodies. When a monk had chosen a moment to die, he went to meditate in an underground chamber and starved himself to death. His body then was smoked inside the chamber, treated, and ultimately moved into a temple where he could be venerated.

In general, the Chinese tradition tended to locate paradisiacal and infernal dimensions of the afterlife in remote areas located beyond the borders of China. Netherworld beliefs were drawn from different traditions and mingled together. After the introduction of Buddhism, which came from the west (India), the mountains located in the western part of the country were considered to be netherworld realms. An important part of the landscape of the afterlife, for example, was Mount T'ai, originally considered the point where life began. Mount T'ai became, during the Ch'in and Han empires, the "administrational" center of the dead, where souls were judged by a lord of the dead, thus reflecting the structure of political power and highly centralized bureaucracy that characterized those dynasties.

When Buddhism spread into China, an even more organized netherworld was developed; a bureaucratic system of palaces and offices emerged in which the officers were the immortals of the Taoist tradition. Prayers came to resemble an official petition within a bureaucracy. A pantheon of divinities ran the system, assigning positions to officers based on their merits. On the other hand, the infernal dimension of the netherworld was a projection of the imperial Chinese prison system, in which criminals were punished and money could be given in the form of bribes to alleviate the punishment. Thus, "spirit money," offered to the dead by the living family, ensured lightening of the punishment for the dead. Ancient Chinese graves were typically filled with items that could ensure assistance and help at the moment of one's judgment in the netherworld.

Neither heaven nor hell were considered to be permanent states for the dead, who were being rewarded or were suffering due to the law of karma. Thus, punishment lasted as long as it was needed, and then one had to reenter the cycle of rebirth. The belief in the possibility of lightening one's pain was an important point in Chinese spirituality, as it increased ethic and moral responsibility and strengthened the idea of compassion. The Chinese also believed in a paradisiacal state identified with the Buddhist Pure Land (introduced by Amitabha Buddha), a realm in which one could easily achieve self-realization and nirvana.

Sources:

Eliade, Mircea, ed. *The Encyclopedia of Religion.* 16 vols. New York: Macmillan, 1987.

MacGregor, Geddes. *Images of Afterlife: Beliefs from Antiquity to Modern Times.* New York: Paragon House, 1992.

Obayashi, Hiroshi, ed. *Death and Afterlife: Perspectives of World Religions.* Westport, CT: Greenwood Press, 1992.

CHRISTIANITY

Christianity's views of the afterlife, immortality, and the soul reflect the influence of the cultures in which it originated and spread during its first centuries in the Mediterranean basin. For example, the idea of **resurrection** (both individual and eschatological) was introduced into Christianity from apocalyptic Judaism (a notion ultimately derived from **Zoroastrianism).** The idea of resurrection developed in tandem with an apocalyptic vision of history that entails the end of the world as we know it and which will result in the defeat of death and evil.

Early Christianity arose as a Jewish sect during the **apocalyptic** period. First century Christians strongly believed in the imminent Second Coming of Christ (during their lifetime), which would be accompanied by the resurrection of the dead, a Judgment Day, and the end of this world. Bodily resurrection was thus the afterlife belief of the earliest Christians. Christ's resurrection (along with the resurrection of the righteous at the end of time) came to be viewed as the victory over death, which, as

THE RAISING OF LAZARUS AT BETHANY.

the antithesis of God, creator of life, is the ultimate enemy. Although the idea of resurrection is Jewish in origin, belief in the immortality of soul came from Greek culture.

When Christianity spread outside of Palestine, it came into contact with the Hellenistic culture of the Romans and the Greeks, who viewed death and the afterlife from a radically different perspective. Greek **Gnosticism,** for example, was based on the principle that the human soul is a divine spark, imprisoned in the body, that since taking embodiment has forgotten its divine nature. By achieving *gnosis* (knowledge of its true identity), the soul can obtain salvation, liberating itself from its bodily prison.

The New Testament, which is composed of 27 books written in different historical contexts in different parts of the world by different people across a period of more than a hundred years, reflects the broad range of views on salvation and afterlife from traditions as diverse as apocalyptic Judaism to Hellenistic religious culture. Whereas Jewish apocalypticism envisioned salvation as union of soul and body at the resurrection, for the Gnostics salvation meant the exact opposite—the eternal separation of the two. Despite their contradictory emphases, the Jewish concept of resurrection and the Gnostic idea of eternal life of the soul merged in the Christian notion of the afterlife, in which the eternal soul is reunited with a transformed physical body at the end of time.

In the New Testament, the idea of how and when salvation could be achieved varied. In one of Paul's letters, for example, the apostle had to cope with the Corinthians' denial of resurrection as it involved reunification of the soul with the flesh (Gnosticism's influence on the Corinthians is clear). The apocalyptic view of the final judgment, however, is found in both of Jesus' parables and, more clearly, in John's Revelation, with its emphasis on the end of time and final salvation of the righteous through resurrection. (Interestingly enough, Revelation was written when Christians were faced with religious persecution for denying the Roman emperor's divinity. As in the antecedent apocalyptic Judaism, envisioning a future world and a new age where good will prevail and evil will succumb encourages those who are facing religious persecution to accept martyrdom in the name of God.)

Because the early Christians believed the end of the world was imminent (for example, they worried about those who were going to die before the Second Coming of Christ), their focus was on converting and changing their present life in preparation for a future communion with the divine.

As the world did not end during the period of the early church, nor even after the year 1000, Christians began to push forward the end-time (along with the Second Coming of Christ and Judgment Day) to a remote future, and religious authorities began to speculate more on the nature of heaven, hell, and purgatory, integrating what was said in the Scriptures with contemporaneous perspectives.

Heaven in the Old Testament was conceived of as the physical sky where God resided. From the period of the New Testament through the Middle Ages, it came to be viewed as a place open to all who were faithful, free from pain and sorrow, and as a blissful state of communion between the divine and the saints. Thomas Aquinas (1225–1274) in particular portrayed heaven as the place where one meets with and knows God.

The original idea of hell, which drew upon the Jewish idea of **She'ol,** was developed as a realm of pain in early Christianity, in opposition to the blissful state of heaven. The Gospels' reference to Gehenna as a place of torment and punishment was used to encourage conversion in this life.

In the Middle Ages, heaven and hell became part of the popular imaginary piety through the graphic depiction of Dante Alighieri's Divine Comedy. **Dante** depicted heaven and hell as a series of multiple concentric spherical heavens and multilayered underground hells, divided into levels in which good people and sinners were rewarded or punished according to the degree of their noble deeds or sins.

Between the two realms, Dante also placed the multiple levels of the mountain of purgatory (from Latin *purgare,* to cleanse), a place of temporary damnation for those who need to be purified before entering into eternal communion with God. Although a few passages from the Scriptures and the early church fathers mentioned a purgatory where one could be purified (traditionally by fire), the existence of purgatory did not become official doctrine until the Middle Ages, with the Councils of Lyon in 1274 and Florence in 1439. Belief in this intermediary stage where one's soul would go if one died in a state of venial sin led to the development of indulgences, which, it was advertised, could free souls from purgatory and prepare them for the theirjourney to the afterlife. It followed that the penance process could also be extended by a living person to a deceased relative through religious offerings. The Catholic church's practice of selling indulgences became such big business that it helped provoke what became the Protestant Reformation under the leadership of Martin Luther (1483–1546).

Although purgatory and the sale of indulgences presumed the notion of retributive justice and the quantification of sin and punishment, the Protestant doctrine viewed salvation as possible *sola gratia,* by faith only. With the Council of Trent (1545–1564), the Roman Catholic church affirmed the doctrine of purgatory and the efficacy of indulgences, thus effecting the definitive separation of the Protestant and Roman Catholic churches. Protestantism has further developed the idea of salvation as occurring through faith and by grace.

Sources:

Eliade, Mircea. *The Encyclopedia of Religion.* 16 vols. New York: Macmillan, 1987.
MacGregor, Geddes. *Images of Afterlife: Beliefs from Antiquity to Modern Times.* New York: Paragon House, 1992.
Obayashi, Hiroshi, ed. *Death and Afterlife: Perspectives of World Religions.* Westport, CT: Greenwood Press, 1992.

CHURCH OF CHRIST

According to the Church of Christ, life is the singular opportunity to declare for God, by believing in Jesus Christ, repenting for sin, confessing faith in Christ, and being baptized. At death, those who have accepted Christ go to a transitory place of blessing where they will wait for the final judgment, in which they will be welcomed by God to live in heaven forever.

People who refuse Christ, are unfaithful, or have a confused life have a different destiny; they will wait for the final judgment in a place of torment, and—when pronounced guilty by God—they will be punished eternally. This will happen to the majority of people, who, succumbing to the temptations of Satan, do not follow the insights of the Scriptures, especially the New Testament.

The church teaches that for those who believe in Christ death is a time of peace before joining eternal life, whereas for those who do not believe or, although believing, dedicate only a marginal part of their life to discipleship, it is one of separation, a prelude to torture and eternal destruction.

Sources:

Johnson, Christopher Jay, and Marsha G. McGee. *Encounters with Eternity: Religious Views of Death and Life After-Death.* New York: Philosophical Library, 1986.

Kastenbaum, Robert, and Beatrice Kastenbaum, eds. *Encyclopedia of Death.* Phoenix, AZ: Oryx Press, 1989.

CHURCH OF ESSENTIAL SCIENCE

The Church of Essential Science was born out of a Spiritualist background. Its founder, Rev. Kingdon L. Brown, received his original ordination from the National Spiritual Aid Association, an organization that offers credential services for independent Spiritualist ministers. In early 1964 Brown began a journey toward a different religious path when he received his first message from what he called the Silent Brotherhood of Ascended Masters. Brown gained a particular mentor from that group, Master Manta Ru, from whom Brown learned the religious system called Essential Science.

Essential Science teaches that divinity can be understood in modern terms as the basic energy of the universe, expressed through the atomic structure. Human beings are made up of body, mind, and soul, and it is the soul that is related to the divine nature. According to Brown, when people decide to concentrate on developing their spiritual nature, that provides the opportunity to progress toward direct contact with the divine essence of the universe and access the power and wisdom of that divinity.

The teaching of Brown through the channeling of Manta Ru and other entities attracted followers who helped found the Church of Essential Science in Detroit, Michigan, in 1965. Members seek to become part of the Silent Brotherhood, that group of souls, whether in this life or in the next life, that have attained a degree of knowledge and awareness. Channeling, healing, and meditation are key tools for followers, who can thereby seek guidance from those spiritually advanced beings who have ascended into the life beyond death. In 1987 Brown, who now goes by the name Brian Seabrook, founded a church-related mystical system called the Knights Templar Aquarian, which teaches a metaphysical interpretation of the Christian Bible and in particular the idea that the Aquarian age, the next step in humanity's evolution, will soon arrive.

Sources:

Brown, Kingdon L. *The Metaphysical Lessons of Saint Timothy's Abbey Church.* Grosse Pointe, MI: St. Timothy's Abbey Church, 1966.

Melton, J. Gordon. *The Encyclopedia of American Religions.* 4th ed. Detroit, MI: Gale Research, 1993.

CHURCH OF JESUS CHRIST OF LATTER-DAY SAINTS (MORMON)

Members of the Church of Jesus Christ of Latter-day Saints (LDS), also known as Mormons, believe that at the end of the **millenium** (a thousand-year period during which Christ will rule the earth), the regeneration of nature will be achieved through the resurrection of the bodies of all beings. The earth itself will experience a sort of death, after which it will be regenerated.

The church actually speaks of two resurrections. The first one will involve those who lived faithfully according to the laws of God, children who died in innocence, and those who died in ignorance. The dead who were not eligible for the first resurrection will be encompassed by the second one, which is universal. At the second resurrection—which includes everyone regardless of age, sex, or virtue—every soul will assume its body and, with spirit and body reunited, will be subjected to the final judgment.

Baptism of the dead, indispensable for all who would seek salvation, is an important element of Mormon doctrine, because it is considered the symbol of burial, to be followed by resurrection. Through baptism of the dead, also, those who have lived and died without knowing the gospel can benefit from the saving laws of the Lord and will not be condemned at the last judgment, whereas the wicked will be sent to eternal punishment.

Sources:

Johnson, Christopher Jay, and Marsha G. McGee. *Encounters with Eternity: Religious Views of Death and Life After-Death.* New York: Philosophical Library, 1986.

Kastenbaum, Robert, and Beatrice Kastenbaum, eds. *Encyclopedia of Death.* Phoenix, AZ: Oryx Press, 1989.

CHURCH OF METAPHYSICAL CHRISTIANITY

The Church of Metaphysical Christianity, based in Florida, is a blending of science and religion drawn from a Spiritualist background and New Thought influence. The church teaches that obedience to natural laws—whether physical, mental, or spiritual—constitutes a pure form of worship. It teaches that spiritual laws are still in force after death, e.g. the law of karma.

Revs. Dorothy Graff Flexer and Russell J. Flexer founded the Church of Metaphysical Christianity in 1958. They were originally ministers in the Spiritualist Episcopal Church, but after that organization suffered internal difficulties, the Flexers went independent. The "natural spiritual laws" that the church focuses on are the law of life, the law of love, the law of truth, the law of compensation, the law of freedom, the law of abundance, and the law of perfection. Such ideas as the law of abundance shows the influence of New Thought.

The church conceives of love as the creative force of life, which does not end with death. The spirit of a person is said to continue after death, and the church places emphasis on giving evidence of that life after death. The spirit of the deceased is thought to still have the ability to communicate with the living, given the right conditions. Church members are given the techniques for developing their own abilities to communicate with those in the next life.

Sources:

Melton, J. Gordon. *The Encyclopedia of American Religions.* 4th ed. Detroit, MI: Gale Research, 1993.
Wade, Alda Madison. *At the Shrine of the Master.* Philadelphia: Dorrance, 1953.

COLLECTIVE UNCONSCIOUS

The term *collective unconscious,* was coined by psychologist Carl Jung after he observed that the basic structures of many symbols and myths are nearly universal, even between cultures with no historical influence on one another. Most traditional societies, for example, tell hero myths, use circles to represent wholeness, believe the sky symbolizes transcendence, and so forth. Jung theorized that this universality resulted from unconscious patterns (genetic or quasi-genetic predispositions to utilize certain symbolic and mythic structures) that we inherited from our distant ancestors. The reservoir of these patterns constitute a collective unconscious, distinct from the individual, personal unconscious that is the focus of Freudian psychoanalysis.

Jung referred to the unconscious, predisposing patterns for particular myths and symbols as archetypes. Hence, we speak of the mandala (circle) archetype, the hero archetype (the latter made famous by the Jungian thinker Joseph Campbell), and so forth. Jung asserted that his notions of the collective unconscious and the archetypes were similar to the theory of instincts (i.e., behavior is the result of certain biological drives).

Jung's ideas have sometimes been invoked to explain certain experiences or certain cultural historical facts that seem to indicate the existence of a spiritual dimension, such as conscious life after death. Thus, reports of similar experiences during **near-death experiences,** for instance, can be explained in terms of universal symbols from the collective unconscious. Similarly, the fact that different cultures at different periods of time all report similar phenomena—such as, for example,

possession and **exorcism**—may merely indicate that such phenomena reflect archetypal patterns in the human mind rather than prove that disembodied spirits really exist.

Sources:

Hall, Calvin S., and Vernon A. Nordby. *A Primer on Jungian Psychology.* New York: New American Library, 1973.

Jung, C. J. *The Archetypes and the Collective Unconscious.* 2d ed. Bollingen Series, no. 20. Princeton: Princeton University Press, 1968.

Samuels, Andrew, Bani Shorter, and Fred Plaut. *A Critical Dictionary of Jungian Analysis.* London: Routledge & Kegan Paul, 1986.

COMMUNICATION WITH THE DEAD

Communication with the dead is accomplished through clairvoyant persons, such as mediums, or mechanical devices, such as the planchette (similar to a ouija board, a pointer moves across a board indicating letters or numbers to spell out words). A talented medium is usually considered the best means for such communication, the reliability of which depends on the medium's sensitivity to normally unperceived entities. This mediumship may take the form of some kind of motor automatism, which manifests itself through everything from the movement of a planchette across a Ouija board to automatic writing and trance-speaking. Other forms of communication from ''the other side'' involve heightened sensory sensitivity such as clairvoyant (psychic sight) or clairaudient (psychic hearing) messages, as well as telepathic messages and symbolic visions. Sometimes multiple communications occur, such as in the case of an exceptionally talented medium who obtains messages from two different entities at the same time, one writing and the other speaking.

Numerous experiments to communicate with the world of the dead through mechanical devices have been attempted. During the 1930s, for instance, a group of British psychical researchers established the Ashkir-Jobson Trianion, which experimented with various devices, such as the communigraph and the reflectograph, to facilitate spirit communication. Other, more recent mechanical devices used include the dynamistograph, the Vendermeulen spirit indicator, and the famous **electronic voice phenomenon,** developed with the idea that voices of dead people can be recorded on a tape recorder, giving verifiable evidence of survival.

Communications allegedly coming from spirits cannot always be trusted. They are often highly improbable, even when they occur through mediums of established reputation, and can often be explained in terms of the subconscious powers of the medium or of the sitters. There are also many instances of fraud, as various researchers and investigators of mediumship phenomena, like those belonging to the **Society for Psychical Research,** have demonstrated.

Sources:

Almeder, Robert. *Beyond Death. Evidence for Life After Death.* Springfield, IL: Charles C Thomas, 1987.

Moore, Brooke Noel. *The Philosophical Possibilities Beyond Death.* Springfield, IL: Charles C Thomas, 1981.
Shepard, Leslie A., ed. *Encyclopedia of Occultism & Parapsychology.* Detroit, MI: Gale Research, 1991.

CONSCIOUS DYING

Conscious dying is an approach to death in which it is regarded as a means of liberation of one's consciousness, as well as the way to achieve enlightenment and immortality. The concept of conscious dying is particularly well developed in two books by **Benito F. Reyes,** *Conscious Dying* (1986) and *The Practice of Conscious Dying* (1990), and in a book by his wife, Dominga L. Reyes, *The Story of Two Souls* (1984).

According to Benito Reyes, death and dying are both aspects of life, the main characteristic of which is its endless and beginningless nature—its immortality and eternity. Death and dying may thus be regarded as transformation of energy on the physical level and alteration of consciousness on the nonphysical plane. The integrity and continuity of human consciousness can be maintained by the individual after dying, through the intermediate state between death and rebirth, and through the process of being reborn **(reincarnation),** including both the intrauterine phase and the birth phase.

Advocates of the concept of conscious dying, which is inspired in particular by The Tibetan Book of the Dead, maintain that most people erroneously live their lives in a completely ''physicalistic'' way by identifying themselves with their physical bodies. At the crucial moment of death, and following death, however, they discover that such attitudes are wrong and that, although the body dies, consciousness continues to live in a nonphysical form. Evidence from investigations of **near-death** and **out-of-body experiences** tend to support such a revelation.

This discovery of continuing consciousness after death has many variations and depends on many elements, such as the kind of death one is undergoing (e.g., gradual or sudden), the quality of consciousness the person possesses, and the quality and degree of help the person is receiving in facilitating the transition from the physical to the nonphysical state of being, during which it is essential to preserve the continuity of consciousness. The transition is characterized by several elements, the most important of which is a sensation of complete separation from the physical body. During this experience the individual can see, hear, feel, and think without the physical body and its organs of perception and thought.

Sources:

Reyes, Benito F. *Conscious Dying: Psychology of Death and Guidebook to Liberation.* Ojai, CA: World University of America, 1986.

———. *The Practice of Conscious Dying: Off-Ramp to Liberation and Freeway to Conscious Immortality.* Ojai, CA: World University of America, 1990.

Reyes, Dominga L. *The Story of Two Souls.* Ojai, CA: World University of America, 1984.

CONTROL

In the context of **Spiritualism,** the term *control* refers to the primary spirit with whom a **medium** works. Thus, while a medium may relay messages or information from any number of different entities, it will be the control who regulates ("controls") which other disembodied entities are allowed to speak. Within the Spiritualist tradition, controls are usually regarded as working with a medium for all of the medium's life.

Mediums need not be consciously aware of their controls. One prominent incident that shows this involved the famous medium **Arthur Ford.** While Ford was in a trance in 1924, a spirit spoke through him, telling the sitter who was present to "tell Ford that I am to be his control and that I go by the name of Fletcher." Ford later learned from Fletcher that they were able to work with each other because Ford had the correct "vibration" for the two of them to communicate.

The medium Gladys Osborne Leonard had a control named Feda who claimed to be an Indian girl who had passed away at the beginning of the nineteenth century. Feda helped Leonard develop into a professional medium. Because Leonard was able to dispatch Feda to obtain information, she was able to describe places she had never seen and relate information taken directly from books located in other rooms.

In at least some instances, controls seem to be secondary personalities of the medium, particularly in cases in which there are marked parallels between the medium's and the control's statements. When, for example, a spirit's knowledge seems to replicate the medium's, one has grounds for suspecting that the "spirit" is merely an unconscious aspect of the medium's own mind. In other cases, controls have been explained as manifestations of the **collective unconscious,** which, if **Jung** was correct, would enable the medium to tap into a storehouse of universal knowledge that far exceeds her or his individual experience.

Sources:

Ford, Arthur, with Marguerite Harmon Bro. *Nothing So Strange: The Autobiography of Arthur Ford.* New York: Harper & Brothers, 1968.

Grattan-Guinness, Ivor. *Psychical Research: A Guide to Its History, Principles and Practices.* Wellingborough, Northamptonshire, England: The Aquarian Press, 1982.

CRAWFORD, WILLIAM JACKSON

William Jackson Crawford (1881–1920), born in Dunedin, New Zealand, was a lecturer in mechanical engineering at Queens University, Belfast, Ireland and a member of the Society for Psychical Research (SPR). His contribution to psychical research consists of his controversial studies of the Goligher Circle. The Golighers were **Spiritualists** who used to sit in **séances** as part of their religious observance. The circle consisted of Goligher, a working man, his four daughters, who were **mediums,** his son, and his son-in-law.

The Golighers communicated with spirits that were believed to be responsible for various effects, such as imitative sounds, **rappings** on the table or the walls, the moving of a trumpet, and the levitation of a table. The effects produced during the séances, which usually took place in a circle around the table, were investigated by Crawford, who used his engineering expertise to analyze the phenomena produced by Kathleen, the most powerful medium in the family. In particular, he set up a battery of five cameras with which he recorded the presence of "psychic rods" or "pseudopods," which were a psychokinetic force emanating from her body that caused the table to rise through a "cantilever principle." He thought that unseen operators were responsible for producing the psychic rods. Crawford published some of these photographs in *The Psychic Structures of the Goligher Circle* (1921).

Another Society for Psychical Research (SPR) researcher who investigated the Golighers during the same period, W. W. Carington, believed that the phenomena were fraudulent, although he was persuaded that what he saw was genuine. The suspicion that the suicide of Crawford, who poisoned himself in 1920, may have had something to do with a discovery about the Golighers, is unavoidable. Crawford's three books, *The Reality of Psychic Phenomena* (1916), *Experiments in Psychic Science* (1919), and *The Psychic Structures of the Goligher Circle* (1921) have had an important influence on psychical research.

Sources:

Barham, Allan. "Dr. W. J. Crawford, His Work and His Legacy in Psychokinesis." *Journal of the Society for Psychical Research* 55 (1988): 113–38.

Inglis, Brian. *Science and Parascience: A History of the Paranormal, 1914–1939*. London: Hodder and Stoughton, 1984.

CROOKES, SIR WILLIAM

Sir William Crookes (1832–1919), one of the greatest physicists of the nineteenth century, was one of the first prominent investigators of Spiritualist mediums. He discovered the element thallium and invented the radiometer, spinthariscope, and Crookes' tubes, among other inventions. For much of his life he was committed to **Spiritualism.**

Crookes, born June 17, 1832, in London, England, was the son of a prosperous tailor. Until age 16, when he entered the Royal College of Chemistry, Crookes had little formal education. Following graduation, he became superintendent of the meteorological department at Radcliffe Observatory, Oxford, in 1854, where he devised an automated method for recording instrument data. The next year he joined the faculty of Chester Training College as professor of chemistry. Because Chester would not provide him with a research laboratory, he resigned in 1856. Most of his life's research was carried out at a home laboratory.

SIR WILLIAM CROOKES. (FROM THE P. LUDOVICI PAINTING IN THE NATIONAL PORTRAIT GALLERY.) COURTESY OF THE ARC.

In the same year in which he resigned from Chester, Crookes married Ellen Humphrey, with whom he had eight children. Crookes initially supported his family by writing and editing articles for photography journals. Eventually, in 1859, he initiated his own periodical, *Chemical News,* which he edited for almost 50 years. Later, he also helped found and edit of the *Quarterly Journal of Science.*

In 1861 Crookes discovered the element thallium and accurately measured its atomic weight. Two years later, he was honored by being elected a fellow of the Royal Society of London for Improving Natural Knowledge.

In 1867 Crookes's youngest brother, Philip, died of yellow fever. He had been close to his brother and was upset by his death. A fellow physicist who was also a Spiritualist, Cromwell Varley, persuaded Crookes to attend a séance and attempt to contact Philip. Crookes believed that he was successful in this attempt and joined the Spiritualist movement. He kept his religious inclinations to himself, however, and never publicly associated himself with the movement.

Crookes found the phenomena associated with Spiritualism fascinating. He systematically studied mediumship from 1869 to 1875 and attended séances with such well-known mediums as D. D. Home, Frank Herne, and Charles Williams. He chose to devote most of his time to the former, perhaps because Home always held séances in good light, as well as welcomed scientific research into his abilities. Also, Home's mediumship was marked by such tangible physical phenomena as levitation, table-tilting, luminous phenomena, and materialization of hands.

Crookes went beyond simple observation to investigate Home's phenomena in controlled, scientific environments. Often he had Home perform one of his remarkable feats of psychokinesis (moving physical objects without touching them) while he and other scientists of repute watched and took notes. Rather than claiming that disembodied spirits were responsible for the observed phenomena, he postulated that they were the result of some sort of psychic force projected by the medium.

Crookes presented this psychic force as supremely worthy of scientific investigation but found other scientists disinterested and even hostile. Some of the other members of the Royal Society rejected his invitation to attend experimental sessions with Home. The society also rejected a paper on his psychic work that he had submitted for publication, so he published it instead in his *Quarterly Journal of Science.* Typical of the attitude of a certain class of narrow-minded rationalists, a critic asserted that the phenomena Crookes described could never have happened because they were impossible. To this charge he responded, "I never said it was possible, I only said it was true."

Crookes is also remembered for his study of Florence Cook. In 1872 Cook requested an investigation after an attendee at one of her séances had grabbed the full-form materialization of her spirit guide, Katie King, and claimed that it was Cook herself. Crookes studied her mediumship closely, and for some four months she lived with him and his family. The research question he posed for himself was whether it was possible to observe both Cook and Katie at the same time. Crookes asserted that he was able to do this, going so far as to take a picture of Katie and Cook together. He took 44 pictures of Katie. He also claimed to have held and measured Katie, observing that she was taller, larger, and more attractive than Cook.

Cook was later caught perpetrating a fraud, however, and it remains an open question as to whether her sessions with the great scientist were genuine or he was duped. Skeptics have suggested that Crookes was having an affair—or was at least infatuated—with Cook, which would explain why a scientist of his stature could have been easily tricked. This "theory," however, is pure speculation, based on little more than circumstantial evidence.

After completing yet another series of investigations of another medium of doubtful reputation, Anna Eva Fay, in 1875, Crookes turned his research talents back to the field of natural science. He lent his support to the Society for Psychical Research (SPR) after its formation in 1882, even serving as president in 1886, but he never became truly active in it.

In 1875 the Royal Society awarded Crookes its Royal Medal. The next year he devised the radiometer, an instrument that measured the impact of radiation on objects in a vacuum, and a special vacuum tube called a Crookes' tube. This line of research led more or less directly to his discovery of cathode rays, which soon led to discoveries (by other scientists) of X rays and the electron.

From 1887 to 1889 Crookes served as president of the Chemical Society. From 1890 to 1894 he also served as president of the Society of Electrical Engineers. In 1897 he was knighted, and in 1898 became president of the British Association for the Advancement of Science. In his presidential address he made a point of asserting that he had nothing to retract with respect to his study of Home and Cook. In 1903 Crookes invented an instrument used in the study of subatomic particles, the spinthariscope. In 1910 he was awarded the Order of Merit, one of England's highest nonmilitary honors. From 1913 to 1915 he served as president of the Royal Society, the same organization that had criticized his psychical research.

Crookes died in London on April 4, 1919. He never wrote the book he was planning on his spirit research. His writings on the subject, however, were collected in an unauthorized booklet, *Researches in the Phenomena of Spiritualism,* initially published in 1874. This publication and other materials were reprinted in *Crookes and the Spirit World* (1972), which was edited by SPR members R. G. Medhurst and K. M. Goldney.

Sources:

Gauld, Alan. *The Founders of Psychical Research.* London: Routledge & Kegan Paul, 1968.

Medhurst, R. G, and K. M. Goldney. *Crookes and the Spirit World.* New York: Taplinger, 1972.

Oppenheim, Janet. *The Other World: Spiritualism and Psychical Research in England, 1850–1914.* Cambridge: Cambridge University Press, 1985.

CROSS-CORRESPONDENCES

Cross-correspondences refer to message fragments, sent by the spirit world to the living through different mediums, that are later combined to form a complete message. They are regarded as providing strong evidence of survival after death. The information, received through trance or automatic writing, makes sense only when the messages are put together, demonstrating that the mediums are not simply fabricating the information.

Cross-correspondences are considered simple when two or more mediums produce the same or related words or phrases. When indirect messages must be decoded, cross-correspondences are considered complex.

Various members of the **Society for Psychical Research,** such as Edmund Gurney, **Henry Sidgwick,** and **Frederic W. H. Myers,** were very interested in cross-correspondences and in the question of survival after death. Myers, in particular, was deeply involved in this subject, and in his *Human Personality and Its Survival of Bodily Death* (1903) he maintained that the dead would know how to produce strong evidence of survival and that this evidence would require a group effort on the part of the dead.

Myers said that he would attempt to communicate posthumously. After he died in 1901, the mediums Mrs. Piper and Mrs. Willett produced separately some scripts they claimed emanated from him. The scripts, some of which have been published in the *Proceedings of the Society for Psychical Research,* are very complicated, often involving classical and literary allusions and topics in which Myers had been interested. Many explanations for the scripts have been suggested, such as unconscious telepathy between the mediums.

Cross-correspondences became more popular after Myers's death. They also became more complex and symbolic, such as in the famous cases known as the Palm Sunday case and the Ear of Dionysius, in which the messages could be understood, or interpreted, only by the individual mediums or only after much analysis of the various clues to links between messages. Sometimes years were spent investigating the communications, and by 1918 the researchers of the Society for Psychical Research concluded that cross-correspondences formed large and linked groups.

There are no "natural" explanations for cross-correspondence phenomena, and many investigators claim that the messages provide true evidence of survival after death. Other researchers maintain that mediums obtain the communications from their own unconsciousness, or through telepathy and clairvoyance. Frank Podmore, one of the founding members of the Society for Psychical Research, asserted that cross-correspondences were the result of the telepathic communication between the living. None of these explanations satisfied hard-core skeptics, who usually chose simply to ignore the careful experiments of the researchers.

Sources:

Gauld, Alan. *The Founders of Psychical Research.* London: Routledge & Kegan Paul, 1968.
Guiley, Rosemary Ellen. *The Encyclopedia of Ghosts and Spirits.* New York: Facts on File, 1992.
Haynes, Renee. *The Society for Psychical Research, 1882–1892: A History.* London: Heinemann, 1982.

Cryonic Suspension

The term *cryonic suspension* (from the Greek *kyros,* icy cold) refers to the practice of maintaining a body in a state of hypothermia for a long period of time and then bringing the body back to life. This phenomenon, also called solid-state hypothermia, is considered a means of overcoming death.

According to Robert C. W. Ettinger, author of the much discussed *The Prospect of Immortality* (1964), most human beings have a good possibility of surviving death through the scientific rejuvenation of their frozen bodies. Human bodies can be preserved at very low temperatures without deterioration, and if damage occurs in death, medical science can repair and rehabilitate them.

The prospect of immortality proposed by Ettinger attracted much attention at the time, but many technical and ethical questions have since been raised. Criticism runs the gamut from psychological to social to moral to economic issues. It has often been argued that it is ethically wrong to deal with life and death in this way and that the procedure does not consider the effects on the lives of the survivors. Cryonic preservation is also expensive, giving rise to ethical considerations such as who should undergo the procedure (e.g., a child with a disease for which a cure is expected in the near future, or anyone who can pay for it, regardless of age or other factors).

Among the most important objections to cryonic suspension are those involving its scientific credibility. Although there is little doubt about future technological advances, the scientific community is divided regarding the rapidity and extent of developments in cryonic suspension. Critics of cryonic suspension maintain that it is impossible to resuscitate a corpse from a solidly frozen state. Damage from freezing may also occur, and a method of freezing has yet to be perfected. Critics also maintain that there is no way to prevent lethal cell loss and that some types of cells do not survive solid freezing.

Proponents of cryonics claim that the technology for both freezing and resuscitating is advancing rapidly. They believe that atom-by-atom manipulation of matter will eventually be possible, allowing repair and maintenance of cells.

Sources:

Kastenbaum, Robert, and Beatrice Kastenbaum. *Encyclopedia of Death.* New York: Avon, 1989.

CULT OF DIONYSUS, THE

Dionysus was the ancient Mediterranean god of wine, and thus the giver of joy, as well as the god of the exceptional. The madness or frenzy induced by wine drinking was viewed as an expansion of the mental powers and possession by the divinity. In ancient **Greece** there were four public festivals in honor of this god: the Anthesteria, the Agrionia, the Dionysia, and the Great Dionysia. The Anthesteria was associated with a myth of the origin of wine concerning the death of Ikarios the peasant, who was the first human to learn from Dionysus the arts of planting the vine and pressing wine. When Ikarios was killed by those who believed they had been poisoned by him, his daughter hung herself, thus casting a mythical shadow on the act of drinking wine—the sacrifice of the father and the maiden. The link between wine and blood is thus very ancient.

All of the Dionysian festivals are associated with the madness induced by drinking wine to excess. This madness overturns the normal social order. According to myth, possessed women, called *maenads,* abandoned their home to go to a mountain, where, in a state of altered consciousness, they dismembered and devoured wild animals. This mythical heritage is reflected in such works as Euripides' play *Bacchae,* in which Agaue, possessed by the divine, is unaware that she is killing her own son, the king Pentheus.

In addition to the public festivals, mysteries and secret esoteric cults devoted to Dionysus developed. The Bacchic mysteries emerged out of the cult of Dionysus—in Italy known as Bacchus, god of wine, ecstasy, and *enthusiasmos,* the state of possession by the divinity (*en theos,* ''in god''). Sexual practices and alcohol use were included in the rituals of the secret mysteries, as the iconography of wine and phallic symbols testifies. Archeological findings and literary sources from the fifth century B.C. onward document the practice, in Greece and southern Italy, of nocturnal Bacchic mysteries, which promised a state of blessedness after death to those who were initiated.

Initiation into the mysteries of Dionysus involved the mystic discovery of what death is all about, that is, knowledge of the postmortem wandering of the dead in the darkness of **Hades** and the processes and rituals that the dead undergo. This initiation thus taught how to properly answer the questions that are put to the deceased, so that he will be able to drink from the waters of remembrance rather than from the waters of forgetfulness in the underworld. The experience of remembering was very important in the mystic Greek milieu, where it represented victory over ignorance. Remembering was also the condition that guaranteed the best postmortem status for the soul. Thus, remembrance revealed to initiates, both men and women, the way to eternal bliss through knowledge and ritual. In this, the mysteries are comparable to the ancient Egyptian belief (found in the Book of the Dead) that the soul, before reincarnation, drinks from the River of Indifference.

The Bacchic mysteries did not constitute a uniform movement. Different variations and implications developed throughout the Hellenistic world. There was no centralized organization or sanctuary to coordinate and establish rituals and mysteries practice. A broad variety of practices were found in different areas and at different times; the cult of Dionysus ranged from friendly gatherings, to initiation rituals, to sexual orgies. In Rome the practice of the Bacchanalia was brutally suppressed in 186 B.C. because of extreme sexual practices. Dionysian initiation survived to symbolize liberation from the routine and pressure of everyday life, and served as a source of energizing forces thought to guarantee a blissful state after death.

Sources:

Burkert, Walter. *Greek Religion.* Cambridge, MA: Harvard University Press, 1985.

Grant, Michael, and John Hazel. *Who's Who in Classical Mythology.* New York: Oxford University Press, 1993.

Tripp, Edward. *The Meridian Handbook of Classical Mythology.* New York: New American Library, 1970.

D

Dante Alighieri

Dante Alighieri (1265–1321), the famous Italian poet, is generally considered a philosopher as well as a theologian. Born of a middle-class family, he played an important role in Florentine civic and political life. After writing his first work, *The New Life,* about his youthful idealistic love for Beatrice Portinari, he took active part in the administration of the commune and was on the imperial side in the struggle between Guelfs and Ghibellines, the partisans of the pope and the emperor, respectively, who were fighting for jurisdiction in Italy. However, when the rival party split into two factions, Alighieri decided to support the antipapal policy of the White Guelfs. After the Blacks took over the city in 1301, under the wing of Charles de Valois, Dante was exiled and his life of wandering from court to court of medieval Italy began.

During his exile, he wrote the *Convivio,* his chief work in Italian prose, which was inspired by Cicero and Boethius; the Latin *De vulgari eloquentia,* a treatise about the preeminence of the Italian vernacular and the definition of the highest form of Italian lyrical poetry, the *canzone;* the *De Monarchia,* an eloquent defense of the imperial principle, which contains Dante's most original contribution to philosophical thought.

The tenor of the times, reflected in the story of his own inner anguishes, represents Dante's primary source of inspiration for *The Divine Comedy,* an allegory of human existence and destiny in the form of a vision of the state of souls after death. Dante himself is the pilgrim in the visionary journey through hell and purgatory to heaven, during a week at Easter in the year 1300 when, at age 35, he feels lost in the "dark wood" of his own moral confusion. The Latin poet **Virgil,** representing secular learning, is his guide through the depths of hell and up the mountain of **purgatory,** and Beatrice, the woman Dante idealized in *The New Life,* representing the higher divine inspiration, leads him to heaven and to the inexpressible divine source of all love "that moves the sun and all the stars."

Hell, in Dante's grand scheme, corresponding to the general medieval view of the world, is portrayed as the place of eternal isolation of souls. It consists of nine concentric circles that, from the hemisphere of Earth and across the river Acheron, progressively diminish in circumference, forming an inverted cone ending in the center of Earth. In each circle, representing the nature and effects of sin, a distinct class of sinners undergo a particular torment according to the nature and gravity of their wrongdoings. In the first circle are placed those individuals unconsciously ignorant of Christianity, such as unbaptized infants and virtuous pagans. The torments of hell begin with the second circle, where the lustful are punished. Circles two to five are designated for sins of incontinence, such as gluttony, avarice, prodigality, and anger.

Then come the walls of the city of Dis, where are contained the sixth circle, with the heretics, and the seventh circle, holding those souls guilty of violence against God, nature, or art, against another's possessions, or against one's neighbors or their possessions. After a still more precipitous descent comes the eighth circle, contained in the pits of Malebolge ("evil pouches"), where are allocated perpetrators of the many variations of fraud and malice. Below this region is a third abyss connecting to the ninth and last circle, the frozen lake of Cocytus, consisting of four divisions for four distinct classes of traitors. In the last of these is fixed Lucifer, imagined as a frosty monster.

A hidden path connects the center of Earth to purgatory, the place of expiatory purification and preparation for the life of eternal blessedness. It is imagined as a mountain formed by the earth, which retreated before Lucifer as he fell from heaven into the abyss of hell, and it is antipodal to Jerusalem and Mount Calvary, in the center of the Southern Hemisphere. After the ante-purgatory, a place holding the excommunicated and the belatedly repentant, and Peter's gate, come seven encircling terraces, which rise in succession with diminished circuit as they approach the summit. Each of the cornices corresponds to one of the seven deadly sins, from which the soul is purged through the expiatory labor of climbing the mountain.

Heaven, in Dante's vision a terrestrial paradise, is reached through a final wall of flames. It contains two streams that wash away the remembrance of sin and strengthen the remembrance of good deeds. Dante's paradise, in accord with the Ptolemaic system of cosmography, consists of nine moving heavens concentric with Earth, the fixed center of the universe, around which they revolve at a velocity proportional to their distance from Earth. Each heaven is presided over by one of the angelic orders and exercises its special influence on human beings and their affairs. The seven lowest are the heavens of the planets: the Moon, Mercury, Venus, the Sun, Mars, Jupiter, and Saturn. The eighth heaven, the sphere of the fixed stars, is the highest visible region of the celestial world. The ninth heaven, the Primum Mobile, governs the general motion of the heavens from east to west, and by it all time and place are ultimately measured. Finally, beyond and outside the heavens, lies the empyrean, where there is neither time nor place, but light only, and which is the special abode of the deity and the saints.

The final intuitive vision of the Divine Will in Dante's poem represents the last step of an itinerary that leads both the author and the reader not only through a process of conversion to which *The Divine Comedy,* in its larger aspect, is an invitation but also through a deep investigation of human nature.

Sources:

Edwards Paul, ed. *The Encyclopedia of Philosophy.* New York: Macmillan, 1967.
Eliade, Mircea, ed. *Encyclopedia of Religion.* 16 vols. New York: Macmillan, 1987
Hastings, James, ed. *Encyclopedia of Religion and Ethics.* Edinburgh, Scotland: T. & T. Clark, 1981.
Jacoff, Rachel, ed. *The Cambridge Companion to Dante.* Cambridge: Cambridge University Press, 1993.
Toynbee, Paget. *Dante Alighieri: His Life and Works.* New York, Harper and Row, 1965.

DAVIS, ANDREW JACKSON

A particular psychic practice that has its origins in the experiences of the early French and American mesmerists consisted of hypnotizing subjects and putting them into an altered state of consciousness that provided them with knowledge they did not have in their conscious state. These subjects often displayed what is known as traveling clairvoyance, the ability to describe events occurring in places at a distance from the hypnotized subject. Andrew Jackson Davis (1826–1910) was a famous example of an individual who manifested this particular ability.

Born into poor circumstances and uneducated, Davis became a celebrity of the nineteenth century because of his profound trance lectures and his many books, dictated while in trance. He claimed that **Emanuel Swedenbörg,** the famous Swedish mystic, dictated his lectures, published in 1847 as *The Principles of Nature, Her Divine Revelations,* and *A Voice to Mankind,* which represented a fusion of Swedenbörg's cosmology and Charles Fourier's socialism. In his time, Davis was regarded as an American Swedenbörg. He was also a spiritual healer.

In *The Great Harmonia: Being a Philosophical Revelation of the Natural Spiritual, and Celestial Universe* (1850–1855), Davis stated that the only way to purify the world of all its evils was by becoming aware that good and evil represent two fundamental elements in God's plan for mankind. The higher stages of development inherent in each human being can be reached by following the harmonious principles of nature.

His writings, particularly those in which he discussed afterlife realms, were said to have influenced the metaphysics of **Spiritualism,** whose proponents adopted him as a ''philosopher'' of Spiritualism. His reports about the existence of spirits in **Summerland** influenced **mediums,** although he minimized the importance of mediumship, considering it unreliable. When the New York State legislature forbade the practice of spiritual healing, Davis decided to study medicine and anthropology, and after graduating, moved to Watertown, Massachusetts, where he gave medical aid to people without regard to their ability to pay.

ANDREW JACKSON DAVIS. COURTESY OF THE ARC.

Sources:

Berger, Arthur S., and Berger Joice. *The Encyclopedia of Parapsychology and Psychical Research.* New York: Paragon House, 1991.

Cavendish, Richard, ed. *Encyclopedia of the Unexplained. Magic, Occultism and Parapsychology.* New York: McGraw-Hill, 1974.

DAY OF THE DEAD

The Day of the Dead, or All Soul's Day, refers to a yearly holiday in which the dead are honored by various practices, including religious rites, feasts, special foods, and even songs and parades. Typically, the Day of the Dead is celebrated as a time when the departed and the living come together for a celebration or to share a meal. The purpose is to remember the dead and, often, to placate them for the rest of the year. Such ceremonies are ancient, and they continue to be practiced across the globe.

In many African traditional religions, the spirits of the dead watch over their living relatives and intercede for them with other kinds of divine spirits. To appease the dead, their families hold feasts for them, and sometimes offer animal sacrifices. The meal is viewed as a kind of communion between the living and the dead.

Hindu ancestor rites take place over the course of 10 days, during which time the soul is offered food so that it can survive the journey through ten hells. Also, on the first new autumn moon, the head of every household conducts rituals commemorating the departed of the preceding three generations.

The traditional Chinese, in particular, conduct ceremonies in the autumn, summer, and spring for the "spiritual" as well as for the lower, "animal" soul of humanity; the lower soul is placated so as not to disturb living descendants, and the spiritual soul is asked to watch over and aid living descendants. The most important of these ceremonies is the two-week Hungry Ghost Festival, which occurs in the fall. According to tradition, the departed who have no living descendants to feed them become hungry ghosts. During the festival, food is offered to these "ghosts," who are represented by lamps made of lotus flowers that are carried in streets and by candles in tiny boats that are put into streams at dusk.

The Feast of Lanterns, the Japanese Day of the Dead (called Obon), takes place between July 13 and 16. Departed souls return home during Obon and are offered food and entertainment. Special ceremonies are held in the household, and special lanterns are placed at entranceways to direct the dead.

The holiday we designate as Halloween (All Hallow E'en or All Hallows Eve) was formerly a Day of the Dead for the ancient Europeans, a day when the "veil" between this world and the otherworld was thought to be unusually thin. The present date of All Hallows Eve was set by the Catholic Church, which took over the ancient Roman Day of the Dead, Feralia, and transferred it to the first of November. The Catholic All Hallows Eve blended with certain northern European beliefs to give the Halloween familiar to most Americans its current associations with the powers of evil. The tradition of costumed children going door to door asking for food is an echo of the ancient practice of providing food for the spirits of the departed.

For the most part, we moderns have forgotten the original meaning of Halloween. Something like the spirit of the original has been preserved in Mexico, where native Indian beliefs and practices blended with the culture of the Spanish conquistadors.

Compelled to convert to Christianity, the native peoples translated their death beliefs and rituals into ceremonies associated with Catholic martyrs. Religious artworks of Mexico (and even popular cartoons) picture death in all its graphic detail. *Calaveras,* or death's heads, can be found in any Mexican gift shop.

El Dia de los Muertes, the official Day of the Dead, is November 2, All Souls' Day. This date was introduced by the conquistadors, but it fit well with traditional corn celebrations. Activities begin somewhat earlier, on October 31—Halloween. Families clean house, prepare great quantities of chicken, tortillas, and hot chocolate, and make candles and bread in the form of animals. They build small clay altars on which they offer food and toys to the *angelitos* (the spirits of dead children). In the middle of the night, the family prays while the Angelitos come, enjoy their gifts, and then leave.

During the next day, All Saints' Day, the children consume the food that had been offered to the angelitos. A larger feast is prepared for the souls of the older dead, who are expected to show up around dawn the next day. The food for this second celebration is spicier, and the altar is larger. This altar contains decorated bones and skulls made from marzipan or a special baked bread. The foreheads of the skulls bear the names of the dead, or sometimes a suitable motto or sentiment. In earlier centuries, real skulls were unearthed for this purpose and then reburied after the festivities were over.

Far from being days of mourning, these holidays are a genuine celebration. The Mexicans enjoy carnival rides, eat candy shaped like bones and tiny coffins, and frequently drink heavily. Rather than dishonoring the dead, such celebrations are thought to make the deceased happy, as the spirits enjoy the same pleasures as living human beings. People go from house to house sharing food and telling stories about the dead, who have gathered to hear what the living are saying about them. Everyone is mentioned, for fear that any of the departed who is neglected may become unhappy or even vengeful. Priests visit their parishioners' homes, praying with the family and giving blessings. The family shrine is often decorated with photos of the deceased and of their patron saints.

The visitations between neighbors go on all night until morning mass the next day, All Souls' Day, when the deceased are thought to return to their graves. On the evening of All Souls' Day, the community travels to the cemetery, where families pray, sing, and share food one more time in a picnic over the graves of the spirits of deceased relatives. The tradition holds that by the end of this last meal the departed are completely satisfied and can be at peace until the next Day of the Dead.

Sources:

Dictionary of Folklore, Mythology and Legend. New York: Funk & Wagnalls, 1949.
Kastenbaum, Robert, and Beatrice Kastenbaum. *Encyclopedia of Death.* New York: Avon, 1989.

DEATH

All religious traditions have invested death with metaphysical and spiritual significance. In a few cases death has been associated with sleep. In ancient **Greece,** for example, death (Thanatos) was considered the child of Night (Nux) and twin brother of Hypnos (Sleep). Often death has been associated with evil and suffering. Throughout the world one can find myths that portray humans as having been at one time **immortals,** possessed of eternal youth. Death came later, the result of the fall of human beings from their original state of perfection and order. This fall has been viewed in various ways, for example, as the result of the primordial death of a mythical divinity (which then extended to humans), the outcome of a war between the

DEATH, FROM THE ENGRAVING *KNIGHT, DEATH, AND DEVIL*, BY ALBRECHT DÜRER, 1513.

gods, the consequence of carelessness or irresponsibility on the part of a divine being or a human being, and as retribution for disobedience to divine authority.

Humankind's fall from an original status of perfection and the loss of immortality as the result of an act of disobedience to divine authority is best exemplified in the Judeo-Christian tradition. According to the biblical account, Adam and Eve were expelled from **paradise** to prevent them from eating from the Tree of Life, which would have given them immortality. Hence, disobedience (and, secondarily, pride) was the primary cause of mortability for humanity.

Various myths in African traditions view death as resulting from carelessness or stupidity. For example, a being (e.g., a chameleon or a goat) sent to humans to inform them on immortality is unaware of the importance of the mission and does not fulfill completely its responsibility. Thus, many traditional societies have portrayed the introduction of death as unfortunate and even as accidental. In other traditions, however, death has also been understood as a necessary component of human life that ensures the end of suffering and aging. In religions such as Christianity, death represents a transition to a better and happier mode of existence—a return to Eden, so to speak—and hence a fate that should be embraced rather than avoided.

An animal that often plays a role in ancient myths related to the origin of death is the snake, whose ability to shed its old skin for a new one creates the impression that it can rejuvenate itself. Snakes have thus become symbols of immortality and eternal youth, as in the Adam and Eve story. In the Mesopotamian epic of **Gilgamesh,** to take a very different example, the hero is able to obtain, after many epic vicissitudes, the herb of eternal youth. The herb is stolen from him by a snake, however, thus forever depriving humans of the gift of immortality. Along these same lines, some myths in Africa and Asia view the snake as a trickster who stole the secret of immortality from divinity or from humanity. Similarly, in some native American myths death is introduced among human beings by a trickster who is often represented as a coyote, rather than a snake.

Sources:

Eliade, Mircea, ed. *The Encyclopedia of Religion.* 16 vols. New York: Macmillan, 1987.
Smart, Ninian. *The Religious Experience of Mankind.* 3d ed. New York: Charles Scribner's Sons, 1984.

DEATH DREAMS

Ethnographic reports indicate that concern with death dreams is as ancient as human culture. In Eastern traditions, where religions arose from an immanent realization of the authentic "self," a wide range of dream interpretations and theories is offered, as well as such unusual practices as dream yoga. Western religious traditions include dreams in which a messenger of God appears, or the soul travels out of its body in the underworld, or a power or magical ability is given to the dreamer.

Death dreams often occur as a result of great stress caused by relationships, school, vocational changes, or the approach of death itself. They may also result from a terminal illness or the death of a loved one, before and after which a member of the family often receives visitations from the departed. Among the most important investigations of death dreams are the psychological studies of Carl G. Jung, according to whom death dreams are linked to the universal primordial imagery of transformation. Jungian psychotherapist Marie Louise von Franz asserts that dreams of dying people can be interpreted as preparation of the consciousness for a deep transformation and for the continuation of life after death.

Among other studies interpreting and classifying death dreams are those of Edgar Herzog, Hendrika Vande Kemp, and Ann Faraday. In *Psyche and Death,* Herzog attempts to trace the associations between dreams and ancient myths and analyzes five types or sequences of death dreams: repression of death dreams, about the dreamer's refusal to face the death situation; dreams about killing, in which the killer comes to terms with death; dreams of archaic forms of the death demon, composed of mythological components; dreams about the land of the dead, in which archaic myths are associated with love, procreation, birth, and rebirth; and dreams of death as an expression of the process of development, in which there is an encounter with death that reflects the dreamer's personality or aids in its development. Another classification of dreams is given by Hendrika Vande Kemp, who delineates the following types of dreams: telepathic, in which the dying person appears in the dreams of friends or relatives; premonitory, in which the dying person appears and announces his or her impending death; hypermnesic, in which the dead person conveys information that has been forgotten by the dreamer's waking memory; predictive, in which the dreamer predicts the time of his or her own death; archetypal, in which death appears in a symbolic form; and revelatory, in which the deceased appears to convey a religious or philosophical truth that the dreamer had promised to announce to the living.

Ann Faraday, in *The Dream Game,* states that death dreams can be considered (1) metaphors expressing that our feeling for someone, something, or an aspect of ourselves is dead; (2) reminders of something in need of resolution; or (3) symbols indicating the need for an old self-image to be transcended.

Sources:

Faraday, Ann. *The Dream Game.* 1974. Reprint, New York: Perennial Library, 1976.

Kramer, Kenneth Paul. *Death Dreams. Unveiling Mysteries of the Unconscious Mind.* New York: Paulist Press, 1993.

DEATH SYMBOLISM

The symbolism of death is a complex subject, and it is important to distinguish between symbols of physical death and symbols of transition to the otherworld. In most traditional cultures, the postmortem passage from this world to the afterlife is not envisioned as a quick, easy process that takes place immediately upon death. Instead, after dying one often undertakes a journey to "the other side." This transition—as opposed to death itself—is symbolized in many different ways, by **rivers** (over which one crosses), **boats, bridges, birds,** and so on. In Western culture, essentially the same notion is expressed in popular folklore by crossing through the Pearly Gates.

Death itself is represented by a very different set of symbols. Skulls and skeletons are natural symbols of death, for obvious reasons, as are certain instruments of death, such as arrows. Other kinds of symbols are derived from funerary customs, such as wreaths and gravestones. Symbols of mortality (a notion closely related to death), such as hourglasses, may also be employed as symbols of death.

Because they are so closely related, symbols of death and symbols of transition are often used interchangeably. In particular, symbols of transition often serve as symbols of death. Again, it is easy to see how the Pearly Gates (a passageway or transition symbol) have been used to symbolize "death proper."

Sources:

Biedermann, Hans. *Dictionary of Symbolism: Cultural Icons and the Meanings Behind Them.* New York: Meridian, 1994.

Cooper, J.C. *An Illustrated Encyclopaedia of Traditional Symbols.* 1978. Reprint, London: Thames and Hudson, 1992.

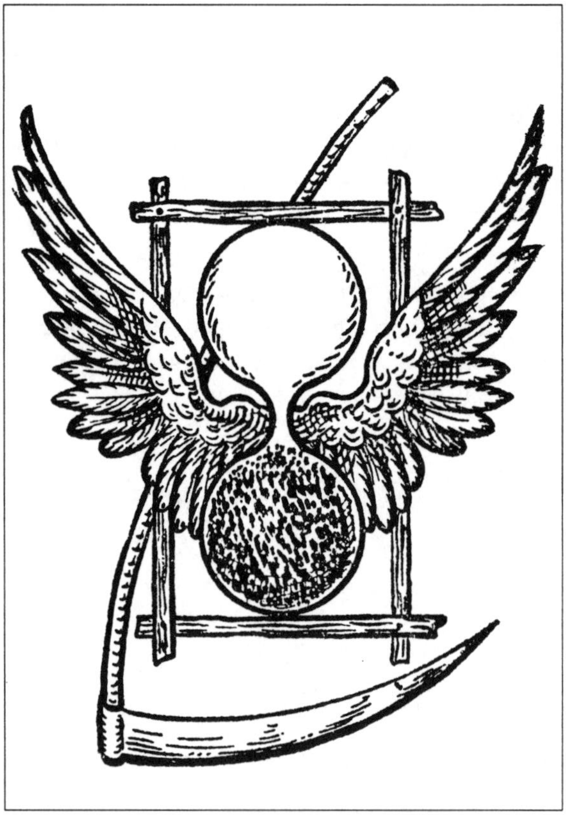

THE WINGED HOURGLASS AND THE SCYTHE, SYMBOLIZING THE FLIGHT OF TIME AND THE CERTAINTY OF DEATH. FROM A ROSICRUCIAN EMBLEM BOOK, 17TH CENTURY.

DEATHBED VISIONS

People very close to death often have visions of deceased relatives or religious figures that exhibit certain characteristics of mystical experiences, like a strong sense of the sacred and a profound feeling of peacefulness. At one time, the subject of deathbed visions was as popular as the contemporary phenomenon of **near-death experiences.** Deathbed visions are usually characterized by radiant lights, scenes of great beauty, and especially, beings of light, such as religious or mythical figures whose purpose is to escort the deceased to the afterworld.

An unusual light or energy in the room and an energy cloud assuming the shape and appearance of the dying are usually perceived by people present during the vision. Also, previews of the afterworld as a beautiful garden are very frequent, and they seldom correspond to the religious beliefs of the dying. Deathbed visions, which have been recorded since ancient times, are considered proof of survival of consciousness after death.

The simplest theory advanced to explain déjà entendu is that the new sounds or conversations we experience during déjà entendu simply resemble familiar sounds or conversations. Another idea is that déjà entendu is a form of psychic experience. Other explanations postulate that at least some déjà entendu experiences represent indistinct memories of past lifetimes. If, for example, one travels to a country one has never before visited and yet feels a sense of profound familiarity with the sounds and the language, it could be postulated that the traveler had lived in that area of the world in another lifetime.

Sources:

Bletzer, June G. *The Donning International Encyclopedic Psychic Dictionary.* Norfolk, VA: Donning, 1986.

Head, Joseph, and S. L. Cranston. *Reincarnation: The Phoenix Fire Mystery.* New York: Julian Press/ Crown, 1977.

DÉJÀ VU

Déjà vu is an experience in which there is a feeling that a completely unknown place is familiar, as if one had been there before, or that a new situation has been experienced before. The core sensation of déjà vu is an eerie feeling of unexpected familiarity. It can involve such things as events, dreams, thoughts, statements, emotions, and meetings. The expression itself is French for "already seen" and was coined by E. Letter Boirac in 1876. No English expression has the same connotations as déjà vu. Déjà vu is a widespread experience; a poll conducted in 1986 reported that 67 percent of Americans had experienced it. Other studies indicate that déjà vu occurs more often to females than males, and to younger than older individuals.

There are many theories that attempt to explain déjà vu. In 1884, for instance, it was theorized that one brain hemisphere registered information slightly sooner than the other hemisphere, and that this could explain the experience. Other researchers have postulated similar partial delay mechanisms, such as the hypothesis that the subconscious receives information before the conscious mind. These biological explanations have not been demonstrated to actually reflect the human physiology. A more widely accepted hypothesis, which certainly accounts for at least some such "already-seens," is that the new places or experiences that we encounter during déjà vu simply resemble familiar places or experiences.

A less widely accepted explanation is that déjà vu is a form of psychic experience. Thus, the new but seemingly familiar places we encounter may be, for example, places we visited while **out-of-body** during sleep. Yet another type of explanation utilizes the notion of a **collective unconscious,** through which one is in touch with the universal experience of the human race. From this frame of reference, a déjà vu experience may simply represent a resonance between a current experience and one of the archetypes in the collective unconscious.

Of particular significance are explanations that postulate that at least some déjà vu experiences represent indistinct memories of past lifetimes. If, for example, one travels to a country one has never before visited, and yet feels a sense of profound familiarity with the landscape and the culture, such an explanation would postulate that the traveler had lived in that area of the world in another lifetime. The great psychiatrist Carl Jung experienced déjà vu when he first traveled to Africa. Gazing at the landscape from the window of his train, he said that he felt like he was coming back to a land he had lived in five thousand years ago. He explained his déjà vu as ''the recognition of the immemorially known.''

Sources:

Head, Joseph, and S. L. Cranston. *Reincamation: The Phoenix Fire Mystery.* New York: Julian Press/ Crown, 1977.

Neppe, Vemon M. *The Psychology of Déjà Vu.* Johannesburg, South Africa: Witwatersrand University Press, 1983.

Wolman, Benjamin B., ed. *Handbook of Parapsychology.* New York: Van Nostrand Reinhold, 1977.

DEMONS AND DEVILS

The notion of some form of conscious, demonic force has been a part of the human imagination since prehistoric times. The belief that malicious entities lie behind natural disasters and other unpleasant aspects of human life is still prevalent in certain traditional societies, in such culture areas as Africa and Oceania. These demonic forces are believed to exist in the form of natural elements (typically as animals or such phenomena as floods) or as spirits of the ancestors. Especially before the development of scientific discoveries that proffered more neutral explanations for the irregularities of nature, demons were believed to be responsible for unexplainable natural disasters and diseases. Although scientific explanations have gradually supplanted metaphysical explanations, demons and devils presently survive in the mythology of Jung's **collective unconscious** and in other schools of the study of the mind that interpret evil forces as projections of human fear or as hallucinations.

Even though the two words often are used interchangeably, their meaning evolved through the centuries and in different religious traditions. Devil (from Greek *dia-ballo,* to throw across, i.e., to accuse) has always had a negative connotation as an evil force, whereas a *demon* (from Greek *daimon,* spirit) may be either good or evil, depending on its individual nature. *Daimones* in ancient Greece were tutelary semidivine spirits of either good or bad nature.

In the early stages of Judaism, demons did not have a major impact on the religious belief system. During the first diaspora, when Jews were in contact with the dualist vision of **Zoroastrianism,** a more defined role for demons was developed within the tradition that reflected the popular rabbinic beliefs. These mythological figures were drawn from the indigenous pagan beliefs and are believed to be either creations of God or offspring of Lilith, the first wife of Adam. In the Cabala of the Middle Ages, the evil forces of Jewish tradition took definite forms, names, and roles, although they were never really fully accepted in Orthodox Judaism.

The Greek word daimon was introduced in the Roman and the Hellenistic world to indicate evil forces, and thus entered early Christian writings with the negative

FROM THE LIMBOURG BROTHERS' *LES TRÈS RICHES HEURES DU DUC DE BERRY* (FRANCE, 15TH CENTURY).

connotation of impure spirits. The Judeo-Christian tradition elaborated the concept of the Devil as the fallen angel who tempted Adam and Eve and was forever banished from paradise. Christian writers also drew upon the belief system of their neighbors in the depiction of the **Apocalypse,** wherein appear demons that recall Jewish, Persian, and Mesopotamian myths.

In the Scriptures the Devil came to be identified with Satan (a name used in the Hebrew Bible to indicate an adversary). The belief in evil powers as the source of sicknesses and problems for humans is found in all the early Christian literature, and Christian theology acknowledges evil as necessary for the fulfillment of free will. From very early, Christianity developed the practice of **exorcism** to expel evil spirits that had taken over control of human individuals. In medieval Europe, belief in the existence of demons came to be associated with witchcraft and thus contributed not only to the practice of exorcism but also to witch-hunting which faded out only after the introduction of the religious skepticism of the eighteenth-century Enlightenment.

Since the early drafting of the Quran, Muslims have also believed in the existence of demonic forces, known as *shaytan,* that are in constant revolt against God. Sometimes these evil forces are identified with animals (such as the snake and the scorpion) or with natural elements. An ambiguous figure, divine and evil at the same time *(jinn),* who partially resembles the Devil of the Judeo-Christian tradition, in that he is also a fallen angel, is Iblis. Believed to be eternally expelled from the garden of heaven for refusing to bow, upon God's order, in front of Adam (a being made of earth), he gradually also came to be called Satan.

The Hindu tradition is rich with mythic figures of divine, semidivine nature, and superhuman nature. In its literature demons are hierarchically ranked in various cosmic layers. Demons that belong to the lower part of the hierarchy are dark beings, such as the *asuras,* that are always adversaries to humankind. *Raksasas* are demons that embody various hostile animals (e.g., snakes, vultures), and who are identified with spirits of the night. They resemble vampires and kill people.

Buddhism, especially at the popular level, inherited the lore of mythological Hindu images, the asuras and other demons. They belong to the category of sentient beings (like humans and gods) and as such are subject to the cycle of **reincarnation.** The Buddhist archfiend is Mara, the Buddhist Satan who in vain tempted Gautama shortly before his enlightenment. Evil forces are encountered in the Burmese Buddhist figures of ghosts that inflict pain on humans. In Mahayana Buddhism demons are alternately good and evil in their effort to keep their devotees in the faith.

Female demonic figures have also been developed to explain children's sicknesses and death. In medieval central and eastern Europe the *lamias,* mythic figures of Greek and Roman origin, were believed to kill all children by drinking their blood; the Hindu Churalin (which embodies the women who died because of childbirth) and the Islamic *ghul* are female demons that lie in wait and practice cannibalism. In Judaism, Lilith, considered to be the first wife of Adam, typically was believed to attack children.

Most of the traditional cultures of the world visualize the universe as a three-tiered cosmos of heaven, earth, and underworld. Heaven is reserved for deities, living human beings occupy the middle world, and demons often reside primarily in the underworld. The spirits of the dead are also often perceived as living underground, perhaps as a result of the custom of burial in the ground.

In Christianity the ancient underworld that originally was the common fate of humanity became a realm of torture in which sinners and unbelievers were tormented for eternity. In the Christian tradition in particular, underworld devils acquired employment tormenting the souls of the damned, although the earliest Christian idea was that stern, righteous angels did that job. As these ideas evolved and the righteous angels were removed from hell, Satan, ruler of all other devils, became king of the underworld.

Sources:

Eliade, Mircea, ed. *Encyclopedia of Religion.* 16 vols. New York: Macmillan, 1987.
Turner, Alice K. *The History of Hell.* New York: Harcourt Brace, 1993.
Zimmer, Heinrich. *Philosophies of India.* New York: Bollingen, 1951.

DESCENT INTO THE UNDERWORLD

In most religious traditions the underworld is thought to be located someplace underneath the earth (e.g., under a mountain, or beyond an ocean that can be reached only by crossing a narrow and dangerous **bridge**). The dark kingdom of the underworld typically contains various spirits, a king and/or a queen, or some other mythical characters that control the souls of the dead.

In the shamanic tradition, which spread from Siberia and Asia to the American continent and the Pacific islands, the descent into the underworld was an important part of the spiritual ideology. The shaman's healing power stemmed from his ability to descend into the underworld to visit the spirits that caused a person's illness. Upon his return, the shaman sang of his journey to the underworld, of crossing a bridge over an ocean, and encountering the spirits. The shaman's task included foreseeing the future or the weather, or finding a person or lost object, or guiding the wandering spirits of the dead to the realm of the dead.

In the ancient Western world some myths recounted the descent into the underworld of a heroic or divine being who aimed to rescue a loved one or to obtain immortality and wisdom. In one of the most ancient accounts of a journey to the underworld, the Sumerian goddess Inanna (in the Akkadian civilization she was called Ishtar) descended into the underworld, where she underwent a sort of initiation process of death and rebirth. During the journey, the goddess went through seven gates, gradually taking off all of her clothes and ornaments. At the end of the journey, the goddess died and the vegetation on earth immediately wilted. When sprinkled with the water of life, the goddess came back to life, thus regenerating the earth.

In the Greek world, a similar myth is the story of **Persephone.** Persephone was kidnapped by Hades. Her mother, Demeter, goddess of grain, mourned the loss of her daughter, which resulted in the death of vegetation and humankind's starvation. The gods eventually agreed that Persephone should be returned to her mother. In the meanwhile, however, Hades had made Persephone eat the fruit of the dead (seeds of pomegranate, symbol of fertility and blood) and had thus bound her to the lower world. The final agreement was that for half of the year Persephone would be the ruling queen of Hades, and for the other half she would live with her mother.

A mythical hero of the ancient Greek world was **Orpheus,** a poet and musician, whose wife, Eurydice, died from the bite of a snake. Orpheus's art was so powerful that he enchanted the king of **Hades** and convinced him to release his wife, although his violation of the condition that he not look at her until they were completely back on earth resulted in the loss of Eurydice. The theme of failure of the hero to complete his task in the underworld realm of the departed represents the effort of the human imagination to come to grips with the inevitability of death.

In the Christian tradition, the underworld is a place of damnation for sinners. In early apocryphal literature, Christ was described as descending into hell to rescue the damned and to demonstrate his victory over the reign of evil. In medieval culture, the first part of *The Divine Comedy,* the *Inferno,* describes **Dante**'s descent into hell under the guidance of the Roman poet **Virgil.** Christian myths also partially influenced the accounts of the journeys to the underworld of Väinämöinen and Lemminkäinen, mythical Finnish heroes. Their descent into the underworld represented, similarly to the shaman's ritual journey, one stage on the path toward wisdom.

The notion of descent into the underworld also developed in the Eastern world. In Japanese Buddhism, for example, monks practiced a technique that led to an ecstatic experience inspired by the mythical priest Chiko: The priest, accompanied by two messengers, was taken to the underworld, where he was dismembered and reconstituted three times before being allowed to return to earth—a standard element of Shamanic initiation, signifying the transformation of death and rebirth.

Sources:

Eliade, Mircea, ed. *The Encyclopedia of Religion.* 16 vols. New York: Macmillan, 1987.
———. *A History of Religious Ideas.* Vol. 1. Chicago: University of Chicago Press, 1978.
Turner, Alice K. *The History of Hell.* New York: Harcourt Brace, 1993.

DIANETICS

Dianetics is a form of popular psychotherapy, a synthesis of modern psychology and Oriental philosophy devised and propagated by L. Ron (Lafayette Ronald) Hubbard (1911–1986), popular fiction writer and founder of the Church of Scientology. In 1948 Hubbard circulated a document entitled *Dianetics: The Original Thesis,* the first statement of a theory that would make him famous as well as controversial. In 1950 he published his most famous book, *Dianetics: The Modern Science of Mental Health.* This work became an instant best-seller, generating numerous articles and discussion groups. It was something of a fad, becoming particularly popular on college campuses and within the movie industry. A brief account of Dianetics therapy can be found near the beginning of Aldous Huxley's novel *Island,* where a young resident of the island helps the protagonist come to grips with a traumatic encounter with snakes.

Because of *Dianetics'* popularity, the Hubbard Dianetics Research Foundation was established in May 1950 in Elizabeth, New Jersey, with offices in Los Angeles, Chicago, Honolulu, and Washington, D.C. Dianetics was opposed by the medical, psychological, and psychiatric professions, which all published articles discouraging its use. Despite these attempts, by late September 1950, more than 750 Dianetics groups were established with more than 250,000 individuals applying the techniques described in *Dianetics.*

The basic concept in *Dianetics* is that the mind has two very distinct parts. Hubbard called the conscious part the "analytical mind." The second part, the "reactive mind," comes into play when the individual is "unconscious"— in full or in part. "Unconsciousness" could be caused by the shock of an accident, the anesthetic used for an operation, the pain of an injury, or the deliriums of illness. According to Hubbard, the reactive mind stores particular types of mental images he called **engrams.** Engrams are a complete recording of every perception present in a moment of partial or full "unconsciousness." This part of the mind can cause unevaluated, unknown, and unwanted fears, emotions, pains, and psychosomatic illnesses. The goal of "auditing"—the application of Dianetics and Scientology processes and procedures—is to rid oneself of the power of the reactive mind.

Dianetics therapy is appealing in its straightforwardness. With the aid of an electrical device that registers emotional reactions (an E-meter, which is based on the same technology employed in lie detectors), individuals undergoing auditing are led to recall repressed memories of painful experiences in vivid detail. When auditing is properly carried out, the recollection is vivid enough that the original experience is, in a certain sense, relived. Much like psychoanalysis, this confrontation releases one from the power of one's repressed past. The ultimate goal of Dianetics therapy is a state termed *clear* (named after the clear command found on calculators) in which one is freed from the warping power of one's engrams. Thus freed, one can become a healthy, fully functioning human being.

Hubbard taught that some engrams are recorded before the individual is born and even during conception. Dianetics theory eventually expanded to include the notion of engrams carrying information from past lifetimes. As Hubbard developed his work, he added "exteriorization" (similar to what parapsychologists call out-of-body experiences) and reincarnation memories to his ideas. The expanded system he called Scientology. The practice of past-life therapy, as performed by contemporary psychologists and psychiatrists, is clearly reminiscent of Hubbard's notion that the sources of some engrams can be found in previous existences.

Although current past-life therapists tend to deny the link because of Scientology's negative reputation, Winafred Blake Lucas, in her definitive *Regression Therapy: A Handbook for Professionals,* acknowledges that Dianetics "has covertly impacted much of the past-life work we know today" (p. 5). Even though highly critical of Scientology, Lucas credits Dianetics with originating

> . . . the proposal, startling at the time, that past lives existed and could be contacted by traveling backwards on an emotional-physical bridge search-

> ing for an engram (an original traumatic situation still influencing behavior). The past lives recovered by this technique that L. Ron Hubbard reported in *Have You Lived Before This Life?* (1958) were in part similar to those found in contemporary regressions (p. 6).

She further notes that even Dianetics' regression technique, namely, "flowing backward on a feeling or physical sensing" (p. 6), is utilized by many current practitioners.

Sources:

Contemporary Authors. New Revision Series, vol. 22. Detroit, MI: Gale Research Inc.

Hubbard, L. Ron. *Dianetics: The Modern Science of Mental Health.* New York: Hermitage House, 1950.

Hubbard, L. Ron. *Have You Lived Before This Life?* Los Angeles, CA: Church of Scientology of California, 1977.

Lucas, Winafred Blake. *Regression Therapy: A Handbook for Professionals.* 2 vols. Crest Park, CA: Deep Forest Press, 1993.

DIRECT VOICE

Direct voice is a form of **mediumship** in which a disembodied entity speaks with an audible voice, independently of the medium. Spirit voices were often amplified with megaphones or trumpets, so direct voice mediums were sometimes called trumpet mediums. The theory behind such phenomena was that a quasi-physical larynx made of **ectoplasm** (a subtle substance emitted from the medium's body) was constructed by the disembodied spirit, and activated by the speaking entity. In the **Spiritualist** heyday of the nineteenth century, this form of mediumship was so widespread that, at one time or another, most mediums utilized it. Direct voice mediums were frequently accused of orchestrating a deception through the use of ventriloquism. Today, direct-voice mediumship is rare.

Sources:

Cavendish, Richard. *Encyclopedia of the Unexplained.* New York: McGraw-Hill, 1974.

Godwin, John. *Occult America.* New York: Doubleday, 1972.

DISCARNATE ENTITY

In classical, nineteenth-century **Spiritualism,** the personality with whom a medium was communicating almost invariably was identified as a disembodied human being. In more recent communications with "the other side," however, **mediums,** and especially New Age **channels,** have claimed to have received information from other, more exotic sources. These include spirits that claim to be animals, extraterrestrials, and even "intelligences" that claim never to have been incarnated. In view of this expanded situation, it has become customary to employ the neutral expression *discarnate entity* to refer to the spirit with whom one is communicating.

SIR ARTHUR CONAN DOYLE. (PHOTO: W. RANSFORD.) COURTESY OF THE ARC.

Sources:

Guiley, Rosemary Ellen. *The Encyclopedia of Ghosts and Spirits.* New York: Facts on File, 1992.
Shepard, Leslie A. *Encyclopedia of Occultism & Parapsychology.* Detroit, MI: Gale Research, 1984.

Doyle, Sir Arthur Conan

Creator of the famous detective Sherlock Holmes, Sir Arthur Conan Doyle (1859–1930) profoundly believed in **Spiritualism** and in the power of **mediums.**

After participating in table-turning séances at the home of the mathematician General Drayson, he became interested in paranormal phenomena and joined the **Society for Psychical Research.** Doyle embraced the faith of Spiritualism after 30 years of study—and started lecturing with his second wife (who also began **automatic writing**—after the loss of her brother during World War I). He lectured in northern Europe, South Africa, the United States, and New Zealand and published *The New Revelation* (1918) and *The Vital Message* (1919).

Doyle supported "spirit photography" and the search for proof of fairies, which had interested him all his life. He was particularly excited by a letter received from a Spiritualist friend who maintained that the existence of fairies could be proven through photographs taken in Yorkshire by two young girls, Elsie Wright and her cousin Frances Griffiths. The Theosophist Edward L. Gardner, who was asked to investigate, pronounced the photographs genuine, although they looked fake.

Doyle's *Coming of Fairies,* published in 1922, contained a full account of the two girls' case and documented other fairy evidence. But upon his return from a trip to Australia, he found out that the photographs had been pronounced false, and that he was the victim of a hoax, admitted later by the two girls.

In 1923 the Doyles were warned against the evil nature of the world by Pheneas, an Arabian spirit with whom Lady Doyle was in contact, and were told that their task was to prepare people's minds for a conflagration that was supposed to happen in 1925. Pheneas later informed them about the details, and Doyle kept notes of the prophesied events. None of these prophesies came about, however, and Doyle began to wonder if he was the victim of a great joke by members of the spirit world.

Sources:

Brandon, Ruth. *The Spiritualists.* New York: Alfred A. Knopf, 1983.

Doyle, Sir Arthur Conan. *Coming of the Fairies.* London: Hodder & Stoughton, 1922.

———. *The Edge of the Unknown.* New York: Berkley Medallion Books, 1968. (Originally published by G. P. Putnam's Sons, 1930.)

Fodor, Nandor. *An Encyclopaedia of Psychic Science.* Secaucus, NJ: The Citadel Press, 1966. (Originally published 1933.)

E

ECKANKAR

ECKANKAR, the Ancient Science of Soul Travel and Religion of the Light and Sound of God, was founded in 1965 by Paul Twitchell, who declared himself the Living 91st ECK Master of the Order of the Vaiargi and established headquarters in Las Vegas, Nevada. He was a former journalist who had been a student of various spiritual teachers, including Sant Mat Master Kirpal Singh, the founder of Ruhani Satsang and teacher of the Divine Science of the Soul.

In 1964 Twitchell began to teach a form of yoga in San Francisco and focused on bilocation, the ability of the conscious soul to separate itself from the body and travel in invisible planes. In this emphasis, he appears to have been drawing on the popularity of the notion of astral projection, although Twitchell claimed his bilocation involved the soul, whereas astral projection was a comparatively low-level phenomenon in which merely the astral body was involved.

With the publication of *The Tiger's Fang,* the organization began growing quickly. The *Shariyat-Ki-Sugmad* is the scripture of ECKANKAR, and the original copy is said to be located in the spiritual city of Agam Des, where it can only be reached in the soul body. According to ECKANKAR, the ultimate state for each human being is that of co-worker with God; inner techniques are more active spiritual exercises than yogic practices, and Eastern austerities are not important.

ECKANKAR teaches that all life flows from the Sugmad, the formless, all-embracing, impersonal, and infinite God, downward to the world. The ECK current is the creative-sustaining reality of all existence and is heard as sound and seen as light. It is necessary for the immortal soul, incarnated and residing in the physical body, to see and hear the spiritual light and sound in order to gain the highest spiritual realms, through precise techniques taught by the ECK masters.

The ECK master leads the adherents, or *chelas,* to the realms of total spiritual freedom through 12 invisible planes, the second of which is the realm of ghosts, spirits, and psychic phenomena. The fifth plane is the first one in which the soul achieves the true God worlds. Followers of ECKANKAR regularly report spiritual travel of the body through imagination, direct projection, and through their dreams while asleep.

Like many other new religious movements, ECKANKAR has been surrounded by controversy. The most serious criticism leveled against the group has been that Twitchell created the religion by reformulating the teachings and practices of Kirpal Singh (one of his spiritual teachers) and simply fabricating the rest.

Sources:

Melton, J. Gordon. *Encyclopedia of American Religions.* Detroit, MI: Gale Research, 1993.
Melton, J. Gordon. *Encyclopedic Handbook of Cults in America.* New York: Garland, 1986.

ECLESIA CATOLICA CRISTIANA

Delfin Roman Cardona was born in Puerto Rico in 1918. He was raised a Roman Catholic but was introduced to Spiritualism as a teenager. He soon developed clairvoyant and healing abilities, and when he later moved to New York City, he continued in that activity. In 1956 he founded the Spiritualist Cristiana Church, which in 1969 he renamed the Eclesia Catolica Cristiana to differentiate its more traditional Christian orientation from that of other Spiritualist churches.

Cardona modeled the Eclesia Catolica Cristiana on the hierarchy of the Roman Catholic church and installed himself as its pope. Doctrinally, of course, the church differs substantially from the Roman Catholic church. Cardona believed that the Roman Catholic church was not as catholic (universal) as it could be, and he therefore developed what he called a universalist catholicism, the Delfinist Doctrine.

The Delfinist Doctrine incorporates elements from many different religious traditions, both organizationally and theologically. Organizationally, Cardona has opened the entire hierarchy to women, teaching that women and men are equal in all important respects. Theologically, he draws primarily upon traditional Christianity and the teachings of Allan Kardec, the French writer and medium who brought Spiritualism to Brazil. The Kardec brand of Spiritualism was distinctive at the time because of its emphasis on reincarnation and karma. The Delfinist Doctrine brings the church's various ideological elements together under a number of unifying concepts, including love, compassion, humility, and faith.

Sources:

Melton, J. Gordon. *The Encyclopedia of American Religions.* 4th ed. Detroit, MI: Gale Research, 1993.

ECTOPLASM

Ectoplasm is a subtle substance on the boundary between physical and nonphysical that, according to researchers into Spiritualism, exudes from the body of certain **mediums.** This quasi-physical material is transformed into the substance that is perceived during so-called materialization phenomena, when limbs, faces, or even whole bodies of spirits appear in a séance.

The term was originated in 1894 by French physiologist and psychic investigator Charles Richet. It is derived from the Greek *ektos* plus *plasma,* usually translated as "exteriorized substance," and is sometimes referred to as psychoplasm or teleplasm. Although the name *ectoplasm* was not introduced until the end of the nineteenth century, ectoplasmic phenomena were reported much earlier, such as vapors **Sir William Crookes** claimed to see in the vicinity of the great materialization medium, D. D. Home in the nineteenth century. Even Swedenbörg reported "a kind of vapor steaming from the pores of my body" during one of his visions.

Ectoplasm can be warm or cold, can be weighed, and often feels like rubber or dough to the touch. It is frequently white, and is said to smell like ozone. Its structure varies widely, from a cloudy mist, to solid rods, to a netlike membrane. Ectoplasm is said to be required for materialization, and the source of this subtle substance seems to be the medium, who "secretes" ectoplasm from one or more body orifices. This phenomenon is said to require low-light conditions, with ectoplasm dissipating—or even snapping back into the body violently—when exposed to light. Skeptics have criticized the low-light requirement as disingenuously convenient.

Ectoplasm is said to play a role in other forms of physical mediumship less dramatic than materialization. It is the substance incorporeal spirits use to "rap" (make knocking noises, especially in response to yes or no questions) and provides a basis for telekinesis (the movement of objects), direct voice (audible spirit voices), and other tangible manifestations.

Rev. Robert Chaney, a medium himself, said that ectoplasm was a kind of spiritual protoplasm that resides in the body in a semiphysical/semispiritual state. During a séance, ectoplasm is unconsciously exuded from the medium, while he or she simultaneously "draws" some of the ectoplasm from the bodies of other séance attendees. The spirit is then able to somehow attract the ectoplasm, using it to communicate audibly or visually with those at the sitting.

The medium Marthe Beraud, in a series of early twentieth century investigations, produced large quantities of gray-white ectoplasm for colleague Juliette Bisson and for the physician Baron Albert von Schrenck-Notzing. Beraud allowed herself to be searched thoroughly before each session. Schrenck-Notzing observed that Beraud's ectoplasm manifested as sticky, gelatinous icicles that dripped from the orifices of her

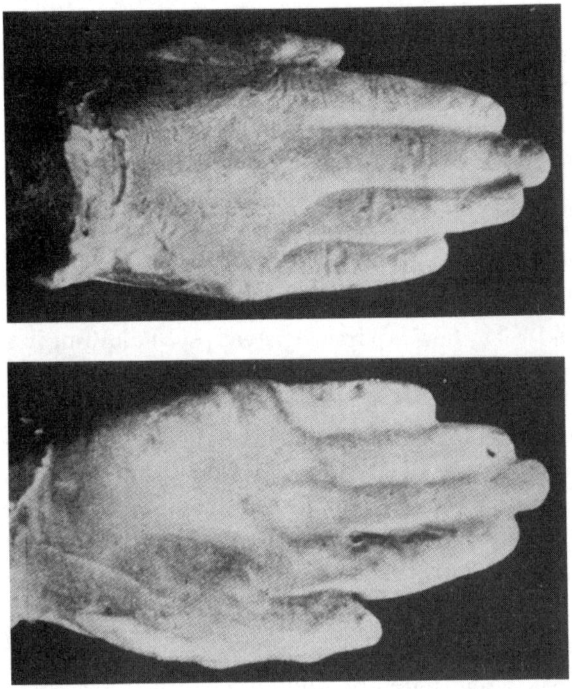

PLASTER CAST OF AN ECTOPLASMIC HAND. COURTESY OF THE ARC.

face and down onto her body. In the light or when touched, these extrusions writhed and were drawn back into her body like the limbs of a turtle. Beraud's ectoplasm could be projected through clothing without leaving a trace. Once secreted, the substance would often form into shapes, some resembling well-known governmental and historical personages.

Between 1917 and 1920 the prominent psychic investigator William Jackson Crawford examined the Goligher family, particularly the daughter Kathleen. He came to believe that Kathleen was able to lift tables and accomplish other tasks via a pseudopod, an ectoplasmic "limb" or rod. Crawford's investigations influenced Dr. LeRoi Crandon to begin experiments with his wife, Mina.

Mina Crandon's abilities included a marked talent with ectoplasmic phenomena. Long streams of ectoplasm were photographed hanging from her ears, nose, and mouth, as well as from between her legs. Crandon's claims were later effectively debunked. The researcher Eric J. Dingwall accused her of hiding "ectoplasm" in her vagina and projecting it with muscle contractions. When she produced a vaguely formed hand, supposedly from her navel, that did not evaporate upon exposure to the light, Harvard biologists examined it and found it to be an animal lung that had been cut into the shape of a hand.

Crandon's effort to fool the world with fake ectoplasm was repeated, unfortunately, by mediums seeking celebrity and the financial benefits that accompany such fame. Fraudulent mediums have been known to produce pseudo-ectoplasm out of everything from cloth and chewed paper to soap and egg whites. These shenanigans tended to discredit the whole field of physical mediumship, and, as a result of this discreditation, spectacular phenomena such as materialization gradually faded from prominence in Spiritualist circles. Contemporary mediums still refer to ectoplasm to explain certain spirit manifestations, but it no longer occupies the position of prominence it once did.

Sources:

Chaney, Rev. Robert G. *Mediums and the Development of Mediumship*. Freeport, NY: *Books for Libraries Press*, 1972.

Doyle, Sir Arthur Conan. *The History of Spiritualism*. 2 vols. New York: Arno Press, 1975.

Shepard, Leslie A. *Encyclopedia of Occultism & Parapsychology*. 2d ed. Detroit: Gale Research, 1984.

EGYPT

If any one place has been known for a preoccupation, even obsession, with the afterlife, it is ancient Egypt during the time of the pharaohs and pyramids. This was a civilization that, according to the voluminous records available to us, maintained basically the same understanding of death and the afterlife for more than three thousand years.

Ancient Egypt was a civilization with a stability and history that staggers the contemporary imagination. As long ago as 4000 B.C. there were significant political and agricultural centers all along the Nile River. Thanks in part to the invention of writing and agricultural developments in the ancient Near East that allowed for greater urbanization, the many city-states in the area of today's Egypt were gradually unified into one dynasty. The Old Kingdom of Egypt was well established by the middle of the third millennium B.C. The Middle Kingdom dates from about 2100 B.C. to about 1786 B.C., and the New Kingdom lasted from about 1580 B.C. to approximately 1080 B.C.

Then began a series of incursions by the Assyrian and Persian Empires, although ancient Egypt was not really brought to an end until after Alexander the Great conquered it in 332 B.C. Knowledge of the beliefs and culture of ancient Egypt soon was lost to the world and remained hidden until the nineteenth century brought the first systematic excavations and the translation of hieroglyphs.

WORSHIP: From about 3000 B.C. Egyptian official religion recognized the pharaoh as the offspring of the sun-god Ra and thus as a god himself. There were many other gods and goddesses in the Egyptian pantheon, whose domains covered everything from natural phenomena like air (the god Shu) to cultural phenomena like writing (the

AMAM (THE DEVOURER, LEFT) AND A CYNOCEPHALUS BABOON (RIGHT), DEMONS OF THE NETHER WORLD.

goddess Safekht). Many gods were represented as an animal or part-human/part-animal, probably the remnant of earlier animal worship. A well-developed and powerful priesthood structure organized the various deities, most of whom were perhaps originally local gods only, into family groupings. The creator-god Ptah (according to Memphis theology), for example, was grouped with the goddess of war, Sakhmet, and the medicine god, Imhotep, in one form of a father-mother-son triad.

Generally, Egyptians gave most prominence to those gods associated with the Nile (Hapy, Sothis, Sebek), the sun (Ra, Re-Atum, Horus), and helping the dead (Osiris, Anubis, Sokaris). During the time of the Old Kingdom, the sun-god Ra was the dominant god. Ra served to give immortality to the collective state through the pharaoh, his son. The sun seemed to the Egyptians and to many other ancients to be clearly immortal, as it "died" every evening, traveled through the underworld, and was "reborn" every morning. The sun was also important to the success of Nile agriculture. Thus, insofar as the pharaoh was identified with the sun-god, the continuity and success of the state was ensured. Further, Ra was the upholder of the moral order of creation and Maat (Truth, Justice, Concord) was his daughter. This gave the masses a code for living and additional means of pleasing the sun-god on behalf of the state and their way of life. This was not an individualistically oriented religion; outside the royal family, there was no hope for an afterlife and little belief that Ra paid attention or offered comfort to the common people as individuals.

Egyptian religious temples were far more than religious sites; they were centers of social, intellectual, cultural, and economic life as well. During the Middle Kingdom and the Egyptian Imperial period the temples surpassed the pyramid as the leading architectural form. The great temple at Karnak covered the largest area of any religious building ever. Its central hall alone could hold most of the Gothic cathedrals of Europe. As with the pyramids, the sheer size of the temples expressed a permanence that was symbolic of the immortality of the pharaoh, the state, and finally the soul as well.

Priests were only one segment of a large number of employed temple personnel, including attendants, scribes, singers, sacrificers, purifiers, readers, prophets, and musicians. At the height of temple architecture around 1500 B.C., several large structures typically surrounded the temples and a broad avenue approaching the area was marked by rows of sphinxes (sculptures with human heads and the bodies of lions) serving as guardians. All could enter the open courtyard, but only a few high priests could enter the inner sanctuary where the god's statue was kept in a shrine kept on a boat. Daily ceremonies in the temples involved the priests' censing the area, then awakening, washing, perfuming, and reclothing the statue of the deity, offering a burnt food sacrifice, then resealing the sanctuary chamber until the next ceremony. In addition to these daily temple ceremonies, there were regular feasts and festivals held throughout Egypt dedicated to various deities. The festival was often held on the occasion of some part of the agricultural cycle. The statue of the deity might be brought out from the sanctuary and paraded through the town and perhaps oversee the festivities. Plays were sometimes enacted, depicting particular events in the life of the deity.

MYTHOLOGIES: One of the primary sources for understanding Egyptian mythologies and approaches to death and the afterlife is the Book of the Dead, now more accurately translated as the Book of Going Forth by Day. This refers to a large number of funeral texts spanning the entire history of ancient Egypt. From these texts and other sources scholars have pieced together the major stories of the gods and patterns of afterlife beliefs. Egyptian mythology was not a tidy, uniform package of stories, but contained a number of mutually exclusive, even contradictory ideas. At least three different gods were given credit for the creation of the earth, there were several sun-gods, and the sky was conceived of variously as supported by posts, a goddess, a god, and a cow. In the process of bringing all the local principalities together in one political and cultural system, Egyptians did not simply delete the local sets of beliefs, but tended to keep them and incorporate them into an ever-growing field of religious heritage.

Toward the end of the Old Kingdom the stories concerning two brothers, Seth and **Osiris,** and their two sisters, Nephtys and Isis, seriously competed with the sun-god for primacy. These four gods were part of a grouping of nine gods that formed the Ennead of Heliopolis, an influential metropolitan center. Egyptian texts refer only to certain episodes of the Osiris myth, and the most complete account comes from Plutarch in the second century A.D.

According to the story, Osiris was a good and popular god-king who was betrayed and killed by his evil brother, Seth. Seth dismembered Osiris into 14 pieces and scattered the pieces in various places. When Nephtys and Isis discovered the deed, Isis (Osiris's wife as well as sister, according to the tradition of royal inbreeding) vowed to find the pieces and put the body back together. Being a "great magician," she was able to do so and even to become pregnant by him, but otherwise she could not bring life to him and had to bury him. When Horus, the posthumous son, grew up, he desired to avenge his father's death. He first tried the legal approach, taking the murder charge against Seth to the court of deities. When the court seemed unable to act, Horus took matters into his own hands and killed Seth in a monumental battle. Horus then went to the land of the dead, where he was recognized as Osiris's legitimate successor and crowned the new king of Egypt. At that point Horus was able to revive Osiris, who became ruler of the underworld, symbolic of resurrection and fertility, and judge of the dead for the rest of eternity.

Originally, the story of Osiris seems to have been merely the story of a vegetative cult, where Osiris's fate represented the flooding of the Nile in the spring and its recession in the fall, and/or the regular agricultural cycle of seed, growth, death, and rebirth. The story began to gain greater significance when Horus became identified with the living pharaoh, which may have happened as early as 2800 B.C. That identification perhaps occurred because the immortality of Osiris might have been deemed useful for reinforcing the royal dynasty: If every living pharaoh is Horus and every recently deceased pharaoh is Osiris, the orderly succession is ensured. The Osiris story, however, also grew in impact because it offered new levels of meaning for the general populace. This was a good story, with good and evil, familial loyalty, tribulations, and triumphs that offered many points of personal connection. It also suggested that resurrection from the dead was part of the natural order in a way that might include ordinary people as well.

DEATH AND JUDGMENT: The Seth and Osiris story underlay Egyptian convictions about what awaited them after death. The moral of the story seemed to be that evil deeds would eventually be repaid and that good would triumph. With Osiris as ruler of the underworld, certainly he would not allow evildoers to pass by him unscathed. Indeed, all funeral preparations became centered on the fateful meeting with Osiris. Unlike nearly all other ancient cultures with rulers of the dead, Osiris was a benign, moral figure. Also unlike most other ancient cultures, Egypt believed in an ethically based judgment after death. Egypt thus represents a major shift in afterlife concepts, and the whole idea of afterlife judgment may well have been pioneered by the Egyptians.

Just to reach the hall where Osiris sat in judgment was a task wherein the newly dead faced many perils. Obviously, people were very concerned that they be able to conduct themselves successfully on this journey, so over time guidebooks were put together to enable people to know what was expected of them, what were the relevant mythologies, how to say the right prayers, which magical formulas to use, and so on. In the beginning, this information was placed on the walls of the burial chamber, and scholars have called these sources The Pyramid Texts. Sometimes the information was placed on wooden sarcophagi, and these sources are called The Coffin Texts. By the time of the New Kingdom, when many more parts of the populace had reason to hope for immortality, it was customary to put the information on a roll of papyrus and place the roll in the tomb. These papyruses form the basis for the Book of Going Forth by Day (or the Book of the Dead). However it was transmitted, the information was considered invaluable for a successful crossing into the afterlife.

The afterlife was experienced in various ways by the different parts of one's self. The tomb was the natural location of the *khaibit,* a shadowy, skeletal figure. The *akh* was a ghost or an illuminated spirit and could live either among humans, usually in the vicinity of the tomb, or in the next world. Relatives tended to address their concerns to the akh. The *ka* was the guardian spirit or life force and looked exactly like the person. This spiritual double tended to hover around the tomb. The ka was the part of the person that dwelt in statues of the person and was the aspect to which mortuary offerings were generally made. The *ba* was the breath or soul, the principle animating the person, both physically and psychically, and was pictured as a human-headed bird. The ba was able to perform all bodily functions, but shared with the *akh* the ability to exist as well among the gods.

The theology indicates that the pharaohs entered the divine realm, that is, the circuit of the sun-god, by right. They did not have to answer to anyone and did not have to visit Osiris in the underworld. Even so, the pharaohs sometimes gave evidence of anxiety about the journey. In general, the newly dead, in the form of their ba and ka, traveled in the boat of Ra the sun-god as he made his way across the sky. In the West, as Ra reached the underworld with his load of new arrivals, the deceased disembarked and proceeded through seven gates, each with a gatekeeper, watcher, and herald. At each gate, and at several other instances, they had to consult the Book of the Dead in order to recite the names and formulas that would allow further progress. (In the tomb of a powerful official from the Old Kingdom is inscribed this boast: ''I am an effective spirit who knows his magic spells'' [Murnane 1992, 41]).

Finally, with the ka clad in white, Anubis (who has been described variously as a jackal-headed god or a faithful dog that guides the soul in his role as psychopomp) would provide escort to the Hall of Justice.

In the court proceedings, Thoth, an ibis-headed god of wisdom, acts as prosecutor, and Osiris sits on the judge's throne, flanked by Isis and Nephthys. Forty-two divine figures sit as jurors. Again using the Book of the Dead and as much

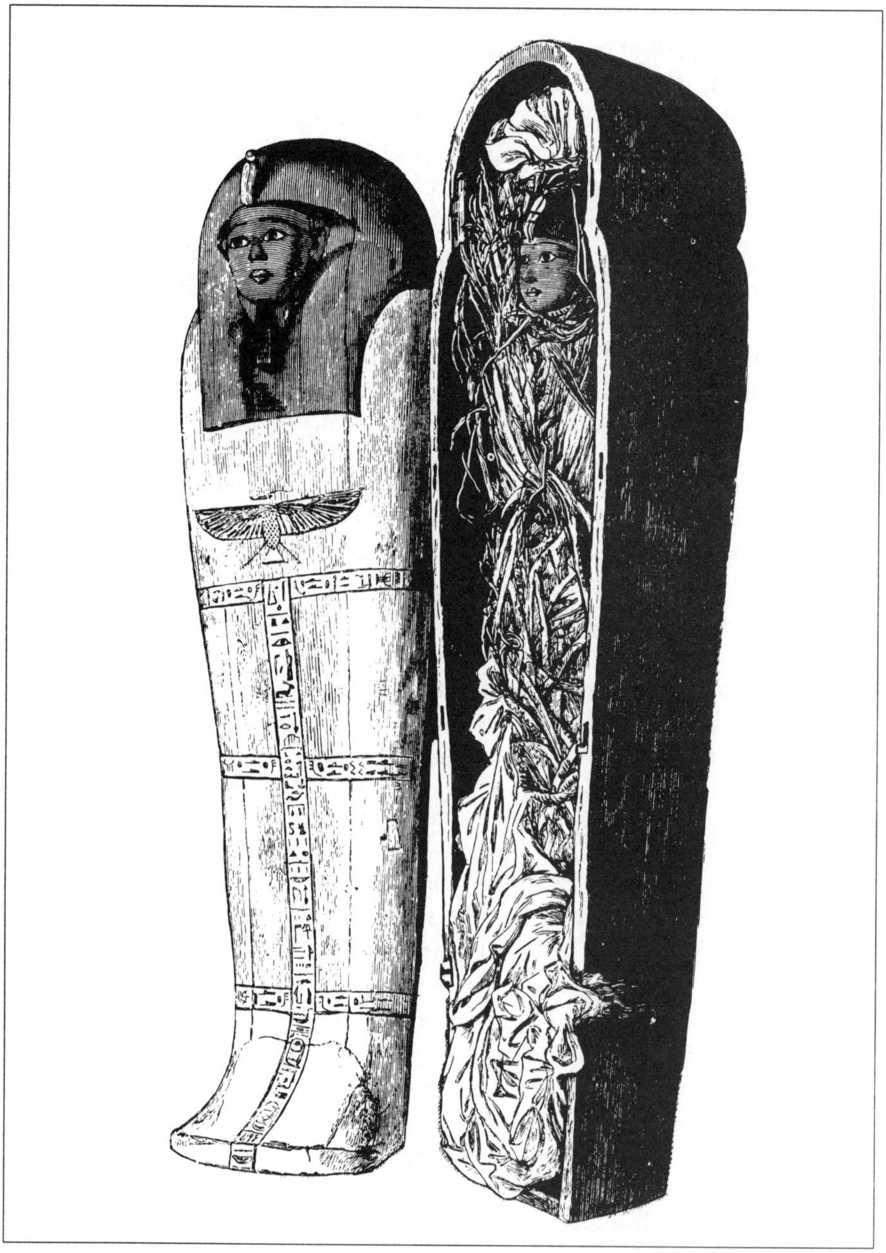

SARCOPHAGUS.

eloquence as they can muster, the deceased make an accounting of their lives. In particular, the dead need to be able to recite a ritual confession of innocence, which might include such lines as the following:

> Hail to thee, great god, lord of Truth. . . .
> I have committed no sin against people. . . .
> allowed no one to hunger.
> I caused no one to weep.
> I did not murder.
> I caused no man misery.
> I did not decrease the offering of the gods.
> I did not commit adultery.
> I did not diminish the grain measure.
> I did not diminish the land measure.
> I did not deflect the index of the scales.
> I did not take milk from the mouth of the child.
> I did not report evil of a servant to his master.
> I did not catch the fish in their pools.
> I am purified four times.
>
> (Nigosian 1990, 30–31)

After the talking was done, the heart of the deceased was placed on a scale vis-à-vis a feather, symbolic of truth. Sometimes instead of a feather an image of Maat, the goddess of truth, was used. If the heart was too heavy, the sinful party would be considered to have failed the test. According to some accounts, the unfortunate person would then be eaten and destroyed by a terrible creature called Ammit. According to other accounts, the person would be placed in a pit of fiery tortures. If, however, the heart balanced the feather, all was well and the person, now with a new body called the *sahu,* was free to enter the happy world of the Sekhet Aaru, or Field of Rushes. The hardest part was over, but there were still some dangers or trials to face, as the sahu was not invulnerable. The Book of the Dead was still useful for spells to protect one from crocodiles, suffocation, and any number of other problems.

The location of the land of the blessed is unclear, but it might have been conceived as up in the sky somewhere. In The Pyramid Texts there is a passage describing the successful journey of the dead pharaoh Pepi II into the afterlife, and its primary imagery is of life in the sky:

> The king ascends to the sky among the gods dwelling in the sky. He stands on the great [dais], he hears (in judicial session) the (legal) affairs of men. . . .
> He (Ra) gives thee his arm on the stairway to the sky.
>
> (Trans. by J. H. Breasted, as quoted in Eliade 1967, 354)

In any case, the place of the afterlife was usually described as a place not unlike the Nile valley, complete with canals, dams, and farms. Once having arrived, the deceased would be able to make use of all the items left for their use in the crypt, such as food, beds, chairs, and utensils. They would choose one of the 15 *aats* or regions of the Field of Rushes in which to live, each region having its own ruler. The deceased could transform themselves into a bird and live that sort of life, or live as in the midst of an orchard, with delicious fruits of never-ending yield. There were magic spells to turn models of servants, or *shabti,* that were left in the tomb into living servants for one's comfort. (King Tut [Tutankhamen] had 414 shabtis in his tomb; the number decreased as did the social level of the deceased.) These servants could also do the work of keeping the canals and dams of paradise in good condition, if the need arose. The ability to turn images of servants into real servants was based on the same principle that led the Egyptians to feed and clothe statues of deities and mummify themselves. They believed that the physical person or representation of a person contained an important part of that person's substance.

TOMBS AND FUNERALS: Early Egyptians believed that the dead could be needful of such items as were useful during life partly because people were conceived of as a composite of body and spirit, and survival beyond death had to involve the body. This meant that the body had to be preserved enough for revivification and that useful and valuable items had to be provided for the corpse, thus the need for mummification and for protected tombs to store valuables and keep the body safe. Preservation of the body and the protection of items of daily use thus served religious convictions that life had not ended. (Some of the oldest mortuary spells ensured the deceased that death was, in the end, an illusion: "It is not in the state of being dead that you have gone away; it is being alive that you have departed" (Murnane 1992, 37).

At first the arid nature of the desert preserved the bodies, but gradually techniques evolved that allowed remarkably sophisticated preservation. Complete mummification involved removing the brain and intestines and inserting wads of linen mixed with sodium, spices, and oil into the cavities. Sodium, spices, and oil were also applied externally, and the body was wrapped in linen. The internal organs were preserved in four jars, said to be protected by the four sons of Horus. The heart was not removed like the other organs, because it was the seat of one's spirituality; thus its use on the scale at the Hall of Justice to judge the deceased. By about 1500 B.C. complete mummification had become affordable beyond the circle of the pharaoh's family, but it was still out of reach of the lower classes.

The first pyramid, constructed around 2700 B.C. was the step-pyramid at Saqqara for King Djoser, the earliest large stone structure built by humans. The idea behind the step formation was probably ascension to the sun and heaven. The pharaohs naturally had the largest tombs and pyramids because they had the power and wealth to create them and because the population was willing enough to expend that energy on behalf of a god-king. It is difficult to describe the immense amount of energy and money that went into building the pyramids. The Greek historian Herodotus estimated that 100,000 workers spent 20 years to complete the single pyramid of Khufu at Gizeh. Those who could afford it set up endowments to pay for grave goods and for the mortuary priests who looked after the well-being of the spirits of the dead. These priests held regular ceremonies in the chapel of the tomb. These conditions, of course, could not be afforded by the poor, but as the notion of immortality was democratized, their hopes were the same. Most of the poor had minimal mummification, and many were buried in pit graves.

Within the tombs were paintings and reliefs of afterlife scenes, typically showing the deceased being honored by peers or being tended to by servants or touring his many lands and possessions. These renditions served several purposes. In addition to providing aesthetic surroundings, they also served as magical "backups" for the deceased. If the priests failed to keep up the mortuary rites, all that might be needed in terms of servants, tools, food, or status, were depicted for the deceased's use. Furthermore, the more solid one's standing in the afterlife, the more likely the descendants would be to look after the tomb and remember the deceased; the immortality of being perpetually remembered by family and friends was an important concern.

Beyond the other kinds of immortality represented in the tomb, some Egyptian festivals were celebrated by extended families and included statues of ancestors. During the Festival of the Valley at Thebes, families opened tombs and presented meals to their ancestors. Families—not content to let the deceased handle their tasks alone—often saw to the maintenance of mortuary rites at the tombs. The families benefited by maintaining access to the deceased for occasional advice or intercession, and by presuming that their descendants would look after their tombs similarly. The robbery or destruction of a tomb was felt as a devastating blow, as the deceased was thereby deprived of so many afterlife resources as well as remembrance by the living. Such a spirit could end up haunting the cemetery or a person or could disappear and lose existence altogether.

Even more important than the tomb or physical enclosure was the spiritual protection provided by proper observance of the funeral rites. If done improperly, the eternal condition of the deceased could presumably be affected. The central act of the burial ceremony was opening the mouth and touching it with an adze (a carpenter's cutting tool). At this time the ba (soul) was breathed back through the mouth in the belief that this made all the bodily faculties available for new life. It was also believed that this enabled the reunion in the next world of the ba and the ka.

Another part of the funeral rites involved empathy with Osiris. The Osiris name might be prefixed to that of the deceased, or the deceased might be depicted with Osirian characteristics in the hope that this would provide some advantage in the trials to come.

THE PHARAOH AND THE PEOPLE: In the beginning, only pharaohs and members of the royal family were considered to have access to eternal life. Since the king was believed to be divine, it was natural to believe that upon the death of his human body he would return to his true home among the other gods. But there was more involved than this. The god-king was the link between heaven and earth, and his sovereignty was key to both the stability of the society and the functioning of the natural order. In some sense he needed to be eternal because he was the guarantor of continued sunshine, soil fertility, and all the things that made the empire flourish. Gradually the pharaoh was identified with the activities of all the important gods. If Ra, the sun-god, was responsible for the regular appearance and activity of the sun day after day, still the pharaoh must be involved in some way. If Osiris was the vegetation god and responsible for the regular cycle of seed, growth, decay, and rebirth, still the pharaoh had to have a hand in it.

The more this theology developed, the more the pharaoh shifted from being merely a divine ruler to being the vital force behind the constant renewal of life. Over time, as the link between Osiris and the pharaoh was elaborated, the meaning of the whole burial process was changed and democratized. Osiris, the vegetation god, was turned into the god of the dead and came to represent the cycles of death and rebirth available to all humans, rather than just to the king. The king was not so much a privileged beneficiary of immortality, but its very principle. He became the universal model for the process that was theoretically open to everyone.

Like all other religions, that of ancient Egypt contained inconsistencies and ambiguities. A case can be made that, over time, at least some ancient Egyptians developed a completely spiritualized concept of the afterlife in which mummification, tombs, and mortuary rites would be unnecessary. Although the spiritualized ideas were there, the major traditions and rituals remained unchanged. This produced some beliefs not altogether compatible. On the one hand was the idea that you could "take it with you," literally. On the other hand was the idea that there was another, nonphysical realm to which the dead made their way. As William J. Murnane has put it, "The otherworldly orbit of the dead was not seen as a bar to their inhabiting their tombs or participating in the feasts of the living" (Murnane 1992, 43). Possible explanations for this are many. There was the power of the priests to maintain their numerous functions, particularly in mortuary cults. Perhaps most people then, like today, did not think systematically about familiar beliefs. Perhaps they recognized incongruities but did not want to cease traditional practices "just in case" they might work after all.

What is certain is that the power of Egyptian afterlife beliefs was felt for many centuries, even after the passage of that great civilization. The myth of Isis and Osiris became the basis for the most popular of the mystery religions of the ancient Near East. Even the idea of the tomb as a replica or miniature house for the dead continued into the early Christian era and in some places into our own times.

It is somewhat surprising that despite the harnessing of so much psychic and economic energy toward the afterlife, the Egyptians did not lead gloomy, otherworldly lives. Rather, they fully enjoyed the pleasures of life and were not in a hurry to see "the day of landing," as the occasion of death was called. They were never completely sure that they had the afterlife figured out. They did, however, think it important to prepare as best they could for the inevitable end of this life.

Sources:

Burns, Edward McNall. *Western Civilizations.* 2 vols. 8th ed. New York: W. W. Norton, 1973.

Eliade, Mircea. *From Primitives to Zen.* New York: Harper & Row, 1967.

Lesko, Leonard H. "Egyptian Religion: An Overview." In Mircea Eliade, ed. *The Encyclopedia of Religion.* 16 vols. New York: Macmillan, 1987.

Murnane, William J. "Taking It With You: The Problem of Death and Afterlife in Ancient Egypt." In Hiroshi Obayashi, ed. *Death and Afterlife: Perspectives of World Religions.* Westport, CT: Greenwood Press, 1992.

Nigosian, S. A. *World Faiths.* New York: St. Martin's Press, 1990.
Parrinder, Geoffrey. *World Religions: From Ancient History to the Present.* New York: Facts on File, 1971.
Smart, Ninian. *The Religious Experience of Mankind.* 3d ed. New York: Charles Scribner's Sons, 1984.
Smart, Ninian, and Richard D. Hecht, eds. *Sacred Texts of the World: A Universal Anthology.* New York: Crossroad Publishing, 1982.
Turner, Alice K. *The History of Hell.* New York: Harcourt Brace, 1993.

ELECTRONIC VOICE PHENOMENA (RAUDIVE VOICES)

In the context of afterlife investigations, the electronic voice phenomenon (EVP) refers to what appear to be the voices of departed spirits that are recorded on audiotape. EVP is also sometimes referred to as Raudive voices, a designation derived from the name of Konstantin Raudive, an EVP researcher. As with everything else in the field of afterlife investigations, electronic voice phenomenon has generated controversy. EVP researchers believe they record communications from the deceased, and sometimes from extraterrestrials. Skeptics, predictably, assert that the ''spirit voices'' either represent the intrusion of broadcasts from radio, television, and CBs, or are imagined from static.

EVP is an interesting innovation in the arena of efforts to communicate with discarnate entities. Such early figures in electrical design as Thomas Edison asserted that it would probably be possible to construct an electronic machine through which one could communicate with the dead. Edison actually worked on such a device, as mentioned in the *Scientific American* issue of October 1920. He failed, however, to complete his EVP machine before his death a decade later. The subject languished for decades until, in 1956, Attila von Sealay, a psychic, cooperated with researchers in an attempt to record spirit voices on tape. Von Sealay asserted that in 1938 he began to sense a ''tiny voice'' near him. He thought the voice was that of his deceased son, Edson. The experiments resulted in what sounded like voices, whistles, and rappings.

In spite of this prior history, Friedrich Jurgenson, a Swedish opera singer, painter, and producer, is usually credited with the discovery of EVP, perhaps because his work became so widely known and influenced so many other investigators. Jurgenson's EVP work began innocently enough when he was tape- recording birds near his Swedish villa. Listening to his recording, he heard a Norwegian voice talking about ''nocturnal bird songs.'' Initially, he thought a radio broadcast had somehow been recorded. He decided to experiment with other recording sessions to see if the same phenomenon would recur. He heard no voices while recording, but many when he played back the tape. These voices provided personal information about Jurgenson, as well as instructions on how to record yet more such communications.

In 1964 Jurgenson discussed his experiences in *Voices from the Universe,* which was published along with a recording of EVP sounds. The next year, he encountered Konstantin Raudive, a philosopher and psychologist who became interested in researching the electronic voice phenomenon. Raudive made more than 100,000 recordings. His research, published in German as *The Inaudible Made Audible,* was translated and published in English as *Breakthrough* (1971). His work was so widely studied that EVP voices became known as Raudive voices.

The greatest contemporary interest in EVP investigation is in the United States and Germany. In Germany, there are two EVP organizations: the Association for Voice Taping Research (VTF), founded in the 1970s, and the Research Association for Voice Taping (FGT). The American Association-Electronic Voice Phenomena was started in the United States in 1982 by Sarah Estep. EVP seminars and conferences are held worldwide. Many of these enthusiasts are electronics experts and engineers who design sensitive and sophisticated equipment for taping the communications.

Estep classifies such communications into three different categories: Class A are clear voices that can be discerned without headphones, and can even be copied onto other tapes. Class B communications are intermediate in clarity and volume. Class C are faint voices that are often difficult to decipher. Beyond the tendency to speak in brief and sometimes cryptic and ungrammatical phrases, EVPs exhibit no particular pattern. The communications come through in different languages, sometimes disregarding the languages of the researchers. At times, the voices will sing in indistinct lyrics. At other times, several or even numerous voices come through simultaneously. Animal sounds have also been taped. Some EVP voices claim that they are able to impress their sounds on tape via **ectoplasm.**

There is no particular way to record EVPs. One may, for example, simply turn on a tape machine and leave it running, particularly at night when the chances of interference from other sources is minimized. Serious investigators use more sensitive microphones and higher-quality tape. One approach to EVP research is to ask questions and leave the recorder on. If this approach works, answers (which are inaudible during taping) are recorded and become audible on playback.

Many otherwise nonskeptical researchers believe that the electronic voice phenomenon can be adequately explained without resorting to the idea that the communications come from departed spirits. In the early 1970s, for instance, the London Society for Psychical Research commissioned D. J. Ellis to examine Raudive voices. He found that, because of the poor quality of most recordings, the interpretation of the "voices" was too subjective, and that these sounds were probably random noises, not supernatural manifestations. Other critics have hypothesized that EVPs result from psychokinesis. In other words, according to this line of interpretation, EVP researchers are so intent on recording spirit voices that they unconsciously imprint sounds on the recording with their own psychokinetic powers. Raudive, who died on September 2, 1974, had no particular theory about the source of EVP.

EVP researchers were tantalized by new possibilities when in 1982 George Meek, a retired engineer, announced that he and William O'Neill, a medium and an electronics expert, had constructed an instrument through which one could communicate with spirits of the dead. Instructions for the device had been given in a séance, and they called it Spiricom. Meek made the information necessary to build Spiricom widely available, but no one who actually put together such an instrument reported that it worked satisfactorily. Some people in the field speculated that Meek's own success with Spiricom was a function of O'Neill's abilities as a psychic medium.

Despite the continued ambiguity of EVP communications, investigators continue to work on producing recordings that will satisfactorily demonstrate survival after death. Similar research using film, video, and even computers has also been pursued.

Sources:

Estep, Sarah. *Voices of Eternity.* New York: Fawcett Gold Medal, 1988.
Ostrander, Sheila, and Lynn Schroeder. *Handbook of Psi Discoveries.* New York: Berkley, 1974.
Raudive, Konstantin. *Breakthrough: An Amazing Experiment in Electronic Communication with the Dead.* New York: Taplinger, 1971.

ELEUSINIAN MYSTERIES

The classical period of ancient Greece saw the development of a form of religious expression that has been referred to as mystery religions. As part of the mysteries, initiates were required to take a vow of secrecy. These secrets were so well kept that we moderns are unable to reconstruct the ancient mystery religions. What we do know is that individuals were attracted to the mysteries because of the promise of a better fate in the afterlife. The most famous of the mystery religious was the Eleusinian mysteries, centered in Eleusis, outside of Athens. In the outer (first stage) mystery, we know from contemporaneous accounts that, under the guidance of a hierophant (''revealer of holy things'') candidates for initiation underwent:

1. A preparatory purification, such as bathing in the sea
2. Instruction in hidden knowledge, often behind closed doors in a mystic hall
3. Ceremonial handling of sacred things
4. Acting out of the central myth or sacred story
5. Crowning of the candidate as a full initiate

The principal figures in the Eleusinian mysteries were Demeter and **Persephone.**

In classical Greek mythology, Persephone was the wife of **Hades,** ruler of the underworld. Hades kidnapped Persephone and took her off to the underworld. Distraught over the loss of her Daughter, Demeter, who was a goddess of fertility, grain, and the harvest, neglected to perform her divine tasks, and the earth became barren. Demeter relented only after she and Hades agreed that Persephone would spend half of the year with her mother, and half of the year with her husband. Fall and Winter are said to be the six months when Persephone is with her husband, and Spring and Summer when she is with her mother. Because of her association with the seasons, Persephone became a symbol of the springtime, renewal, and rebirth. Like **Orpheus,** Persephone was one of the few mythological figures to enter the realm of the dead and return. This characteristic of returning from the dead seems to have been the primary reason why Persephone and Demeter her mother became the central figures in the Eleusinian mysteries.

By the time of the development of the Eleusinian mysteries, the Greek conception of the afterlife had developed to the point where not all of the dead met the same drab fate of an endless, boring life in the realm of the dead. In the later Greek view the departing soul went to the underworld to stand before the throne of Peresphone and be sentenced to reward in the Elysian Fields, or to punishment in Tartarus. Apparently the whole point of being initiated at Eleusis was that one was thus adopted as a child of Demeter; hence when one stood before Demeter's daughter Peresphone, she would judge one as a family member, not as a stranger—a status which made all the difference in Greek society. This may be why such concepts as adoption and sonship are emphasized in some New Testament writings. In any event, this Greek belief is one of the major sources of the Christian concept that each person is judged and sentenced immediately after dying.

Sources:

Grant, Michael and John Hazel. *Who's Who in Classical Mythology.* New York: Oxford University Press, 1993.

Tripp, Edward. *The Meridian Handbook of Classical Mythology.* New York: New American Library, 1970.

ELIXIR OF IMMORTALITY, THE

Mythic tales of the quest for **immortality,** eternal youth, and longevity are found in every major cultural and religious tradition. Every major tradition explains why or when death or aging was introduced, explanations that also reveal the human desire to discover or invent something to prevent old age and mortality from occurring. Some techniques involve physical practices, such as the **yoga** exercise of channeling energy along the spine through the seven chakras, or taking an elixir of immortality—a potion or herb often dispensed as some kind of secret formula.

The Tree of Life in the Garden of Eden, whose fruit guarantees eternity, is described in Genesis. A similar Hindu myth tells of a magic tree whose fruit protects the people of Uttaruku from sickness and aging. In India the ancient system of Ayurvedic medicine also includes the study of a purifying and rejuvenating potion, the *soma* (''drink of non-death''). According to different traditions, the soma is obtained either by mixing specific ingredients following certain precise procedures or by extracting it from a single plant. Whatever the origin, the soma is supposed to give youth and longevity.

The waters of the Ganges river in India are also believed to give the gift of immortality, conceived of as liberation from the wheel of **karma** (i.e., from future **reincarnations**). An old Hindu myth explains why the waters of these two rivers are sacred: the *amrita* (nectar of eternal life), created in the Ganges by gods and demons working together, was then fought over by the two groups. Eventually, some drops fell into the water and were spread by the river to four cities, which alternately celebrate the Festival of the Pottery Jar with immersion in the sacred waters of those rivers.

Belief in the rejuvenating or immortality-granting power of certain waters was not confined to India. In some ancient Greek sources it was reported that magic fountains and springs were believed to exist in Ethiopia. Also, at the time of the Spanish conquest of the New World, an expedition was conducted to discover the Fountain of Youth. In ancient Greece, ambrosia and nectar were considered the food of the gods, the food that ensured them eternal life.

When Westerners came into contact with the Arabs, they learned the principles of alchemy (an Arabic word) in an effort to discover or create an elixir (*al iksīr,* in Arabic), or philosophers' stone—the basic principle or substance that allows one to transmute ordinary metals into gold. This metallic transmutation was symbolic of immortality and longevity. Francis Bacon believed that human life could be prolonged through the secret arts of alchemy and the philosophers' stone. The learned alchemist, magus, and physician Paracelsus (1493–1541), also tried to create an elixir of immortality.

Alchemical studies aimed at achieving longevity or immortality were known much earlier in eastern Asia, particularly in the Chinese Taoist tradition, dating from several centuries B.C. Asceticism was coupled with potions in an attempt to give immortality to those willing to withdraw from society and lead a spartan existence.

Sexual practices have also been used in Taoism, as well as in Tantrism (a southern Asian strand of spirituality), to prolong life by tapping sexual energy for the purpose of rejuvenation. The human imagination has also drawn from the animal world to find models and sources for longevity. Typically, insects (e.g., scarabs, a type of beetle) and other organisms that in their simplicity seem to be gifted with immortality have been studied to discover the basis of their longevity.

Sources:

Eliade, Mircea, ed. *The Encyclopedia of Religion.* 16 vols. New York: Macmillan, 1987.

———. *A History of Religious Ideas.* 16 vols. Chicago: University of Chicago Press, 1978.

ENGRAM

Engram is a **Dianetics** term referring to the unconscious residue of a past experience that exercises a harmful influence over the present. The concept is somewhat similar to the Hindu/Buddhist notion of *samskara,* although the latter is a more comprehensive term referring to the residues of all prior experiences. In contrast to samskara, an engram is, in the words of L. Ron Hubbard, the founder of Dianetics, "a mental image picture which is a recording of a time of physical pain and unconsciousness. It must by definition have impact or injury as part of its content." The goal of Dianetics therapy (termed auditing) is to clear an individual of the warping effects of engrams.

As originally formulated, engrams encompassed only memories of this life. However, individuals undergoing auditing would sometimes relate present difficulties to traumatic events experienced in previous lifetimes. Hubbard found that auditing was just as effective with these past-life engrams as it was with those of this life, and work with earlier incarnations was integrated into Dianetics therapy. In this way engrams came to be linked to the notion of **reincarnation.** This aspect of dianetics therapy makes it the predecessor of **past-life therapy.**

Sources:

Hubbard, L. Ron. *Dianetics: The Modern Science of Mental Health.* New York: Hermitage House, 1950.
———. *Have You Lived Before This Life?* Los Angeles, CA: Church of Sciencetology of California, 1977.

ESCHATOLOGY

Eschatology ("the study of the last things," from the Greek *eschatos,* last), is the study of the end of time or the end of the world as we know it. Eschatology involves the idea of redemption or salvation and is part of the doctrine of most world religions. It can be subdivided into individual eschatology (concerned with the fate of individual souls, or the judgment of the dead and their ultimate destination) and cosmic eschatology (which can be either restorative of the old pure primordial order, or utopian—establishing a perfect system that never before existed).

In the South Asian traditions, individual eschatology involves liberation of the soul (*moksa* for Hindus and *nirvana* for Buddhists) from the endless cycle of deaths and rebirths that are experienced on the wheel of reincarnation. Hindu and Buddhist cosmic time is divided in four primary ages (*yugas*). We are said to be living in the fourth of these ages (the Kali Yuga). The appearance of an avatara (an incarnation of a Hindu deity) or of a new Buddha will signal the end of the kali yuga and the beginning of a new cosmic cycle.

In Chinese Buddhism, upon the end of the present age of inexorable decline, the appearance of Buddha Maitreya will inaugurate a new, utopian kingdom. Other Chinese millennialist notions that emphasize the restoration of the old, pure origins draw upon Taoist and Confucian beliefs.

Zoroastrianism is one religion in which individual and cosmic eschatologies merge. The souls of the dead are provisionally assigned a state of bliss or suffering. Their final status is determined at the end of the world. Once the forces of light have completely overturned darkness, the resurrection of the dead will occur. This optimistic vision of the end of the world is an original contribution to the religious thought of the Western world.

Early Jewish eschatology as documented in the prophecies of the Old Testament aimed at the restoration of an earlier golden age. Persian and Hellenistic ideas influenced Judaism, leading to the development of a variety of messianic or apocalyptic ideas. These sometimes contradicted one another, and only in later centuries were they harmonized into a coherent system. The expected Messiah is a descendant of the House of David and/or a divine being referred to as the Son of Man. He represents the redeemer of a peaceful world. In contrast, advocates of the Apocalypse envision the annihilation of the present age.

ANGEL FROM HEAVEN ANNOUNCING THE END-TIME.

Judaism influenced the eschatology of early Christianity, providing the notion that the Messiah will usher in a new age. The Messiah is to replace the present age with the Kingdom of God upon Judgment Day and the resurrection of the righteous.

Throughout the centuries, various Christian movements have developed their own millenarian doctrines that anticipate the end of the world and the coming of a new golden age.

In the early development of Islam, the notion of final universal judgment and the end of the world (as a historical process) were important elements in the religious experience of Mohammed. Often in the later history of Islam, the messianic figure of the Mahdi has been introduced to inaugurate the beginnings of a new age, especially in Shiite Islamic groups.

Sources:

Eliade, Mircea. *Encyclopedia of Religion.* 16 vols. New York: Macmillan, 1987.
Van Der Leeuw, G., trans., *Religion in Essence and Manifestation.* Vol.1. Gloucester, MA: Peter Smith, 1967. (Originally published 1933.)

ESSENES

The Essenes were a Jewish monastic sect made famous by the discovery of the Dead Sea Scrolls—the Essene monastery's library, which had been hidden in caves near the Dead Sea—in 1947. A good deal of excitement was initially generated by the scrolls' mention of a "Teacher of Righteousness," which some early investigators mistakenly thought might be a reference to Jesus. The Essenes had also been romanticized by certain occult/metaphysical writers who thought they perceived an ancient mystery school in Josephus's and other authors' writings about this group.

Further investigation into the scrolls, however, indicated that the Essenes were an apocalyptic Jewish sect descended from the pietists (Hasidim, not to be confused with contemporary Hasidism) of the Maccabeean era. They withdrew from society and established a monastery on the shores of the Dead Sea at Qumran in the middle of the second century B.C., where they had a community until attacked during the Roman-Jewish War of A.D. 66–70.

In stark contrast to other forms of **Judaism** and to early **Christianity,** the Essene sect believed in the notion of an immortal **soul.** In their very un-Jewish antagonism toward the flesh, as well as in certain of their notions of soul, they appear to have been influenced by **Gnosticism,** or by one of the other Neoplatonic mystery religion of the Hellenistic period. Their beliefs about the soul and the afterlife were described by Josephus in *The Jewish War:*

> It is indeed their unshakable conviction that bodies are corruptible and the material composing them impermanent, whereas souls remain immortal forever. Coming forth from the most rarefied ether, they are trapped in the prison house of the body as if drawn down by one of nature's spells; but once freed from the bonds of the flesh, as if released after years of slavery, they rejoice and soar aloft. Teaching the same doctrine as the sons of Greece, they declare that for the good souls there waits a home beyond the ocean, a place troubled by neither rain nor snow nor heat, but refreshed by the zephyr that

blows ever gentle from the ocean. Bad souls they consign to a darksome, stormy abyss, full of punishments that know no end. (Turner 1993, 43)

Sources:

Eliade, Mircea, ed. *The Encyclopedia of Religion.* 16 vols. New York: Macmillan, 1987.
Turner, Alice K. *The History of Hell.* New York: Harcourt Brace, 1993.

Evolution of the Soul

Traditional religions have tended to emphasize the sharp transition from a nonenlightened or nonsaved state to an enlightenment or salvation. In contrast, contemporary occult/ metaphysical spirituality emphasizes gradual growth, expansion of consciousness, and learning across time, including growth across many different lifetimes. Thus, in contrast with traditional **Hinduism** and **Buddhism**—which view **reincarnation** negatively, as a cycle of suffering out of which one should strive to liberate oneself—the contemporary metaphysical subculture views reincarnation positively, as a series of opportunities for expanded spiritual growth. This gradual spiritual expansion constitutes a kind of evolution of the soul, and the metaphor of spiritual evolution is often expressed in the literature of this subculture.

Sources:

Shepard, Leslie A. *Encyclopedia of Occultism & Parapsychology.* Detroit, MI: Gale Research, 1984.
Zimmer, Heinrich. *Philosophies of India.* 1951. Reprint. New York: Macmillan, 1987.

Exorcism (Depossession; Releasement)

Exorcism is the driving out of spirits or other entities, most often conceived of as evil (or at least undesirable), from a human being. This expulsion may involve a formal, ritual procedure or a less formal process, depending on the tradition. Exorcisms may also range from dramatic struggles to friendly persuasion. The afflicted person is said to be **possessed.** Notions of possession and exorcism practices are found worldwide, in every major religious and cultural tradition. As a result of certain popular movies (particularly *The Exorcist,* an American movie made in the early 1970s), many people have a basic familiarity with the notions of possession and exorcism. Beyond the exorcisms that are sometimes performed in a few Christian churches, certain alternative therapists—most notably Edith Fiore, author of *The Unquiet Dead*—have seriously proposed that certain psychologically disturbed individuals are being bothered (if not actually possessed) by spirits of the dead.

Exorcism, from the Greek *exorkizein* (to bind by oath), means something along the lines of placing the possessing spirit under oath—invoking a higher authority to compel the spirit—rather than an actual "casting out." This placing under oath implies a kind of binding. Catholic exorcisms begin, *Adjure te, spiritus nequissime, per Deum omnipotentem*. . . which means "I adjure thee, most evil spirit, by almighty God. . . ."

The practice of exorcism is both ancient and universal. In some societies in which spirits were thought to intrude often into human affairs, exorcism became a part of everyday life, so that one might consult an exorcist for spirit-induced problems much as one would a medical doctor for health problems. Exorcisms may be performed by ministers, shamans, priests, rabbis, lamas, or witches. In a less literal manner than the approach taken by Edith Fiore, the treatment of psychological disorders in which one is dealing with alternate personalities (however unreal) may be conceptualized as exorcisms.

In Christianity, possession and exorcism are associated with evil. In this tradition, priests and ministers perform most exorcisms, and the process is often dramatic and even violent. The possessed person is often in pain, undergoing physical contortions, cursing, vomiting, and so forth. As in the movies, objects in the room where the exorcism is occurring may fly around, endangering those present. As a struggle between representatives of Satan and representatives of Christ, an exorcism in the Christian tradition is viewed as a fight over the soul of the possessed, and the outcome of the conflict will determine the eternal fate of the victim.

Traditionally, exorcists used prayer, commands, holy water, fumigations, and unpleasant-tasting preparations in their practice. Attar of roses, hellebore, and rue also were said to work quite well. Salt, which in the medieval period represented spiritual purity, was also utilized in exorcism rituals. Wine, as the blood of Christ, was also employed. Catholicism's exorcism ritual, the Rituale Romanum, dates back to 1614. Protestant exorcism manuals are less well known, but at one time or another were propagated by many of the major Protestant traditions.

Roman Catholicism is the most famous denomination to practice exorcism, but the contemporary Catholic church has downplayed possession and exorcism. Always on the search for sensationalistic stories, however, ABC broadcast a live exorcism, by a priest, of a young girl in 1991 on the show "20/20." Despite previous psychiatric treatment, the victim still seemed to be afflicted by what seemed to be a demon. Parents and church officials decided to attempt an exorcism. The possessed girl regurgitated, exhibited fits, and even cursed in a voice that seemed not to be her own for the TV audience. The exorcism was much less dramatic, however, than people were accustomed to viewing in the movies. It also failed to produce lasting effects, and the victim went back to psychiatric treatment.

Among Protestant denominations, the notions of possession and exorcism are particularly important to Pentecostals (sometimes also referred to as charismatics), a

DEMON LEAVING THE BODY OF A POSSESSED WOMAN.

type of spirituality best known for its emphasis on glossolalia (speaking in tongues) and other "gifts of the Spirit." Some Pentecostal groups engage in a practice of casting out demons via the laying on of hands. Similar to other forms of exorcism, the exorcist (who may or may not be a minister), assistants, and sometimes a whole congregation pray and command the possessing spirit to leave. If the procedure is successful, the demon is forced out. The confrontation has some resemblance to other forms of Protestant exorcism, however, the possession and the exorcism are often more a symbolic language for understanding, confronting, and ridding oneself of a particular weakness. Thus, for example, as the possessing spirit departs, it may call itself by name, such as Greed or Anger.

Exorcism is mentioned in Hebrew Scriptures (the Old Testament) in I Samuel where Saul becomes possessed and David exorcises the spirit by playing his harp. Early rabbinical literature also makes reference to exorcism. As recorded in the Gospels, exorcism played a significant role in Jesus' ministry. Perhaps the best known of his exorcisms is when he cast out unclean spirits from a madman. These spirits then possessed a herd of pigs that in turn charged over a cliff to drown in the waters below.

In religious traditions outside of the Judeo-Christian-Islamic complex, a broad spectrum of different kinds of spirits can possess a person, causing a wide variety of illnesses, both physical and psychological. Possession, in other words, need not always be by evil demons, and as a consequence exorcism need not be viewed as a struggle for the eternal fate of the possessed soul.

The Western Christian tradition does not have formal rituals for exorcising spirits from *spaces* (i.e., there are no rites for ridding spirits from ''haunted houses'' and the like). In traditional China, by contrast, there were highly developed rites for clearing a haunted house. Taoist priests would initially set up an altar in a space the spirit frequented. After lighting incense and tapers, the priest entered the building dressed in an elaborate costume and carrying an exorcism sword. The sword was held over beds and other places in the house where one wished to drive out the unwanted supernatural. The sword was made of special wood, and an exorcism spell was carved on the blade.

After placing the sword on the altar, the priest would prepare and burn an exorcism scroll. The ashes were then collected in a glass of water. Sword and cup in hand, he would first step to the left and then step to the right, saying, ''God of heaven and earth, invest me with the heavy seal, in order that I may eject from this dwelling-house all kinds of evil spirits. Should any disobey me, give me the power to deliver them for safe custody to the rulers of such demons.'' He would then command the ghost to leave the house, put down the sword, and grasp a bunch of willow and dip in the glass. The priest would then proceed to sprinkle the water mixed with the ashes of the scroll into the corners of the building. After the ritual was completed, he would go to the entrance and declare the home free of spirits.

The contemporary period has seen what amounts to a revival of interest in possession and exorcism, although current perspectives on such phenomena are more moderate than traditional Christian views. For example, the American psychologist and doctor Carl Wickland believed that such spirits were more confused than demonic, and were simply ''caught'' in the energy of the person whom they appeared to be afflicting. As a result of this entrapment, they caused what appeared to be schizoid symptoms and other types of aberrations. Wickland found simple persuasion was often enough to effect an ''exorcism.'' He described his findings in *Thirty Years Among the Dead* (1924). Other people who became interested in the possession phenomenon, such as Anglican priest Canon John D. Pearce-Higgins and Dr. Martin Israel, who was a University of London lecturer in pathology, are in basic agreement with Wickland.

More recently, psychiatrist Ralph Allison noted that certain of his patients, particularly those with multiple personality disorder, appeared to be possessed, and that both exorcism and therapy were necessary to effect a cure. A contemporary term for exorcism is *releasement,* a word that seems to imply Wickland's view, which is that discarnate spirits become trapped in the possessed person's aura. Some therapists and mediums who deal with such problems prefer the term because it does not bear the same connotations with evil as does *exorcism.*

In releasement-type exorcisms, an intuitively gifted individual enters into communication with the discarnate entity that is possessing someone or causing a disturbance. The revenant is sometimes a disoriented person who died suddenly and is unaware that death has occurred, and at other times is someone who is attempting to complete unfinished business. The "exorcist" attempts to learn the discarnate being's "story," which in itself is sometimes sufficient to enable the spirit to go on to the otherworld. In other situations, the spirit must be persuaded to leave. In this procedure, the exorcist performs one of the tasks that **shamans** undertake in traditional cultures.

Exorcism has also been termed *depossession,* a word coined in the field of **past-life therapy** (dealing with current psychological problems by tracing their roots to previous incarnations). Clients in this form of therapy are sometimes exorcised from the influence of spirits that can cause a wide range of physical, emotional, and mental problems. As with other contemporary therapists, past-life practitioners do not consider most of the obsessing spirits to be demonic. One of the more popular accounts of contemporary spirit obsession and depossession is *The Unquiet Dead: A Psychologist Treats Spirit Possession* (1987), by psychologist and past-life therapist Edith Fiore. Fiore estimates that as many as 70 percent of all her clients are being bothered by at least one discarnate spirit. She attributes most serious mental disorders as well as substance abuse to spirit obsession.

Some therapists who take discarnates seriously have categorized such influences as follows:

> *Attachment.* Spirit simply hangs out near person; connection is loose.
>
> Oppression. Spirit invasive with respect to living person's energy; effects are mild or intermittent.
>
> *Obsession.* Spirit enters person's body, influencing the individual's personality so that it is overshadowed by the personality of the obsessing spirit.
>
> *Possession.* Spirit actually takes over the living body so as to displace the living person's personality.

Discarnate spirits that possess people most often belong to the departed. Conditions that invite possession are substance abuse and negative emotions. People who have been through releasement often say they feel lighter and negative conditions cease.

Sources:

Crabtree, Adam. *Multiple Man: Explorations in Possession and Multiple Personality.* New York: Praeger, 1985.

Ebon, Martin. *The Devil's Bride, Exorcism: Past and Present.* New York: Harper & Row, 1974.
Eliade, Mircea. *Shamanism.* Princeton, N.J.: Princeton University Press, 1964.
Fiore, Edith. *The Unquiet Dead: A Psychologist Treats Spirit Possession.* Garden City, NY: Dolphin/Doubleday, 1987.
Wickland, Carl A. *Thirty Years Among the Dead.* North Hollywood, CA: Newcastle Publishing, 1974. (Originally published 1924.)

EXTRATERRESTRIAL INCARNATIONS

Most variations in the theory of **reincarnation** include the notion that one may incarnate in a variety of different forms, human or animal. In classical **Hinduism,** an ordinary human being could even incarnate as a demigod, such as **Yama.** As ideas about extraterrestrials and the inhabitants of UFOs were adopted by the West's metaphysical subculture and integrated into its ideology, it was natural that speculation about possible incarnations on other planets also would eventually be integrated into this subculture's general worldview. In more recent communications with ''the other side,'' New Age **channels** have even claimed to have received information from, among other sources, extraterrestrials. Thus, although extraterrestrial incarnation is generally overshadowed by the more exotic notion of extraterrestrial **walk-ins,** it is not uncommon to speak with people who claim to have had such lifetimes.

Sources:

Guiley, Rosemary Ellen. *The Encyclopedia of Ghosts and Spirits.* New York: Facts on File, 1992.
Shepard, Leslie A. *Encyclopedia of Occultism & Parapsychology.* Detroit, MI: Gale Research, 1984.

EXTRATERRESTRIAL WALK-INS

A **walk-in** is an entity that occupies a body that has been vacated by its original soul. An extraterrestrial walk-in is supposedly one from another planet. The walk-in situation is somewhat similar to **possession,** although in possession the original soul is merely overshadowed—rather than completely supplanted—by the possessing entity. The contemporary notion of walk-ins was popularized by **Ruth Montgomery,** who developed the walk-in notion in her 1979 book *Strangers Among Us.* In 1983 Montgomery published another book, *Threshold to Tomorrow,* containing case histories of 17 walk-ins. According to Montgomery, walk-ins are usually highly evolved souls here to help humanity that, to avoid the delay of spending two decades growing up, contact living people who, because of the frustrating circumstances of life or for some other reason, no longer desire to remain in the body. The discarnate

RUTH NORMAN (1900–1993), HEAD OF THE UNARIUS ACADEMY OF SCIENCE, WHOSE TEACHINGS STRESS EXTRATERRESTRIAL INCARNATIONS. COURTESY OF MICHAEL GRECCO.

entity finds such people, persuades them to hand over their body, and then begins life as a walk-in. These ideas became extremely popular in New Age circles, and for a while it seemed that almost every hard-core New Ager was claiming to be some kind of walk-in.

In a later book, *Aliens Among Us* (1985), Montgomery developed the notion of extraterrestrial walk-ins—the idea that souls from other planets have come to earth to take over the bodies of human beings. This notion dovetailed with popular interest in UFOs, which had already been incorporated into New Age spirituality. Some inhabitants of UFOs are viewed negatively, but others are viewed positively, as embodying a wisdom higher than most earthlings are capable of. Extraterrestrial walk-ins are viewed by New Agers as part of the larger community of advanced souls that have come to earth to help humanity through this time of crisis.

Sources:

Montgomery, Ruth. *Aliens Among Us.* New York: Putnam's, 1985.

———. *Strangers Among Us: Enlightened Beings from a World to Come.* New York: Coward, McCann & Geoghegan, 1979.

———. *Threshold to Tomorrow.* New York: Putnam's, 1983.

F

Family Karma

Karma is the moral law of cause and effect (As you sow, so shall you reap) through which individuals who have performed good or bad actions are rewarded or punished according to their actions. Thus, for example, if someone is generous with money, he will eventually be rewarded with comparable recompense, either in this lifetime or in a future lifetime. This understanding of karma is very old and is fundamental to such religious traditions as **Hinduism** and **Buddhism.**

The term *family karma* has also been applied to groups of people who reincarnate together as families in particular areas and time periods. The idea here is that, as a result of the karmic complexities arising from interactions in prior lifetimes, people who have been together before must return together in order to reap the effects of past interactions. Because of the comparatively long periods of time in which family members interact, it is natural that there might be an unusually large number of debts and dues in the "karmic bankbook." According to this view, fathers and sons, for example, might have reverse roles in successive lifetimes to balance out the karmic bankbook.

Sources:

Guiley, Rosemary Ellen. *The Encyclopedia of Ghosts and Spirits.* New York: Facts on File, 1992.
Shepard, Leslie A. *Encyclopedia of Occultism & Parapsychology.* Detroit, MI: Gale Research, 1984.

Fear of Death

The notion of some sort of continued existence after death has been assumed worldwide in almost every religion and society. However, increased understanding of natural science and the subsequent expansion of scientific explanations of natural phenomena since the early modern period of the West have made it possible to conceive of reality as a completely physical realm, requiring no spiritual agencies to explain the world as we experience it in our everyday lives or to suggest continued spiritual existence after corporeal death.

Many people have come to embrace contemporary science as the sole arbiter of truth, despite its rather dismal picture of human life as devoid of ultimate purpose and meaning. Some individuals in this camp, especially those who had unpleasant experiences with religion in their childhood, are harshly critical of anything that suggests that the human being might be something more than a physical-chemical organism. In particular, belief in any kind of afterlife is dismissed as wishful thinking, motivated by fear of death.

This evaluation of afterlife beliefs as stemming from nothing more than fear of death is too simplistic to constitute anything close to a definitive explanation. For example, many people are raised in religious communities within which such ideas about the beyond are simply assumed. Also, many otherwise skeptical individuals have had ''spiritual'' experiences that have led them to accept the ''reality'' of a nonphysical realm. Thus, adherence to afterlife beliefs is not always connected with fear of death.

Sources:

Bletzer, June G. *The Donning International Encyclopedic Psychic Dictionary.* Norfolk, VA: Donning, 1986.
Kastenbaum, Robert, and Beatrice Kastenbaum. *Encyclopedia of Death.* New York: Avon, 1989.

FINAL JUDGMENT (LAST JUDGMENT)

In religious traditions that distinguish between the afterlife fates of morally good and morally bad individuals, there are different mechanisms by which souls can be sent to happy or unhappy states. In Christianity and related religions the judgment of souls is believed to occur upon death of the individual, who will be assigned either eternal condemnation or reward (hell or heaven) or, in some Christian churches, purgatory. Beyond this particular judgment, Western religions also propagate the idea of a final Judgment Day, held at the end of time, which usually culminates in the resurrection of the righteous for life in paradise and the resurrection of sinners for either extinction or eternal damnation.

In Western religions the notion of a final judgment originated in Zoroastrianism. The religion of Zoroaster is best known for its dualism. The god of light and his angels are locked in a cosmic struggle with the god of darkness and his demons. At the end of time, after a great final battle between good and evil, there will be a general judgment in which everyone will be put through an ordeal of fire (a river of molten metal), in which good individuals will have their dross burned away and evil people will be consumed. Thus, the souls of the damned will trade their ongoing torment in hell for a painful annihilation. The souls of the blessed, on the other hand, will be resurrected in

THE LAST JUDGMENT. (FROM THE BAMBERGISCHE HALSGERICH TSORDNUNG, 1510.) THE QUOTATIONS READ: "FOR WITH WHAT JUDGMENT YE JUDGE, YE SHALL BE JUDGED" (MATTHEW 7:2) AND "THE LORD EXECUTETH RIGHTEOUSNESS AND JUDGMENT FOR ALL THAT ARE OPPRESSED" (PSALMS 103:6).

physical bodies, which Ahura Mazda (the Supreme Being) will make both immortal and eternally youthful.

Many of the components of this vision of the end times—e.g., a final battle between good and evil, judgment of the wicked, resurrection of the dead—were adopted by Jewish apocalyptic thinkers. From texts composed by these apocalypticists, such notions were adopted by Christianity and Islam. Although the Judgment Day seems to be a dreadful event, many believers throughout the centuries have looked forward to it as the day on which their suffering for the faith would be vindicated and their persecutors and ridiculers punished. This prevalent "revenge" motif finds expression in, for example, the church father Tertullian, who, as Turner (1993, 76–77) says, "could scarcely wait for the great moment":

> What a panorama of spectacle on that day! What sight shall I turn to first to laugh and applaud? Mighty kings whose ascent to heaven used to be announced publicly, groaning now in the depths with Jupiter himself who used to witness the ascent? Governors who persecuted the name of the Lord melting in flames fiercer than those they kindled for brave Christians? Wise philosophers, blushing before their students as they burn together, the followers to whom they taught that the world is no concern of God's, whom they assured that either they had no souls at all or that what souls they had would never return to their former bodies? Poets, trembling not before the judgment seat of Rhadamanthus or of Minos, but of Christ—a surprise? Tragic actors bellowing in their own melodramas should be worth hearing! Comedians skipping in the fire will be worth praise! The famous charioteer will toast on his fiery wheel. . . . These are things of greater delight, I believe, than a circus, both kinds of theater, and any stadium.

Sources:

Eliade, Mircea. *Encyclopedia of Religion.* 16 vols. New York: Macmillan, 1987.
Turner, Alice K. *The History of Hell.* New York: Harcourt Brace, 1993.
Van Der Leeuw, G., trans. *Religion in Essence and Manifestaton.* Vol. 1. Gloucester, MA: Peter Smith, 1967. (Originally published 1933.)

FORD, ARTHUR AUGUSTUS

The American medium Arthur Augustus Ford (1897–1971) was internationally famous for his ability to communicate with the spirit world through a control named Fletcher. He was also well known for the role he played in the American Spiritualist movement, through which he tried, with little effect, to convince mainstream churches to adopt Spiritualist beliefs. From the time he was a boy, he prayed for the dead because of his conviction that he could help deceased people that way, although he did not agree with orthodox church doctrines about life after death, particularly the concepts of heaven and eternal punishment in hell.

Born in Titusville, Florida, of a Southern Baptist family, Ford started having profound psychic experiences, such as frightening voices and visions, during his army stint as a young adult. His first clairvoyant experience concerned his brother George, who that same day became very ill and died shortly thereafter.

Ford later developed his extrasensory ability, as Dr. Elmer Snoddy suggested to him at Transylvania College in Lexington, Kentucky. After graduation, he was ordained a minister of the Disciples of Christ Church in Baurbonville, Kentucky, where he gained great popularity for his preaching. He then left the church to join the Swarthmore Chatauqua Association of Pennsylvania, where he started giving lectures about Spiritualist topics and, in a half-hypnotized state, delivered messages from the dead to people in the audience.

After he met the person he considered to be his guru, Hindu Swami Yogananda, Ford was able to achieve a Yogic trance state that permitted him to control the effects of the voices he could hear. In 1924 he began to communicate with his spirit guide, Fletcher, a former friend who was killed during World War I. With his help, Ford's psychic ability increased so much that he impressed audiences all over the world, even some of his harshest critics, who used to challenge him in public. Only after his death did evidence of trickery surface—from his private papers.

One of Ford's most famous communications with the dead occurred in 1929, when he sat with Harry Houdini's wife and received the coded message Houdini and his wife had agreed to before Houdini's death in their effort to prove or disprove life after death.

After a traumatic automobile accident in 1930, Ford also had out-of-body experiences while on morphine. As a consequence of his addiction to morphine, taken to have out-of-body experiences and to combat insomnia, he became alcoholic and his psychic powers started to diminish. Despite his illness, he continued to have psychic experiences, including the famous séance on television for Bp. James Pike, and to work for various Spiritualist organizations.

Sources:

Bletzer, June G. *The Donning International Encyclopedic Psychic Dictionary.* Norfolk, VA: Donning, 1986.
Cavendish, Richard. *The Encyclopedia of the Unexplained.* New York: McGraw-Hill, 1967.
Guiley, Rosemary. *The Encyclopedia of Ghosts and Spirits.* New York: Facts on File, 1992.

Fox Sisters

The origin of modern **Spiritualism,** a religion centered around communications with the spirits of the deceased, is usually attributed to a poltergeist case in 1848 when two American girls began to hear **rappings** in their family home, as well as other inexplicable noises.

Margareta and Kate Fox, then ages 15 and 12, lived with their parents, John, a Methodist farmer, and Margaret, in a wooden house in Hydesville, near Rochester, New York. From the time the family moved there near the end of 1847, the Foxes had

THE FOX SISTERS: (L. TO R.) MARGARETTA FOX-KANE, KATE FOX-JENCKEN, AND LEAH UNDERHILL. COURTESY OF THE ARC.

been disturbed and kept awake at night by unexplainable sounds, such as raps and bangs, which were imputed to the presence of spirits in the house.

This belief received support when, on the night of March 31, 1848, Maggie and Katie began to clap their hands and were answered by rappings imitating the pattern of their claps. The rappings, later witnessed by neighbors, resolved into alphabetical messages that allegedly came from Charles Rosa, a peddler who claimed to have been murdered for his money by a former occupant of the house and to have been buried in the cellar. Some human remains were, in fact, found in the cellar, as John Fox subsequently maintained.

The phenomenon became very popular, and the two sisters, who then went to stay with their elder sister, Leah, in Rochester, began to give public demonstrations of their ability to communicate with the spirit world. They were soon followed by other **mediums,** and they provided a fertile ground for a new way of looking at life and a new "religious" movement, during a period in which mesmerism and Swedenbörgianism were already very popular.

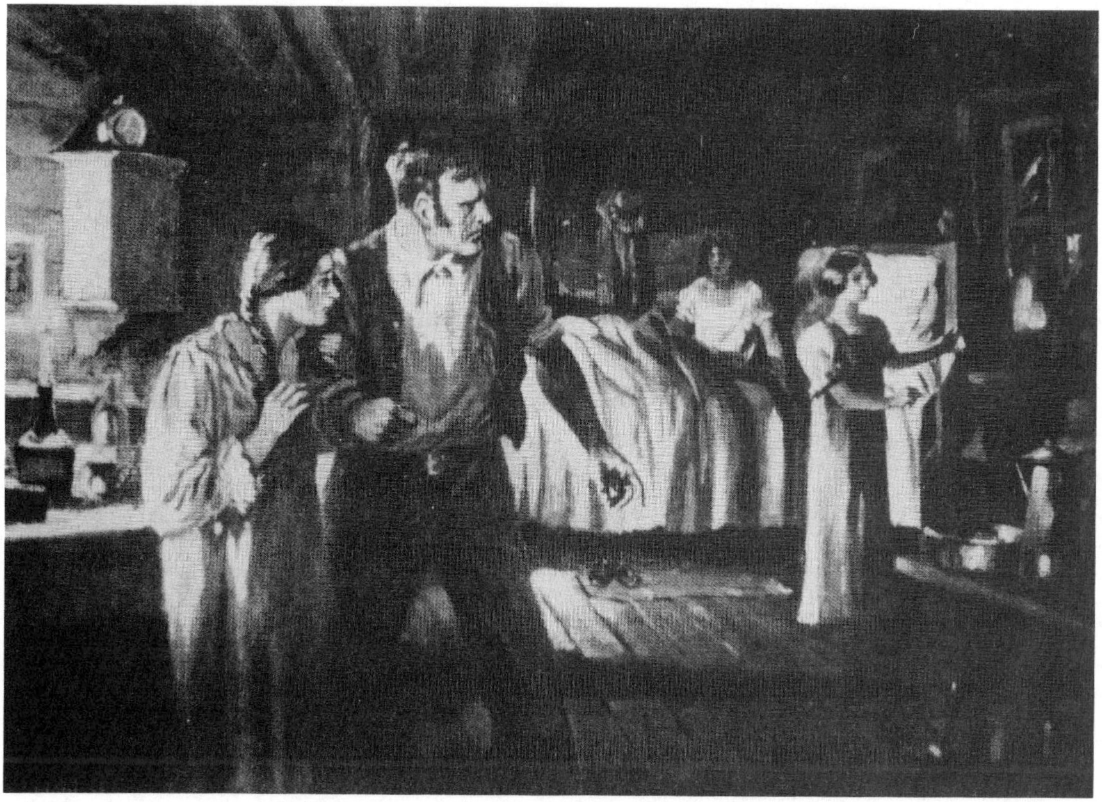

KATIE FOX RECEIVES AN ANSWER TO ONE OF HER SIGNALS. (FROM A DRAWING BY S. DRIGIN.) COURTESY OF THE ARC.

Leah became the manager of Maggie and Kate, who toured many cities and held séances in parlors, charging fees. During their elaborate performances, tables moved, objects materialized, and spirits joined in. Their fame, however, began to decline by 1855, when Maggie and Kate were facing the problem of alcoholism. They were then abandoned by Leah, who, after remarrying, retired from the stage acts.

Performances became irregular due to drinking, and investigations of fraud increased. Maggie herself denounced Spiritualism as a fraud during a public appearance in 1888, during which she confessed that the rappings were created by toe cracking. The confession was later recanted, however.

After their deaths, both in the early 1890s, a skeleton buried in the cellar of their cottage was discovered, and was claimed by Spiritualists to be the proof of the truth of the Fox sisters' early phenomena, although critics maintained that the human remains probably had been planted.

Sources:

Brandon, Ruth. *The Spiritualists.* New York: Alfred A. Knopf, 1983.

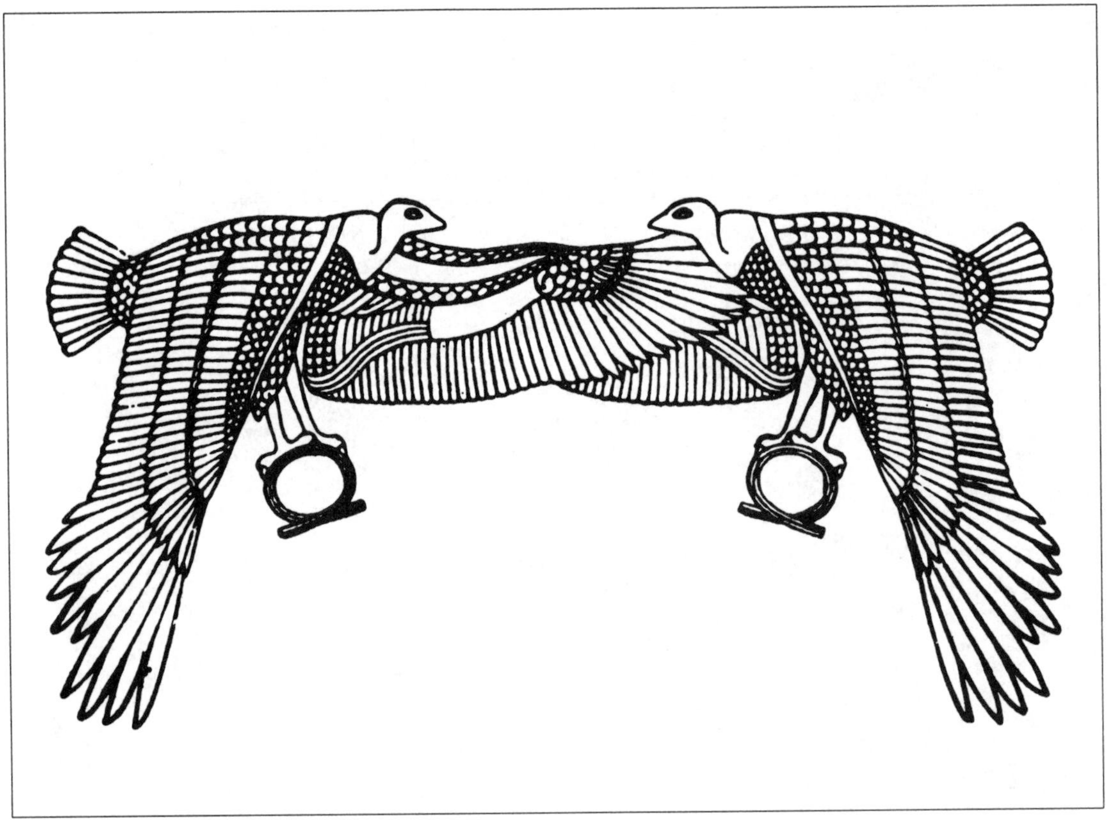

VULTURES: EGYPTIAN FUNERAL BIRDS.

Jackson, Herbert G., Jr. *The Spirit Rappers.* Garden City, NY: Doubleday, 1972.
Moore, R. Laurence. *In Search of White Crows.* New York: Oxford University Press, 1977.

FUNERAL RITES

Traditionally, the aim of funeral rites throughout the world has been to secure a good afterlife for the deceased, to console the survivors through a period of mourning, and to reestablish the order (social and/or cosmic) that has been disrupted by someone's death. Although ancient practices have evolved and changed under the pressures of modernity and secularization, funeral rites still carry the symbolism of a rite of passage to another dimension.

Rituals of purification over the dead person are universally practiced to secure a positive afterlife destiny. With variations in different cultures, this usually involves washing and dressing the corpse. (If not carried out properly, the spirit of the departed is thought to suffer in some way in the afterlife.) Afterward, the corpse is displayed, again in myriad cultural variations, for the mourners' wake. During this occasion the mourners pray, referring to the dead's journey in the afterlife. In some cultures mourners provide food or offer sacrifices, either at the time of wake or upon burial. A common meal is typically organized in some non-Western cultures in order for the mourners to be together, and in some cases to be with the dead, who also somehow participate at the banquet (a plate or a seat is designated for the deceased, for instance).

Finally, many cultures introduce methods to preserve the body from decay (e.g., mummification, the coffin), whereas others enhance the decomposition, for example, by exposing the corpse to dogs (in Tibet) or to vultures (a practice of the Zoroastrians). The process of mummification, used in ancient Egypt and in precolonial South America, was developed to ensure immortality of their royal figures. Burial of the dead in cemeteries, in various positions and orientations, religiously represents a return to mother earth. A common alternative to burial since the early stages of civilization has been cremation.

Sources:

Eliade, Mircea, ed. *Encyclopedia of Religion.* 16 vols. New York: Macmillan, 1987.
Smart, Ninian. *The Religious Experience of Mankind.* 3d ed. New York: Charles Scribner's Sons, 1984.

G

Ghost Dance

Since the beginning of European colonization of America in the seventeenth century, native Americans developed a resistance ideology that was reflected in emergent millennial religious systems. These new religions partially integrated and partially rejected the values of the invaders. The prophets Popé (of the Tewa tribe) and Neolin (a Delaware) were the earliest formulators of such systems of millennialist resistance.

In 1890 Wovoka (a.k.a. Jack Wilson), a **shaman** (''medicine man'') who had received a millenarian revelation, began teaching what became known as the Ghost Dance of 1890. The dance was an attempt to evoke the dead, whose return to the realm of the living would be accompanied by reinstitution of the pre–Anglo-American world. Influenced by the Christian religion of the invaders, the dance was a syncretistic blend of shamanistic elements (e.g., evocation of spirits, a trance state) other indigenous practices (e.g., the Paiute round dance), and Christian values (e.g., prohibitions against drunkenness, murder, adultery, and lying) and concepts (e.g., an eschatological expectation of salvation). From its place of origin in the Plains, the practice of the ghost dance spread to other tribes, both to the west and the east. The large-scale practice of the ghost dance ended tragically in the massacre at Wounded Knee, South Dakota, where native American men, women, and children were killed indiscriminately in the same year, 1890.

Sources:

Kehoe, Alice Beck. *The Ghost Dance: Ethnohistory and Revitalization.* New York: Holt, Rinehart and Winston, 1989.

Lewis, James R. "American Indian Prophets." In Timothy Miller, ed., *When Prophets Die: The Postcharismatic Fate of New Religious Movements.* Albany: State University of New York Press, 1991.

Mooney, James. *The Ghost-Dance Religion and the Sioux Outbreak of 1890.* Chicago: University of Chicago Press, 1965. (Originally published 1896.)

GHOST HUNTING

Ghost hunting is the investigation of such alleged phenomena as ghosts, apparitions, and poltergeists. Often, apparently supernatural manifestations have natural explanations, such as tricks of light and shadow, hallucinations, peculiar atmospheric conditions, geological or electromagnetic influences, and animal noises.

A set of guidelines for such investigations was established by the **Society for Psychic Research,** which defined haunting phenomena as unaccountable movements of objects, unaccountable noises and smells, apparitions, mysterious lights and shadows, unaccountable touches and pushes, unaccountable feelings of heat and cold, and feelings of fear and horror of unseen presences. Possible natural causes of these phenomena, may be mechanical (such as machinery vibrations, lights, and the like) or personal (subconscious or deliberate effects caused by people). The effects are considered paranormal when, once all possible natural causes have been eliminated through an accurate examination, members of the scientific community agree that they are not caused by ordinary means.

The basic investigative techniques include describing, detecting, and experimenting with the observed phenomena. Observation may involve everything from eyewitness accounts to the psychic testimony of a medium—the value of which varies widely among investigators—to see if their impressions coincide. Detection techniques include such procedures as securing rooms and objects to test their disturbance, setting up electronic surveillance equipment, and spreading flour, sugar, or sand on floors to detect footprints.

The book *The Most Haunted House in England,* published in 1940, includes the results of the ghost investigations made by Harry H. Price, who was among the first to use modern technologies, steel tape measures, still cameras, remote-control movie cameras, fingerprinting equipment, telescopes, and portable telephones.

Despite the techniques and the great precautions taken by investigators, ghost hunting is still considered imprecise by critics, and scientists have little knowledge about the nature and laws of hauntings.

Sources:

Bletzer, June G. *The Donning International Encyclopedic Psychic Dictionary.* Norfolk, VA: Donning, 1986.
Guiley, Rosemary Ellen. *The Encyclopedia of Ghosts and Spirits.* New York: Facts on File, 1992.
Shepard, Leslie A., ed. *Encyclopedia of Occultism & Parapsychology.* Detroit, MI: Gale Research, 1991.

GHOSTS

Belief in the existence of ghosts is found throughout history and in all cultures. Etymologically, *ghost* is linked to the German word *Geist,* meaning spirit, thus indicating a broader connotation for the root word than for its derivative. In fact, ghosts have been viewed variously as souls, as breath, and as good and evil, to name a few. Most cultures have believed ghosts to be souls of the dead that have returned from the afterlife to the living world for a variety of reasons, such as avenging their own deaths, reclaiming their goods, accomplishing some unfinished task, revealing some sort of truth, or protecting their families.

In more traditional cultures, particularly in Africa, ghosts have sometimes been considered cruel spirits that steal children. In other cultures, a lonely, wandering ghost may be the restless soul of someone who committed suicide, of a woman who died giving birth, or of someone paying a nocturnal visit to the grave of a loved one who died tragically. Also, in some cultures those who, for whatever reasons, did not receive the traditional burial rites remain in a restless, wandering state as ghosts. Where there is cult of the ancestors, as, for example, in traditional Chinese culture, the existence of ghosts is a given.

In the West, the appearance of ghosts has usually been considered frightening, an indication of evil, or demonic forces. In eastern Europe, much of the popular lore concerns ghosts that come back to attack the living in the form of vampires. In Indian culture, both Hinduism and Buddhism acknowledge some sort of ghosts. Like evil spirits, they haunt cemeteries and live in trees. Certain festival days are occasions for casting off evil forces, such as those embodied by ghosts. Those who die a violent death need particular funeral rites to cast off the evil energy. In Burmese Buddhism, the ghost stage is the third of four stages achieved by a dead person (after being an animal and a demon), immediately preceding the next reincarnation.

Within Christianity, the Holy Ghost, often depicted as a dove, represents the Spirit of God, which empowers human beings. On the other side of the coin, the practice of **exorcism** to cast out evil demonic spirits dates back to biblical times. Some of the practices of shamans and other healers also aimed to cast out evil entities that had possessed a sick person.

A new approach to ghosts developed in the nineteenth century with the birth of **Spiritualism,** which advocates use of **Mediums** (intermediaries who communicate with the spirits) to help ghosts, thought to be souls of the dead, often confused and trapped somewhere, to find their way out.

Although it is typically believed that ghosts appear at night, there are many traditions in which they make daylight or twilight appearances. Various theories have been offered to explain the phenomenon of ghosts, the most widely accepted proposing that they are tricks of light and shade or one's imagination. Psychological theories tend to explain ghosts as dreams, projections of one's subconscious, or hallucinations.

Sources:

Cavendish, Richard, ed. *Encyclopedia of the Unexplained: Magic, Occultism and Parapsychology.* London: Arkana Penguin Books, 1989.

Shepard, Leslie A., ed. *Encyclopedia of Occultism & Parapsychology.* Detroit, MI: Gale Research, 1991.

GILGAMESH

Humanity is thought to have made the transition from tribal life-styles to the more complex forms of social organization we call civilization along four great river basins located in China, India, Egypt, and the Middle East, along the Tigris and Euphrates Rivers. The Middle Eastern basin (in modern Iraq), which hosted a series of sequentially related civilizations that together we refer to as **Mesopotamia,** is the oldest of these four, antedating the high culture of Egypt by thousands of years.

The Mesopotamians wrote on clay tablets, many of which have survived to the present. This ancient literature contains, among other compositions, *The Epic of Gilgamesh.* This epic, which is humankind's oldest recorded hero tale (dating from at least 2000 B.C.), is built around the quest of Gilgamesh, a legendary king who ruled the city-state of Uruk around 2600 B.C. for immortality. Said to be the son of the goddess Ninsun and king Lugalbanda, Gilgamesh was not exempt from mortality despite his divine heritage on his mother's side.

The first part of the epic relates the events leading up to Gilgamesh's meeting with Enkidu. Enkidu, who begins life as a naked wild man, is eventually tamed and becomes Gilgamesh's best friend. Together they travel off and slay Humbaba, the giant of the pine forest. The triumphant Gilgamesh is so attractive that the goddess of love herself, Ishtar, proposes that she and the young king become lovers. Gilgamesh responds by recounting the ill fortune her previous partners have met with and rejects her proposal. Ishtar does not take the rebuff very well; in fact, she is so upset that she persuades the Bull of Heaven to come down from the sky and punish Uruk. Gilgamesh and Enkidu, however, make short work of the bull.

Unfortunately, slaying the Bull of Heaven evokes the ire of the gods, who decide that one of the two friends must die as punishment. They chose Enkidu for this unpleasant fate, and he sickens and eventually dies. Gilgamesh is distraught by the death of his best friend, but he also begins to consider his own mortality.

In Mesopotamian thought, the gods constructed humanity out of clay to be their servants on earth. Pragmatists, they did not bother to include an immortal soul as part of the package. The Mesopotamians thus saw the afterlife as a pale shadow of earthly life, much like the Jewish **She'ol** or the Greek **Hades.** At one point in the Gilgamesh epic, Enkidu dreams about the other world and offers the following description:

> There is the house whose people sit in darkness; dust is their food and clay their meat. They are clothed like birds with wings for covering, they see no light, they sit in darkness. I entered the house of dust and I saw the kings of the earth, their crowns put away forever. . . . (Sandars 1972, 92)

As in other cultures that buried the dead in the ground, the Mesopotamians conceived of the otherworld as being a dark, dusty, unpleasant underworld.

With this frightful vision before him, Gilgamesh resolves to set out on a quest for immortality. He has heard that the mortal man Utnapishtim (the Mesopotamian Noah) was granted immortality by the gods. To discover how Utnapishtim obtained such a favor, Gilgamesh undertakes an arduous journey. When he finally arrives, Utnapishtim relates how the gods, in a fit of anger, destroyed all of humankind in a great flood. Only the wise divinity Ea had the foresight to warn Utnapishtim, who built a great boat in which he and his family survived.

The gods quickly realize the error of their ways, but only after the fact; human beings ''feed'' the gods, and without humanity they will starve. Utnapishtim, however, is able to make the appropriate offerings, and the gods are able to eat. Out of gratitude, they grant immortality to him and his wife.

As for Gilgamesh, Utnapishtim requires that, as a test to determine his worthiness for immortality, he stay awake for a week. Gilgamesh promptly fails the test and, instead, sleeps for a week. Good host that he is, however, Utnapishtim gives Gilgamesh a ''consolation prize,'' namely, a plant with the powers of rejuvenation (the next best thing to immortality). Unfortunately, on the journey back a snake eats the plant, so Gilgamesh arrives home empty-handed.

Although his quest was a failure, Gilgamesh is able to return to Uruk and get on with the business of life. His mourning for Enkidu is finally over, and having done his best in the quest for immortality, he seems content to assume his place as a mortal man. The lesson, if there is one, seems to be that death is part of the natural order, and humans must, as a consequence, accept death as part of life and enjoy this life as best we can.

Sources:

Black, Jeremy and Anthony Green. *Gods, Demons and Symbols of Ancient Mesopotamia: An Illustrated Dictionary.* Austin: University of Texas Press, 1992.

McCall, Henrietta. *Mesopotamian Myths.* Austin: University of Texas Press, 1990.

Sandars, N. K., trans. *The Epic of Gilgamesh.* Rev. ed. New York: Penguin, 1972.

GNOSTICISM

Gnosticism was primarily a movement and school of thought prominent in the Hellenistic Mediterranean world and influenced paganism, Judaism, and Christianity. Its core teachings were that this world, and especially the human body, were the products of an evil deity—the Demiurge—who had trapped human souls in the physical world. Our true home is the absolute spirit (the *pleroma*), and hence we should reject the pleasures of the flesh as a way of escaping this prison. Unlike Christianity, in which one is saved by faith, in this school of thought one was saved by proper intellectual insight, or *gnosis.* Gnosticism in its original sense died out before the Western Middle Ages, although the term continued to be used to refer to any deviations the Church deemed excessively world-denying, or that seemed to stress mental insight over faith as the essential mode of salvation.

Although many mystery religions and other religious movements in antiquity emphasized a dualism between the body and the soul, none went to the extreme of Gnosticism. Rather than yearning for immortality in this life, the Gnostics viewed living in this world as a kind of hell. Like the southern Asian religions, which may have influenced this school of thought, Gnosticism saw human beings as trapped in a cycle of reincarnation and believed that even suicide could not release one from bondage to the flesh.

Sources:

Eliade, Mircea. *Encyclopedia of Religion.* 16 vols. New York: Macmillan, 1987.
Turner, Alice K. *The History of Hell.* New York: Harcourt Brace, 1993.

GREECE (ANCIENT CLASSICAL)

The religion of classical Greece is famous for its humanistic orientation. For the first time, the gods were pictured as naturalistic human beings, not as beast-persons nor even as stylized persons. Greek gods were, for the most part, like very beautiful, capricious people, albeit immortal and superhumanly powerful. Their lives, filled with loves, jealousies, and rivalries, were analogous in many ways to the lives led by ordinary people. Although serious followers of the gods needed to pay the proper attention through various sacrifices and rituals so as not to commit offense, these gods did not project primarily fearful images. Greek religion, like the rest of Greek life, was concerned with the exploration of human capacities, and was suffused with a positive, straightforward spirit. Any obstacles to be overcome were handled by human strength, discipline, and virtue. Magic was largely absent in classical Greece; the mythical hero Hercules freed the land of monsters by the power of his humanity—writ large, of course.

The Greeks, in making the gods in their own image, saw nothing in the nature of things to make one cower in fear or to feel subject to otherworldly demands. For them, the dark forest contained playful nymphs, not horrible dangers. Stories were told of only two witches, Circe and Medea, and they both were young and beautiful. Neither was the world of the dead something to be feared. The focus of Greek life was so much on the living that the activities of the dead were of relatively little concern. In the *Odyssey,* the spirits of the dead are called "piteous," because their existence so paled in comparison to the existence of the living. Nevertheless, the dead held a certain place in the Greek imagination, and more than one concept of the afterlife was present in the popular imagination.

HOMER: The foundation for Greek classical religion was set in the Homeric poems, the *Iliad* and the *Odyssey,* which themselves were the inheritors of older heritages from the Mycenaean-Minoan culture. The Minoan civilization on the island of Crete was known to have reached great heights of sophistication and achievement. From roughly 1800 B.C. to 1200 B.C. the Minoans had one of the freest and most artistic cultures in the world. Their leader was known as minos (similar to the title of pharaoh), and he oversaw a society in which women and men had a general social parity. The chief deity was the Mother Goddess, who brought both good and evil, but she was not feared because even the apparent evil was understood to be part of the natural cycle of things. This included death, which was believed to be essential for new life. The Mother Goddess herself was ruler of the nether regions and thus a key element in the cult of the dead. At Argos she was known as Hera (the Lady), at Eleusis she was known as Demeter (Mother Earth), at Sparta she was Orthia, and at Ephesus she was Artemis.

The epic poem the *Iliad,* dating to about 800 B.C. and traditionally assigned to the authorship of Homer, signals the ascendancy of the Olympian gods brought by the Hellenic people and the submerging of the cult of the Great Mother. Aspects of her religion that continued in classical Greece, aside from the co-opting of the mother figures for the Greek pantheon, include the relatively benign nature of the gods and the nonterrifying nature of death. The Homeric gods lived on Mt. Olympus, a peak in northern Greece. Zeus, a sky god from Indo-European sources, was, at least theoretically, the chief of the gods.

The Olympian gods served as the national pantheon of Greece, the gods that all Greeks shared in common. Each local area also had a regulated worship of a parochial deity, and this is where the religion of the average person was probably most intensely felt. This local deity may have been a heroic figure who, after death, was venerated as a protector. If the hero died away from the area, it was thus important to recover his remains and bury them in a locally accessible tomb.

Perhaps because the local deities remained local, the Greeks were remarkably free of ties to powerful religious institutions. In the *Odyssey,* when the hero Odysseus is begged by a priest and a poet to spare their lives, he kills the priest without a thought, but spares the poet as someone who had been given his art by the gods. The poet, in other words, had more influence in the divine realm than the priest. Homer thought that priests were relatively unimportant, and in no sense did he show them to be a vital means of easing the transition from this life to the next. He seemed to imply that people could accomplish whatever rites were necessary for themselves, as in Book XI of the *Odyssey,* where Odysseus needed to seek advice from a seer in the land of the dead. To do this, he sailed to the far west (in several cultures this is where the sun "dies" daily, thus the location of the land of the dead) and upon reaching land made a sacrifice of sheep covered with honey, milk, water, and wine. The sacrifice brought forth some ghosts (or shades) of the dead, who were able to converse with Odysseus only after drinking the blood of the sheep.

For several reasons, including the limited power of the priests, the psychological distance between local worship and the Olympic gods, and the increasingly secular Greek outlook, the Greeks had a surprising ease in their relationships with the gods, and even felt comfortable laughing at some of their antics. Zeus, who was constantly trying to keep his extramarital affairs secret from his wife, Hera, was an excellent source of comedy. The one god who tended not to be a topic of easy conversation was **Hades** (or Pluto), a brother of Zeus who ruled over the land of the dead with his wife,

Persephone. This region was called the House of Hades, which after the classical period was shortened to Hades. The god Hades was not feared in the sense that in death there was judgment and retribution (although acceptance of this idea grew over time), but rather in the sense that being dead was not considered a very meaningful existence. Homer had the shade of Achilles tell Odysseus that he would rather be a peasant serf on earth than a king among the dead.

The House of Hades was pictured as a large cavern somewhere under the earth or in the far west beyond the river Oceanus. It was not a happy place, but shrouded in mist and darkness, and figures moved about as in a dream. Hades was separated from the land of the living by five rivers—Lethe (the river of forgetfulness), Styx, Phlegethon, Acheron, and Cocytus. The entrance was guarded by **Cerberus,** a terrifying dog with three heads and serpents around each neck. The psyche (or life essence, shade, or ghost) of the deceased would leave the dead body and travel to that place to lead a pallid, weak, melancholy existence. Heroes might be able to continue, in a reflective way, activities of the previous life.

Hades was not a **heaven** or **hell,** but a place that almost everyone went to regardless of their behavior on earth. The *Iliad* does offer the belief that gods punished or rewarded souls at death, but the mythology is not consistent about this. Occasionally mentioned are the Elysian Fields, or Isles of the Blessed, a wonderful, pleasurable place where certain special people get to go. This would seem to indicate, after all, a system of rewards and punishments, but its few inhabitants tended to be people who were simply chosen by the gods rather than people who "deserved" it. Menelaus, for example, was not particularly virtuous or heroic, but was able to enter the Elysian Fields because he was Helen's husband and the son-in-law of Zeus. Some shades suffered in Hades, not so much because of a judgment on their life, but because they were not properly buried or nourished by sacrificial food offerings. In the story of Tantalos in the *Odyssey,* every time he reached for fruit, ravenously hungry, the wind would blow the fruit away; every time, desperately thirsty, he sought water, it would evaporate.

The Homeric poems provided the classical Greek period with a generally understood and accepted idea of how the afterlife worked. Basically, the vital part of a person survived death and continued an existence of sorts in the House of Hades, which was under the earth or far to the West. If funeral rites were not held, the spirit might not make it to the land of the dead and would be doomed to a nonexistence. (In the *Iliad,* for instance, the ghost of Patroclus asked Achilles to bury his body for that reason.) The shade of the deceased was believed to have no physical body, but retained recognizable features of its former self. A spirit could sometimes be contacted, particularly if it was a troubled spirit (e.g., the victim of murder) in the immediate vicinity of the tomb. In this case an offering such as food or drink might gain its assistance or appease it and turn it from causing mischief.

PLAYWRIGHTS: The playwrights of classical Greece (especially around the fifth century B.C.) were the primary interpreters of their culture's mythic heritage, and they were by no means restricted to images of the afterlife provided by Homer or

Hesiod. The authors felt free to combine these images with local practices or change things altogether to suit their purposes. There was no hint of treating the *Iliad* or *Odyssey* as sacred texts containing ideas that must not be altered in any way. Indeed, the playwrights introduced a steady stream of changes in the concept of the afterlife, particularly with regard to differentiation between the virtuous and the sinner. Even in Homer there are a few references to the more notorious evildoers receiving punishment in the hereafter. With this idea also grew the idea of a more ethically conscious and consistent Zeus. This Zeus gradually displaced the amoral, capricious, often comic Zeus, until finally Dio Chrysostom described him in the second century A.D. as "Our Zeus, the giver of every good gift, the common father and saviour and guardian of mankind" (Hamilton 1961, 14).

There were numerous scenes in Greek tragedies that involved **necromancy,** or consultation of the dead. Many Greek theaters in fact had tunnels running from behind the stage building to a trapdoor in the orchestra so that an actor could appear to rise from beneath the earth, or the land of the dead. In *The Persians,* by Aeschylus, Darius is called forth from the dead by means of offerings of wine, milk, honey, and other libations at his tomb. Darius is not presented as an omniscient being, and in fact he has to be brought up to date on the events that have transpired and must be told why he has been called upon. He then is able to offer some prophecies and words of wisdom. In the story of the tragic Agamemnon and his family, told in a trio of plays by Aeschylus, much is made of the belief that the victim of murder can call for vengeance from the grave. Agamemnon and his mistress, Cassandra, are murdered by Agamemnon's wife, Clytemnestra. She in turn is murdered by their son, Orestes, who has called upon the aid of Agamemnon's spirit, or *daimon,* and of the Furies, who are supposed to avenge such blood crimes. *Eumenides,* the last of the Agamemnon trinity of plays by Aeschylus, gives evidence of further development of the idea that the afterlife involves moral judgment. Clytemnestra, in death, calls upon the Furies to avenge her, even while complaining that the other spirits avoid her as a murderer. This suggests that even though the evil and the virtuous end up in the same place, it may be a very lonely place for the former. In the same play the statement is made that "the Lord of Death (Hades) is mighty in holding mortals to account beneath the earth, and he surveyeth all things with his recording mind" (North 1992, 63, n. 3). This places Hades in the role of moral judge of the dead and creates the expectation of varied treatment of their souls depending on the conduct of their life on earth.

Some playwrights underscored the importance of proper burial. In *Ajax,* by Sophocles, the hero Ajax tries to kill Odysseus and other leaders who are mounting an attack on Troy. Failing in his plans, Ajax commits suicide. His brother wants to arrange a burial, but others try to prevent it. Finally, it is left to Odysseus to decide, and he votes for burial. The grand scale of Odysseus's character was thus shown, as he would not let personal enmity get in the way of providing this ritual. It was not considered simply human decency, but the will of the gods. If the body was not properly tended to, it might contaminate offerings to the gods, and the gods would seek retribution. Improper care of the body was not, apparently, something that the deceased could or would take vengeance for on their own.

In *Alcestis,* by Euripides, the heroine, Alcestis, has volunteered to die in place of her husband, King Admetus, that he might escape, at least temporarily, the death date set for him by fate. Her preparations for death include a ritual bath, a prayer to Hestia (the spirit of the hearth) on behalf of her children, that they may be happy, and a farewell to family and friends. She describes a vision of **Charon,** ferryman of the dead, who is calling out to her impatiently, and finally she dies. These scenes include stock elements with which the audience would likely have been familiar. Euripides then injects into the story a surprise dramatic element: Hercules, grateful to King Admetus for earlier favors, decides to save Alcestis. He goes to the tomb to confront Death (Thanatos). In his words, ''I sprang and caught him in my hands'' (North 1992, 56). At the end of a successful struggle, Hercules was able to take Alcestis back to a grateful Admetus.

MYSTERY RELIGIONS: Homeric mythology was adapted by the mystery religions and mixed with secret rituals so as to provide a personal dimension to religion not available in the traditional practices and beliefs. The two most important mystery religions were the Orphic and **Eleusinian mysteries.** In Greek mythology, Orpheus was the son of Calliope, a muse, and his singing to the lyre could charm animals and even rocks and trees. When his wife, Eurydice, died, he was permitted to lead her back from Hades, provided he did not turn to look at her until they arrived safely in the upper world. He did look at her, however, and she had to return to Hades.

Because Orpheus was one of the few figures in Greek mythology to visit Hades and return safely, he became symbolic for many of the possibility of new life after death. He was also known for sexual purity, which gave him an aura of asceticism. The Orphic mysteries claimed Orpheus as their founder because his story seemed to fit the message of their version of the Dionysian myth. Dionysus was the god of wine and fertility, and in the sixth and fifth centuries B.C. was the center of a cult known for its violent, ecstatic, and orgiastic rites. This notion of Dionysus was quite the opposite of the Orphic orientation, however.

The Orphic mysteries identified Dionysus with Zagreus, the son of Persephone and Zeus. In one story, Zeus wished for Zagreus to rule the world but was opposed in this by the Titans, an ancient race of giant gods. They killed Zagreus and ate him, and in retaliation Zeus sent lightning bolts that burned all the Titans to ashes. The human race was then formed from those ashes, which meant that humans are partly bad (the Titans' ashes) and partly good (Zagreus's ashes). But this was not the end of Zagreus. The goddess Athena managed to rescue his heart from the Titans and returned it to Zeus. Zeus swallowed the heart and Zagreus was later reborn as the son of the earth goddess Semele, with whom Zeus was having a relationship. Through union with Zagreus (Dionysus), the once dead, now reborn god, humans could also hope for a rebirth after death.

Because the activities of the mystery religions were secret, we know few details of their beliefs. However, the Orphic cult (active by at least the sixth century B.C.) emphasized a body–soul dualism and urged followers to liberate themselves from dependence on their bodies through various ascetic practices, particularly abstention from eating meat. This approach was summarized in the famous Orphic phrase *soma sema* (the body is a tomb). Unlike the mainstream of classical Greek life, Orphic followers believed that existence in this world was inherently troubled and sorrowful and life in the next world was to be preferred. The next world was not necessarily the last, since the Orphics believed in **reincarnation.** In the process of reincarnation the soul would be judged and the next life would reflect a reward or punishment. If, however, a soul were advanced enough to lead a pure life and faithfully follow all the ascetic rituals, it might be possible, they believed, to exit the cycle and return to its original divine state. This was the ultimate goal.

The actual number of Orphic devotees was rather small, but they had an impact on Greek philosophy and culture far beyond their numbers. A similar impact, from a much larger devotee base, came from the Eleusinian mysteries. The myth of this cult focused on Demeter, the vegetation deity. Her daughter, Kore, was carried off by Hades, ruler of the dead. Demeter, not knowing where Kore was, searched through many lands for her, growing ever more despondent. She finally arrived at Eleusis, on the Attica coast not far from Athens, and refused to allow anything to flower or bear fruit. The devastation produced by the barren landscape was so terrible that the gods persuaded Zeus to retrieve Kore from the underworld. Hermes was sent to accomplish the task, and Hades relented, but not before persuading Kore to eat a pomegranate, symbolic of marriage and a promise of return. This trickery forced Zeus into a compromise, by which Kore would have to spend one-third (or one-half, depending on the source) of each year in the underworld, the part of the year when Demeter is once again sorrowful and nothing grows. Thus did Kore, a fertility figure by relation to Demeter, become identified with Persephone, the wife of Hades and a figure of death.

The main festival of the Eleusinian mysteries was held in the fall and lasted many days. Beginning with a procession from Athens, the rituals and ceremonies revolving around re-enactments of the myth were designed to have a powerful psychological and spiritual effect. Only the initiates, or *mystae,* were allowed to experience the inner secrets of the mysteries, which were closely guarded. The autumn festival grew so popular that by the late fifth century B.C. it was open to the entire Greek world and was basically incorporated into the religion of the city-state of Athens. The ultimate point of the cult was to enable the follower to identify with Kore so as to become one with the processes of life and death, with the promise of immortality.

PHILOSOPHERS: Further consideration of the nature of death and the afterlife was provided by the philosophers. It is not known how many Greeks followed any particular school of philosophy, but many of the philosophers' views had far-reaching influence. The philosophers offered a very different means of thinking about death and afterlife issues, as their starting point was not mythology but observation or logic. The atomists, such as Democritus, believed that the universe is composed of different combinations and kinds of atoms, themselves indestructible. At death, they claimed, there is no personal continuation of any kind because the atoms simply disperse, eventually joining other groups of atoms in forming other animals or objects.

Pythagoras, in the sixth century B.C., promoted a mixture of philosophy and religion, and his beliefs shared some characteristics with the Orphic mysteries. Pythagoras migrated from Samos to Croton in southern Italy and established a philosophical/religious community. He taught that in order to pursue the contemplative life (the highest good), one must deny the powers and distractions of the flesh. He drew sharp distinctions between spirit and matter, harmony and discord, good and evil. He also taught reincarnation (metempsychosis) as the path pursued by the eternal soul, and even claimed to remember all of his incarnations. The story was told, probably by a satirist, that Pythagoras once cried out to someone, ''Stop beating that dog—I recognize him by his voice as a friend of mine!'' (Werblowsky 1989, 23). Pythagoras was undoubtedly a powerful force in making dualism and reincarnation legitimate philosophical/ religious options (if minority ones) in the Greek culture. Empedocles in the following century announced his belief in reincarnation, stating, ''I have been a boy and a girl, a bush and a bird and a dumb sea-fish'' (North 1992, 57).

Socrates, whom we know only through **Plato,** insisted that the most important aim in life is the care of the soul, even if one does not know for sure what the end of life might bring. In his *Apology* to the court that was about to sentence him (in 399 B.C.) to death for corrupting the youth of Athens with his new teachings, Socrates (according to Plato) declared as follows:

> To be afraid of death is only another form of thinking that one is wise when one is not; it is to think that one knows what one does not know. No one knows with regard to death whether it is not really the greatest blessing that can happen to a man (Hamilton and Cairns, 1961, 15).

Elsewhere in the *Apology,* Socrates muses about the possibilities beyond the grave. If there is only nothingness, what is so wrong with that? If, on the other hand, one can meet and converse with the spirits of the dead, especially the great minds and heroes, what a wonderful prospect! At the end of his defense, Socrates states that it ''is certain that nothing can harm a good man either in life or after death, and his fortunes are not a matter of indifference to the gods'' (p. 25), suggesting that he was, after all, hopeful that the hemlock would not have the final word.

As with Socrates, Plato's final stance on the existence and nature of the afterlife is hard to ascertain. His discussions of the issues of immortality and the afterlife always had a conversational, rather than declaratory, style. In his explorations of the world, he freely used traditional myths, stories, metaphors, and his own imagination to spark ideas. Plato did believe that ideas are immortal, and that the soul is like ideas and therefore also immortal. As Hamilton and Cairns put it, ''Plato thus clearly believed in the imperishability of the soul *(psyche)* as the activating principle of change. Physical objects come and go but the activating power of Being is constant''

according to their actions. Thus, for example, if someone is generous with money, she will eventually be rewarded with comparable recompense, either in this lifetime or in a future lifetime. This understanding of karma is very old and is fundamental to such religious traditions as **Hinduism** and **Buddhism.**

Group karma is a more recent term that can be applied to any kind of group or association, although it is most often applied to nation-states. The basic idea of group karma is the same as individual karma, except that it is applied to the actions of groups, which are rewarded or punished according to past actions. This idea modifies the notion of karma to explain such events as great disasters. Rather than saying that everyone killed during a great earthquake, for instance, must have individually had that fate written in their karmic record, one can assert that the disaster was the fate of a particular geographical area, and that many individuals in the area died simply as a result of their membership in the larger community.

The term *group karma* has also been applied to groups of people who reincarnate together in particular areas and time periods. The idea is that, as a result of the karmic complexities arising from interactions in prior lifetimes, people who have been together before must return together in order to balance out the ''karmic bankbook.'' These groups can be as small as single nuclear families or as large as entire towns.

Sources:

Guiley, Rosemary Ellen. *The Encyclopedia of Ghosts and Spirits.* New York: Facts on File, 1992.
Shepard, Leslie A. *Encyclopedia of Occultism & Parapsychology.* Detroit, MI: Gale Research, 1984.

GROUP SOUL

The expression *group soul* may refer to more than one notion. In the case of a group of people who, because of past **karmic** interactions, tend to reincarnate together lifetime after lifetime, one may speak of the shared destiny of the group. In this case, the group of distinct individuals is being regarded as a self-contained spiritual unit.

A more unusual notion is that two or more individuals who seem distinct because they occupy separate bodies have, in fact, but one soul among them. In more sophisticated formulations, this single group soul is conceived of as having several different aspects or facets, each of which incarnates in a distinct series of embodiments. (This is one of the theories behind the idea of **soul mates,** a couple who are the two halves of one soul.) The reason for such multiple embodiments is explained in different ways. If the purpose of a series of incarnations is to gain experiences that will help one to grow spiritually, then clearly the ability to enter into several different embodiments simultaneously allows one to speed up the process of spiritual growth.

Sources:
Guiley, Rosemary Ellen. *The Encyclopedia of Ghosts and Spirits.* New York: Facts on File, 1992.
Shepard, Leslie A. *Encyclopedia of Occultism & Parapsychology.* Detroit, MI: Gale Research, 1984.

GUARDIAN SPIRIT (GUARDIAN ANGEL, TUTELARY SPIRIT, SPIRIT GUIDE)

Guardian spirits, which in Western societies are called guardian angels, are a familiar concept in many cultures. The function of these tutelary spirits is to watch over and protect individuals. In some cultures, they are believed to be attached to a person from birth; in others, they are acquired later, making themselves known through a vision or dream. The manifestations of these spirits' guidance varies from vague ''hunches'' and intuitions to visions and audible voices. Cross-culturally, the conceptualization of the nature of tutelary spirits runs the gamut from animal spirits to the spirits of departed relatives.

Among societies in which individuals acquire guardian spirits later in life, one of the more striking traditions for seeking such guardians is the ''vision quest'' of certain native American groups. In these societies, a standard component of puberty rites (the formal transition from childhood to adulthood) is a ritual quest for a ''revelation'' (in the form of a dream or a vision) from the spirit world that gives the young person a sense of purpose or vocation for adult life. This ritual sometimes involves treks into the wilderness where questing individuals fast or engage in other activities likely to bring on visionary experiences. As part of their vision, initiates often acquire spirit helpers—helpers who are animal spirits, deceased relatives, or personifications of the forces of nature. This link-up (meeting the spirit guardian) may be conceived of as a new encounter or as the ultimate realization of a relationship that had existed since birth.

Shamans, who may find their vocation during their adolescent vision quest—or, later, during a separate encounter with the otherworld—often have many spirit helpers. These helpers run the gamut, from animal spirits to the spirits of departed shamans. With respect to animal helpers (one's *power animals,* to use contemporary terminology) the relationship may be a totemic one, meaning that the initiate in some way exhibits the nature of the animal; in other words, a person with an eagle spirit helper becomes ''eaglelike,'' someone with a bear helper, ''bearlike,'' and so forth.

A phenomenon with certain parallels to shamanism is contemporary **Spiritualism.** Among Spiritualists, whose religion is built around communication with the dead, one finds similar notions of spirit guides or helpers—helpers who are often, but not always, deceased relatives. Individual **mediums** (people with exceptional sensitivity to the otherworld) often have many guides, much as the shaman has many spirit helpers. Despite this multiplicity, mediums usually have one principal spirit—a master guide or ''control''—who regulates contact with other spirits, and who thus serves as a kind of guardian spirit for the medium.

Sources:

Eliade, Mircea, ed. *Encyclopedia of Religion.* 16 vols. New York: Macmillan, 1987.

Guiley, Rosemary Ellen. *The Encyclopedia of Ghosts and Spirits.* New York: Facts on File, 1992.

Hultkrantz, Ake. *Conceptions of the Soul Among North American Indians.* Stockholm: Ethnographic Museum of Sweden, 1953.

H

Hades

Hades originally referred to the Greek god of the underworld and king of the dead. Later, Hades became, by extension, the name of the land of the dead itself. Hades the god was the son of Rhea and Chronos. After defeating the Titans (a family of giants who ruled the earth), Hades and his brothers, Zeus and Poseidon, divided the world among themselves. Poseidon received the seas, Zeus the sky, and Hades the underworld. Considered so unfortunate that even the mention of his name was regarded as unlucky, the god of the underworld is rarely the subject of mythological tales. The only narrative of any length is the story of his abduction of Persephone and their subsequent marriage.

The daughter of Zeus and Demeter, Persephone was exceptionally beautiful. To protect her, Demeter kept Persephone isolated on the island of Sicily. With the consent of his brother, Zeus, Hades kidnapped Persephone while she was picking flowers and took her off to the underworld. When Demeter finally discovered her daughter's whereabouts, she demanded that Persephone be returned to the earth. Persephone had eaten food while in the underworld (a few pomegranate seeds), however, which prevented her from ever being entirely free of the underworld. Distraught over the loss of her daughter, Demeter, who was a goddess of fertility, grain, and the harvest, neglected to perform her divine tasks, and the earth became barren. The dispute between Hades and Demeter was finally resolved when they agreed that Persephone would spend half of the year with her mother and half with her husband. This arrangement was said to explain the seasons; fall and winter occur when Persephone is with her husband (and Demeter mourns), and spring and summer when she is reunited with her mother.

Although Hades and his realm are grim, the Greek god of the underworld bears little resemblance to the Devil who rules over a fiery Hell in the traditional Christian

HADES.

concept. With the exception of the heroes granted immortality by the gods, the realm of Hades is the destination of all the departed, whether good or evil. The Greek underworld is more like a musty closet than a furnace; it is a dark, sterile, and humorless realm, where the departed wander about aimlessly as shades of their former selves—the dead seem more devitalized and bored than tormented.

Sources:

Grant, Michael, and John Hazel. *Who's Who in Classical Mythology.* New York: Oxford University Press, 1993.

Tripp, Edward. *The Meridian Handbook of Classical Mythology.* New York: New American Library, 1970.

HALLOWEEN

All Hallow's Eve (All Hallow E'en), also known as Halloween, is a pagan festival of fire, the dead, and the powers of darkness. It is celebrated on October 31, the night before the Christian festival of All Hallows' or All Saints' Day, which commemorates the saints and martyrs and was first introduced in the seventh century. On November 2,

Roman Catholics celebrate All Souls' Day and pray for rest and peace for the souls of the departed.

Bonfires are one of the rituals of Halloween, symbolically retaining the light and warmth of summer and early autumn in contrast with cold winter. The origins of Halloween are in the ancient four great fire festivals of Britain, which used to take place on the first of November. Halloween is still known in Ireland as Samhein or La Samon (the Feast of the Sun) from the name of one of the two great fire festivals of the pagan Celts—Beltane and Samhain, which marked the beginning of summer and winter, respectively.

In Scotland, Halloween is believed by some to be a night on which the invisible world has considerable power and malignant witches may be seen cleaving the air on broomsticks. Throughout Europe, Halloween has traditionally represented not only the night that marks the transition from autumn to winter but also the time of year when the souls of the departed revisit their old homes and warm themselves in the kitchen or the parlor, enjoying the company of their family and their friends. Halloween was thus a European version of the **Day of the Dead.** In many parts of Europe, and not only in Celtic countries, Halloween, as the beginning of winter, which called to mind the cold blackness of the grave, was a night in which the departed walked the countryside. Food and drink were offered to the ghosts, who passed by to the west, the direction of the dying sun.

Fairies were also believed to appear on Halloween. They were usually identified with the dead and moved from one hill to another with the music of bells and elf horns. Other dark and cold creatures, such as demons and witches, populated Halloween, and the fires helped to keep them away. People used to go from house to house, singing and dancing and wearing grotesque costumes and masks in order to keep evil away. Their appearance was also a visible representation of the ghosts and goblins that sneaked about in the night.

In the United States, Halloween has become a special occasion in which the costumes and masks have been transferred to the children, who visit their neighbors seeking a "trick or treat." They thus keep alive, although in a trivial manner, the ancient association of Halloween with demons and the souls of the dead.

Sources:

Bletzer, June G. *The Donning International Encyclopedic Psychic Dictionary.* Norfolk, VA: Donning, 1986.
Guiley, Rosemary Ellen. *The Encyclopedia of Ghosts and Spirits.* New York: Facts on File, 1992.
Kastenbaum, Robert, and Beatrice Kastenbaum. *Encyclopedia of Death.* New York: Avon, 1989.

HARROWING OF HELL

In Christian denominations that adhere to the Apostles' Creed, there is an unusual line which asserts that after Jesus was crucified, "He descended into hell." This line—obscure to most contemporary Christians but an important piece of the new faith to

CHRIST TOPPLING THE GATES OF PURGATORY. (DERIVED FROM A 13TH CENTURY FRENCH MANUSCRIPT.)

early believers—refers to the widely accepted doctrine that Christ invaded hell during the period between his death and resurrection.

As recounted in the Gospel of Nicodemus, which had been accepted on par with the other Gospels until after the New Testament was canonized, Satan arranged to imprison Jesus in hell following his execution, only to have the plan backfire. Technically, Christ harrows (violates or despoils) the **Limbo** (an intermediate containing the Old Testament patriarchs), rather than hell, as the patriarchs are merely being held as prisoners rather than being tortured in a realm of fire and sulfur. Rather than being imprisoned, Jesus does battle with Satan and his minions, defeats them, and frees everyone in hell, from Adam and Eve to Moses.

The Gospel of Nicodemus was popular long before the full development of the notion of purgatory, which eventually supplanted the idea of Limbo. Limbo had been necessary because Christians of the first few centuries of the common era imagined that only Christian souls could go to heaven. This, however, creates the problem of what happened to such righteous and deserving individuals as the Old Testament patriarchs (e.g., Abraham, Moses), who died before the Christian gospel was preached? Placing them in a Limbo realm, from which Christ later rescued them and conducted them to heaven, solved this problem.

The story of the Messiah's harrowing of hell and rescue of infernal prisoners is actually older than Christianity. In the pre-Christian Testament of the Twelve Patriarchs, for example, the future Messiah rescued captives from a hell ruled by Beliar (Baal). Later compositions, such as the Gospel of Bartholomew, the Gospel of Nicodemus, and the Teachings of Silvanus, merely placed Jesus in a role that had already been carved out in earlier narratives.

From a broader perspective, the motif of a human being descending to the underworld for the purpose of rescuing someone's soul is widespread in world culture. In particular, in shamanic cultures sick people are sometimes diagnosed as having lost their soul. The attending shaman then performs a ritual and enters a trance state in order to seek out the lost soul, which has often wandered off to the realm of the dead (often an underworld). If the rite is successful, the wandering spirit is persuaded to return, and the ill person recovers. This seems to be the cross-cultural archetype to which the story of the harrowing of hell adheres.

Sources:

Eliade, Mircea, ed. *Encyclopedia of Religion.* 16 vols. New York: Macmillan, 1987.
Eliade, Mircea. *Shamanism: Archaic Techniques of Ecstasy.* Princeton, NJ: Princeton University Press, 1964.
McDannell, Colleen, and Bernhard Lang. *Heaven: A History.* Reprint, New York: Vintage, 1990.
Turner, Alice K. *The History of Hell.* New York: Harcourt Brace, 1993.

HART, HORNELL NORRIS

The sociologist and psychical researcher Hornell Norris Hart (1888–1967) was born in St. Paul, Minnesota, of a Quaker family. He received his Ph.D. from the State University of Iowa in 1921 and later became professor of social economy and of ethics, before being appointed professor of sociology in 1938 at Duke University, where J. B. Rhine's Laboratory of Parapsychology was located.

The early death of his son Robert and his personal religious convictions stimulated Hart's interest in psychical research in general and in the question of survival after death in particular. His textbook *The Science of Social Relations* (1927) and the paper "Visions and Apparitions Collectively and Reciprocally Perceived," written with his wife and published in the *Proceedings of the Society for Psychical Research* in 1933, deal with psychical phenomena. The paper, in particular, includes quantitative analyses and comparisons of various forms of apparitions, some of which can be considered **out-of-body experiences (OBEs),** which Hart called reciprocal apparitions. Other Hart publications about OBEs and apparitions include several papers in the *Proceedings of the Society for Psychical Research* as well as the *Journal of the American Society for Psychical Research.* His 1956 paper "Six Theories about Apparitions," on the idea of a "psychic fifth dimension," is considered a classic.

During the last years of his life, Hart wrote his only book devoted entirely to psychical research, *The Enigma of Survival: The Case For and Against an After Life* (1959), in which he tried to reconcile the two points of view on the evidence of apparitions and mediumship through his "persona" theory. According to Hart, a projected "persona," (projected from the person asking questions, not from the medium) which interacts with the perception of the percipient and the unconscious of a **medium,** produces the reported effects. Therefore, what appears and attempts to communicate is not the deceased person but the projected persona. Hart also introduced the term *super-ESP,* which refers to a hypothetical ESP ability extending beyond the bounds established in laboratory experimentation or field work with everyday psychic experiences. Among his last works about psychical research are the monograph *Toward a New Philosophical Basis for Parapsychological Phenomena* (1965) and the manuscript of a book that he completed shortly before his death, "Survival After Death" (1967).

Sources:

Guiley, Rosemary Ellen. *The Encyclopedia of Ghosts and Spirits.* New York: Facts on File, 1992.
Pleasants, Helene, ed. *Biographical Dictionary of Parapsychology.* New York: Helix Press, 1964.

HAUNTING

The term *haunting,* which has the same root as *home,* refers to the manifestation of unaccountable phenomena attributed to spirits or ghosts. They usually occur where people and animals, to whom the spirits belong, used to live, or in places merely frequented by the deceased, or at the sites of violent deaths.

Hauntings may involve inexplicable apparitions, noises, smells, tactile sensations, or extremes in temperature and movement of objects. Haunting places are generally characterized by a heavy atmosphere, and the paranormal phenomena, which can be perceived only by individuals with particular psychic qualities, may last for a short period or can continue for even centuries. In hauntings that include apparitions, the ghosts are typically clothed in period costumes and usually wear the same garment at subsequent appearances. Some of them change their appearance, and others are horrific, missing some body parts.

Much scientific inquiry has been devoted to hauntings over the last hundred years, since the first investigations of the founders of the **Society for Psychical Research,** whose members proposed some definitions of haunting. **Frederic W. H. Myers,** for instance, defined *ghost* as "a manifestation of a persistent personal energy," and Eleanor Sidgwick asserted that hauntings could be considered a form of psychometry, vibrations of events and emotions contained in a house, site, or object. Other proposed theories hypothesized the inability of the spirits of the deceased to leave the earth plane.

Various techniques are employed to investigate hauntings, usually including description through eyewitness accounts, experimentation involving a medium to corroborate the accounts, and detection, by observing or recording the phenomena. Despite the accuracy of new technologies used by investigators, including various electronic devices, the interpretation of results is often subjective and inconclusive, and very little is really known about the nature of hauntings and why they happen.

Sources:

Bletzer, June G. *The Donning International Encyclopedic Psychic Dictionary.* Norfolk, VA: Donning, 1986.

Cavendish, Richard. *The Encyclopedia of the Unexplained.* New York: McGraw-Hill, 1967.

Fodor, Nandor. *An Encyclopaedia of Psychic Science.* Secaucus, NJ: The Citadel Press, 1966. (Originally published 1933.)

Heaven and Hell

Every human society draws distinctions between right and wrong. Contrary to what the human heart might wish, however, adherence to good does not always bring reward, nor does evil always result in an ignoble fate. Afterlife notions may allow for adjudication, at least at the level of the imagination, of the inequities of this life by providing a realm in which the righteous are rewarded and the wicked punished.

In societies that postulate a process of **reincarnation,** the righteous and the unrighteous may reap the fruits of their actions in future lifetimes. This possibility is most fully developed in southern Asian religious traditions, in which the principle of **karma**—the moral law of cause and effect—ensures that even the slightest credit or debit in the ''Karmic bankbook'' is balanced out before individuals are permitted to close their accounts. In **Zoroastrianism** and in the traditions influenced by Zoroastrianism (particularly **Judaism**), the dead are **resurrected** at the end of history and everyone is judged by the Supreme Deity. Subsequently, the righteous live in a renewed world and the unrighteous are snuffed out.

One of the more popular and certainly among the best-known ''solutions'' to the problem of how to adjudicate right and wrong in the afterlife is to postulate a realm of reward for the good (heaven) and a realm of punishment for evildoers (hell). This schema is often merged with a concept of the universe that pictures the cosmos as consisting of three levels: an upper world beyond the sky (above the ''heavens'') in which the gods of light dwell, a middle realm occupied by humanity, and a lower world beneath the earth in which gods of darkness reside. In certain religious traditions, particularly the familiar Western faiths, the god(s) of light became ''good'' and the gods of darkness became demons. A natural consequence of this moral division is that the realm of reward was placed in the upper world with god(s) and the realm of punishment in the lower world with the demons.

In the Christian tradition in particular, underworld devils acquire employment tormenting the souls of the damned. The popular association of hell with fire appears to originate in the linking of hell with volcanic activity, during which the ''underworld'' belches up liquid fire in the form of molten lava. And, of course, the popular image of heaven as a realm where the deceased have wings and sit around on clouds is a direct result of associating the abode of the righteous dead with the upper world.

INFERNAL PUNISHMENT FOR THE SEVEN DEADLY SINS. THE LUSTFUL ARE SMOTHERED IN FIRE AND BRIMSTONE. (FROM *LE GRANT KALENDRIER ET COMPOST DES BERGIERS*, PRINTED BY NICOLAS LE ROUGE, TROYES, 1496.)

Notions of heaven and hell realms are sometimes mixed with other possibilities. In popular **Hinduism** and **Buddhism,** for example, the notion of punishment in hell worlds (and, to a lesser extent, reward in heaven worlds) emerged to supplement—rather than supplant—earlier notions of karmic punishment. Many of the torments of Hindu and Buddhist hell worlds, such as being tortured by demons, resemble the torments of more familiar Western hells. Unlike Western hells, however, southern Asian hell worlds are not final dwelling places. They are more like **purgatories** in which sinful souls experience suffering for a limited term. After the term is over, even the most evil person is turned out of hell to once again participate in the cycle of reincarnation.

In the Christian tradition the notions of heaven and hell are mixed in a somewhat confused manner with earlier ideas about the resurrection of the body. The notion of resurrection—in which the deceased person remains in the ground until Judgment Day—was popular in Jesus' lifetime, and this is the notion of the afterlife that the founder of Christianity taught. However, the Christian tradition very early adopted the Greek idea of an eternal soul that went to a realm of punishment or a realm of reward after the body died. Hence, resurrection in later Christianity involves reuniting the soul, which obviously has to leave heaven to accomplish this purpose, with the reconstructed body on earth.

Another issue with which serious thinkers have grappled across the centuries is the fate of souls that, although not moral athletes, have nevertheless not committed outrageous sins. This has led to the development of ideas of ''intermediate'' afterlife abodes in which ''mixed'' souls are purified and made fit for heaven. Catholic purgatory is the most well known of these realms, but the same basic idea is incorporated in other ways into other traditions.

Yet another solution is to postulate a series of multiple heavens and hells, or levels of heaven and hell, in which good people and sinners are rewarded or punished according to the degree of their noble deeds or sins. One of the most well known examples of the latter is found in Dante's *Inferno.* Dante presents a picture of a complex, nine-layered hell. Virtuous but unbaptized souls reside at the top, suffering only the emotion of hopelessness. At the very bottom of hell, undergoing the worst punishment, are those who committed the very worst sin, which in Dante's ethical schemata is treason. Ranged in between is a moral hierarchy of sinners, all experiencing a punishment appropriate for their crime. Dante's heaven is somewhat different: Although there are concentric spheres of light and nine levels of angels, righteous souls are not ordered according to a hierarchy of virtue.

The case is different in other visions of the afterlife. Mormons, for example, believe in a hierarchically ordered heaven. (For further information on heaven and hell notions in particular religious traditions, consult the relevant entries.)

Sources:

Eliade, Mircea, ed. *Encyclopedia of Religion.* 16 vols. New York: Macmillan, 1987.
McDannell, Colleen, and Bernhard Lang. *Heaven: A History.* Rev. ed. New York: Vintage, 1990.

Turner, Alice K. *The History of Hell.* New York: Harcourt Brace, 1993.
Zimmer, Heinrich. *Philosophies of India.* New York: Bollingen, 1951.

HINDUISM

Hinduism is a blanket term for the indigenous religious tradition of the Indian subcontinent. To be considered "within the fold," one must nominally acknowledge the authority of the four Vedas, ancient religious texts that express concepts and values bearing little resemblance to current Hinduism, much as the first five books of the Old Testament express a religious ideology at variance, on many points, with that of current Christianity. Indian religions that reject the authority of the Vedas—particularly Jainism, Buddhism, and Sikhism—are regarded as non-Hindu. What remains even after these other religions are excluded, however, is a broad diversity of beliefs and practices that, at their extremes, bear little resemblance to one another. For example, a villager sacrificing a goat during a Kali festival in Bengal is as much a Hindu as the office worker engaged in quiet meditation in his suburban Bombay home.

Hinduism's sometimes mind-boggling diversity is at least partially a result of India's complex history. Over the millennia, the Indian subcontinent has been subjected to innumerable influxes of different peoples. Rather than serving as a "melting pot" in which various ethnicities were completely submerged into the preexisting culture, India has tended to allow each new group of migrants to maintain at least some of their distinctiveness. A new social category (subcaste) was created for each group, a social institution that simultaneously incorporates and draws a boundary around intruders. Thus, new ideas, practices, and gods could be at least partially retained within the invaders' communities, thereby contributing to Hinduism's complexity.

Another trait of the Hindu tradition is that earlier strands of spiritual expression tend to be retained rather than discarded as new religious forms emerge. Thus, in the wake of a devotional reform movement, for example, certain segments of the population might be persuaded to abandon older practices and ideas in favor of something new, but other members of the community would continue in the old ways. As a result of this characteristic, ideas and practices that are very ancient—sometimes thousands of years old—are still practiced by at least some contemporary Hindus.

Humanity is thought to have made the transition from tribal life-styles to the more complex forms of social organization we call civilization along four great river basins—in China, India, Egypt, and what is today Iraq. A civilization that thousands of years ago existed along the Indus River in western India left ruins of sophisticated cities. One of the ruins was uncovered near Harappa; hence, this civilization is sometimes referred to as the Harappan civilization. Because their written records were apparently composed on perishable materials, we know very little about them or about their religious beliefs. Scholars have surmised, however, that some of the basic

KALI, FROM AN ALBUM PAINTING, RAJASTHAN, 18TH CENTURY.

beliefs of classical Hinduism, such as the doctrines of **reincarnation** and **karma,** are probably Harappan in origin.

One of the reasons we know so little about the Harappans is that around

1000–1500 B.C. a group of aggressive pastoral peoples from central Asia invaded India through the northern mountain passes, conquered the Harappans, and destroyed whatever records might have remained from the original civilization. These peoples, who called themselves Aryans ("noble"), originated around the Caspian Sea. For unknown reasons, groups of Aryans took off in every direction, subjugating indigenous peoples in every area of the world from India to Ireland (the names Iran, Ireland, and Aryan all derive from the same root). The Indo-European family of languages is one of the legacies of this expansion.

The worldview of the Aryan invaders of India was preserved in the Vedas. The religious vision of the Vedas, unlike that of classical Hinduism, focused very much on this world. The gods were ritually invoked to improve one's situation in this life, so that priests became something approaching magicians. After settling down in the Indian subcontinent, the Aryans became more introspective, started asking questions about the ultimate meaning of life, and developed an ideology centered around release or liberation (**moksha**) from the cycle of death and rebirth (*samsara*). The various disciplines that are collectively referred to as **yoga** developed out of this introspective turn, creating a new vision of reality, first expressed in the *Upanishads,* that superseded the Vedic worldview. Because some of the figures that survive from the Harappan period appear to be human beings in yogic meditation poses, it is likely that the Aryans picked up these practices from the indigenous peoples. Classical Hinduism culminated in innumerable devotional movements that swept across the subcontinent and shaped the face of contemporary popular Hinduism.

Three "layers" of the Hindu tradition—Vedic ritualism, Upanishadic release, and devotional salvation—were marked by divergent afterlife beliefs and practices. Thomas Hopkins (1992) provides a schema in "Hindu Views of Death and Afterlife" that correlates these three layers with the three traditional paths of salvation—ritual action (*karmayoga*), metaphysical knowledge (*jnanayoga*), and devotion (*bhaktiyoga*).

I. VEDIC HINDUISM: The Vedic Indians did not believe that the soul migrated from one lifetime to another in a series of incarnations, but that it migrated at the body's death to the World of the Fathers (in Sanskrit, *pitri-loka),* an afterlife realm never clearly described in Vedic literature. To reach his new home in the afterlife, the deceased had to obtain a new body after cremation consumed the old one. The problem of creating an "afterlife body" occupied priestly thinkers, who developed various postcremation rituals for this purpose. These special rites, referred to as *sapindikarana* and usually performed by the oldest son, had the function of creating as well as maintaining the new body for the deceased in pitri-loka. Successful transition to the afterlife and maintenance therein is thus heavily dependent on proper ritual performances by one's descendants. These rites may have had their roots in more ancient forms of **ancestor worship**; even if they do not, the basic idea of assisting or pleasing the ancestors with certain specific ritual actions (such as "feeding" them) qualifies these rites as a form of ancestor worship. Despite the development of other notions of the afterlife in the post-Vedic period, sapindikarana rites continued to be practiced. They are still widely practiced today, particularly by upper caste Hindu families.

Although little is known about the Vedic World of the Fathers, an interesting composition in the Rig Veda (the oldest and most important of the four Vedas) does give a glimpse into that realm. In this passage, Yama—the first man to die and now god, king, and judge of the deceased—is honored by those who have gather around a funeral pyre:

> Honor with thine oblations the King, Yama, who gathers men together.
>
> Who travelled to the lofty heights above us, who searches out and shows the path to many.
>
> Yama first found for us a place to dwell in: this pasture can never be taken from us. . . .
>
> Meet Yama, meet the Father, meet the merit of free and ordered acts, in highest heaven.
>
> Leave sin and evil, seek anew they dwelling, and bright with glory wear another body.
>
> (Rig Veda, X, 14:1–2, 7–8)

The portrayal of Yama as "finding" the realm that became the World of the Fathers seems to allude to a mythic tale about his search for an appropriate dwelling place after death, a myth that has not survived the millennia. As a people who cremated rather than buried their dead, Vedic Hindus pictured the realm of the dead as being in the sky (where the smoke ascends during cremation) rather than under the earth. In later Hinduism, Yama is still king of the dead, although he acquires different aspects through the centuries.

II. UPANISHADIC HINDUISM: Around 800 B.C., Vedic Hinduism, with its heavy dependence on ritualistically knowledgeable priests, was challenged by a more individualistic form of spiritual expression that rejected many of the basic views and values of Vedism. This emergent view was expressed in a set of religious texts collectively referred to as the Upanishads. In contrast to the risky, tenuous afterlife body that it was the function of sapindikarana rituals to create and maintain, the Upanishads postulated an eternal, changeless core of the self called as the **Atman,** which appears to have originally referred to the breath. (As the invisible part of the person that stopped once life had departed, the breath was often associated with—and sometimes even identified with—the soul in many different world cultures.) This soul or "deep self" was viewed as being identical with the unchanging godhead, referred to as Brahma (the unitary ground of being that transcends particular gods and goddesses). The deep self was equated with the ultimate in innumerable ways, such as in the Upanishadic formula *Tat tvam asi* ("Thou art that!"), meaning that the essential "you" is the same as that indescribable ("wherefrom words turn back") essence of everything:

> He who, dwelling in all things, yet is other than all things, whom all things do not know, whose body all things are, who controls all things from within—
> He is your soul, the Controller, the Immortal.

Untouched by the variations of time and circumstance, the Atman was nevertheless entrapped in the world of samsara (the cycle of death and rebirth). *Samsara* is the southern Asian term for the world we experience in our everyday lives. This continually changing, unstable world stands in contrast to the spiritual realm of Atman/Brahma, which is stable and unchanging. Samsara also refers to the process of death and rebirth (reincarnation) through which we are "trapped" in this world. Unlike Western treatments of reincarnation, which tend to make the idea of coming back into body after body seem exotic, desirable, and even romantic, Hinduism, Buddhism, and other southern Asian religions portray the samsaric process as unhappy. Life in this world means suffering.

What keeps us trapped in the samsaric cycle is the law of karma. In its simplest form, this law operates impersonally like a natural law, ensuring that every good or bad deed eventually returns to the individual in the form of reward or punishment commensurate with the original deed. It is the necessity of "reaping one's karma" that compels human beings to take rebirth (to reincarnate) in successive lifetimes. In other words, if one dies before reaping the effects of one's actions (as most people do), the karmic process demands that one come back in a future life. Coming back in another lifetime also allows karmic forces to reward or punish one through the circumstances to which one is born. Hence, for example, an individual who was generous in one lifetime might be reborn as a wealthy person in the next incarnation.

Moksha is the traditional Sanskrit term for release or liberation from the endless chain of deaths and rebirths. In the southern Asian religious tradition, it represents the supreme goal of human strivings. Reflecting the diversity of Hinduism, liberation can be attained in a variety of ways, from the proper performance of certain rituals to highly disciplined forms of yoga. In the Upanishads, it is proper knowledge, in the sense of insight into the nature of reality, that enables the aspiring seeker to achieve liberation from the wheel of rebirth.

What happens to the individual after reaching moksha? In Upanishadic Hinduism, the individual Atman is believed to merge into the cosmic Brahma. A traditional image is that of a drop of water that, when dropped into the ocean, loses its individuality and becomes one with the sea. Although widespread, this metaphor does not quite capture the significance of this "merger." Rather than *losing* one's individuality, the Upanishadic understanding is that the Atman is *never separate* from Brahma; hence, individuality is illusory, and moksha is simply waking up from the dream of separateness.

The most that the classical texts of Hinduism say about the state of one who has merged with the godhead is that the person has become one with pure "beingness," consciousness, and bliss. From the perspective of world-affirming Western society, such a static afterlife (if it is even proper to refer to the liberated state as an "afterlife") appears distinctly undesirable. Furthermore, this concept cannot even be said to have wide appeal among ordinary Hindus.

III. DEVOTIONAL HINDUISM: The third "layer" of the Hindu tradition introduced a devotional approach to the divine, in which the nature of the human/divine relationship—as well as the Hindu vision of the afterlife—was reconceived.

Beginning at least several centuries B.C., devotionalism rejected the impersonalism of both the ritual strategy of Vedism and the intellectual emphasis of the Upanishads. Instead, God was approached as a personal, supremely loving deity who would respond to devotional worship. The gods of the Vedic pantheon, as with the deities of ancient Greece and Rome, were not particularly concerned with human affairs. And, although the Upanishadic sages accepted the existence of the Vedic gods, the focus of their reflections was the godhead—the abstract ground of being that transcended the gods.

By way of contrast, the focus of devotional theism was on the great gods/ goddesses of classical Hinduism. In the wake of the devotional movements that swept across the subcontinent, various strands of "sectarianism" developed, focused on the worship of Vishnu/ Krishna, Shiva, Durga/ Kali, or some other form of the divine. The deity of one's sect was portrayed as *the* supreme god or goddess, and the other divinities envisioned as demigods or demigoddesses, inferior to the supreme. This high god or goddess deity was also seen as the creator, a creator concerned with his or her creation, and particularly concerned with the fate of human beings. As Hopkins (1992, 154) observes:

> The world is thus not an impersonal or unreal realm, but the arena of divine activity and divine encounter. Vishnu incarnates himself in the world as Rama and Krishna to save the world from unrighteousness, Shiva manifests himself in the world in theophanies to save his devotees, and the goddess enters the world to defeat demons who threaten its security.

Despite these modifications, the samsaric cycle of death and rebirth was still viewed as unattractive, and the goal was still to achieve release from the cycle. By the time of Buddha (approximately 600 B.C.), the Indian consensus was that it was desire (passion, attachment, want, craving) that kept one involved in the karmic process, and hence desire that kept one bound to the death/rebirth process. Consequently, the goal of getting off the ferris wheel of reincarnation required freeing oneself from desire.

To reduce the possibility of karma-producing actions, followers of the Upanishadic tradition had tended to view asceticism or monasticism as the mode of life best suited to achieving release from samsara. However, by the time of the **Bhagavad Gita,** the earliest important work of devotional theism, another possibility had been thought through. Because it was the craving associated with activity that set the karmic process in motion, rather than the activity itself, the author(s) of the Bhagavad Gita developed an alternative approach of remaining in the everyday world while performing one's deeds with an attitude of dispassionate detachment. In the Gita, this detachment is discussed in terms of detachment from the "fruits of actions," meaning that actions are not undertaken for personal gain. Although achieving detachment may be difficult, Krishna, who in the Gita is the principal spokesperson for this point of view, asserts that such a frame of mind is indeed possible if one constantly maintains an attitude of devotion to God. When successful, one can even engage in such activities as war (as long as one is fighting because it is one's duty) and avoid the negative karma that normally results from such actions. In the words of the Gita:

> Set thy heart upon thy work, but never on its reward. Work not for a reward; but never cease to do thy work. Do thy work in the peace of Yoga and, free from selfish desires, be not moved in success or in failure. Yoga is evenness of mind—a peace that is ever the same. . . .
>
> . . . Seers in union with wisdom forsake the rewards of their work, and free from the bonds of birth they go to the abode of salvation. (2:47–48, 51)

The afterlife (the "abode of salvation") in devotional theism is not the static, abstract bliss of merging into the ocean of Brahma. Rather, the devotional tradition views the liberated soul as participating in a blissful round of devotional activities in a heaven world that is comparable, in certain respects, to the heaven of Western religions.

Along with heaven realms, Hinduism also developed notions of hell worlds in which exceptionally sinful individuals were punished. In earlier stages of the development of the Hindu tradition, the impersonal force of karma carried out punishment for evil deeds through the circumstances into which one was reborn and through the unfortunate events one experienced while incarnated in a body. By the period of the *Puranas* (the mythological texts of classical Hinduism), written chiefly from A.D. 300 to A.D. 750, however, the notion of punishment in hell worlds emerged to supplement—rather than to supplant—earlier notions of karmic punishment. Many of the torments of Hindu hell worlds, such as being tortured by demons, resemble the torments of more familiar Western hells. Unlike Western hells, however, Hindu hell worlds are not final dwelling places. They are more like **purgatories** in which sinful souls experience suffering for a limited term. After the term is over, even the most evil person is turned out of hell to once again participate in the cycle of reincarnation.

In fact, in all the diverse strands of Hinduism following the Vedic period, reincarnation is accepted as an almost unquestioned assumption regarding the nature of reality. For this reason, death is not as significant in the Hindu tradition as it is in many other world religions. As Hopkins (1992, 154) points out,

> It is not coincidence that there are no massive monuments to the dead in Hinduism, no tombs, sarcophagai, or pyramids to mark the final resting place of the dead, because death is not in any sense a final stopping point. All beings that die will be reborn as long as they are still engaged in the karmic process, so their physical remains are only a transient and insignificant reminder of their passing; and all beings similarly have the possibility of final salvation, although this may be many lifetimes in the future.

Sources:

Bhagavad Gita. Juan Mascaro, trans. Baltimore, MD: Penguin, 1970.

Feuerstein, Georg. *Encyclopedic Dictionary of Yoga.* New York: Paragon House, 1990.

Hopkins, Thomas. "Hindu Views of Death and Afterlife." In Hiroshi Obayashi, ed., *Death and Afterlife: Perspectives of World Religions.* Westport, CT: Greenwood Press, 1992, 149–64.

MacGregor, Geddes. *Images of Afterlife: Beliefs from Antiquity to Modern Times.* New York: Paragon House, 1992.

Zimmer, Heinrich. *Philosophies of India.* 1951. Reprint, New York: Macmillan, 1987.

HOME CIRCLE (HOME SITTING)

A home circle or home sitting is a séance that is, as the name indicates, held in a private home with the aim of communicating with the dead. Such circles were highly popular in the late nineteenth and early twentieth centuries when **Spiritualism** was something of a fad. Home circles were frequently held without the assistance of professional mediums. In the wake of the frenzied publicity surrounding the **Fox sisters** in the mid-nineteenth century, many ordinary people organized circles with their family and friends in an effort to manifest Spiritualistic phenomena. In England in the 1870s the weekly magazine *The Spiritualist* went so far as to provide guidelines for such grass-roots activity. It was usually possible to find at least one individual in every such gathering with the necessary mediumistic abilities.

The group sat in a circle or around a table, often holding hands. Medium James M. Laughton advised using the same room over and over for the best effects. Another medium, Clifford L. Bias, advised a circle composed equally of men and women, with each sex alternating. Yet other items of advice were to begin circles at the same hour each time and to keep the meeting place comfortably cool. Like the ceremonies in contemporary Spiritualist churches, such gatherings often started with prayers and hymns. The home circle, which had made Spiritualism a popular movement exending well beyond Spiritualist denominational boundaries, faded in relative obscurity early in the present century.

Sources:

Brandon, Ruth. *The Spiritualists.* New York: Alfred A. Knopf, 1983.

Chaney, Rev. Robert G. *Mediums and the Development of Mediumship.* Freeport, NY: Books for Libraries Press, 1972.

HOSPICE MOVEMENT

The term hospice has its origins in the Middle Ages, when hospices were refuges where pilgrims were sheltered and fed during their journey to the Holy Land. It now refers to an approach toward dying people established in England by Dr. Cicely Saunders in 1967 that grew out of awareness that the medical system was ignoring the basic human needs of terminally ill people and exposing them to physical and psychological discomfort.

The distinctive purpose of hospice programs is to help both ill people—often cancer victims who are expected to live only for a short period—and their families to deal positively with death and experience it with dignity. Hospice services provide continuous care consisting of relief of physical pain and treatment of a variety of psychological factors, such as depression and anxiety about the welfare of loved ones.

Aggressive techniques to preserve life are usually discontinued, for they are thought to increase discomfort and isolate dying people from their families. Also, when death occurs, hospice services are extended to the members of the patient's family. It is suggested that families, who are seen not only as fundamental sources of support for the dying person but also as individuals who are experiencing stress and who need attention, should have the opportunity to discuss death with the staff and should have privacy with the dying person both before and immediately after death.

Therefore, the focus of hospice philosophy is not the disease, but respect for the individual's needs, fears, hopes, and expectations. Hospice philosophy developed out of the Christian tradition, which is still often in evidence, although all religious orientations are respected, as well as preferences for agnosticism or atheism. Any suggestion to modify the dying person's beliefs in any direction is considered unacceptable, particularly in matters regarding the afterlife.

Sources:

Kastenbaum, Robert, and Beatrice Kastenbaum. *Encyclopedia of Death.* Phoenix, AZ: Oryx Press, 1989.

Roy, F. Hampton, and Russel Charles, eds. *The Encyclopedia of Aging and the Elderly.* New York: Facts on File, 1992.

Saunders, Cicely, ed. *Hospice: The Living Idea.* London: Edward Arnold, 1981.

HOUDINI, HARRY

Harry Houdini (1874–1926), born Ehrich Weiss in Budapest, Hungary, was brought to the United States as a child, where he later became a famous escapologist and magician. He took his name from Jean Eugene Robert Houdin, a nineteenth-century French illusionist who exposed fake performers of religious marvels.

He married Wilhelmina Beatrice Rahner in 1894, and from that time on they worked together as the Houdinis. He developed a series of challenge acts, escaping from handcuffs and ropes brought by spectators, from prison cells, and from boxes. His amazing feats included walking through a wall, a vanishing elephant act, and the famous escape from a Chinese water torture cell—a large tank filled with water in which he was immersed head downward after his feet were locked up.

In his later years, Houdini was highly critical of **mediums,** mind readers, and others who claimed supernatural powers, as the title of his book *Miracle Mongers and their Methods* (1920) suggests. He replicated a variety of alleged phenomena by mechanical methods. He completely rejected the Spiritualist idea that those who have died continue to live in some spiritual world and that they can communicate with us under suitable conditions through the instrumentality of particular individuals.

Houdini contended that thought is a function of the brain, and death consists of the cessation of life activities, with nothing beyond. He also maintained that his training and experience had led him to the conclusion that communications with spirits were purely human fabrications, all delusion and trickery.

Before his death Houdini made a pact with his wife, as a last test of **Spiritualism;** if spirit survival was possible, he would communicate with her by a series of coded messages. She attended various séances in order to receive messages from him, but after years of trying to communicate through Spiritualism with her husband without any result, she declared the experiment a failure.

Sources:

Ernst, Bernard M.L., and Hereward Carrington. *Houdini and Conan Doyle. The Story of a Strange Friendship.* London: Hutchinson & Co., 1933.

Shepard, Leslie A., ed. *Encyclopedia of Occultism & Parapsychology.* Detroit, MI: Gale Research, 1991.

I

Immortality

Immortality, the trait of being eternal, is often attributed to divinities and is one of the central traits that distinguishes human beings from gods. In the human realm, immortality can refer to the ability to indefinitely prolong the life of the physical body. Primarily, however, the term is usually taken to refer to eternal existence in some type of afterlife realm. As such, immortality is a characteristic of the soul rather than the body. Most world religions accept the notion of the immortality of the soul, the chief exceptions being **Buddhism,** which explicitly rejects the idea (the doctrine of **anatta**), and **Judaism,** in which the **resurrected** dead lead eternal lives in immortal physical bodies.

Sources:

Eliade, Mircea, ed. *The Encyclopedia of Religion.* 16 vols. New York: Macmillan, 1987.
Smart, Ninian. *The Religious Experience of Mankind.* 3d ed. New York: Charles Scribner's Sons, 1984.
Turner, Alice K. *The History of Hell.* New York: Harcourt Brace, 1993.

Incarnation

The literal meaning of incarnation is "in the flesh." It is related to words like **reincarnation,** which means to reenter the flesh. Customary usage in English and other Western languages has restricted incarnation to refer specifically to Christ's embodiment, although it is sometimes used to refer to other instances in which the soul or spirit "takes flesh."

Sources:

Eliade, Mircea, ed. *Encyclopedia of Religion.* 16 vols. New York: Macmillan, 1987.
Shepherd, Leslie A. *Encyclopedia of Occultism and Parapsychology.* Detroit, MI: Gale Research, 1985.

THE BRANCH OF IMMORTAL LIFE (ASSYRIA). COURTESY OF THE ARC.

INCAS

Far from being a single culture, the original peoples of the Americas created a series of complex cultures that often bore little resemblance to one another. Of particular interest are the so-called high cultures of Mexico and Peru, three "citied" civilizations that, at least at an earlier period, maintained links with one another: the Mayan on the Yucatán Peninsula, the Incan in the highlands of Peru, and the Aztecan (and its predecessors) in central Mexico. These cultures all seem to have begun their unusual course of development around 500 B.C., actually evolving from small-scale societies to citied civilizations with written records. Although these societies were largely destroyed by Spanish conquistadors, their less-than-extensive writings in combination with the observations of their early conquerors allow us to partially reconstruct their worldview and religious beliefs.

As with the Aztec in Mexico, the Inca were but the most recent tribal group to rule the Andean region. Much of their material culture was taken from peoples they conquered. The Inca apparently resisted adopting the religions of subject peoples, and instead imposed worship of the sun god Viracocha throughout the empire. It is difficult to tell to what degree Spanish observers imposed their own views when interpreting aboriginal religion, but it seems that the Inca believed in a bifurcated afterlife, one in which "bad" people went to a frigid realm of punishment in the bowels of the earth, where they had nothing but stones to eat, and "good" people went to a happy realm, much like this one, in the heaven of the sun deity.

According to some early accounts, the dead had to cross a **bridge** made of hair over a large **river** to reach the "the silent land." One of the better-known items of information about the Inca is the elaborate burials of their kings. Rulers were interred with their possessions. As in many other royal funerals in other areas of the world, wives, servants, and others close to the king were expected to commit suicide and accompany the ruler to the other world.

Sources:

Eliade, Mircea, ed. *The Encyclopedia of Religion.* 16 vols. New York: Macmillan, 1987.

Hultkrantz, Ake. *The Religions of the American Indians.* 1967. Reprint, Berkeley: University of California Press, 1979.

Marzal, Manuel M. "Andean Religion at the Time of Conquest." In Gary H. Gossen, ed., *South and Meso-American Native Spirituality.* New York: Crossroad, 1993.

INDO-EUROPEANS

Most of the languages of Europe, as well as some from as far away as India, belong to the same family and are referred to as Indo-European languages. Similarities of vocabulary among this family abound, as, for example, in the Sanskrit/Hindi word *nam,* which means name. To explain this phenomenon, scholars have postulated that these similarities are the result of a group of peoples who spoke the original (now lost) Indo-European language.

These peoples, who called themselves Aryans ("nobles"), originated in the steppes of southern Russia, in the region stretching from the Black Sea to the Ural Mountains. For unknown reasons, groups of Aryans took off in every direction, subjugating indigenous peoples in every area of the world from India to Ireland (Iran, Ireland, and Aryan all derive from the same root). The Indo-European family of languages is one of the legacies of this expansion.

Efforts to reconstruct Indo-European religion and mythology, especially the work of George Dumézil, have focused on finding common elements in the myths and religious practices of Indo-European peoples that are not found in other cultures. It has been established, for example, that the Indo-Europeans divided their society into three groups of people, and that this tripartite division was reflected in their myth system, as in the myth of the three tasks or "sins" of the warrior (offenses against each of the three orders of society)—a theme about which Dumézil has written.

This three-part social stratification of Indo-European society was also reflected in burial practices. Members of the ruling class were buried in richly furnished tombs built in the form of houses *(tumuli),* whereas other classes were interred under far poorer circumstances. The afterlife itself, which was apparently much like the present life, was viewed positively, in terms of reunion with one's ancestors. As preserved in the ancient Vedic texts of **Hinduism,** and also in the myth systems of other Indo-European societies, the Indo-Europeans believed that the afterlife otherworld was founded by the first mortal (to Hindus, **Yama**; to Indo-Europeans, Yemo).

Sources:

Eliade, Mircea, ed. *The Encyclopedia of Religion.* 16 vols. New York: Macmillan, 1987.
Eliade, Mircea. *A History of Religious Ideas, Vol. I.* Chicago: University of Chicago Press, 1978.

Initiation (Initiatory Death)

Initiation in the most general sense refers to a rite in which the initiate undergoes a transformation in religious or social status. The most widespread initiatory ritual is the puberty rite, in which the individual becomes an adult member of the community. To contemporary Westerners, the bar mitzvah is perhaps the most familiar of such rites. Depending on the perspective one takes, other rites of passage, such as marriage, can also be viewed as initiations. The second widely practiced rite classified as an initiatory ritual is initiation into a specialized group, particularly initiation into a secret society. Although not universal, such societies are widespread in traditional cultures. To contemporary Westerners, initiation into a group like the Masons is the most familiar of this class of rituals.

A third and final class of rites and experiences classified as an initiation is the transformation of an individual into a **shaman** or medicine man. Shamans are the religious specialists of certain traditional societies who act as healers and diviners. There are different traditional ways in which one becomes a shaman. Often the role is simply inherited, and the shaman is initiated in public. At other times, the person is chosen by spiritual forces. Sometimes the chosen individual does not particularly wish to take up a shamanic vocation, and this "supernatural" election frequently involves a serious illness in which the person comes close to death. The death theme is emphasized in certain traditions in which the individual has a vision of being slain, dismembered, reconstructed, and revived. There are no well-known parallels to this form of initiation in contemporary Western societies.

Certainly the most striking aspect of most traditional initiations is the manner in which the initiate is symbolically slain. Often the person undergoing the ritual is made to feel pain—pain as might actually be experienced if the person were killed. This suffering can be as mild as the discomfort of fasting, or as excruciating as having an incisor knocked out.

Such death symbolism may seem foreign to modern civilization. Partially as a result of the idea of "progress," those of us who live in contemporary, industrialized

INITIATORY DEATH.

societies are accustomed to the notion of gradual development. Widespread acceptance of this notion in Western culture is comparatively recent, however, dating from some time in the nineteenth century. In relatively stable traditional societies, transformation from one stage of life to another is viewed differently. As a caterpillar appears to have to "die" in order to give "birth" to a butterfly, so it seems natural that one's old self must be slain before the individual can fully be reborn as a new self, whether that new self be a "born again" Christian, or a shaman.

Another possible explanation for initiation rites that sometimes seem to actually bring the initiate to the point of death is that, at least in their original form, such rites were actually meant to induce a **near-death experience.** According to near-death researchers, people who have had such experiences emerge with an unshakable faith in their own immortality. After they have recovered, they live transformed lives; they no longer fear death, they sense the importance of love in ways they had never before experienced, they feel a connection with all things, and they acquire a thirst for learning, especially for spiritual understanding. Given the profundity of near-death experiences, they may actually have been a factor in the institution of such "death" rites.

Sources:

Eliade, Mircea. *Encyclopedia of Religion.* 16 vols. New York: Macmillan, 1987.
Moody, Raymond A., Jr. *The Light Beyond.* 1988. Reprint, New York: Bantam, 1989.
Van Der Leeuw, G., trans. *Religion in Essence and Manifestation.* Vol. 1. Gloucester, MA: Peter Smith, 1967. (Originally published 1933.)

International Association for Conscious Dying

The International Association for Conscious Dying was founded by **Benito F. Reyes** (1914–1992) in 1990 in Ojai, California, in observance of the sixteenth anniversary of the foundation of the World University of America. Its main activity is conducting a series of seminars dealing with the techniques and implications of **conscious dying, near-death experiences,** conscious **out-of-body experiences, past-life therapy,** and human **immortality.**

According to Reyes, the general objectives of the conscious dying conferences and workshops are to help liberate the human mind from ignorance and fear produced by the erroneous "physicalistic" interpretation of life and death (reducing everything to physical explanations, including apparently "spiritual" phenomena) by creating a nonphysicalistic way of understanding those events; to help develop a way of dying with dignity and wisdom; and to focus on the worldwide problem of **AIDS** as a unique opportunity for understanding conscious dying. The seminars are taken mainly by medical and health care professionals and educators.

The association also publishes a newsletter, *The Clear Light.*

Sources:

Reyes, Benito F. *Conscious Dying: Psychology of Death and Guidebook to Liberation.* Ojai, CA: World University of America, 1986.

International Association for Near-Death Studies

The International Association for Near-Death Studies was founded in 1981 as a nonprofit organization for understanding the nature and scope of human consciousness in its relationship to life and death, through empirical observation and through near-death experiences. It is a professional organization that promotes scholarly study of the near-death experience through conferences, grants, and international networking. It grew out of the studies, in the 1970s, of psychiatrists **Elisabeth Kübler-Ross, Raymond Moody, Jr.,** and George Ritchie. In the 1980s their research was extended through the findings of **Kenneth Ring,** Michael Sabom, and

INTERNATIONAL ASSOCIATION FOR CONSCIOUS DYING (IACD) OPEN FORUM. SEMINAR SPEAKERS INCLUDED (L. TO R.) **DR. KENNETH RING,** DR. CLAUDIA JENSEN, **DR. RAYMOND A. MOODY,** DR. BRUCE GOLDBERG, SUSAN STORCH, AND DR. DOMINGA L. REYES. COURTESY OF THE INTERNATIONAL ASSOCIATION FOR CONSCIOUS DYING (IACD).

Bruce Greyson. These studies have shown that the near-death experience (NDE) is perceived more as a spiritual or psychological event than as a physical phenomenon. Also, there is evidence that the experience exhibits the same patterns regardless of the individual's cultural, religious, or psychological background. The association publishes the scholarly *Journal of Near-Death Studies* and issues a quarterly newsletter, *Vital Signs.*

International Church of Ageless Wisdom

The International Church of Ageless Wisdom was born of the controversy in American Spiritualist organizations over the belief in reincarnation. Rev. Elizabeth R. Hand, the organizer of several Spiritualist congregations, heard Paramahansa Yogananda (founder of the Self-Realization Fellowship) speak when he visited the United States in 1924 and eventually became convinced of the truth of reincarnation. This belief provoked much strife within her congregations and throughout the larger Spiritualist groups to which they were related, and she was forced to move into independent ministry, founding the Church of Ageless Wisdom in Philadelphia in 1927.

Soon thereafter, Hand met Rev. George C. O. Haas, who had recently founded the Universal Spiritual Church in New York City and shared her views on reincarnation. He was also founder and director of the Institute of Hyperphysical Research. Hand affiliated her work with his and sought a formal union when his church received a charter from New York State in 1929. Although that union was not forthcoming, the congregations remained allied.

Hand shaped the church on eclectic terms, taking parts of Hindu, Buddhist, and occult traditions and adding them to a Christian foundation. The church teaches that Jesus was the Wayshower, the model for humans to follow to become one with God. Souls are understood to be immortal and are under the universal laws of reincarnation and karma, which provide a means by which even the most evil soul can eventually be saved. The church encourages further understanding of these spiritual truths through use of whatever psychic abilities may be available.

Reverend Haas received independent episcopal consecration from John Beswarwick of the Free Protestant Episcopal Church in 1956 and in turn consecrated Hand on July 22, 1958. Despite this additional communion, Hand still did not receive a formal union with Haas and finally became independent of his work. She did, however, continue in the episcopal line by consecrating Muriel E. Matalucci-Ley in 1960. Matalucci-Ley succeeded Hand as archbishop upon Hand's death in 1977.

Sources:

Melton, J. Gordon. *The Encyclopedia of American Religions*. 4th ed. Detroit, MI: Gale Research, 1993.

Ward, Gary L., Bertil Persson, and Alan Bain, eds. *Independent Bishops: An International Directory*. Detroit, MI: Apogee Books, 1990.

ISIS *See:* OSIRIS

ISLAM

The notions of resurrection, heaven, and hell have been part of Islam since the time of Mohammed. Both the Koran (Islamic scriptures) and the Hadith (the sayings of the Prophet Mohammed) refer to the afterlife.

The human being, created in God's image, is composed of a body, the outer shell of which originated in clay, and spiritual breath, which can communicate with God and which is located at the center of the body. This is the microcosmic reflection of the Islamic macrocosm, which is viewed as a globe of infinite dimensions whose center is full of light, the purest of God's creations. Its outer shell is made of clay, which represents darkness. The human soul (*nafs*) resides within the human being some-

ASCENT OF MOHAMMED, FROM THE *KHAMESH*, NIZAMI, INDIA (16TH CENTURY).

where between these two opposite principles—light and darkness—and is a mixture of the two, unique to each individual, while the spirit that resides at the center (being of godlike nature) is the same for everybody.

When human beings die, they remain in a sort of interworld (*barzakh*), a realm located closer to the luminous cosmic center, until the day of resurrection. In this interworld, which somewhat resembles dreaming, the soul of the deceased, liberated from its bodily layers, can awaken and become aware of its true nature. The interworld period is important in preparing for the day of resurrection, which occurs at the end of time, that is, when human possibilities and potential have been exhausted. The day of resurrection (*qiyama,* the return, or *ba'th,* awakening), which constitutes one of the essential beliefs of the Islamic faith, is believed by some to last thousands of years. On this day the souls, rejoined with their bodies, will be assigned eternal life either in paradise (literally, ''garden'') or in hell (fire), depending on their merits.

Although the figure of the Madhi is more central to Shiite Islam, it is a popular belief among many Sunni Muslims that a righteous leader (a Madhi, or ''rightly guided one'') will reign for a brief period in the last days. He will be followed by an impostor messiah (parallel to the Christian notion of the Antichrist) who will attempt to lead the world astray. Finally, however, the prophet Jesus will appear to usher in the final judgment. On Judgment Day the earth will quake and mountains become a heap of sand: ''When the stars shall be extinguished, when heaven shall be split, when the mountains shall be scattered . . . (Arberry 1969, 318).'' As in the Judgment Day scenarios of other Middle Eastern religions, the dead are resurrected.

> Upon the day when the Caller shall call unto a horrible thing, abasing their eyes, they shall come forth from the tombs as if they were scattered grasshoppers, running with outstretched necks to the Caller. The unbelievers shall say, ''This is a hard day!'' (Arberry 1969, 247)

And the dead are judged:

> Then he whose deeds weigh heavy in the Balance shall inherit a pleasing life, but he whose deeds weigh light in the Balance shall plunge in the womb of the Pit. (Arberry 1969, 348)

Paradise (*al-Jannah*) is located at the macrocosmic center of light and is composed of eight levels (or, according to some authorities, as many as the number of souls inhabiting paradise). It is thought to be a garden where all kinds of delights are prepared for the saved. On the far outer part of the macrocosm lies hell *(an-nar),* arranged in seven layers, where the soul's punishment consists of being far from God, which is considered to be the worst chastisement. More so than Judeo-Christian Scriptures, the Koran contains vivid descriptions of both paradise and hell. For instance, in the chapter entitled ''The Terror,'' the Koran says:

> [T]hey are brought nigh the Throne, in the Gardens of Delight upon close-wrought couches reclining upon them, set face to face, immortal youths going round about them with goblets, and ewers, and a cup from a spring and such fruits as they shall choose, and such flesh of fowl as they desire, and wide-eyed houris as the likeness of hidden pearls, a recompense for that they labored. (Arberry 1969, 254)

Equally vivid descriptions of hell can be found throughout the Koran, as in the chapter "The Pilgrimage":

> [G]arments of fire shall be cut, and there shall be poured over their heads boiling water whereby whatsoever is in their bellies and their skins shall be melted; for them await hooked iron rods; as often as they desire in their anguish to come forth from it, they shall be restored into it, and taste the chastisement of the burning. (Arberry, 1969, 29)

Islamic theologians, particularly those of the Asharite school, believed that if a believer entered hell, God could forgive his sins or nonconformities and remove him, either immediately or after a certain period during which imperfections had been "burned away." The basis for this doctrine is the Hadith: "He shall make men come out of hell after they have been burned and reduced to cinders." In addition to this purgatory of suffering, there is another Muslim limbo—*al-A'raf* (the "heights" or "ramparts"), described in a chapter of the Koran by that name—in which those souls reside that do not merit damnation yet are unable to enter paradise.

Beyond certain commonalities, the views of Shiites and Sunnis (the two principal Muslim "denominations") on the destiny of the body and the soul differ greatly. Shiites hold that the human being is a spirit, the *ruh* (spiritual breath, which is immortal by nature), which uses the body as instrument. Upon death the spirit, liberated from the body, can rediscover its true nature. The souls of those who believed in God live until the day of resurrection, enjoying the vision of God. On the day of resurrection the bodies of the righteous will join their soul and will enter paradise forever, whereas the unbelievers' souls will suffer until the last day and, once rejoining with their bodies, will suffer eternal punishment.

Sunnis, in contrast, consider the human being a material compound of body and soul. Upon death, both body and spirit die and spend a certain period in the grave, where they undergo a personal judgment by two angels and a divine judge. This personal judgment is followed by a second death, which is abrogated, however, for those who died in the name of God. Souls are then believed to vanish, and to appear again on Judgment Day, when they rejoin their original bodies.

Sources:

Arberry, A.J. *The Koran Interpreted.* 1955. Reprint, New York: Macmillan, 1969.

Eliade, Mircea, ed. *The Encyclopedia of Religion.* 16 vols. New York: Macmillan, 1987.

Glassé, Cyril. *The Concise Encyclopedia of Islam.* 1989. Reprint, San Francisco: Harper San Francisco, 1991.

Obayashi, Hiroshi, ed. *Death and Afterlife: Perspectives of World Religions.* Westport, CT: Greenwood Press, 1992.

J

JAMES, WILLIAM

William James (1842–1910) was a well-known American psychologist and philosopher, perhaps best remembered as an advocate of the philosophy of pragmatism. **Spiritualism** was a popular movement during his lifetime, and he made significant contributions to what we would today call psychical research. He was fascinated by the phenomenon of **mediumship** and studied many mediums.

He was born into a wealthy New York family. His father was the equally famous Henry James, who was an adherent of the ideas of Emanuel Swedenbörg. James graduated from Harvard University with a medical degree at age 27, and within a few years was teaching physiology, psychology, and philosophy at his alma mater. An interesting blend of scientist and spiritual seeker, James was interested in religious experiences and mystical states. He is justly celebrated for his *Varieties of Religious Experience,* a book that is still a standard reference for scholars in that field.

James was also interested in paranormal phenomena, an interest that manifested as early as 1869. While in London in 1882, he encountered—and even participated in the research of—the new **Society for Psychical Research** (SPR). He especially appreciated the notion of the subliminal self developed by Frederic W. H. Myers. Myers's secondary self was similar to James's own idea of a ''hidden self,'' which he had developed before encountering Myers. His appreciation of the British society was such that, in 1885, he helped found the American Society for Psychical Research. Psychical research was also carried on at the Lawrence Scientific School, which James founded at Harvard. He was deeply committed to the goal of subjecting so-called psychic phenomena to scientific methods.

James was particularly interested in mental mediums, such as Boston medium Leonara Piper. (Mental mediums are psychics or clairvoyants that do not manifest such phenomena as materialization or levitation, which are referred to as physical mediumship.) James gave a famous lecture called the White Crow lecture in 1890 in which he asserted that "to upset the conclusion that all crows are black, there is no need to seek demonstration that no crows are black; it is sufficient to produce one white crow; a single one is sufficient." He further asserted that Ms. Piper was such an exception (i.e., to the many phony mediums).

James was also deeply interested in the question of the survival of the soul after death. He never asserted that survival had been proved beyond a shadow of a doubt, but he cited Spiritualist phenomena as strongly supporting such a view. This point was well argued in several essays. James died at his summer home in Chocura, New Hampshire, on August 26, 1910. Current mediums and channels often claim contact with James, and relay his supposed teachings from "the other side."

Sources:

Burkhardt, Frederic, and Fredson Bowers, eds. *The Works of William James: Essays in Psychical Research.* Cambridge, MA: Harvard University Press, 1986.

James, William. *The Will to Believe and Other Essays in Popular Philosophy* and *Human Immortality.* 1897, 1898. Reprint (2 vols. in 1). New York: Dover, 1956.

Murphy, Gardner, and Robert O. Ballou, eds. *William James on Psychical Research* . New York: Viking Press, 1960.

Myers, Gerald E. *William James: His Life and Thought.* New Haven, CT: Yale University Press, 1986.

JIVA

Jiva, related to the English words *live* and *life,* is a Sanskrit term for the impermanent, changing part of the self that carries our distinct personality traits from one lifetime to the next. Its antonym in the **Hindu** tradition is **atman,** which refers to the deeper, eternal self that remains unchanged during the process of reincarnation. From the standpoint of classical Hinduism, the atman is eternal, whereas the jiva is not.

It is relatively easy to see how one might equate, or at least associate, the trait of unchangeableness with that which is eternal and most "real," even if we do not agree with the equation. Southern Asians, however, have relied heavily on this association, making it a basic presupposition of their religious thinking for millennia. The corollary of this premise is, logically enough, that whatever changes is not eternal and is thus ultimately illusory.

Because the self we normally experience is in a constant state of flux, this gives rise to the concern that we are not eternal, immortal beings. In reflecting on the concern, early southern Asian thinkers postulated that the self can be subdivided into a changeable, mortal self (the jiva), and an unchanging, immortal self (the atman). Buddha later criticized this distinction, pointing out that, with a little honest self-reflection, it is not possible to find anything that does not change within ourselves.

Sources:

Feuerstein, Georg. *Encyclopedic Dictionary of Yoga.* New York: Paragon House, 1990.

Zimmer, Heinrich. *Philosophies of India.* New York: Bollingen, 1951.

JIVAN-MUKTA

Jivan-mukta (also rendered as *jivanmukta, jiva mukti,* and other variations) is a Sanskrit term that can be translated roughly as "liberated in life." The expression refers to the enlightened person who has been liberated from the bondage of the cycle of death and rebirth while still in a physical body. To understand this notion, one must first be aware that southern Asian religions hold that life in this world—a life that the process of **reincarnation** continually brings us back to by the force of our **karma**—is painful rather than pleasant. Thus, the goal of **Hinduism, Buddhism,** and other Indian religions is to break free of this cycle. A jivan-mukta is an individual who, usually through various spiritual practices, has been liberated from the necessity of reincarnating. The person is thus "liberated while yet in this life."

Sources:

Feuerstein, Georg. *Encyclopedic Dictionary of Yoga.* New York: Paragon House, 1990.
Zimmer, Heinrich. *Philosophies of India.* New York: Bollingen, 1951.

JOURNAL OF REGRESSION THERAPY (JRT)

The Journal of Regression Therapy (JRT), a biannual periodical that has been published since 1986, is the official journal of the **Association for Past-Life Research and Therapies** (APRT). APRT is an association concerned with research into **reincarnation** and the advancement of methods that involve accessing past lives as part of therapy. Composed primarily of mental health professionals and others interested in the advancement of **past-life therapy,** APRT has been less concerned with general reincarnation research than with matters directly relevant to therapeutic intervention. Most of the association's research has arisen directly out of clinical settings.

Winafred Blake Lucas, the second editor of *JRT,* has written that the journal was initiated by APRT to "give cohesion to the association and to provide an opportunity to share therapeutic procedures, experiences, and research." *JRT* has also "helped to define the nature and parameters of the regression field." Contributions have run the gamut from reports of physical healings resulting from past-life therapy to articles on depossession (**exorcism**).

The employment of "**regression**" rather than "past life" in the journal's title might have been intended to enhance its professional image, as the term *regression* has other, nonmetaphysical meanings in the discipline of psychology. *JRT* also adheres to the traditional conventions of what a professional journal is "supposed" to look like. It is, in fact, for all intents and purposes, an academic periodical, although its exotic subject matter has kept it out of the psychological mainstream.

Sources:

Lucas, Winafred Blake. *Regression Therapy: A Handbook for Professionals, Vol. I.* Crest Park, CA: Deep Forest Press, 1993.

JUDAISM

The core of Judaism is a covenant relationship—which is both a contractual agreement and a "marriage" of love—between Yahweh and his chosen people. Because Judaism is built around a relationship involving agreements and promises in *this* life, the afterlife is less essential for Judaism than for other world religions. It would, in fact, be relatively easy to imagine Judaism without any afterlife beliefs whatsoever. In marked contrast, the promise of a postmortem paradise lies at the very core of the believer's religious life in traditions like **Christianity** and **Islam,** so that to delete afterlife beliefs would be to delete an ingredient essential to these faiths. Because of the noncentrality of the afterlife for Judaism, this tradition has been able to entertain a wide variety of different afterlife notions throughout its history, more so than perhaps any other religion.

The ancient Hebrews emphasized the importance of the present life over the afterlife. As with both the ancient Greeks and Mesopotamians, the afterlife, if it was considered at all, was conceived of as a pale shadow of earthly life, much like the Greek **Hades.** Also similar to the Greek Hades, in the Hebrew afterlife no distinction was made between the treatment of the just and the unjust after death. Instead, rewards and punishments were meted out in the present life, and in the covenant "contract" Yahweh promised to do just that.

One of the few stories in Hebrew Scriptures (the Old Testament) that mentions the afterlife is the tale of the so-called Witch of Endor. King Saul had banished, under threat of death, "all who trafficked with ghosts and spirits" (I Samuel 28:3). However, faced with a superior army and believing himself in a desperate situation, Saul, in disguise, consults a woman whom today we would refer to as a **medium.** This woman, who lived at Endor, summoned the spirit of the prophet Samuel from **She'ol,** the Hebrew equivalent of Hades. When Samuel arrived, he asked Saul, "Why have you disturbed me and brought me up?" (I Samuel 28:15) By making a directional reference ("brought me *up*"), the clear implication is that She'ol is underneath the surface of the earth.

Samuel told Saul that he should never have turned away from God, that he was on the verge of defeat, and, furthermore, that "tomorrow you and your sons will be with me" (I Samuel 28:19). By asserting that Saul's soul will soon be residing in the same resting place, the clear implication is that moral distinctions do not influence one's afterlife fate—the spirits of the good (e.g., Samuel) and the spirits of morally bad people (e.g., Saul) both end up in the same place, presumably under much the same conditions.

Although this is the general Old Testament view, reflection on the inequalities of this life and on the apparent failure of Yahweh to make good on his covenant promises led serious religious thinkers to consider the option of **resurrection.** The resurrection of ordinary human beings seems to have originated in the Persian (Iranian) religion of **Zoroastrianism.** As a result of several centuries of Persian control of the Middle East region, Jews were brought into contact with Zoroastrian religious ideas and the notion of resurrection. Zoroaster combined resurrection with the idea of a final judgment, in which the entire human race is resurrected and individuals rewarded or punished. This concept clearly appealed to Jewish religious thinkers of the time as an adequate way of coming to grips with the injustices that were so apparent in this life, and was incorporated into such late writings as the Book of Daniel.

The Book of Daniel was composed during the time of the Maccabees, around 165 B.C., when Judaism was suffering the first major, specifically religious persecution in its history. The Seleucid ruler Antiochus IV, descendant of one of Alexander the Great's generals, attempted to impose Hellenistic culture on his subjects in an effort to unify his realm. Although Hellenizing measures had been imposed for many years, it was not until 167 B.C. that the practice of Judaism was actually forbidden. Forbidden practices included temple sacrifices, circumcision, Sabbath observance, kosher restrictions, and possession of sacred books. Jews were even forced to eat foods that the Torah classified as impure and to sacrifice at Greek altars that were set up across the country. The death penalty was imposed upon refusal to comply with any of these requirements. The final insult occurred in December of 167 B.C., when a pig was sacrificed on an altar erected to Zeus in the temple. A successful revolt, led by the Maccabees, soon followed. This event is celebrated by the holiday of Hanukkah.

The Book of Daniel, which addresses these circumstances, envisions an apocalyptic notion of resurrection in its scenario of the end-time:

> Many of those who sleep in the dust of the earth shall awake, some to everlasting life, and some to shame and everlasting contempt (12:2).

Although the Jewish resurrection entails a type of afterlife, it is peculiar in that it is an afterlife that returns the deceased to this life. It is thus, in a sense, more of a continuation of the present life than a true afterlife. This peculiarity saves the original covenant relationship, and, hence, divine justice, by allowing Yahweh to reward devout Jews in what amounts to an extension of *this* life. Adopting this notion of resurrection also allowed Jews to maintain their notions about the essential goodness of this world and this life.

Resurrection is also mentioned in such apocryphal books as Second Maccabees, where it is described as a "wonderful reward" (II Maccabees 12:45). In postbiblical rabbinic Judaism, acceptance of the doctrine of resurrection became one of the essentials of the faith. The Mishnah even states, "All Israel has a portion in the world-to-come" (the postresurrection world) except "one who says, 'There is no resurrection of the dead'" (San. 10.1). In the standard basic prayer of the rabbinic liturgy, still recited daily by observant Jews, the second benediction of the Standing Prayer ('Amidah) praises God for the resurrection:

> You, O Lord, are mighty forever, you give life to the dead, you have great power to save. You sustain the living with loving kindness and revive the dead with great mercy; you support those who fall, heal those who are sick, release those who are captive, and keep your faith with those who sleep in the dust. Who is like you, powerful Master, and who resembles you, O King who kills, gives life, and brings forth salvation? You are faithful to bring the dead to life; blessed are You, O Lord, who revives the dead. (Goldberg, 1992, 107)

The belief in resurrection deeply affected early Jewish attitudes toward burial, and it was considered a Jew's duty to drop everything else and bury an exposed corpse, should one be encountered along the road. Such untended bodies were referred to by the rabbis as *met mitzvah,* which, roughly translated, means an obligatory corpse (one that a person is "obliged" to bury).

The remains of the body were considered a sort of "seed" from which Yahweh would later reconstruct the body. As an extension of this idea, the notion developed that a small bone in the spine, referred to as the *luz,* never completely disintegrated and formed the nucleus around which the body would be resurrected. This notion, in turn, filtered into Jewish folklore and was elaborated in practices associated with the need to protect the luz from accidental destruction. People who perished at sea, for instance, were regarded as having suffered an unspeakable fate, endangering their chances of resurrection. The need to preserve the remnants of the body also explains the Jewish aversion to the practice of cremation.

Following the Maccabean revolt, edicts against the practice of Judaism, which had been issued by Antiochus IV in an attempt to impose Hellenistic culture on his subjects and thus unify his realm, were repealed. The country continued to be involved in various fights and political intrigues until annexed by Rome during the first century B.C. Under Roman rule, various sects with differing notions of the afterlife proliferated. Both the early Christians and the pious Pharisees held what became the mainstream view of resurrection. The Sadducees, a group of older landowners that included many priests, emphasized the authority of the first five books of Hebrew Scriptures (the books of Moses) and emphatically rejected the notion of an afterlife, particularly the notion of a resurrection. As a privileged class, they were comfortable with the ancient Hebrew idea that God's rewards and punishments were meted out in the present life.

The most unusual sect with the most unusual (for Judaism) notion of the afterlife was the **Essenes,** a strict Jewish monastic group that awaited the apocalypse in a monastery at Qumran near the Dead Sea. In stark contrast to other forms of Judaism, the Essenes believed in the notion of an immortal **soul** that would be rewarded or punished in an afterlife **heaven** or **hell.** In their very un-Jewish antagonism toward the flesh, as well as in certain of their notions of soul, they appear to have been influenced by **Gnosticism.**

In the first century A.D., the Egyptian Jewish philosopher Philo also expressed belief in an afterlife of disembodied souls. In this idea, Philo was influenced by Neoplatonism rather than by the Essenes. Maimonides, the great medieval Jewish philosopher, expressed a similar belief, although accusations of blasphemy led him to write an essay in which he defended himself and asserted his belief in the resurrection.

In addition to these various views, a notion of limited **reincarnation,** termed *gilgul,* was espoused in Cabalistic (Jewish mystical) circles. In this view, people who had committed extraordinary sins were given an opportunity to return to life in order to set things right. More particularly, they were reincarnated in circumstances similar to those of their previous incarnation. Thus, Moses and Jethro, for example, were supposed to be the *gilgulim* of Cain and Abel.

As implied in the Book of Daniel, the Jewish notion of resurrection in the Maccabeean period was tied to a notion of judgment, and even to separate realms for the judged. In rabbinical thought, the model for heaven was Eden. The rabbinic word for hell, Gehenna, is taken from the name of a valley of fire where children were said to be sacrificed as burnt offerings to Baal and Moloch (Semitic deities). Jewish legend paints hell with all of the vividness that medieval Christians did, even associating particular tortures with particular sins, as in the following description:

> Some sinners were suspended by their eyelids, some by their ears, some by their hands, and some by their tongues. In addition, women were suspended by their hair and their breasts by chains of fire. Such punishments were inflicted on the basis of the sins that were committed: those who hung by their eyes looked lustfully upon their neighbors' wives and possessions; those who hung by their ears listened to empty and vain speech and did not listen to the Torah; those who hung by their tongues spoke foolishly and slanderously; those who hung by their hands robbed and murdered their neighbors. The women who hung by their hair and breasts uncovered them in the presence of young men in order to seduce them. (Cohn-Sherbok, 1987, 29)

At later points in this same account, sinners are stung by scorpions and lashed with fiery chains by Angels of Destruction.

Heaven is described with the same kind of vividness, although its pleasures are far more restrained than the tortures of hell. The following, found in Midrash Konen (part of the *Midrash,* or commentary) emphasizes the fine buildings and great expanse of heaven:

> The Gan Eden at the east measures 800,000 years (at 10 miles per day or 3,650 miles per year). There are five chambers for various classes of the righteous. The first is built of cedar, with a ceiling of transparent crystal. This is the habitation of non-Jews who become true and devoted converts to Judaism. They are headed by Obadiah the prophet and Onekelos the proselyte, who teach them the Law. The second is built of cedar, with a ceiling of fine silver. This is the habitation of the penitents, headed by

Manasseh, King of Israel, who teaches them the Law. (Cohn-Sherbok 1987, 27)

Other increasingly brilliant chambers made of gold and precious stones are also described.

In contemporary Judaism, the traditional, mainstream view of resurrection is maintained by the Orthodox, but generally not by the non-Orthodox. Outside the Orthodox fold, ordinary believers often accept the notion of an immortal soul, not unlike the notion held by most Christians. And many secular and Reform Jews continue to view themselves as part of the tradition of Judaism, without adhering to any sort of afterlife belief.

Sources:

Cohn-Sherbok, Daniel. "Death and Immortality in the Jewish Tradition." In Paul and Linda Badham, eds., *Death and Immortality in the Religions of the World.* New York: Paragon House, 1987.
Eliade, Mircea. *The Encyclopedia of Religion.* 16 vols. New York: Macmillan, 1987.
Goldberg, Robert. "Bound Up in the Bond of Life: Death and Afterlife in the Jewish Tradition." In Hiroshi Obayashi, ed., *Death and Afterlife: Perspectives of World Religions.* Westport, CT: Greenwood Press, 1992.
Mendenhall, George E. "From Witchcraft to Justice: Death and Afterlife in the Old Testament." In Hiroshi Obayashi, ed., *Death and Afterlife: Perspectives of World Religions.* Westport, CT: Greenwood Press, 1992.
Nielsen, Niels C., Jr., et al. *Religions of the World.* New York: St. Martin's Press, 1983.
West, James King. *Introduction to the Old Testament.* New York: Macmillan, 1981.

JUDGMENT OF THE DEAD

Not all cultures differentiate between the afterlife fates of morally good and morally bad individuals. In traditions in which such a distinction *is* made, the mechanism by which good souls are sent to happy states and evil souls directed to unhappy states may operate in different ways. Sometimes this dichotomization occurs automatically, as in southern Asian traditions in which the net effect of one's accumulated **karma** propels the departed soul to reincarnate in pleasant or unpleasant circumstances. Similarly, the religious notion of metempsychosis, the process by which souls enter a new body in the Pythagorean doctrine as well as in ancient Druid and Irish literature, is related to the belief in immortality and indirectly implies a judgment on the fate of the souls.

In Zoroastrianism and in certain other religions, the deceased must cross a bridge, which presents an easy passage for good souls but is difficult for evil souls. Here, again, the mechanism by which this occurs is impersonal. As the nomenclature Judgment of the Dead implies, the determination of the fate of the dead is often portrayed in more personal terms in which the deceased is brought into a kind of otherworldly courtroom to have judgment passed on the person's life by a divine or semidivine being.

References to the judgment of the dead are rather meager in Mesopotamian civilization. In ancient Egypt, tomb inscriptions from the Old Kingdom refer

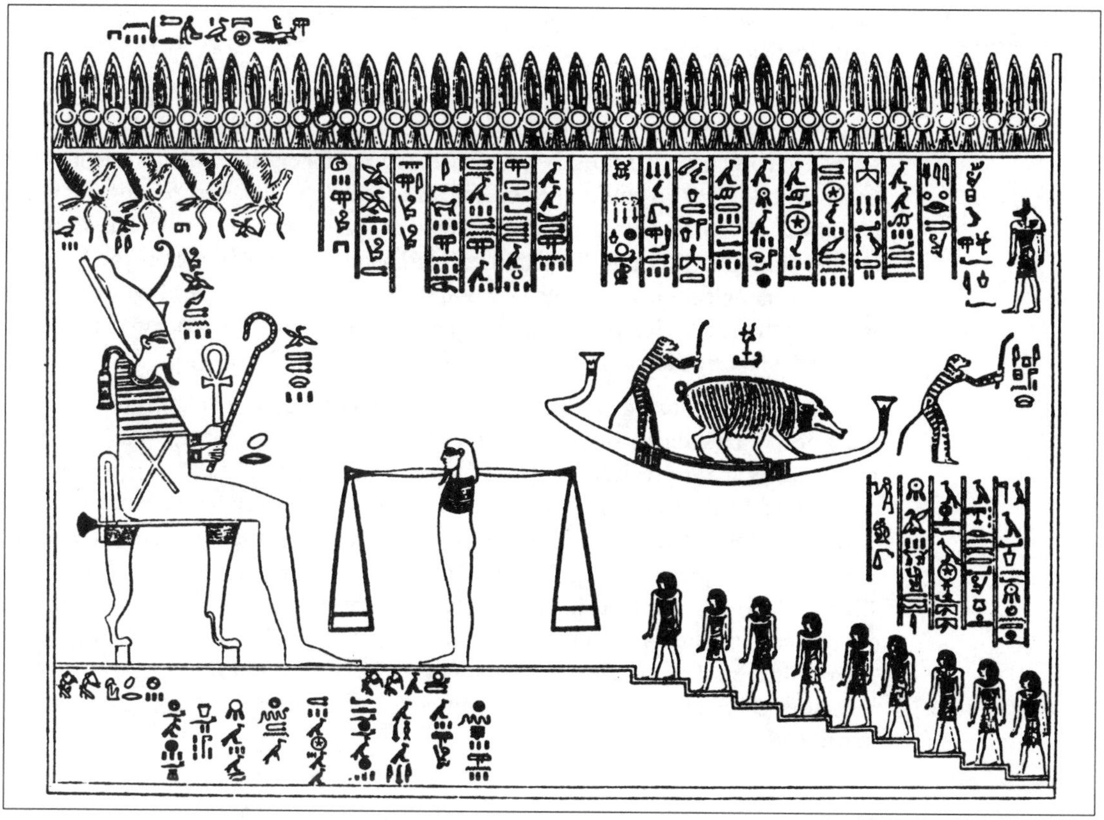

THE JUDGMENT HALL OF OSIRIS, ACCORDING TO THE BOOK OF GATES. (FROM CHAMPOLLION, MONUMENTS DE L'ÊGYPTE.) COURTESY OF THE ARC.

indirectly to an afterlife judgment. Religious texts in the Middle Kingdom (e.g., *Instruction for Merikare*) are explicit about an afterlife judgment for sinners, whose sins will be laid beside them in a heap. Another Egyptian religious text, the *Book of the Dead,* contains magic spells for protecting oneself from divine judgment. According to this book, the deceased recite a "negative confession" in which they must declare that they have not sinned during life. The soul is judged by **Osiris** (the judge of the underworld), who weighs on a balance the heart of the dead person against a feather to determine whether the dead deserves eternal beatitude. Souls who do not measure up are consumed by the devourer of the dead.

In the ancient Vedic texts of India a distinction was made by the underworld judge, King Yama, between those who had been sincere and liars. A weighing of good and evil is also mentioned in later Brahmanic texts. In Chinese Mahayana Buddhism the judge of the dead (Yen-lo Wang), along with other divinities of Chinese origin, determine the fate of the dead. In Japanese Buddhism one also finds a judge of the dead, known as Enma-ō. According to Chinese Taoism, in the judgment of the dead the soul is assigned to one of many hells or paradises found on the Chinese mythological landscape.

In the ancient Greek world, Hades was an underworld kingdom that hosted the shadows of the dead, whereas the Elysian Fields were accessible only to the righteous. In the Homeric poems, Minos is mentioned as a regulator rather than a judge of the dead. With the development of Pythagorean doctrine, a true afterlife judgment was conceived in Pythagoras's notion of reincarnation. Orphism (a Greek mystery religion) introduced the afterlife judgment of Rhadamanthus, Triptolemos, and Aiakos in its mythological system. **Plato** mentions the judgment of the dead by these three figures at the conclusion of *Gorgias.* In ancient Roman literature one finds judges of the dead who originated in Greece, Rhadamanthus, and Minos.

In early Judaism the deeds of the dead were recorded and a judgment of the dead mentioned to establish punishment for the sinners or reward for the righteous (culminating in resurrection). In Christianity the judgment of the soul is believed to occur upon death of the individual, who will be assigned either eternal condemnation or reward (Hell or Heaven) or, in some Christian churches, purgatory. Some texts also mention a final judgment day, held at the end of time by God or by the Son, Jesus Christ, which will culminate in the resurrection of the righteous and eternal damnation for sinners. In Islam a notion of an imminent judgment day draws primarily from Jewish literature; in the *Quran* a description of a trial of the soul refers to a scale weighing good and evil deeds, and consequently to eternal reward (Paradise) or penalty (Hell).

Sources:

Eliade, Mircea. *Encyclopedia of Religion.* 16 vols. New York: Macmillan, 1987.

Van Der Leeuw, G., trans. *Religion in Essence and Manifestation.* Vol. 1. Gloucester, MA: Peter Smith, 1967. (Originally published 1933.)

JUNG, CARL GUSTAV

Carl Jung, the famous Swiss Psychologist (1875–1961), was born at Kesswil, Thurgau, Switzerland. He is considered to be the originator of analytical psychology. Jung studied medicine at the University of Basel, Switzerland, and took his M.D. degree in 1902 at the University of Zurich. Between 1907 and 1913 he became a disciple of Freud, but their collaboration did not last. They both studied dreams, but Jung advanced an approach that did not depend heavily on sexual problems, in contrast with Freud, who insisted upon sexual roots for neuroses. Jung was more interested in the archetypal symbols that appeared in dreams, rather than in what dreams revealed about personal wishes and repressed fears.

Also, Jung, whose thought was deeply influenced by his own Christian background and commitment to religious humanism, believed that religion was a fundamental element of the psychotherapeutic process and of life itself, whereas Freud insisted upon an entirely biological understanding of psychoanalysis. The paper *Symbols of the Libido,* which appeared in 1913, marked Jung's break with

Freudian theory, and the psychology that emerged afterward focused on the division between the conscious and unconscious and on the personal unconscious as a branch of the tree of the **collective unconscious.** According to Jung, one could bring unconscious contents into consciousness through a process of individuation, or journey of the soul, which he called Heilsweg. Jung's analytical psychology emphasized the importance in this spiritual journey of archetypal symbols, which have a universal application in human life, as well as individual symbols, which appear in both waking and dreaming life.

After the break with Freud, Jung went through a period of inner disorder and seeking, during which he carried out a journey of exploration into his own unconscious mind. He published only a few works during that period, such as his *Psychology of the Unconscious* and *VII Sermones ad Mortuos* (Seven Sermons to the Dead), written in three evenings in a semiautomatic way and published anonymously. In the same period, Jung's household seemed to be bothered by ghostly entities. In his interpretation of the spiritual journey of the human being, he also drew upon Eastern philosophies and various occult ideas, such as alchemy. The supernatural was an object of preoccupation for Jung, and it played a considerable part in his life. He had visions during his childhood as well as later life, and had an experience with the spirit medium Miss S. W. that encouraged his reading into the philosophical aspects of occultism. Some of his reminiscences are recorded in *Memories, Dreams, Reflections,* an autobiographical memoir that, like *The Soul and Death,* deals with death and afterlife.

Although Jung always refused to assert overtly that there was life after death, he usually insinuated that this was the case. He believed in a spiritual survival beyond physical death, and this conviction was strengthened by his belief that the psyche, as dreams evidence, behaves as if it will continue to exist. According to Jung, death dreams are linked with a primordial set of archetypes, and through their analysis it is possible to conclude that there will be a human existence after death that will be characterized by the level of consciousness attained by one while alive. Thus, earthly life is highly significant, and what a human being brings over at death is very important, for it helps the person to achieve the upper limit of knowledge and awareness in the afterlife.

Jung maintained that the assumption that there is an afterlife means a great deal for most people and allows them to live more sensibly and more at peace. Even though there is no way to prove a continuance of the soul after death, some experiences can incline us toward that view, such as myths and the hints and figurative allusions sent to us from the unconscious through dreams. According to Jung, death usually appears as a catastrophe, which is brutal not only as a physical event, but also psychically. But if one believes in eternity, death can be regarded as a joyful event, a wedding in which the soul joins its missing half with the wholeness.

Among Jung's other most significant works are *The Theory of Psychoanalysis* (1916), *Psychological Types* (1923), *Modern Man in Search of a Soul* (1933),

Psychology and Religion (1938), *Psychology and Alchemy* (1953), *The Interpretation of Nature and the Psyche* (1955), and *Archetypes and the Collective Unconscious* (1959).

Sources:

Cavendish, Richard, ed. *Encyclopedia of the Unexplained: Magic, Occultism and Parapsychology.* London: Arkana Penguin Books, 1989.

Jung, Carl Gustav. *Memories, Dreams, Reflections.* New York: Vintage Books, 1965.

Kramer, Kenneth Paul. *Death Dreams. Unveiling Mysteries of the Unconscious Mind.* New York: Paulist Press, 1993.

K

KARDEC, ALLAN

The French doctor Hippolyte Leon Denizard Rivail (1804–1869) was the founder of spiritism, also called Kerdecism, which differs from Anglo-American **Spiritualism** primarily because of its emphasis on reincarnationist beliefs. His pseudonym, Allan Kardec, is attributed to information he received about past lives during which his name was Allan and Kardec. This information was received through Celina Japhet, a professional somnambulist with whom he participated in **séances.**

Many of Kardec's scripts, produced while he was in trance, called for compulsory reincarnation, and *The Book of the Spirits,* published in 1856, explained these concepts. Its 1857 revision became the guidebook of spiritist philosophy, and, with Kardec's other works, *The Book of Mediums* (1864), *The Gospels According to Spiritism* (1864), *Heaven and Hell* (1865), *Genesis* (1867), *Experimental Spiritism and Spiritualist Philosophy,* and *The Four Gospels* (1881), have had a particular influence in Brazil.

According to Kardec, reincarnation through many lives is necessary to achieve spiritual progress. Also, the interference of past incarnations may be the cause of such problems as epilepsy, schizophrenia, and multiple personality disorders, so that understanding past lives may help heal these disorders. This, it should be noted, is the basic premise of **past-lives therapy,** which Kardec anticipated by a century.

Kardec encouraged the practice of healing/therapy through the acceptance of spirit communications. He also criticized contemporaneous psychical research through the monthly magazine *La Revue Spirite* and the Society of Psychologic Studies, of which he was president.

Sources:

Doyle, Sir Arthur Conan. *The History of Spiritualism, Vol. I and II.* New York: Arno Press, 1975.

ALLAN KARDEC. COURTESY OF THE ARC.

Fodor, Nandor. *An Encyclopaedia of Psychic Science.* Secaucus, NJ: The Citadel Press, 1966. (Originally published 1933.)
Guiley, Rosemary Ellen. *Harper's Encyclopedia of Mystical and Paranormal Experience.* San Francisco: Harper, 1991.

KARMA

The wide variety of southern Asian (especially Indian) religious systems all assume the basic validity of the law of karma. In its simplest form, this law operates impersonally like a natural law, ensuring that every good or bad deed eventually returns to the individual in the form of reward or punishment commensurate with the original deed. The term derives from the Sanskrit root word *kr,* which means to act, do, or make.

Karma originally referred to ritual action, which in the Hindu tradition produces concrete results if properly performed (the priest controlled the gods if his rituals were correctly carried out). Traditionally, some of the discourse about karma was carried out in terms of agricultural imagery—in which the original action is the ''seed'' of later "fruit"—suggesting the region's long-standing agrarian economy as a source for the notion. The concept of karma was later extended to refer to proper action in general.

The notion that one's actions set loose forces that eventually return to the actor is subject to more than one level of interpretation. When initially transferred from the ritual to the moral sphere, the notion of karma operated independently of the actor's intentions. Thus, if a pedestrian stepped out in front of a speeding truck (or a speeding chariot, to place it in the ancient Indian context) and was killed, the driver incurred the same negative karma as if he or she had intentionally murdered the pedestrian. However, as karma was a staple of Indian thought, centuries of reflection on the concept resulted in more sophisticated notions, and earlier ideas that saw a person creating karmic reactions as a result of unintended actions were discarded.

Karma also refers to both the personality patterns that result from past actions and the forces at large in the cosmos that bring reward or retribution to the individual. In yogic psychology, the personality patterns—in the sense of the subconscious motivators of action—shaped by karma are referred to as **samskaras.** Where karma ties in with afterlife notions is in the southern Asian tradition, in which it is karma that compels human beings to "take rebirth" (**reincarnate**) in successive lifetimes. In other words, if one dies before reaping the effects of one's actions (as most people do), the karmic process demands that one come back in a future life. Coming back in another life also allows karmic forces to reward or punish one by determining the circumstances in which one is born. Hence, for example, an individual who was generous in one lifetime might be reborn as a wealthy person in the next incarnation.

For the most part, mainstream southern Asian thinking does not view the cycle of death and rebirth as attractive. Hence, the ultimate goal of most Indian religions is to escape the cycle of death and rebirth (**samsara**). Although many contemporary Westerners view the prospects of reincarnation positively, the traditional southern Asian view is that returning to live another life is distinctly undesirable. That is, since life in the physical body always involves suffering, we should strive to escape the wheel of rebirth. By the time of Buddha (approximately 600 B.C.), the Indian consensus was that it was desire (passion, attachment, want, craving) that kept one involved in the karmic process, and hence desire that kept one bound to the death/rebirth process. Consequently, the goal of getting off the ferris wheel of reincarnation necessarily involved freeing oneself from desire.

To reduce the possibility of karma-producing actions, the Indian tradition has tended to view asceticism/ monasticism as the mode of life best suited to achieving the goal of release from samsara. However, by the time of the **Bhagavad Gita** (composed sometime around the beginning of the Christian era), another possibility had been thought through. Because it was the craving associated with an activity that set the karmic process in motion, rather than the activity itself, the author(s) of the *Bhagavad Gita* developed an alternative approach that called for remaining in the everyday world (rather than retreating to a hermitage) while performing one's deeds with an attitude of dispassionate detachment. Difficult though this may be, Krishna, who in the *Gita* is the principal spokesperson for this point of view, asserts that such a frame of mind is indeed possible if the individual constantly maintains an attitude of devotion to God. When successful, one can even engage in such activities as war (as long as one is fighting because it is one's duty) and avoid the negative karma that normally results from such actions.

Sources:

Feuerstein, Georg. *Encyclopedic Dictionary of Yoga.* New York: Paragon House, 1990.
Zimmer, Heinrich. *Philosophies of India.* New York: Bollingen, 1951.

KÜBLER-ROSS, ELISABETH

The contemporary physician Elisabeth Kübler-Ross is one of the most eminent authorities on the subject of death and dying. She was born in Switzerland, where she worked as a country doctor and volunteered to assist escaped refugees during World War II. A visit to the concentration camps after the war encouraged her to help people who were facing death, and to extend her medical background by improving her knowledge about the human psyche. After moving to the United States, she formally started working with terminally ill patients in 1965 as a faculty member at the University of Chicago. She continued in this line of work at the Manhattan State Hospital in New York, where she investigated life after death, giving particular attention to accounts by patients who reported out-of-body experiences.

Kübler-Ross's books include *On Death and Dying* (1974), *Death: The Final Stage of Growth* (1975), *To Live Until We Say Goodbye* (1978), *Living with Death and Dying* (1981), and *Children and Death* (1985). Death, like birth, involves great changes and adjustments, such as inconveniences and pain, but also joy, reunion, and a new beginning. Her books attempt to answer some of the questions posed by her audiences, usually regarding the different ''languages'' that terminally ill adults and children use when they try to convey their inner needs. She also deals with family problems after death has occurred, as well as with the problems faced by doctors, nurses, and others who take care of terminally ill patients.

She distinguishes five stages of death through which each person passes and which last longer or shorter according to the individual's personality and experience. The first stage is that of denial, in which a person refuses to face the idea of death. This is followed by anger. As anger is released, the person experiences a period of bargaining. At this stage the individual is overwhelmed by the pain of parting, the recognition of unrealized goals, and the fear of death, and usually asks for some kind of help. The next stage is that of preparatory depression, the lowest point of the journey, in which the individual feels powerless and tired of struggling and needs an inner adjustment. This stage increases personal awareness and helps the individual to reestablish contact with others. The last step is acceptance, rebirth, and increased self-reliance. At this stage people usually experience a very deep feeling of peace, and they often relive experiences from their life.

Sources:

Kübler-Ross, Elisabeth. *Living with Death and Dying.* New York: Macmillan, 1981.

———. *Questions and Answers on Death and Dying.* New York: Macmillan, 1974.

Parrish-Harra, Carol W. *The New Age Handbook on Death and Dying.* Santa Monica, CA: IBS Press, 1989.

Shepard, Leslie A., ed. *Encyclopedia of Occultism & Parapsychology.* Detroit, MI: Gale Research, 1991.

L

Life Reading

In metaphysical circles, the word *reading* is used in the specialized sense of referring to the information one receives from a **medium** or psychic, although sometimes it can also be used to refer to the information one receives from a palmist, astrologer, or tarot reader. In this context, the expression *life reading* refers to a psychic reading in which the psychic doing the reading supposedly looks back into one's past lives and provides information on who one was and what one did in prior incarnations. Life readings, in contrast to **past-lives therapy,** are more focused on providing information than on providing therapeutic insights, although people often seek such a reading in order to understand current problems or to discover potential talents. Critics have observed that often the past lives uncovered during such readings portray the person receiving the reading as having been a general or a queen, and almost never a stableman or a bar maid.

Sources:

Bletzer, June G. *The Donning International Encyclopedic Psychic Dictionary.* Norfolk, VA: Donning, 1986.

Head, Joseph, and S. L. Cranston. *Reincarnation: The Phoenix Fire Mystery.* New York: Julian Press/Crown, 1977.

Limbo

Limbo literally means borderland (from Latin *limbus,* border) and refers to a realm where souls of the departed who for some reason have not made it to the other world are "stuck," usually temporarily. **Virgil,** for example, placed souls who had not been properly buried in a Limbo realm where they had to wait a hundred years before being admitted to the Land of the Dead.

DESCENT INTO LIMBO BY GIOVANNI BELLINI (1429–1516).

The notion of the dead as stuck in a transitional realm is very ancient. In most of the world's religious traditions, the journey from this world to the abode of the dead is not thought of as a step that one takes immediately upon death. Instead, following death, spirits must find their way to the otherworld. In many cases souls are unable or unwilling to undertake the journey to the realm of the dead and continue to linger around their living relatives, often bothering the living in some way. As spirits that are no longer part of the realm of the living and yet cannot or will not find their way to the realm of the dead, these "haunting" spirits exist in a kind of borderland—or Limbo—between life and death.

In religious traditions that postulate a heaven and a hell as the final abode of the soul, serious thinkers have grappled with the fate of those who, although not ethical exemplars, have been more or less good and not guilty of truly evil actions. This has led to the development of ideas of intermediate afterlife abodes in which souls are purified and made fit for paradise. The most famous of such intermediate realms is Catholic **purgatory.** Prior to the elaboration of the notion of purgatory, the early Christian community had accepted a less-developed idea of Limbo. Limbo provided a realm to which unbaptised babies could go without having to be condemned to hell.

Another question Limbo answered for the early Church concerned the fate of righteous people who had passed away in the eras before the good news of Christianity. That is, Christians of the first few centuries A.D. imagined that only Christian souls could go to heaven. But where does that leave such righteous and deserving individuals as the Old Testament patriarchs (e.g., Abraham, Moses)? Placing them in a Limbo realm, from which Christ later rescued them and conducted them to heaven, solved this problem.

Sources:

Eliade, Mircea, ed. *The Encyclopedia of Religion.* 16 vols. New York: Macmillan, 1987.
Eliade, Mircea. *Shamanism: Archaic Techniques of Ecstasy.* Reprint. Willard R. Trask, trans. Princeton, NJ: Princeton University Press, 1972.
McDannell, Colleen, and Bernhard Lang. *Heaven: A History.* 1988; New York: Vintage, 1990.
Turner, Alice K. *The History of Hell.* New York: Harcourt Brace, 1993.

LINGA SHARIRA (SUBTLE BODY)

While many religious traditions work with a simple dualism of body and soul, other traditions postulate one or more subtle, secondary "bodies" in which the soul is clothed. This subtle body constitutes a kind of intermediary level between the physical body and the soul proper. Because it is nonphysical (in the ordinary sense of physical), it survives the death of the physical body. Some traditional cultures have gone so far as to map out the anatomy of the subtle body. The best known of these is the Chinese—with acupuncture, which maps the vessels (meridians) along which a form of subtle energy (the *chi*) flows. When the flow of energy is disturbed, bodily illness results. The practice of acupuncture is devoted to correcting these energy imbalances.

Undoubtedly the most complex understanding of the subtle body is provided by the Hindu yoga tradition, in which the subtle body is referred to as the *linga sharira* (Sanskrit for "body of characteristics"). Similar to acupuncture, this tradition postulates an intricate map of energy channels (*nadis*) along which subtle energy (*prana*) flows. Additionally, the ancient yogis described a series of energy centers (the *chakras*) arranged along the spinal column. Unlike the Chinese acupuncturists, the Hindu yogis were less interested in healing than they were in achieving release from the cycle of death and rebirth, and traditional discussions of the linga sharira revolve around ways of regulating the prana so as to achieve this end.

Sources:

Feuerstein, Georg. *Encyclopedic Dictionary of Yoga.* New York: Paragon House, 1990.
Zimmer, Heinrich. *Philosophies of India.* New York: Bollingen, 1951.

LORDS OF KARMA

Karma, the moral law of cause and effect, is often described as an impersonal principle (like the law of gravity) that ensures that every good or bad action is

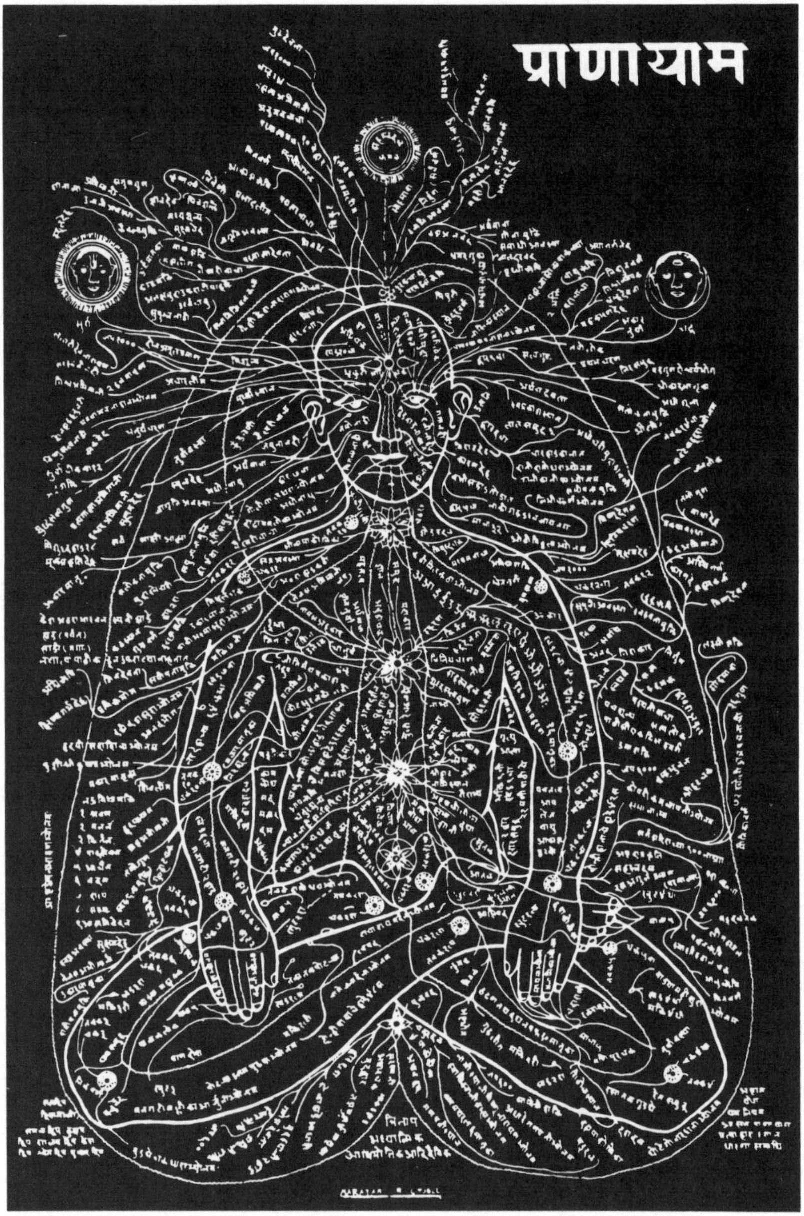

TRADITIONAL SOUTH ASIAN DIAGRAM OF THE SUBTLE BODY. COURTESY OF THE ARC.

eventually rewarded or punished, either in the present lifetime or in a future incarnation. Certain religious thinkers, however, have not been satisfied with the notion of an impersonal principle and have postulated intelligent agents who regulate the operation of the law of karma. Particularly in the Western esoteric tradition (the most visible manifestation of which has been the Theosophical Society), it has been postulated that such agents—sometimes referred to as lords of karma—adjust the effects of karma so that individual souls may learn from their mistakes, and hence eventually develop into better people.

Sources:

Bletzer, June G. *The Donning International Encyclopedic Psychic Dictionary.* Norfolk, VA: Donning, 1986.
Drury, Nevill. *Dictionary of Mysticism and the Esoteric Traditions.* 2d ed. Dorset, England: Prism, 1992.

M

MANICHAEISM

Manichaeism was a religious movement that arose in the third century and spread across the Mediterranean world. Founded by Mani (a Persian born into a Christian and Jewish community in Assyria in A.D. 215), Manichaeism was a mixture of **Gnosticism,** Zoroastrianism, and Christianity that spread across the Western world and lasted for the better part of a thousand years (it may even have lasted until the twentieth century in China). Its central teaching was a severe dualism between spirit and matter, soul and body. St. Augustine, the most influential of the church fathers, converted to Christianity from Manicheism, and some have said that Christianity's antagonism toward the flesh was influenced by Augustine's former religion. Although this movement died out during the Western Middle Ages, the term Manichaeism continued to be used to refer to any sect or teaching that seemed to overemphasize the struggle between good and evil.

Mani began preaching his new religion at age 24. He was eventually executed by orthodox Zoroastrians around the year 276. Mani's extreme dualism was similar to certain strands of Gnosticism, which emphasized the antagonism between the body and the soul. The soul was a fallen divine spark from the realm of light, while the body was the creation of the evil god and his associates, the archons. Also as in Gnosticism, Mani saw human beings as trapped in a cycle of reincarnation that not even suicide could end. Manichaeism preached a rather severe asceticism, especially with regard to the sexual instinct.

Through ascetic living and following Mani's teachings, the elect *(perfecti)* were thought to be able to ascend directly into the light. Everyone else reincarnated until they completely purified themselves. However, at Christ's return, the unrepentant were to be thrown into flames that would engulf the material world.

Sources:

Crim, Keith, ed. *The Perennial Dictionary of World Religions.* 1981. Reprint, New York: Harper & Row, 1989.

Eliade, Mircea, ed. *The Encyclopedia of Religion.* 16 vols. New York: Macmillan, 1987.

Turner, Alice K. *The History of Hell.* New York: Harcourt Brace, 1993.

MARTYRDOM

Martyrs are people who voluntarily offer up their life in sacrifice for their group. Their central motive is altruism, and they focus the ideology of their group on the meaning of life in relation to death.

In early Christianity the martyr, a human sacrifice whose soul had intercessory ability, was guaranteed eternal life in heaven and was even exempted from the Judgment Day proceedings, since all of his sins were automatically forgiven. Thus, the martyr, who died convinced of his legitimate authority as the incarnation of the

MARTYRDOM: THE STONING OF STEPHEN.

death experience, an extreme emotional shock, or profound grief. Mediumistic practices include the diagnosis and cure of diseases, some of which have been pronounced incurable. Most parapsychologists claim that some mediums possess striking psychical abilities, whereas most **Spiritualists** believe that all individuals are mediums, although in varying degrees.

According to the Spiritualist theory, mediumistic phenomena are produced by the spirits of the dead through the agency of the medium. The attempt to communicate with spirits of the dead and the gods through mediums has occupied a special place throughout history, in all cultures in every area of the world. In ancient times mediumship was the craft of oracles, seers, shamans, and prophets—that is, of those individuals who were the intermediaries between this world and the spirit realm. Ancient Egyptian priests and priestesses, Chinese emperors, Shinto shamans, Greek oracles, as well as the founders of major religions claimed to have communicated with disembodied souls and to have received instructions from them. Among the best-known mediums in recorded history is the oracle of Delphi, in Greece, to which people would travel to seek advice from the god Apollo, who was believed to communicate through the medium Pythia. Contact with the spirit world became suspect with the rise of monotheism, which admitted only communication from the one God through prophets. The New Testament also contains many accounts of glossolalia, visions, apparitions, and disembodied voices.

The modern Spiritualist movement, which began in the United States in 1848, when the Fox sisters of Hydesville, New York, began to receive alleged communications from the spirit world through rappings, has played a prominent role in advancing mediumship. The early rappings developed into more elaborate manifestations, such as table-turning, which became a popular means of communicating with deceased individuals.

During this period several charismatic mediums achieved notoriety, such as Andrew Jackson Davis, who reported conversations with the ancient Greek physician Galen and with the spirit of the deceased Swedish scientist and religious writer Emanuel **Swedenbörg.** The most successful of the physical mediums was the Scotchman Daniel Dunglas Home, who moved objects without contact, materialized various objects, and levitated heavy furniture. He held séances before French, Prussian, and Dutch sovereigns and in 1864 was expelled from Rome as a sorcerer. He is the subject of Robert Browning's poem "Sludge the Medium" (1864).

Levitations, supernatural lights, and apports (materializations) were among the manifestations produced by **Rev. Stainton Moses.** He also produced automatic writing, through which he claimed that his spirit controls dictated his work *Spirit Teachings* (1894). The slate-writing of "Dr." Henry Slade and William Eglinton were quite popular, as were the manifestations produced by important mediums such as Eusapia Palladino and a Mrs. Piper.

Many publications reputedly written by spirits through mediums appeared during the later decades of the nineteenth century, such as the 900-page book entitled *Oahspe,* Frederick S. Oliver's *A Dweller on Two Planets,* and **Helena Blavatsky's** books *Isis Unveiled* and *The Secret Doctrine.* One of the most famous investigations into this area was Frederic Myers's *Human Personality and Its Survival of Bodily Death,* in which the author postulates that **cross-correspondences** represent valid proof of the survival of human consciousness after bodily death.

After 1900, interest in mediumship declined because numerous frauds were exposed by investigators, such as those belonging to the **Society for Psychical Research,** founded in England in 1882, and the American Society for Psychical Research, established in 1884. Several physical mediums were caught using stage magic tricks or impersonating the spirits they were supposed to be materializing. Fraud also existed in mental mediumship, particularly around the mid-twentieth century, but all of the phenomena that occurred could not be explained as trickery.

Sources:

Cavendish, Richard, ed. *Encyclopedia of the Unexplained: Magic, Occultism and Parapsychology.* London: Arkana Penguin Books, 1989.

Shepard, Leslie A., ed. *Encyclopedia of Occultism & Parapsychology.* Detroit, MI: Gale Research, 1991.

Zolar's Book of the Spirit. Englewood Cliffs, New Jersey: Prentice-Hall, 1987.

MESMER, FRANZ ANTON

Franz Anton, or Friedrich Mesmer (1734–1815), was born at Iznang on Lake Constance, Germany, and studied medicine at the University of Vienna, where he put forward the theory that a magnetic fluid surrounds and links all things and beings on earth and in the heavens.

The idea of such a fluid, which has its origins in ancient times in both the West and the East, is the approximate equivalent of the Hindu notion of *prana,* the Chinese *chi,* and the Japanese *ki.* It was argued that through this force one person could influence the organism and psyche of another, and that the influence exerted by the fluid on living creatures was comparable to the effect produced by the common magnet, to which medicinal powers were attributed. The fluid was called animal magnetism.

Mesmer, following the ideas of the English physician Richard Mead about the power of the sun and moon on the human body, wrote *De Planetarum Influxu* (Planetary Influence), which greatly influenced Father Maximilian Hehl. Hehl believed in the influence of planetary magnetism on physical health and used magnets to treat pain and magnetic imbalances of the body.

Mesmer, who also started using magnets, maintained that sickness was the result of an obstacle to the flow of the fluid through the body, which could be controlled by mesmerizing or massaging the body's magnetic poles and, after inducing a crisis, restoring the harmony of man with nature. During his practices, Mesmer was able to induce sleep, later called hypnosis or great sleep, during which various forms of psychical phenomena occurred, such as communication with the dead or with distant spirits, which sent messages through the fluid to the patient's internal sixth sense.

Although Mesmer was not directly concerned with matters of the afterlife, the association of his methods with spirit communication makes him an important figure in the birth of **Spiritualism.**

Mesmer later found that the vital energy could be transmitted directly from healer to patient through touch or with the help of iron rods or wands. In 1778 he founded in Paris a fashionable hospital, which he maintained until 1789, although his fortunes declined after Louis XVI established two commissions that investigated Mesmer's practices and found no evidence to support the existence of animal magnetism. The French Revolution forced him to leave the country. He died at Lake Constance in 1815.

Sources:

Darnton, Robert. *Mesmerism and the End of the Enlightenment in France.* New York: Schocken Books, 1970.

Guiley, Rosemary Ellen. *Harper's Encyclopedia of Mystical & Paranormal Experience.* San Francisco: HarperCollins, 1991.

Mitchell, Edgar D. *Psychic Exploration. A Challenge for Science.* New York: G. P. Putnam's Sons, 1974.

Vasiliev, Leonid L. *Mysterious Phenomena of the Human Psyche.* New York: University Books, 1965.

MESOPOTAMIA

Mesopotamia is the ancient civilization—or, perhaps better, the series of related civilizations (e.g., Sumeria, Babylonia, Assyria)—that occupied the valley of the Tigris and Euphrates Rivers up until the fourth century B.C. After Alexander the Great's conquest, the area lost much of its cultural and religious distinctiveness, becoming part of the Greek cultural sphere. More than a thousand years later, it was the center of the Islamic empire during the height of Muslim classical civilization. The boundaries of present-day Iraq, correspond roughly to those of ancient Mesopotamia.

Relatively little was known about Mesopotamia until about 150 years ago, when archaeologists began unearthing the area's ancient cities. As a result of Babylonia's conquest of ancient Palestine—and, as a consequence, the negative attention Mesopotamia received in the Hebrew Bible—much of what *was* known was not particularly favorable. The judgment of Babylon in Judeo-Christian scriptures was so harsh that even today the mention of Babylon evokes images of moral decadence.

Because the Mesopotamians wrote on clay tablets, many of which have survived the centuries, it has been possible to reconstruct many of their religious beliefs. In common with most traditional religious systems, the Mesopotamians populated the cosmos with a rather large (some sources say several thousand) pantheon of gods and goddesses. Some of these were distinguished as the patron deities of particular city-states, so the importance of various gods tended to vary in different time periods according to the relative strength of their respective cities. Thus Marduk, patron of Babylon, rose from the status of a rather obscure divinity to become king of the gods with the rise of Babylon's political fortunes.

Mesopotamia

Like the gods of the Greek and Roman pantheons, Mesopotamian divinities were pictured as human beings ''drawn large.'' The gods were, in other words, not much more than strong human beings, possessing magical powers and immortality. Humanity, for its part, was created out of clay to serve the gods. Unlike the case in Judaism, Christianity, and Islam, this creation did not include the fashioning of an immortal soul; hence, the afterlife was conceived of as a pale shadow of earthly life, much like the Jewish **She'ol** or the Greek **Hades.** The Mesopotamian afterlife is described in an oft-cited passage from *The Epic of Gilgamesh* in which Enkidu, **Gilgamesh's** servant and companion, relates a dream of the otherworld:

> There is the house whose people sit in darkness; dust is their food and clay their meat. They are clothed like birds with wings for covering, they see no light, they sit in darkness. I entered the house of dust and I saw the kings of the earth, their crowns put away forever. (Sandars 1972, 92)

As was the case with the Greek notion of Hades, mainstream Mesopotamian thought about the afterlife made no distinction between the treatment of the just and the unjust after death. The chief distinction was between the state of those who receive proper burial and memorial services and those who do not. When these matters were attended to properly, the soul rested easily. When neglected, the dead became agitated ghosts who haunted the living. In at least certain periods of Mesopotamian history, this notion appears to have been taken quite literally. For example, when in 646 B.C. Ashurbanipal of Assyria conquered the capital city of Assyria's long-standing enemy Elam, he wrote a letter in which he bragged as follows:

> I tore down, demolished and exposed the tombs of their ancient and recent kings who did not revere Ishtar, my queen. I took their bones to the city of Assur, inflicting unrest upon their ghosts and depriving them of memorial rites and libations. (Cooper 1992, 28)

Mesopotamians, as did many of the other traditional peoples of the world, imagined the universe as a three-tiered cosmos of heaven, earth, and underworld. Heaven was reserved for deities, most of whom resided there; living human beings occupied the middle world; and the spirits of the dead (*gidim*) resided beneath the earth. The literal identification of the realm of the dead with a region beneath the surface of the earth is reflected in a myth in which a hole is punched in the earth, allowing Gilgamesh to communicate with his deceased friend Enkidu. There were numerous names for the realm of the dead, many of which meant simply ''ground'' or ''earth.'' Other designations were ''desert,'' ''lower world,'' and ''land of no return.'' Various sources pictured the journey to the underworld as a descent on a stairway along which one passed through one or more gates guarded by underworld officials. Other sources referred to an underworld river across which one passed to the underworld in a boat, comparable to the Greek concept of the underworld.

Again similarly to the Greek Hades, the Mesopotamian underworld was described as dark, dusty, and unpleasant. The deceased wandered aimlessly about, unclothed or dressed in feathers, with nothing but dirt to eat. Certain demons and dead gods also shared the underworld with deceased human beings. The chief deity of this realm was the goddess Ereshkigal, who seduced the upper world god Nergal into remaining in the underworld as her consort. Although she could be harsh, Ereshkigal was not a devil or Satan figure. The dead stood before her and she pronounced their death sentence. Simultaneously, their names were entered in the ranks of the dead by the scribe Geshtinana. Other, lesser divinities served Ereshkigal as her minister (Namtar), administrator (Pabilsag), majordomo (Nigishzida), and gatekeeper (Neti). Rather than enjoying her job, the queen of the underworld was portrayed as saddened by the fate of many of her subjects, as reflected in the following remarks:

> I weep for young men forced to abandon sweethearts.
> I weep for girls wrenched from their lovers' laps.
> For the infant child I weep, expelled before its time.
>
> (Dalley 1989, 156)

One of the more widespread Mesopotamian stories involved the descent of the goddess Ishtar to the underworld. The first version of this tale was recorded by the Sumerians, whose name for Ishtar was Inanna. The second version was a later, Akkadian text. Ishtar was the most important goddess in all periods of Mesopotamian history, the parallel of the Mediterranean Aphrodite/ Venus. Unlike her classical parallels, however, Ishtar was a goddess of war. While Ishtar was queen of heaven and earth, Ereshkigal, her sister, was, as mentioned, queen of the underworld. Precisely why Ishtar should have undertaken such a perilous journey is obscure. Some interpreters have speculated that Ishtar wished to usurp her sister and extend her rule to the underworld; others that she simply wished to visit her sister.

The Sumerian version begins with Inanna looking longingly toward the underworld:

> From the summits of heaven
> she looked into the pit,
> She was a god on the summits of heaven
> but her heart was in hell.
>
> (Sandars 1971, 135)

The Akkadian retelling of the story portrays Ishtar quite differently, picturing her more as a belligerent aggressor. When she arrives at the outer gate to the underworld, for instance, Ishtar demands entrance:

> If you do not open the gate for me to come in,
> I shall smash the door and shatter the bolt. . . !
>
> (Dalley, 1989, 155)

In both versions, before embarking, Ishtar has the wisdom to inform her chief minister that she is about to undertake a journey to the underworld and instructs him to appeal to the gods in heaven to intervene should it become necessary to retrieve her from her sister's realm. As she descends, Ishtar/ Inanna passes through seven gates. She is required to surrender some item of her finery to the guardian of each gate so that, when she finally arrives before her sister, she is naked. In the Sumerian version:

> Naked Inanna dropped on her knees, for great Ereshkigal had mounted the throne.
> In her presence the Seven Judges pronounced the sentence.
> They fastened their eyes on her, eyes of death.
> They spoke the sentence of the accused.
> They uttered the cry of the accursed.
> Inanna instantly sickened to death,
> and her body became a corpse that hung on a spike.
>
> (*Sandars 1971,* 141–142)

The Akkadian retelling has Ereshkigal command her vizier to afflict Ishtar with 60 diseases. Because Ishtar is the goddess of sex and therefore the goddess of fertility, her absence from the earth is immediately noticed:

> No bull mounted a cow, no donkey impregnated a jenny.
> No young man impregnated a girl.
> The young man slept in his private room.
> The girl slept in the company of her friends.
>
> (Dalley 1989, 158)

To reactivate the natural forces of life and reproduction, the gods in heaven are forced to come to Inanna/ Ishtar's aid. Ereshkigal reluctantly permits her sister to leave, but only on the condition that she supply someone else to take her place in the underworld. For this purpose Inanna/Ishtar chooses her shepherd consort, who is called Dumuzi in Sumerian and Tammuz in Akkadian. In the Sumerian version, Dumuzi is chosen because he seems not to have missed Inanna and did nothing to help secure her release from the underworld. The Akkadian retelling of the story provides no explanation, and Ishtar's choice of Tammuz seems senseless.

This tale embodies the first recorded version of a worldwide mythic motif, namely, the descent of a living human being into the underworld. These myths are sometimes referred to as Orpheus tales, after the Greek musician who attempted to retrieve his deceased wife from the underworld. In their most archaic form, Orpheus tales seem to be derived from—or at least influenced by—**shamanism,** in particular from the shaman's role as *psychopomp* (one who leads the confused souls of the departed to their proper home in the otherworld). Depth psychologists (therapists in the the general lineage of Freud and Jung that take account of unconscious, or depth, motives) have interpreted such stories as symbolizing one's ''descent'' into the unconscious (where the past lies buried, so to speak). The Mesopotamians also told several variants of another, more upbeat, story of descent to the underworld, the tale of Nergal and Ereshkigal.

In this story, Nergal, as a consequence of an affront to Ereshkigal's vizier, is required to appear in the queen of the underworld's court to offer an apology. Unlike Ishtar, Nergal is not required to strip himself of his regalia in order to appear before Ereshkigal; rather, it is the queen of the netherworld who strips. Ereshkigal finds herself attracted to this upper world god and attempts to seduce him by allowing Nergal to see her undress for a bath. He resists her charms at first, but gives in on her second try. After a full week of lovemaking, Nergal steals away before dawn. When she hears that he has abandoned her, Ereshkigal falls to the ground and cries. She then sends her vizier to heaven, demanding that they return Nergal to her:

> Ever since I was a child, I have not known the companionship of other girls. I have not known the romping of children. As mistress of the dead, I am not pure enough to take my rightful place among the other great gods. I have dwelt alone in sadness, but the god whom you sent to me has opened my heart to love. Return him to me! Return him to me or I shall raise up the dead, and they will eat the living, until the dead outnumber the living!
>
> (Dalley 1989, 173)

In one version of this myth, Ereshkigal threatens to kill Nergal. Nergal responds by invading the underworld, assaulting its queen, and forcing her to marry him. In other versions, however, Nergal returns for a happy reunion:

> Laughing joyously, he entered her wide courtyard and approached her. He pulled her from the throne, and began to stroke her tresses. The two embraced, and went passionately to bed.
>
> (Dalley 1989, 176)

Subsequently, Nergal becomes Ereshkigal's consort.

Yet another myth recounts what happens when Nergal tarries so long in his wife's bed that he neglects to perform his function as god of war and killing. This story begins with an image of Nergal (who in this story is referred to by his Akkadian name of Irra or Erra—"scorched earth") lying awake in bed beside his wife, experiencing a rather restless night. At length, the silence of the nuptial chamber is disturbed by the voice of his weapon, Sibittu. Sibittu calls Nergal to embark on a campaign of war, citing the general decline of the world as evidence that the equilibrium of things has been disturbed.

According to Sibittu, lions and wolves, no longer hunted by Nergal, attack the cattle and carry them away. The shepherds, although watchful, are powerless to stop them. Other creatures invade the fields and carry away the grain. Most important, because Nergal has failed to exercise his function as god of war and death, the population of men and animals has multiplied to the point where the earth groans from the weight of them. The increased population has also made the earth so noisy that the celestial gods cannot get any peace.

Recognizing the truth of Sibittu's observations, Nergal resolves to embark on a campaign of violence, but it is an unusual kind of conflict in which the normal order of things is inverted:

> He who knew nothing of weapons drew his dagger. He who knew nothing of projectiles drew back the arrow in his bow. He who knew nothing of war engaged in hand-to-hand conflict. He who did not know how to run flew like a bird. The weak defeated the strong. The cripple outstripped the swift.
>
> (Dalley 1989, 303)

It is a world turned upside down, in which even sunlight has turned to shadow. After the task of destruction is complete, the cosmos is reborn as a fresh creation. The various versions of the story (only a few of which are cited here) exemplify the renewal symbolism that one finds worldwide in the myths and rituals of traditional societies. The "logic" of such myths/rituals is that the old must be destroyed before the new can grow, and if the old is not periodically obliterated, then the cosmos will decay and run down.

Taken together, these stories embody a fairly sophisticated understanding of death and its relation to life. In the story of Ishtar's descent to the underworld, Ishtar as the embodiment of the life principle wishes to conquer death. However, once she has entered her sister's realm, Ishtar finds herself powerless. The Gilgamesh epic expresses a similar desire to overcome death and live forever. The story of Nergal imaginatively tackles the same problem from the opposite direction: What would life on earth be like if the death principle were to be eliminated? Without death, the narrative asserts, it would be impossible to stop predators and the earth would become overpopulated. Death, in other words, is part of the natural order, and humanity must, as a consequence, accept death as part of life.

Sources:

Black, Jeremy, and Anthony Green. *Gods, Demons and Symbols of Ancient Mesopotamia: An Illustrated Dictionary.* Austin: University of Texas Press, 1992.

Cooper, Jerrold S. "The Fate of Mankind: Death and Afterlife in Ancient Mesopotamia." In Hiroshi Obabyashi, ed., *Death and Afterlife: Perspectives of World Religions.* New York: Greenwood Press, 1992.

Dalley, Stephanie. *Myths from Mesopotamia.* New York: Oxford University Press, 1989.

Sandars, N. K., transl. *The Epic of Gilgamesh.* Rev. ed. New York: Penguin, 1972.

Sandars, N. K., transl. *Poems of Heaven and Hell from Ancient Mesopotamia.* New York: Penguin, 1971.

MILLENARIANISM (MILLENNIALISM)

The terms *millenarianism* and *millennialism* derived from Christian theology, refer to the paradisiacal thousand-year period—the millennium—in which, according to the Book of Revelation, history and the world as we know it will terminate (it is sometimes conceived of as the reestablishment of the Garden of Eden). The expression *millenarian movement* is applied to groups of people who expect the imminent emergence of the millennium and whose religious life is saturated by this

THE HOLY CITY OF JERUSALEM DESCENDING FROM HEAVEN.

expectation. Although the term originated in the Christian tradition, by extension other, non-Christian religious movements that are characterized by such an expectation may be referred to as millenarian. Other terms for these types of groups are *crisis cult* and *messianic movement.* Some researchers have argued that all religions with historically specific origins began as millenarian movements, movements that, after they became established, lost much or all of their millennial enthusiasm.

Norman Cohn, in his classic study *The Pursuit of the Millennium (1957),* outlined five traits that characterize the way in which millennialist movements picture salvation. According to Cohn, millenarian salvation is envisioned as follows:

> Collective, in the sense that it is to be enjoyed by the faithful as a collectivity;
>
> Terrestrial, in the sense that it is to be realized on this earth and not in some other-worldly heaven;
>
> Imminent, in the sense that it is to come both soon and suddenly;

> Total, in that it is utterly to transform life on earth, so that the new dispensation will be no mere improvement on the past, but perfection itself;
>
> Miraculous, in the sense that it is to be accomplished by, or with the help of, supernatural agencies.

Although formulated in the context of a study of Western millennialism, these characteristics are found in similar movements in other parts of the world.

Millenarian movements in the so-called third world often arise in situations of contact between very different kinds of cultures, as when a Western nation intrudes into an area and disrupts the patterns of life of the indigenous people. The response to this crisis is frequently a religious one in which the disrupted culture attempts to apply traditional understandings to a radically new situation. More often than not, this creative response is articulated by a single individual (a prophet or a messiah) who receives a millenarian vision. In some cases the vision is a hostile one in which the community is counseled to resist the intruders and to adhere to the tradition of earlier generations (this subcategory is usually termed a nativisitic movement). In other cases the vision is a syncretistic response in which elements of both cultures are wedded into a new spiritual synthesis. Also, in some visions millenarians are advised to wait patiently for redemptive, supernatural intervention; in others the community or group is encouraged to help bring about the millennium by some type of religious practice.

In the traditional Christian understanding of the millennium, the dead are **resurrected** in new bodies. The living and the dead are judged, with evil people being either condemned to hell or snuffed out, depending on one's interpretation of the Book of Revelation. Non-Christian millenarian movements often include similar return-of-the-dead and final judgment themes in their end-time scenarios. The native American Ghost Dance religion, for example, included a renewal of the earth in which the spirits of the dead returned to earth. The millennium was to be preceded by a general catastrophe (an **apocalypse**) that would destroy Euroamericans and their material culture. Specifically, righteous native Americans would be lifted off the planet, and a new earth rolled down across the surface, burying Euroamericans and unrighteous Indians.

Sources:

Cohn, Norman. *The Pursuit of the Millennium.* London: Oxford University Press, 1957.

Eliade, Mircea, ed. *The Encyclopedia of Religion.* 16 vols. New York: Macmillan, 1987.

Lanternari, Vittorio. *The Religions of the Oppressed: A Study of Modern Messianic Cults.* New York: Mentor, 1956.

Mooney, James. *The Ghost-Dance Religion and the Sioux Outbreak of 1890.* 1896. Reprint, Chicago: University of Chicago Press, 1965.

MOKSHA

Moksa (from Sanscrit *muc,* release) appeared originally in the Vedic texts of the Upanishads (in these texts it was called *mukti*) in the sixth century B.C. It referred to the status of release or detachment from the endless chain of deaths and rebirths (reincarnation or *samsara*), the cycle of suffering one is bound to by the weight of one's actions during embodiment (**karma**). The concept thus conveys a sense of liberation from worldly concerns before one's physical death occurs. In the southern Asian religious tradition, it represents the supreme goal of human strivings.

In the earliest religious literature, *moksa* could be interchanged with terms that implied immortality, escape from the cycle, or attaining unity with the godhead. The term *moksha* was systematically introduced in the Indian Middle Age in commentaries on the ancient Vedic texts, and thereafter it was absorbed into contemporary Indian philosophy.

Traditionally, particularly in nontheistic systems, liberation could be obtained by following the three spiritual paths of ritual (*karmayoga*), metaphysical knowledge (*jnanayoga*), and devotion (*bhaktiyoga*). In theistic systems, particularly in the postclassical *bhakti* (devotional) movements of more recent Indian history, moksha is viewed as something that can occur purely as a result of divine intervention, independently of the merit of one's deeds, simply by practicing meditation and repeating mantras (magic verbal formulas).

Sources:

Feuerstein, Georg. *Encyclopedic Dictionary of Yoga.* New York: Paragon House, 1990.
Zimmer, Heinrich. *Philosophies of India.* New York: Bollingen, 1951. Macmillan, 1987.

MONROE, ROBERT

Among the best-known accounts of **out-of-body experiences** (OBEs or OOBEs) by individuals who claim to have learned how to leave their bodies virtually at will is that provided by Robert Monroe (1915-). He is famous for his publications *Far Journeys* (1985) and *Journeys Out of the Body* (1971).

OBEs can be defined in terms of their psychological characteristics. During these experiences a person feels completely conscious, with normal mental functioning, but physically located at a different place. Monroe became interested in occult or mystical subjects after his first OBE in 1958. He was able to intentionally induce OBEs with repeated inhalations of chemical fumes, and through self-hypnosis. The symptoms were represented by a cramp or constriction, followed by catalepsy and a vibratory sensation accompanied by witnessing electrical sparks and hearing a soft high-pitched "hiss."

During his later OBEs, Monroe became aware of having a second body (a subtle body, or, in yogic terminology, a **Linga Sharira**), with characteristics very similar to those of the physical one. This body had weight, was subject to gravity, could be seen, felt, and touched, was very plastic, and seemed to be connected to the physical body by a cord. According to Monroe, the existence of this second body and its ability to travel without the physical one could be demonstrated by the familiar falling dreams, during which the second body, which had traveled some distance away, "falls back" into the physical one.

Monroe also asserts that he can leave the physical plane and go into other various levels of consciousness and astral dimensions, such as a postmortem, parallel universe, similar to ours, where he once encountered his father. He says he was sometimes attacked by other entities and had difficulties returning to his body. He founded the Monroe Institute to teach people how to have OBEs and to do research into OBEs and related phenomena, such as altered states of consciousness.

Sources:

Berger, Arthur S., and Joice Berger. *The Encyclopedia of Parapsychology and Psychical Research.* New York: Paragon House, 1991.

Mitchell, Edgar D. *Psychic Exploration: A Challenge for Science.* New York: G. P. Putnam's Sons, 1974.

Moore, Brooke Noel. *The Philosophical Possibilities Beyond Death.* Springfield, IL.: Charles C Thomas, 1981.

Ring, Kenneth. *Life at Death: A Scientific Investigation of the Near-Death Experience.* New York: Quill, 1982.

MONTGOMERY, RUTH

The American journalist Ruth Montgomery (1912–), born Ruth Schick in Princeton, Indiana, claims to be able to communicate with spirit guides via **automatic writing,** in her case automatic typing. She has written about **reincarnation,** magnetic healing; Atlantis and Lemuria (antediluvian civilizations); Earth changes (upheavals); and visits from spirits.

After being introduced to the occult in 1956 by the medium Malcolm Pantin, she started using a **Ouija board,** which enabled her to make contact with various spirits, including her dead father. In 1958 she met trance medium **Arthur Ford,** who suggested she write about life after death and who told her that she had the ability to do automatic writing, through the help of spirit guides. In 1960 an entity appeared that announced itself as Lily and said it would communicate material for books from the world beyond the grave.

Montgomery calls her guides mysterious pen pals and describes them as souls currently in the spirit plane after having had many previous lifetimes and claims they dictate information about the stages of eternal life after death. According to Montgomery, Lily has known her well in two of her previous incarnations, once as a friend and the other time as the father of Arthur Ford and herself. She also asserts that all three of them will have to reincarnate many more times before achieving perfection.

Her publications include the following: *A Gift of Prophecy* (1965), about Jeanne Dixon; *A Search for the Truth* (1966), about her spiritual explorations; *Here and Hereafter* (1968), the result of an investigation of reincarnation undertaken with the help of her guides; *A World Beyond* (1971), a book about life after death written after the death of Ford, who she believed joined Lily's group of guides; and *Companions Along the Way* (1974), in which she maintains that she lived during the lifetime of Jesus, when she was supposedly a sister of Lazarus.

The book *Strangers Among Us* (1979) includes her famous theory of **walk-ins,** which are supposed to be highly developed discarnate entities that take over the body and personality of an incarnate adult in order to raise spiritual consciousness and help humankind. Hundreds of thousands of walk-ins are said to be on earth, most as ordinary people. Most keep their identities secret, but some have announced themselves publicly to various groups and societies. Some of them come from other planets and some from the ''sixth dimension.''

Sources:

Berger, Arthur S., and Joice Berger. *The Encyclopedia of Parapsychology and Psychical Research.* New York: Paragon House, 1991.

Guiley, Rosemary Ellen. *Harper's Encyclopedia of Mystical & Paranormal Experience.* San Francisco: HarperCollins, 1991.

Montgomery, Ruth. *Companions Along the Way.* New York: Coward, McCann & Geoghegan, 1974.

MOODY, RAYMOND

During his training as a doctor, Raymond Moody (1944–), professor of psychology at West Georgia College, found that many patients claimed to have **near-death experiences** (NDEs). He put together the stories of about 50 cases in the book *Life After Life* (1975), which became a best-seller in the United States and throughout the world. This successful book was followed by *Reflections on Life After Life* (1977).

Moody gathered the reports of people who were resuscitated after having been pronounced clinically dead, people who came very close to death because of accidents or severe injury, and persons who, as they died, told their experiences to other people who were present. Moody found great similarities among the reports of near-death experiences and was able to identify many recurrent motifs, such as undergoing a feeling of ineffability, hearing the news of one's own death, having feelings of floating out of the body, seeing the resuscitation team working, experiencing feelings of peace, hearing ringing noises, entering a dark tunnel, and encountering other spirits, including a being of light who helps the person to evaluate his or her life.

Moody's findings, which depended on the memories of people who came to him with their reports, were very similar to the findings of other researchers, such as Elisabeth Kubler-Ross, and appeared to offer evidence of life after death. Moody stated that he was not trying to offer decisive proof, however, and that his informal, anecdotal study could not be regarded as scientific. Moody himself has indicated some plausible alternative explanations for the recurrent elements of the near-death experience, referring to, for instance, the results of isolation studies, hallucinations produced by drugs, and cerebral anoxia. He was not satisfied with those explanations, however, and has asserted that the key elements were the uniformity of the descriptions and the reported vividness of near-death experiences. More recently, Moody has shifted his focus away from NDEs, and has begun to research communication with the dead.

DR. RAYMOND MOODY. (PHOTOGRAPH BY LLOYD ANDREWS.)

Moody has left many issues unexplained, including the relationship between the core experience and the condition that brings it about and the role of an individual's religious belief system in shaping the near-death experience. Nevertheless, he stimulated scientific studies by other clinical, psychological, and parapsychological researchers for whom near-death experiences became a major subject.

Sources:

Alcock, James E. *Parapsychology. Science or Magic? A Psychological Perspective.* Oxford, England: Pergamon Press, 1981.

Ring, Kenneth. *Life at Death. A Scientific Investigation of the Near-Death Experience.* New York: Quill, 1982.

Wilson, Ian. *The After Death Experience. The Physics of the Non-Physical.* New York: William Morrow, 1987.

MORTIFICATION

The Latin word *mortificare* (to mortify, kill) appears in St. Paul's New Testament letters as the spiritual ability to kill the desires of the flesh, enforcing a dualist vision of body and spirit as separate, incompatible entities. In the first centuries of **Christianity,** mortification represented an imitation dei, a death that emulated God's (Christ's) death on the cross. This emulation came to include self-inflicted pain, such as wearing rough clothes and the practice of scourging. The concept of mortification was later reconceptualized and applied to ascetic practices that enable an individual to detach from material egocentric needs and to discipline the body for the purpose of spiritual attainment. Both within the Christian and the Hindu traditions, the ascetic practice of mortification typically involves fasting and chastity.

A different concept of mortification is found in archaic societies in connection with the initiation rituals and preparation for initiation. Deprivation of food, sleep, or water, or, at times, exposure to extreme heat or cold, were viewed as techniques for disciplining the body in order to achieve a higher state.

Initiation mortification practices, which sometimes included punishment or torture, represented the death of the old identity in preparation for the birth of a new being. On a broader level, cosmic renewal was brought about in certain civilizations through the process of mortifying, or killing, the king. Mortifying the king reached its fullest expression in the story of Jesus, whose passion and death were meant for humankind's salvation. The expression *mortificatio regis* (mortification of the king) survived and emerged in Renaissance alchemy to indicate the disintegration of matter.

Sources:

Eliade, Mircea, ed. *The Encyclopedia of Religion.* 16 vols. New York: Macmillan, 1987.

Smart, Ninian. *The Religious Experience of Mankind.* 3d ed. New York: Charles Scribner's Sons, 1984.

MOSES, REV. WILLIAM STAINTON

The medium William Stainton Moses (1839–1892), born in Donnington, Lincolnshire, England, is known for having received many spirit communications via **automatic writing.** After graduating at Exeter College, Oxford, he was ordained a minister of the

REVEREND W. STAINTON MOSES. (FROM A LONDON SPIRITUALIST ALLIANCE PORTRAIT.) COURTESY OF THE ARC.

Church of England at age 24 and was sent to Kirk Maughold, near Ramsey, on the Isle of Man.

In 1872 Dr. Stanhope Templeman Speer, who had taken care of Stainton when he was seriously ill, induced him to attend **séances,** although Moses was not very interested in **Spiritualism** at that time. His interest in communicating with the spirit world increased after the séance, however, and within about six months he started showing astonishing paranormal abilities. Among the phenomena attributed to him are levitations of himself, apports (materializations), telekinesis, table-tiltings, and mysterious lights, sounds, and scents of varying description. These phenomena included materializations of luminous hands and columns of lights with human shape.

Stainton's automatic writing began in 1872, when, with the guide of a group of spirits called Imperator, he started recording a series of scripts that became the basis for the newspaper *The Spiritualist,* published under the pseudonym M. A. Oxon, and for his works *Psychography* (1878), *Spirit Identity* (1879), *Higher Aspects of Spiritualism* (1880), *Ghostly Visitors,* (1882), and *Spirit Teachings* (1883), a book that became known as ''the Spiritualist's Bible.''

Stainton joined the **Society for Psychical Research** for a short time, which was established in 1882 by a group of researchers and Spiritualists to investigate **mediumship.** The critical attitude displayed by the researchers, however, induced him to quit the society and to dedicate himself to the London Spiritualist Alliance (LSA), which he had founded in 1884 and which had its own journal, *Light.* This journal is still published today by what became the successor to the LSA, the College for Psychic Studies. Moses died in 1892, of complications brought on by Bright's disease, and after his death allegedly joined the ''Imperator'' group of spirits with whom he had communicated through the American trance medium Leonora E. Piper.

Sources:

Gauld, Alan. *The Founders of Psychical Research.* London: Routledge & Kegan Paul, 1968.

Myers, F. W. H. "The Experiences of W. Stainton Moses—I." *Proceedings of the Society for Psychical Research* 9 (1894): 245-352.

Oppenheim, Janet. *The Other World: Spiritualism and Psychical Research in England, 1850–1914.* Cambridge: Cambridge University Press, 1985.

MOVIES, THE AFTERLIFE IN POPULAR

Stories of ghosts and creatures coming from beyond the grave have been a part of popular entertainment since the beginning of moviemaking, and an increasing number of recent movies have focused on people who have returned from the dead—awakened zombies, reincarnates, vampires, and the like. However, the motion picture industry has made only a relatively small philosophical contribution to understanding death as a passage to another form of consciousness.

Most of the movies about death focus on the loss of everything to which one has been attached in earthly life and support the idea that physical death is the first and only death. The few exceptions are the existentialist and eschatological films of Kurosawa (*Ikiru*), Bergman (*The Seventh Seal [1956]*), and De Sica (*Umberto D [1955]*). The early Russian films, such as those of Alexander Dovzhenko, show a particular sensitivity to the spiritual dimension of human dying, portraying not only loss in terms of biological continuity but also examining the quality of consciousness. In Dovzhenko's *Earth* (1930), the philosophical key is the ancient belief, shared by many cultures, that death is merely a prelude to rebirth, and that the cosmos is divided into a visible reality and an unseen mysterious higher plane beyond evil where the human soul continues to live.

This ancient view of death is not implied in most contemporary films in Western countries, where the possibility of extinction, brought on by such elements as the hole in the ozone layer and **AIDS,** has increased the fear of death and has created a need for reassurance of survival in another form. In general, these films serve as a means of ameliorating those fears, and media fascination with near-death and after-death phenomena reflects people's basic incapacity to believe that death could happen to them, or, if it could, that it represents the termination of consciousness.

The latest movies about afterlife top decades of postmortem fantasies, including the seemingly endless horror films, which are ultimately about death, and out-of-body illusions, from the 1940s *It's a Wonderful Life* (1946), in which James Stewart was able to see what life would have been like had he not been born, to *Here Comes Mr. Jordan* (1941), and Warren Beatty's 1978 *Heaven Can Wait,* in which the protagonist was called to heaven prematurely.

Some movies center on themes of revenge and justice, like *Darkman* (1990), in which the central character, who is alive but is presumed murdered in a lab explosion, returns as a mysterious figure, and *Ghosts Can't Do It* (1990), in which the dead man plans to return to his wife by entering another man's body. Other movies employ a return from the otherworld as a pretext for romantic themes, conveying a reassuring sentimentality (regaining what has been lost is quite appealing). Among the most recent movies of this kind are *Always* (1989), Steven Spielberg's remaking of *A Guy Named Joe; Eternity* (1990), in which the protagonists must resolve a romance in a past lifetime in order to find happiness in the present; and *Ghost* (1990), in which Patrick Swayze's spirit comes back to save his wife Demi Moore from danger.

In *Jacob's Ladder* (1990), which is an attempt to represent hell in contemporay everyday terms, Jacob's idea of heaven is the apartment he once shared with his wife and children. In this film, as in *Ghost,* the prospect of death is positive, providing the protagonist, who is a soldier mortally wounded in Vietnam, with the opportunity to take stock of his life and correct mistakes made in the past. In *Flatliners* (1990), a group of medical students temporarily arrest their heartbeats, take a look at the other side, and come back to life through the jolts of a **defibrillator.** The combination of romance and justice arrived at after death is also presented in such films as *Ghost Dad* (1990), in which Bill Cosby returns to life from beyond the grave in order to watch his kids and to be the good father he never was, and *Switch* (1991), which deals with the consequences of life for a male chauvinist who is reincarnated as a woman. Among other recent popular movies dealing with death and afterlife are *Heart Condition* (1990), *Hello Again*(1987), *Almost Heaven,* and *All Dogs Go to Heaven* (1989), in which a dead puppy gets another chance.

Sources:

Howe, Desson. "Death Takes a Holiday. Why Are We Just Dying to See Movies About the Afterlife?" *Washington Post,* August 26, 1990.

Hurley, Neil P. *Theology Through Film.* New York: Harper & Row, 1970.

Klady, Leonard. "The Hopeful Dead. They Come From Beyond the Grave ... to Find Life at the Box Office." *American Film* Vol 15: no. 6 (March 1990).

Maslin, Janet. "Hollywood Goes in Quest of Spiritual Reward." *New York Times,* November 11, 1990.

MURPHY, BRIDEY

One of the most famous cases of possible **reincarnation** began on November 29, 1952, when 29-year-old Virginia Tigue, wife of an insurance salesman, was hypnotized in Pueblo, Colorado. The hypnotist, Morey Bernstein, encouraged her to go back to memories of a previous existence. Suddenly, Virginia, who had never been outside the United States, began speaking with a soft Irish accent and described herself as Bridey Murphy, a young girl living in Cork, Ireland, during the early years of the nineteenth century.

She claimed that she had been born Bridget Kathleen Murphy on December 20, 1798, that her father was a Protestant barrister named Duncan Murphy, and that she lived in an area called The Meadows outside Cork. She further asserted that she had married the teacher Sean Brian Joseph MacCarthy at age 20 and that she had died in Belfast at age 66. She spoke as though she were completely familiar with the details of traditional Irish life.

Records in Ireland were researched to uncover documentary evidence for the existence of Bridey Murphy or other members of her family. The investigations failed, although that might have been because Ireland had no registrations of births, marriages, and deaths during the period of the Bridey memories.

Later, the *Chicago American* decided to investigate Virginia Tigue's true identity and revealed that she spent part of her childhood in Chicago with an Irish aunt from whose stories she might well have provided the background material for her Bridey accounts. Nevertheless, the Bridey Murphy case stimulated further research on hypnotic regression to past lives, which some believe to be the key to proving that experience continues beyond death.

Sources:

Cavendish, Richard, ed. *Encyclopedia of the Unexplained: Magic, Occultism and Parapsychology.* New York: McGraw-Hill, 1974.

Moore, Brooke Noel. *The Philosophical Possibilities Beyond Death.* Springfield, IL: Charles C Thomas Publisher, 1981.

Wilson, Ian. *The After Death Experience: The Physics of the Non-Physical.* New York: William Morrow, 1987.

MYERS, FREDERIC WILLIAM HENRY

Frederic W. H. Myers (1843–1901), a founding and leading member of the **Society for Psychical Research,** was born in Keswick, Cumberland, England, of a religious family. During the years he spent at Trinity College, Cambridge, studying classical literature, he experienced a deep religious crisis that led him to the loss of faith.

In the summer of 1871, Myers and **Henry Sidgwick** had a profound discussion about the possibility of achieving valid knowledge of the unseen world through the study of psychical phenomena. In 1872 Myers began to attend numerous **séances,** the most important of which was one led by the medium **William Stainton Moses** in 1874. After this event, Myers, Sidgwick, and Edmund Gurney established a group to investigate the phenomenon of **mediumship** and founded the Society for Psychical Research in 1882. Myers served on investigatory committees, such as the Literary Committee, and he participated in the investigations of Leonora Piper and of Eusapia Palladino, two well-known mediums.

FREDERIC WILLIAM HENRY MYERS. COURTESY OF THE ARC.

Myers developed the concept of the "subliminal consciousness" to describe the source of conscious thought. According to Myers, who anticipated Sigmund Freud's idea of the "unconscious," the subliminal consciousness receives extrasensory inputs and survives physical death. He was convinced that there was survival after death, and this belief was strengthened by the mediumistic communications he had received from the woman he had passionately loved in his youth, his cousin's wife, Annie Hall Marshall, who committed suicide in 1876 and who inspired his *Fragments of an Inner Life.*

In the classic book *Human Personality and Its Survival of Bodily Death* (1903), which was completed and published after his death, he systematized the findings of psychical research. His other books include *Phantasms of the Living,* accounts of apparitional experiences written in 1886 with Gurney and Frank Podmore, *St. Paul* (1867), *Essays, Classical and Modern* (1885), and *Science and a Future Life* (1893).

Cross-correspondence, a type of communication that Myers and others allegedly originated from the grave, involves messages sent to different mediums that make sense only when put together, leaving no doubt that the communicators have survived death. Such messages represent a unique proof of survival after death in the mediumistic literature about the afterlife.

Sources:

Gauld, Alan. *The Founders of Psychical Research.* London: Routledge & Kegan Paul, 1968.
Haynes, Renee. *The Society for Psychical Research, 1882–1892: A History.* London: Heinemann, 1982.
Oppenheim, Janet. *The Other World: Spiritualism and Psychical Research in England, 1850–1914.* Cambridge: Cambridge University Press, 1985.

MYSTERY RELIGIONS

Mystery religions, sometimes referred to as mystery "schools," were quite common in the Mediterranean world during the Hellenistic period. The classical religions of Greece and Rome were more concerned with securing the goodwill of the gods in this life, particularly as the gods affected the fate of the country, than in the hereafter. The few ideas of the afterlife they did entertain were distinctly unpleasant: The departed wandered about aimlessly as devitalized shades of their former selves in a dark, sterile, and humorless realm beneath the earth.

In the late classical period, people became progressively more interested in their eternal fate, and there emerged certain new religions that, although not rejecting the old gods, focused on individual salvation. Most of these new religions involved initiating new converts into certain secrets or "mysteries" that would enable them to secure a pleasant afterlife for themselves. The most famous of these ancient mystery schools was the **Eleusinian mysteries.**

Sources:

Grant, Michael, and John Hazel. *Who's Who in Classical Mythology.* New York: Oxford University Press, 1993.
Tripp, Edward. *The Meridian Handbook of Classical Mythology.* New York: New American Library, 1970.

N

NATIONAL SPIRITUAL SCIENCE CENTER

The National Spiritual Science Center grew out of the activities of the Spiritual Science mother church, founded in New York in 1923 by Julia O. Forrest. Forrest had been a Christian Scientist and upon converting to Spiritualism wanted to create a church modeled after the Christian Science Mother Church in Boston.

A prominent student of Forrest, Alice W. Tindall, founded the National Spiritual Science Center in 1941 as an integral part of the Ecclesiastical Council within the Spiritual Science mother church. The National Spiritual Science Center, under the leadership of Tindall, fostered ecumenical spirit among Spiritualists by helping to found the Federation of Spiritual Churches and Associations. In 1968 Tindall added to her duties by taking over the *Psychic Observer,* a Spiritualist journal that had lost almost all of its support after exposing the fraudulent behavior of Mabel Riffle and other mediums at popular Camp Chesterfield in Indiana.

In 1969 Tindall became disabled and turned over the leadership of the National Spiritual Science Center to two of her protégés, Rev. Henry J. Nagorka and Rev. Diane S. Nagorka. In the 1970s, under the Nagorkas and with Tindall still involved but with lower profile, the center became independent of the Spiritual Science mother church and established itself in Washington, D.C., as a prominent player among Spiritualist organizations. Meanwhile, the *Psychic Observer,* now with the help of the Nagorkas, regained much of its former luster, and the center encouraged other publishing activity through ESPress.

The death of Henry Nagorka in 1986 dealt a heavy blow to the center, and its publishing channels were shut down. Nevertheless, the center has remained vital, with more than a dozen related congregations. The center's statement of beliefs defines God as the impersonal, creative energy of the universe, which is always growing and changing. The goal of human life is to unfold one's particular creativity and unite with

God. As a Spiritualist organization, emphasis is of course placed on the belief in human immortality and the ability of those in this life to communicate with the spirits of the deceased.

Sources:

Melton, J. Gordon. *The Encyclopedia of American Religions.* 4th ed. Detroit, MI: Gale Research, 1993.
Nagorka, Diane S. *Spirit as Life Force.* Washington, DC: ESPress, 1983.

NATIONAL SPIRITUALIST ASSOCIATION OF CHURCHES

The Spiritualist phenomenon of the nineteenth century was not immediately one that lent itself to a great deal of structure. The movement began with the mediumship of the Fox sisters in 1848 and spread quickly as individuals discovered their own psychic abilities and became professional mediums, attracting crowds with public exhibitions or giving private sessions. Local Spiritualist churches were formed around various leaders, but there was nothing widespread or ecumenical. The only kind of larger organization for many years was that of Spiritualist summer camps, held in numerous places throughout the country, which provided a comfortable meeting and training place for both professional and lay Spiritualists and a vacation-like atmosphere for proselytizing the public through lectures and demonstrations.

Over time, however, Spiritualism came under attack, with charges of fraud leveled against several mediums. Henry Slade, a famous slate (see **slate writing**) medium, was caught in trickery several times, and in 1888 the Fox sisters themselves confessed to fraud. Spiritualism also experienced controversy from within because of different interpretations of the meaning of Spiritualism. In response to these issues, the National Spiritualist Association of Churches (NSAC) was created in 1893 in Chicago, led particularly by two former Unitarian clerics, Harrison D. Barrett and James M. Peebles, and a well-known medium and author, Cora L. Richmond. They put together a presbyterial structure, with various state associations of member congregations and an annual national convention.

The NSAC immediately set about establishing standards for Spiritualist ministry and investigating reports of fraud. Even today, with several other Spiritualist organizations in existence, the NSAC maintains the highest standards for ordination. The NSAC has also spent a great deal of time and energy on establishing a common statement of Spiritualist beliefs. In 1899 it adopted a Declaration of Principles with six articles; three other articles were added at a later time. The full nine articles are as follows:

1. We believe in Infinite Intelligence.
2. We believe that the phenomena of Nature, both physical and spiritual, are the expression of Infinite Intelligence.
3. We affirm that a correct understanding of such expression and living in accordance therewith constitute true religion.

4. We affirm that the existence and personal identity of the individual continue after the change called death.
5. We affirm that communication with the so-called dead is a fact, scientifically proven by the phenomena of Spiritualism.
6. We believe that the highest morality is contained in the Golden Rule: "Whatsoever ye would that others should do unto you, do ye also unto them."
7. We affirm the moral responsibility of the individual, and that he makes his own happiness or unhappiness as he obeys or disobeys Nature's physical and spiritual laws.
8. We affirm that the doorway to reformation is never closed against any human soul here or hereafter.
9. We affirm that the precept of Prophecy and Healing contained in the Bible is a divine attribute proven through Mediumship.

The last three articles, added later, reflect the later move away from an emphasis on remarkable phenomena and toward an emphasis on philosophical development. Besides these nine articles, the NSAC has also established common definitions of Spiritualist terms and practices. The two major definitional controversies of the twentieth century have centered on the questions of whether Spiritualists are also Christians and whether Spiritualists believe in reincarnation. In 1930 the NSAC specifically condemned belief in reincarnation, but not without repercussions in the form of lost memberships. The controversy over Christian identity has not been as clear-cut. Spiritualism in general has historically drawn most of its membership from the Christian denominations, and most Spiritualists identify with some form of primitive Christian practice in the sense that they believe that Jesus was a master medium and Spiritualist healer. If, however, asked to identify themselves as Christians in a more traditional sense, in the context of denominations and historic creeds, most are reluctant to do so. The NSAC has generally taken the position that Spiritualists are not also Christians. Those who wish to identify as Christians have tended to gravitate to other Spiritualist organizations.

Sources:

Barrett, H. D. *Life Work of Cora L. V. Richmond.* Chicago: Hack & Anderson, 1895.

Melton, J. Gordon. *The Encyclopedia of American Religions.* 4th ed. Detroit, MI: Gale Research, 1993.

National Spiritualist Association of Churches. One Hundredth Anniversary of Modern American Spiritualism. Chicago: National Spiritualist Association of Churches, 1948.

Ward, Gary L., ed. *Spiritualism I: Spiritualist Thought.* New York: Garland Publishing, 1990.

NEAR-DEATH EXPERIENCE

A near-death experience (NDE), sometimes also called a pseudo-death experience, is a seemingly supernatural experience undergone by individuals who have suffered apparent death and then been restored to life. The systematic, scientific study of NDEs is recent, although accounts can be found in literature and historical documents dating back hundreds of years, such as those of ancient philosophers, like **Plato,** and of modern writers, like Melville and Tolstoy. A small number of cases were collected by interested investigators beginning in the late nineteenth century, especially by such pioneers of psychical research as Edmund Gurney, Sir William Barrett, and James H. Hyslop, who also studied **deathbed visions,** which are a common element of NDEs. However, it was only after the advent of medical techniques of resuscitation, like modern cardiopulmonary resuscitation measures, that NDEs became a widespread phenomenon.

The main impetus for modern studies of NDEs was the publication in 1975 of the book *Life After Life,* by psychiatrist **Raymond A. Moody,** which followed earlier research on this topic by such physicians as **Elisabeth Kübler-Ross** and Russell Noyes. NDEs also had been discussed earlier as a subcategory of **out-of-body experiences,** which in turn became a topic of widespread discussion with Robert Crookall's *Out of Body Experience* (1970), as well as Robert A. Monroe's popular *Journeys Out of the Body* (1972). At the time, out-of-body experience was the newly coined parapsychological term for what an earlier generation of occultists had called **astral projection**—the practice of extracting one's consciousness from the physical body and traveling to a different, nonphysical dimension location in a nonphysical form.

Moody's *Life After Life* describes the results of more than 11 years of inquiry into NDEs and is based on a sample of about 150 cases, including persons who were resuscitated after having been thought or pronounced clinically dead by their doctors; persons who came very close to physical death in the course of accidents or severe injury or illness; and persons who, as they died, told their experiences to other people who were present. Moody outlines nine elements that generally occur during NDEs:

1. A *buzzing or ringing noise,* while having a sense of being dead. At this initial stage of the NDE, the dying are confused and try, unsuccessfully, to communicate with other people at the scene.
2. *Peace and painlessness.* While people are dying, they may be in intense pain, but as soon as they leave the body the pain vanishes and they experience peace.
3. *Out-of-body experience.* The dying often have the sensation of rising up and floating above their own body while surrounded by a medical team and watching it down below, feeling very detached and comfortable. They experience the feeling of being in a spiritual body that looks like a sort of living energy field.
4. *The tunnel experience.* The next experience is that of being drawn into darkness through a tunnel, at an extremely high speed, or going up a stairway (or some other symbol of crossing a threshold) until reaching a realm of radiant golden-white light.
5. *Rising rapidly into the heavens.* Instead of a tunnel, some people report rising suddenly into the heavens and seeing the earth and the celestial sphere as they would be seen by astronauts in space.
6. *People of light.* Once on the other side of the tunnel, or after they have risen into the heavens, the dying meet people who glow with an inner light. Often

they find that friends and relatives who have already died are there to greet them.

7. *The being of light.* After meeting the people of light, the dying often meet a powerful spiritual being whom some have called an angel, God, or Jesus. Also, although they sometimes report feeling scared, they do not sense that they were on the way to hell or that they fell into it.
8. *The life review.* The being of light presents the dying with a panoramic review of everything they have done. In particular, they relive every act they have ever done to other people and come away feeling that love is the most important thing in life.
9. *Reluctance to return.* The being of light sometimes tells the dying that they must return to life. Other times, they are given a choice of staying or returning. In either case, they are reluctant to return. The people who choose to return do so only because of loved ones they do not wish to leave behind.

Moody's work was anecdotal, and he was careful to point out that it should not be regarded as a scientific study, since the case history material presented was highly selective and the data were not subjected to any statistical analysis. The first scientific investigation of NDEs was psychologist **Kenneth Ring's** *Life at Death* (1980), which was based on interviews with 102 near-death survivors. Statistical analysis was supplemented by extensive qualitative materials in evaluating Moody's prior findings. Ring was concerned with comparing NDEs of illness victims, accident victims, and suicide attempters, and his book showed that NDEs varied little over different causes of near-death and that they had a high incidence of occurence in all categories studied.

Increasing interest in near-death studies resulted in the establishment of the **International Association for Near-Death Studies** in 1981, and early in the following year two major scientific studies on NDEs were published. Cardiologist Michael B. Sabom's *Recollections of Death* reported the results of interviews with 116 near-death survivors, and George Gallup's *Adventures in Immortality* reported the results of a national survey in which the incidence of NDEs was documented in about 5 percent of the adult population, or 8 million Americans.

After they recover, people who have undergone NDEs usually live transformed lives. They no longer fear death, they sense the importance of love in ways they had never before experienced, they feel a connection with all things and people, and they experience a renewed appreciation of learning, especially spiritual learning, while rejecting the priority of material things.

NDEs have frequently been regarded as evidence of immortality of the soul or, at the least, of life after death. Such experiences can be seen as powerful proof of the belief in a soul as a separate entity from the body in which it lives and develops throughout life, an entity that survives the death of the physical body.

Some skeptics, however, have been quick to dismiss NDE research as subjective and as inadequate proof of life after death, and the significance of the near-death experience has been hotly debated. It has been argued that it is not reasonable to consider NDEs as evidence of survival unless other naturalistic causes for these experiences can be excluded. It is possible that all NDEs can be explained by naturalistic causes, such as psychological, physiological, neurological, or pharmacological manifestations. Religious beliefs, wishful thinking, or medications such as morphine may facilitate the experience. Also, disturbance of brain functions and cerebral anoxia are known to cause hallucinations, which may occur in nearly all dying patients.

In response to critics who consider NDEs to be mere hallucinations, supporters of the out-of-body thesis have pointed out that NDEs have regularly been experienced by people registering flat EEGs (electroencephalograms), meaning that all brain activity had stopped. Supporters of the out-of-body thesis argue that, because even hallucinations produce brain wave activity, someone registering a flat EEG while going through an NDE must be out of the body at the time.

Other critics have asserted that the **tunnel** experience is a memory of our experiences traveling down the birth canal and being drawn into the bright light of the delivery room. During the stress connected with being near death we regress to these memories, which are given a religious interpretation in order to escape the fear associated with death. Such explanations are convincing to those who are intent on dismissing the "metaphysical" implications of NDEs, and unconvincing to those who view NDEs as "proof" of life after death. This mixed evaluation can be generalized to cover the entire NDE phenomenon—convincing to those who are already inclined to accept a spiritual dimension as real, and unconvincing to those who are predisposed to reject spiritual explanations.

Sources:

Gallup, George. *Adventures in Immortality.* New York: McGraw-Hill, 1982.

Greyson, Bruce, and Charles P. Flynn, eds. *The Near-Death Experience: Problems, Prospects, Perspectives.* Springfield, IL: Charles C. Thomas, 1984.

Moody, Raymond A. *Life After Life.* New York: Bantam, 1976.

———. *The Light Beyond.* Reprint. New York: Bantam, 1989.

Shepard, Leslie A., ed. *Encyclopedia of Occultism & Parapsychology.* Detroit, MI: Gale Research, 1991.

NEAR-DEATH EXPERIENCES AMONG CHILDREN

The term **near-death experience** was coined in 1975 by **Raymond Moody** in the book *Life After Life,* in which he gathered the reports of people who were resuscitated after having been pronounced clinically dead, people who came very close to death because of accidents or severe injury, and persons who, as they died, told their experiences to other people who were present.

Moody's work was soon followed by other investigations of near-death experiences (NDEs). Some of these studies focused on NDEs among children. The purpose of one such study, reported in the *American Journal of Diseases of Children,* was to eliminate the hypothesis that NDEs are the result of drugs or sleep deprivation or are merely bad dreams. According to the study, which included interviews with children who had once been pronounced clinically dead, NDEs—including **out-of-body experiences,** traveling to other realms, telepathic communication, and encounters with dead friends and relatives—were found in the great majority of critically ill children who were not being treated with any hallucinogenic medications. The finding is especially significant because children are considered to be a "pure" research sample population, too young to have absorbed adult ideas about death and the afterlife, which otherwise could have affected the accounts of their NDEs.

Sources:

Berger, Arthur S., and Joyce Berger. *The Encyclopedia of Parapsychology and Psychical Research.* New York: Paragon House, 1991.

Morse, Melvin. *Closer to the Light: Learning from the Near-Death Experiences of Children.* New York: Ivy Books, 1990.

Ring, Kenneth. *Life at Death: A Scientific Investigation of the Near-Death Experience.* New York: Quill, 1982.

NEAR-DEATH EXPERIENCES AND TRANSFORMATION

The **near-death experience (NDE),** reported by individuals who have suffered apparent death and have then been restored to life, began to gain public attention with the publication of **Raymond Moody's** *Life After Life* in 1975. This work, which is based on interviews with 150 death survivors, delineates some common traits of the NDE, such as the powerful sensation of being drawn through a long, dark tunnel with a bright light at the end; a feeling of joy, peace, and painless freedom from the body; **out-of-body experiences**; the perception of a being of light; and an encounter with deceased relatives or friends.

Subsequent works have emphasized methods more scientific than Moody's, whose book was anecdotal. **Kenneth Ring's** *Life at Death,* and Michael Sabom's *Recollections of Death* have stressed the importance of scientific rigor and of the application of statistical methods to NDE samples. The studies have unequivocally shown that NDEs have substantial social, moral, cultural, and even political implications, regardless of whether or not they are actual journeys into life beyond physical death.

Most of the research that has dealt with near-death experiences suggests that profound transformations occur in the patients, particularly loss of the fear of death. In Kenneth Ring's *Life at Death,* for instance, considerable evidence supports the thesis that surviving a near-death episode does indeed lead to profound personal changes. Usually these changes are mediated by the individual's interpretation of the NDE, which often acquires definite spiritual or religious overtones and is interpreted as proof of the existence of joyous and pain-free life after death.

A person who has survived a near-death experience has been given a second chance to live, and his or her life represents a continuing testimony to the profundity of that event. Although the existing literature contains relatively little research on such transformations, it has been observed that substantial value transformations usually occur, especially if a life review was experienced as part of the NDE. Persons who have undergone NDEs generally live life more fully and love more openly; they deemphasize the values related to conventional definitions of success, such as money and outer accomplishment, and stress values such as kindness, compassion, and unconditional love for others.

Another important transformation is represented by greater willingness to accept others, by removing social boundaries and recognizing the equality of all people and by having a less judgmental approach to others. Closely related to concern for others is what are usually considered the three major changes associated with near-death experiences: (1) stronger belief in life after death, (2) loss of fear of death, and (3) stronger religiousness or spirituality.

Other changes in the lives of people who undergo NDEs include stronger feelings of self-worth, decreased need to impress others, and an awakening or enhancement of psychic sensitivities. NDEs provide the basis for significant development of moral consciousness, and their long-term effects often prove to be very salutary.

Sources:

Greyson, Bruce, and Charles P. Flynn, eds. *The Near-Death Experience: Problems, Prospects, Perspectives.* Springfield, IL: Charles C Thomas, 1984.

Moody, Raymond A., Jr. *The Light Beyond.* Reprint, New York: Bantam, 1989.

Morse, Melvin. *Transformed by the Light.* New York: Ivy Books, 1992.

Ring, Kenneth. *Life at Death: A Scientific Investigation of The Near-Death Experience.* New York: Quill, 1982.

NECROMANCY

Necromancy, divination with the aid of the dead, is generally condemned as evil. It dates back to ancient Persia, Egypt, and Rome and is still practiced in some cultures (e.g., Haiti). In Greece, it signified descent into Hades in order to consult the dead, who supposedly had great prophetic powers. During the Middle Ages, when it was associated with what was called sorcery, it was believed to be widely practiced by magicians and witches. When a great persecution of witches occurred between the late Middle Ages and the beginning of Renaissance, for instance, necromancy was one of the crimes of which witches were accused. Numerous accounts of necromancy are mentioned in the Bible and in the Talmud, as well as in myths, legends, and literary works in cultures across the globe. One of the best-known necromancers was the biblical Witch of Endor, who summoned the shade of the dead prophet Samuel for King Saul.

From the Greek *nekros* (dead) and *manteia* (divination), *necromancy* means divination by the spirits of the dead or divination through the use of corpses. It presupposes belief in a form of life after death, and involves either the calling back to life of a corpse or, more commonly, the summoning of the spirit to persuade it to provide information, usually about the future. The practice of necromancy is based on the assumption that the dead, no longer bound by the limitations of mortality, are in some sense all-knowing and all-seeing. According to occult theory, the departing soul leaves some of the body's energy in what is called the astral corpse. The astral corpse can sometimes be induced to return to the physical world by the power of magic, because of its great desire to live again. It has also been suggested that the soul, in ascending to a higher level of existence, moves on a shadowy plane surrounding the physical one, from which it can see everything. In the Western magic tradition of necromancy, the period during which the soul is supposed to remain in the vicinity of its grave, and consequently the period during which necromantic practices can be performed, is twelve months following death.

The rituals of necromancy in traditional Western magic presuppose the conviction that the dead return only for some special reason and that communication with them can be achieved only through particular techniques and precautions, which are very similar to those employed for conjuring demons. These methods involve magic circles, incantations, wearing clothes stolen from corpses, meditations upon death, preparations lasting for days or weeks, the choice of the proper time, and a suitable place for the practice.

Sources:

Cavendish, Richard. *The Black Arts.* New York: G. P. Putnam's Sons, 1967.

———, ed. *Man, Myth & Magic: The Illustrated Encyclopedia of Mythology, Religion and the Unknown.* New York: Marshall Cavendish, 1983.

Eliade, Mircea, ed. *The Encyclopedia of Religion.* 16 vols. New York: Macmillan, 1987.

Gettings, Fred. *Encyclopedia of the Occult: A Guide to Every Aspect of Occult Lore, Belief and Practice.* London: Rider, 1986.

NEW AGE

New Age is a synthesis of many different preexisting movements and strands of thought. Direct lines of influence are especially easy to draw between certain nineteenth-century movements of the occult/metaphysical type—(e.g., **Spiritualism, Theosophy,** New Thought), and New Age. A significant proportion of New Agers are baby boomers, people who two decades earlier were probably participating, at some level, in the phenomenon known as the counterculture movement. As the counterculture faded away in the early 1970s, many former hippies found themselves embarking on a spiritual quest—one that, in many cases, departed from the Judeo-Christian mainstream. Thus, one of the possible ways to date the beginning of the New Age movement is to designate it as the period of the rather sudden appearance of large numbers of unconventional spiritual seekers in the decade following the 1960s.

In the early 1970s, the movement's focus was somewhat different from what it would become by the mid-1980s, when the media began to pay attention. Those early years were characterized by the prominence of newly imported Asian groups, although many of the older occult metaphysical organizations were also experiencing a growth spurt. These various groups, in combination with a significant number of less formally affiliated individuals, constituted a fairly substantial spiritual subculture that became the successor movement to the counterculture. In this initial phase of the New Age movement, followers looked forward to the transformation of society, but did not emphasize many of the things that outside observers now regard as quintessentially New Age (phenomena such as channeling and crystals).

The diverse, decentralized nature of the movement frustrates any attempt to characterize it in a final, decisive manner. It is, nevertheless, still possible to discuss in broad general terms certain New Age traits as they pertain to the afterlife. The basic New Age afterlife notion is **reincarnation,** although this process is regarded somewhat differently by New Age groups than by Asian religions. Whereas in a tradition like **Buddhism,** for example, reincarnation is viewed negatively, as a process that brings one back into the world to suffer, in the metaphysical New Age subculture reincarnation is viewed as part of an extended learning process that one undergoes across many lifetimes. Whereas earlier generations of people who dabbled in occult metaphysical spirituality were often interested in learning about their past lifetimes in the hope of discovering that they were some famous or otherwise exalted personality, the New Age emphasis on healing has led the most recent generation of seekers to examine past lives for insights into current psychological problems. It is thus in the wake of the impact of the New Age movement that the practice of **past-lives therapy** has been able to emerge as a serious treatment.

The larger metaphysical culture has also given birth to some unique concepts about the nature of spiritual reality, such as the idea of **soul mates** (the notion that two individuals are ''made for each other'' and seek union with the other across the course of many lifetimes). New Age has further generated the idea of **walk-ins** (entities that occupy bodies vacated by their original soul). The walk-in situation is similar to **possession,** although in possession the original soul is merely overshadowed— rather than completely supplanted— by the possessing entity. An extraterrestrial walk-in is supposedly one from another planet. These ideas became extremely popular in New Age circles, and for a while it seemed that almost every hard-core New Ager was claiming to be some kind of walk-in.

Sources:

Barker, Eileen. *New Religious Movements.* London: Her Majesty's Stationery Office, 1990.

Bednaroski, Mary Farrell. *New Religions and the Theological Imagination in America.* Bloomington: Indiana University Press, 1989.

Ellwood, Robert S. and Harry B. Partin. *Religious and Spiritual Groups in Modern America.* Englewood Cliffs, NJ: Prentice-Hall, 1988.

Lewis, James R., and J. Gordon Melton, eds. *Perspectives on the New Age.* Albany: State University New York Press.

NIRVANA

Nirvana is a term that was introduced in Buddhist scriptures in the second or third century B.C. to indicate the achievement of ultimate enlightenment. It is a Sanskrit word that literally means extinction. Buddha, who preferred to express himself in the vernacular language of his day, used the Pali term *nibbana.* Later Buddhist writers, who were attracted by the greater status of the Sanskrit language, introduced *nirvana* into Buddhist discourse.

Buddha accepted the basic Hindu doctrine of reincarnation as well as the notion, common to most southern Asian religions, that the ultimate goal of the religious life is to escape the cycle of death and rebirth (reincarnation, or **samara**). Whereas many contemporary Westerners view the prospects of reincarnation positively, the traditional southern Asian view is that returning to live another life is distinctly undesirable; because life in the physical body always involves suffering, we should strive to escape the wheel of rebirth.

Buddha asserted that what kept us bound to the death/rebirth process was desire, desire in the generic sense of wanting or craving anything in the world of samsara. Hence, the goal of getting off the ferris wheel of reincarnation necessarily involves freeing oneself from desire. Achieving nirvana, the final state, requires the extinction of all craving.

Sources:

Feuerstein, Georg. *Encyclopedic Dictionary of Yoga.* New York: Paragon House, 1990.
Zimmer, Heinrich. *Philosophies of India.* New York: Bollingen, 1951.

NORTH AMERICAN INDIANS (TRADITIONAL)

The native peoples of North America represent a number of different cultural spheres, separated by broad differences in language and environment. It is customary, for example, to speak of Algonquian tribes (members of a language division that includes a broad variety of groups, from the Shawnee to the Delaware). It is also customary to speak of the Eastern Woodlands tribes, the Plains tribes, and so forth. These various subdivisions indicate that, far from being a monolithic culture, American Indians are actually a complex variety of different cultures, often bearing little in common beyond the constants that all traditional, small-scale human communities the world over share.

Traditional societies do not depend upon written accounts or sacred texts to transmit rituals and beliefs, but rely on elders, or particular authoritative persons, to pass on their worldview from one generation to the next. The communities of belief so formed are small-scale, usually related to particular ethnic populations. Thus, within any one region there may be represented dozens or even hundreds of different religious traditions, along with different linguistic and cultural histories. Traditional societies are oriented around either hunting/ gathering or agriculture, and these two pursuits in turn influence the shape of their cultures, including religious beliefs.

Therefore, it is difficult to make generalizations about *the* Native American belief in the afterlife, because one can find exceptions to almost every generalization. Scholars of American Indian religions have nevertheless often made generalizations,

GHOST-DEMON FROM A PUEBLO BOWL.

such as Ake Hultkrantz's observations on the native American attitude toward death in *The Religions of the American Indians* (1979, 129):

> For the American Indians as well as for most other "primitive" peoples religion primarily serves the present life; it protects livelihood, health, and success. The thought of life's termination is pushed aside. . . . Death is an anomaly, a disturbing and frightening element of existence.

Sam Gill, another well-recognized scholar of American Indian religions, makes diametrically opposed observations in his *Native American Religions* (1982, 110):

> Death is a major subject in Native American oral traditions. . . . death in old age is often not an imbalance in cosmic forces or the final failure of efforts to ward off ill health but a passage that has been prepared for throughout the journey along life's road.

Both these attitudes toward death can be found in a wide variety of Native American cultures.

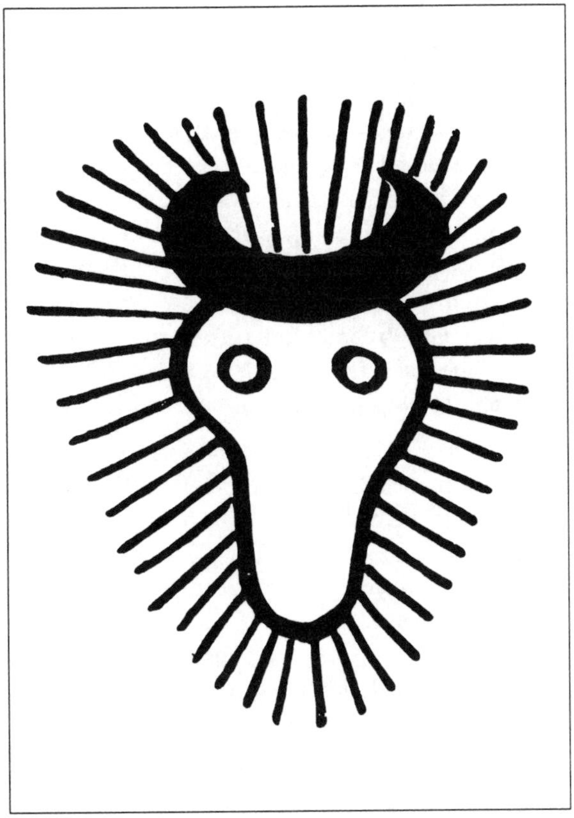

NORTH AMERICAN INDIAN SPIRIT OF HEAVEN AND HELL

Despite the intrinsically problematic nature of making generalizations about such a broad variety of different peoples, we can, nevertheless, discuss afterlife beliefs that are found in many—not necessarily all—American Indian cultures. We can, for example, assert with confidence that most traditional Native Americans believed in some sort of survival after death. In all areas of traditional North America except the Southwest, we can also assert that there were beliefs about the human being having more than one "soul"—a "free" soul that can detach itself from the physical body, still maintain its individuality, and survive death; and a vital soul, often identified with the breath, that animates the body and does not survive death.

Locations of the abode of the deceased vary widely, from quite nearby to great distances. The realm of the dead is also characterized quite differently among Native American societies. In many cultures, the otherworld is a lively copy of the present world. Giving rise to the Anglo stereotype of the American Indian afterlife as a "happy hunting ground," many traditional Plains Indian societies imagined the deceased as "existing on a rolling prairie, successfully hunting buffalo, living in tipis, feasting and dancing" (Hultkrantz 1979, 134). In other native American societies, the afterlife is a pale, gloomy realm, not unlike **Hades** or **She'ol** (the Hebrew abode of the dead). Yet other traditional North American cultures, such as the Eskimo, accept the notion of **reincarnation** as their primary concept of what occurs after death.

The aboriginal peoples of the Americas were influenced by the complex of ideas and practices known as **shamanism,** a fairly specific set of ideas and practices that revolve around religious figures known as shamans. Characteristically, shamans are healers, psychopomps (someone who guides the souls of the dead to their home in the afterlife), and, more generally, mediators between their community and the world of spirits—who are most often animal spirits and the spirits of the forces of nature, but are sometimes also the spirits of the dead. Shamans also have different helping spirits, which may take different forms, from animals to personified forces of nature to the spirits of the dead. The religious specialists of traditional American Indian societies that people sometimes refer to as medicine men are examples of shamans.

As a system, shamanism frequently emphasizes contact and communication with spirits in the otherworld, healing practices in which the shamans search for lost souls of the living, and rituals in which shamans guide the spirits of the deceased to the realm of the dead. As a consequence, certain afterlife beliefs of American Indian societies naturally reflect shamanistic themes. For example, the notion that after death the departed must undertake a more or less arduous journey to the land of the dead is widespread in both North and South America, and reflects the shamanic practice of undertaking special rituals to guide souls to the otherworld.

The deceased require assistance when either they cannot find their way to the realm of the dead or they want to remain around the family for some reason, and as a consequence do not even begin the journey. When a lingering spirit begins to bother the living, the shaman is called in. Entering a trance state, the shaman convinces the deceased to leave the living alone, and then conducts the spirit to the city of the dead. Often the Milky Way is viewed as the path souls take during this journey.

The motif of a human being descending while yet alive to the underworld is widespread in world culture. In certain kinds of shamanic healing, the sick person is diagnosed as having lost his or her soul. The attending shaman then performs a ritual in which he or she enters a trance state in order to seek out the lost soul, which has often wandered off to the realm of the dead (often an underworld). If the rite is successful, the wandering spirit is persuaded to return and the ill person recovers.

Shamanic healing, as well as the shaman's role as psychopomp, appears to provide the backdrop of ideas for what Ake Hultkrantz has referred to as the North American Orpheus tale, a mythological motif that derives its name from ancient Greek myths associated with **Orpheus.** Orpheus was the legendary musician who journeyed to the underworld in a vain attempt to bring his deceased wife, Eurydice, back to the land of the living. He was allowed to lead Eurydice out of the underworld on the condition that he not look back at her until after they had emerged entirely from the realm of death. As they approached the entranceway, however, Orpheus could no longer restrain himself, and he glanced back at his wife. She immediately disappeared back to Hades, and Orpheus found the path back to the underworld blocked.

Similarly, in story after story found among traditional native Americans, a living person seeks out a departed relative. Successful completion of the quest often entails Orphic-like prohibitions, such as neither touching nor looking at the deceased. When these conditions are violated—as they always are—the quest has permanently failed, in the sense that, as for Orpheus, there are no second chances. Such stories thus carry the message that death is inevitable.

The Pawnee story of the man who originated the whistle dance is a good example of an American Indian Orpheus tale. In the Pawnee tale, a man whose young wife has passed away encounters an elderly woman living in a tipi covered with fox skins, eagle feathers, and sage. She provides him with four balls of mud and tells him that he can use the mud balls to attract his wife's attention in the realm of the dead. With the help of the wind, he travels to land of the dead, successfully attracts his wife's attention, and then returns with her to the land of the living.

On their way back, they encounter the old woman, who provides the man with various items and teaches him the whistle dance (also called the elk dance) to help people remain aware that in the future they will eventually reside in the realm of the dead. With the help of the old woman's magic, the man becomes a great warrior, and he soon takes a second wife. One day, while visiting his new wife, he speaks harshly about his old wife. Returning home, the man finds that all that remains of his first wife are her bones. Despite various efforts to communicate with her, she does not respond, indicating that she is forever lost to him.

Sources:

Eliade, Mircea, ed. *The Encyclopedia of Religion.* 16 vols. New York: Macmillan, 1987.

Gill, Sam D. *Native American Religions: An Introduction.* Belmont, CA: Wadsworth, 1982.

———, and Irene F. Sullivan. *Dictionary of Native American Mythology.* Santa Barbara, CA: ABC-CLIO, 1992.

Hultkrantz, Ake. *The Religions of the American Indians.* 1967. Reprint, Berkeley: University of California Press, 1979.

O

Order of the White Rose

Jesse Charles Fremont Grumbine (1861–1938) was an important figure in turn-of-the-century Spiritualism and occultism in the United States. In the 1890s he founded the Order of the White Rose in Chicago, Illinois, as a Rosicrucian-style Spiritualist organization. The Spiritual Order of the White Rose was the name of the exoteric or outer branch of the group, and the Spiritual Order of the Red Rose was the name of the esoteric, inner branch. All members, whether following the White Rose or Red Rose path, aimed at attaining the celestial form of the order.

Grumbine's understanding of God is as universal spirit, not as a personal figure separate from the universe. The universal spirit is the energy vortex from which individual or personal spirits gain their life. Individual spirits are given form and definition through being connected with a physical body. Grumbine believed that personal spirits are themselves subject to temporal and other limitations. As a Spiritualist, he believed that after the death of the physical body it was possible to converse with the excarnate spirit. This, however, was a revelation not so much of the immortality of a personalized spirit but of the presence of divinity, or universal spirit, within each individual spirit.

The Order of the White Rose endeavored to teach followers the means of gaining access to the divine part of themselves while yet in the physical body. An important part of this was the development of psychic abilities such as clairvoyance, telepathy, and healing. These were understood to be, not special talents available only to certain people, but innate powers of divinity and thus abilities that everyone could develop. The order, centered variously in Chicago, Boston, Cleveland, and Portland, used Grumbine's numerous books as texts for spiritual development. The order apparently did not survive the passing of its founder.

Sources:

Grumbine, J. C. F. *Melchizedek or the Secret Doctrine of the Bible.* Boston: Order of the White Rose, 1919.

Melton, J. Gordon. *The Encyclopedia of American Religions.* 4th ed. Detroit, MI: Gale Research, 1993.

ORPHEUS

Orpheus was a legendary Thracian (Greek) musician, the son, according to which myth one reads, of Oeagrus, Apollo, or a Thracian king, and the muse Calliope. His music was so beautiful that he could charm wild beasts—even trees and stones were enamored of his music. Orpheus played an important role in Jason's quest for the Golden Fleece. On his return from that journey, he married the Naiad nymph Eurydice, with whom he was passionately in love.

Jason is best known for his **descent to the underworld.** Not long after Jason's marriage, the amorous Aristaeus chased Eurydice across a field. In her haste to escape, she stepped on a viper whose bite was so poisonous that she died. Orpheus was so disconsolate with grief that he was no longer able to sing or play his lyre. Unable to reconcile himself with his wife's death, he eventually made his was to Taenarum in Laconia, where there was an entranceway to **Hades.** When he reached **Charon,** the ferryman of the underworld, and **Cerberus,** the watchdog of Hades, he was able to charm them so with his music that they allowed him to pass. The grim shades of the dead paused to listen. Even Hades and Persephone were charmed and granted Orpheus an unprecedented favor: He would be allowed to lead Eurydice out of the underworld, on the condition that he not look back at her until after they had emerged entirely from the realm of death. As they approached the entranceway, however, Orpheus could no longer restrain himself, and he glanced back at his wife. She immediately turned into a wraith of mist and disappeared back to Hades. When Orpheus tried to follow her, he found his way barred so that even his music could no longer secure passage for him. For the rest of his life he was a recluse, never recovering from his loss. In historical Greece, Orphism, a mystery religion (a school of thought or religion in which secrets are revealed to the individual aspirant at the moment of initiation) was named after him.

The motif of a human being descending while yet alive to the underworld is widespread in world culture. It appears to derive from **shamanism.** Shamans are characterized by an ability to enter a trance state and travel (out-of-body) to both the upper world and the underworld. In certain kinds of shamanic healing, the sick person is diagnosed as having lost his or her soul. The attending shaman then performs a ritual in which he or she enters a trance state in order to seek out the lost soul, which has often wandered off to the realm of the dead (often an underworld). If the rite is successful, the wandering spirit is persuaded to return and the ill person recovers. It is easy to see how this pattern forms the basis for the Orpheus story.

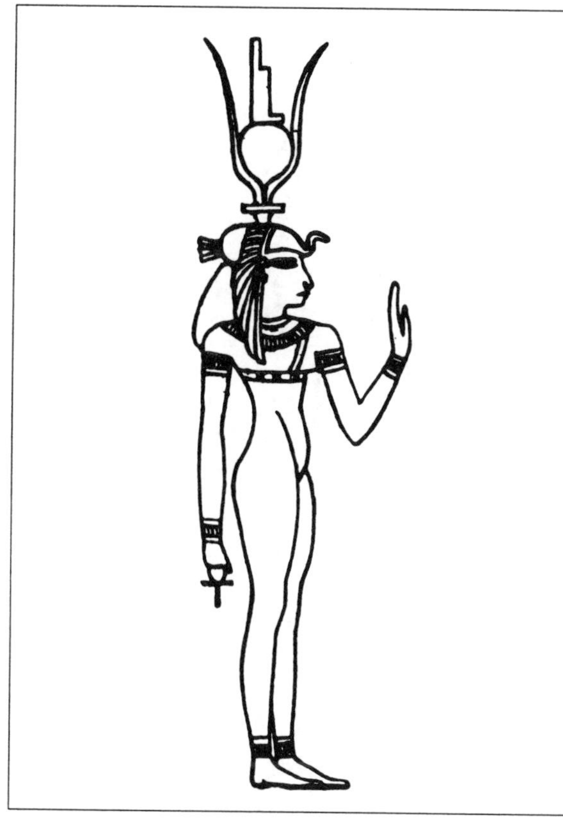

ISIS.

Sources:

Grant, Michael and John Hazel. *Who's Who in Classical Mythology.* New York: Oxford University Press, 1993.

Tripp, Edward. *The Meridian Handbook of Classical Mythology.* New York: New American Library, 1970.

OSIRIS

Toward the end of the Egyptian Old Kingdom, the brothers Seth and Osiris and their two sisters, Nephtys and Isis, emerged to compete seriously with the sun god for primacy. These four gods were part of a grouping of nine gods that formed the Ennead of Heliopolis, an influential metropolitan center. Egyptian texts refer only to certain episodes of the Osiris myth, and the most complete account comes from Plutarch in the second century A.D.

According to the story, Osiris was a good and popular god-king who was betrayed and killed by his evil brother, Seth. Seth dismembered Osiris into 14 pieces and scattered them. When Nephtys and Isis discovered the deed, Isis (Osiris's wife as well as sister, in keeping with the tradition of royal inbreeding) vowed to find the

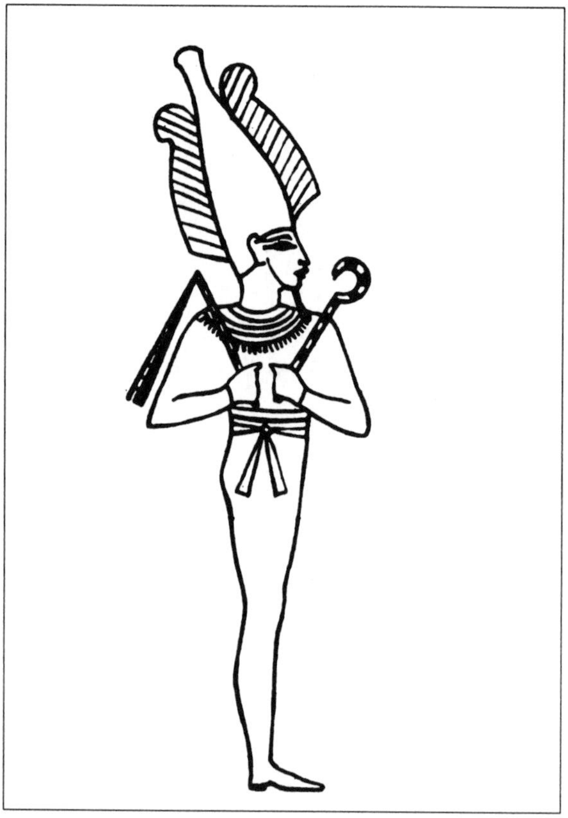

OSIRIS.

pieces and put the body back together. Being a "great magician," she was able to do so and even to become pregnant by him, but otherwise she could not bring life to him and had to bury him. When Horus, the posthumous son, grew up, he desired to avenge his father's death. He first tried the legal approach, taking the murder charge against Seth to the court of deities. When the court seemed unable to act, Horus took matters into his own hands and killed Seth in a monumental battle. Horus then went to the land of the dead, where he was recognized as Osiris's legitimate successor and crowned the new king of Egypt. At that point Horus was able to revive Osiris, who became ruler of the underworld, symbolic of resurrection and fertility, and judge of the dead for the rest of eternity.

Originally, the story of Osiris seems to have been merely the story of a vegetative cult, where Osiris's fate represented the flooding of the Nile in the spring and its recession in the fall, and/or the regular agricultural cycle of seed, growth, death, and rebirth. The story began to gain greater significance when Horus became identified with the living pharaoh, which may have happened as early as 2800 B.C. That identification perhaps occurred because granting immortality to Osiris would have reinforced the royal dynasty. If every living pharaoh was Horus and every recently deceased pharaoh was Osiris, orderly succession would be ensured. The Osiris story also grew in impact because it offered new levels of meaning for the general populace. It was a good story, with good and evil, familial loyalty, tribulations, and triumphs that offered many points of personal connection. It also suggested that resurrection from the dead was part of the natural order in a way that might include ordinary people as well.

Very little is known of the origin of Isis, whose name simply means "seat" or "throne" (of Osiris). Isis became progressively more important in the period when Greek kings, and later the Romans, ruled Egypt. From humble beginnings, she acquired characteristics of a mother goddess, and also became a goddess of love. As a mystery religion her role as reviver of the dead was emphasized, and the cult of Isis became popular throughout the Hellenistic world and the Roman Empire, despite attempts by Rome to repress Egyptian religious cults.

Sources:

Eliade, Mircea, ed. *The Encyclopedia of Religion.* 16 vols. New York: Macmillan, 1987.

Murnane, William J. "Taking It With You: The Problem of Death and Afterlife in Ancient Egypt." In Hiroshi Obayashi, ed., *Death and Afterlife: Perspectives of World Religions.* Westport, CT: Greenwood Press, 1992.

Smart, Ninian. *The Religious Experience of Mankind.* 3d ed. New York: Charles Scribner's Sons, 1984.

Turner, Alice K. *The History of Hell.* New York: Harcourt Brace, 1993.

OTHERWORLD

The basic idea of one or more "spiritual" otherworlds existing alongside the world of our ordinary, everyday experience in what we might call a different "dimension" is taken for granted in almost every religious and cultural tradition. For many of these traditions, the spiritual realm is more important, and often more real, than the physical realm. Cross-culturally and across many different historical periods there is widespread agreement on certain important traits of this otherworld.

One of the more significant points of agreement is that some essential part of the human being survives death and goes on to reside in the other realm. Another broad area of agreement is that communication between this world and the otherworld—between the living and the dead—is possible, although such communication is often not viewed positively. Dreams, which often seem to be experiences of a confused parallel world, are frequently the medium of communication. Yet another shared theme is that living human beings—or their spiritual essences—can journey to the otherworld without having to die. This is particularly true of the many cultures influenced by **shamanism.**

Although viewed as being somehow "alongside of" the world of our ordinary experience, the otherworld is also, paradoxically, seen as being located above and/or below the human realm. A widespread schema is a cosmos consisting of three levels: an upper world beyond the sky (above the "heavens") in which the gods of light dwell, a middle realm occupied by humanity, and a lower world beneath the earth in which gods of darkness reside. In certain religious traditions, particularly the familiar Western faiths, the god(s) of light are "good" and the gods of darkness are demons, but in other cultures moral dividing lines are more ambiguous. When the otherworld is above or below this world, journeys to the other side are naturally viewed as ascents or descents. **Orpheus,** for instance, descended into **Hades** through the entrance to the underworld at Taenarum. On the other hand, the widespread image of the soul as a **bird** (or as having wings) alludes to the individual's ascent to heaven.

Sources:

Eliade, Mircea, ed. *The Encyclopedia of Religion.* New York: Macmillan, 1987.
Turner, Alice K. *The History of Hell.* New York: Harcourt Brace, 1993.

OUIJA BOARD

Ouija boards—*ouija* being a combination of the French (*oui*) and German (*ja*) (yes)—are commercial products that present themselves as half game and half **séance** instrument. The board itself is much like a checker board, except, rather than squares, it contains numbers, the letters of the alphabet, and the words *yes* and *no.* The board also comes with a pointer, usually referred to as a *planchette,* on which the game players/ séance participants lightly place their fingertips. In response to verbalized questions, the planchette moves across the board—supposedly under the influence of a disembodied spirit—pointing to "yes" or "no," or spelling out words. Professional **mediums** and psychics tend to look askance at Ouija boards, regarding them as being too likely to be controlled by "low spirits," more interested in playing games with the participants than in providing accurate information.

Sources:

Berger, Arthur S., and Joyce Berger. *The Encyclopedia of Parapsychology and Psychical Research.* New York: Paragon House, 1991.
Bletzer, June G. *The Donning International Encyclopedic Psychic Dictionary.* Norfolk, VA: Donning, 1986.

OUT-OF-BODY EXPERIENCE

Out-of-body, or ecsomatic, experiences (OBEs) involve perceiving the world from a position different from the one occupied by one's physical body. During OBEs, people often have the experience of quitting their bodies and then viewing them as if from outside.

Those who undergo OBEs are usually dying or injured persons, either asleep or apparently unconscious under anesthetics, although OBEs may also occur under ordinary circumstances. Some people claim to have experienced OBEs since adolescence or early childhood. The similarity of reports of OBEs—often widely separated by geography and even history—is sometimes proffered as proof of the reality of travel of consciousness out of the body. OBEs have also been explained as hallucinations resulting from underlying physiological causes.

OBEs may manifest in a variety of forms. In the most elaborate, people perceive their consciousness to be escaping from their body, which is then observed as a lifeless object. Usually a mist or ball of light or ethereal body seems to surround the escaping consciousness and to be attached to it by a silvery or white cord.

It has been asserted that, if consciousness really can leave the body before death, then OBEs can be regarded as valid proof of survival after death. However, the possibility that these experiences may actually be departures of one's mind or imagination from the body is not contemplated in the professional medical literature. The tales found in popular and Spiritualistic literature are usually not considered a valid source of information, owing to their lack of corroboration and documentation. A considerable number of such studies are reported in parapsychological literature. Some of these studies have been published by the Society for Psychical Research.

Among the most interesting OBE phenomena are those collected by Celia Green, in particular the case of a person who was sitting peacefully on a double-decker bus and found himself looking at himself from the stairs of the bus. All of his senses seemed to be on the stairs, whereas only his physical body remained at the seat. Celia Green distinguishes between parasomatic experiences, in which the subject finds himself in an alternative body that resembles his physical one, and asomatic experiences, in which the subject is not associated with any spatial entity at all. In his highly popular book *Journeys Out of the Body,* Robert Monroe gives instructions on how to produce one's own OBEs. He also discusses the history of his OBEs, which began with intentional repeated inhalations of chemical fumes and continued through self-hypnosis.

An experiment performed by Professor C. Tart on a subject with an allegedly high ability for OBEs was considered very promising. The subject, presumably informed by out-of-body vision, reported correctly a five-digit number thought to be hidden from her view. The experiment was not conclusive, however, because Tart discovered that there were other ways in which the subject might have determined the number.

Acceptable scientific proof of the ability of human consciousness to leave the physical body has yet to be demonstrated.

Sources:

Brooke, Noel Moore. *The Philosophical Possibilities Beyond Death.* Springfield, IL: Charles C Thomas, 1981.

Green, Celia. *Out-of-the-Body Experiences.* London: Hamish Hamilton, 1968.

Monroe, Robert A. *Journeys Out of the Body.* Garden City, NY: Anchor Press, 1977.

P

PALO

Palo is the generic name applied to several closely related Afro-Cuban religiomagic systems that use non-Yoruba, Bantu-derived languages in their rituals. This little-known magic sect is widespread among Hispanic and Caribbean communities in the United States. It is frequently, although erroneously, equated with the better-known Santeria. Palo utilizes human remains in its rites, for which *paleros* (Palo practitioners) must often rob graves. Paleros do not consider their corpse-taking to be grave robbing. In an important article on Palo, Raul Canizares (1993, 91) cites an informant who made the following comment: ''We don't steal no graves, we ask the deceased if he wants to work with us. I went through more than one hundred graves before I found one dead guy who wanted to work with me.''

This set of Afro-Cuban traditions might have originated among a people who called themselves Ganga. This term later became interchangeable with the iron cauldron and its contents (chiefly human remains), which is at the center of Palo practice. In contrast with Santeria, which has retained its essentially Yoruba character, Palo is an amalgam of several different traditions. Multicultural fusion is evident both in the materiel utilized in Palo rituals and in its philosophy. For example, Palo exhibits a good/evil duality not found in Santeria.

Among Afro-Cubans, Palo is equated with magic, whereas Santeria is regarded as a religion of devotion to the higher powers. Another contrast is that Santeria has been mostly politically neutral, not a vehicle for social protest, whereas Palo has a long history of resistance. Generally speaking, paleros devote significantly less time to the worship of saints and deities than do the *santeros* (Santeria practitioners). Most of a palero or palera's religious time is spent caring for his or her *prenda,* the spirit of the disinterred corpse.

Palo is frequently regarded as witchcraft, and it is easy to see why. The palero's iron cauldron is a frightening instrument, associated in the Western mind with black magic and cannibalism. Following is a description of the making of a ganga, from Migene Gonzalez-Wippler's *Santeria: The Religion* (1989, 244–45).

> The [palero] waits until the moon is propitious, and then he goes to a cemetery with an assistant. Once there, he sprinkles rum in the form of a cross over a pre-chosen grave. The grave is opened, and the head, toes, fingers, ribs, and tibias of the corpse are removed. . . . the [palero] insists on having a head in which the brain is still present. . . . After the macabre remains are removed from their graves, they are wrapped in a black cloth and the [palero] and his helper return to the [palero's house]. . . . [After] the spirit of the [corpse] takes possession of [the palero,] [t]he assistant asks the spirit if it is willing to work for the [palero]. . . . Once the spirit accepts the pact, the grisly ceremony is ended. The [palero then] writes the name of the dead person on a piece of paper and places it at the bottom of a big iron cauldron, together with a few coins. . . . The body's remains are added to the cauldron, together with some earth from the grave. The [palero] then makes an incision on his arm with a knife that must have a white handle, and lets a few drops of blood fall into the cauldron, so that the [ganga] may drink and be refreshed. . . . After the . . . blood has been sprinkled on the remains, the [palero] adds to the cauldron the wax from a burnt candle, ashes, a cigar butt . . . some lime[,] . . . a piece of bamboo . . . filled with sand, sea water, and quicksilver . . . [as well as] the body of a small black dog. . . . Next to the dog, a variety of herbs and tree barks are placed inside the cauldron. The last ingredients to be added are red pepper, chili, garlic, ginger, onions, cinnamon, and rue, together with ants, worms, lizards, termites, bats, frogs, Spanish flies, a tarantula, a centipede, a wasp, and a scorpion.

This necromantic sect has a fascinating history that is too involved to develop here. It exhibits a fusion of practices deriving from a wide variety of different traditions. First and foremost a magic system, Palos cosmogony and theology takes second place to its techniques for supernaturally manipulating the environment in order to obtain specific results.

Sources:

Canizares, Raul. "Epiphany and Cuban Santeria." *Journal of Dharma* 15 (October–December 1990): 309–13.

———. "Palo: An Afro-Cuban Cult Often Confused with Santeria." *Syzygy: Journal of Alternative Religion and Culture* 2 (Winter/Spring 1993): 89–96.

Gonzalez-Wippler, Migene. *Santeria: The Religion.* New York: Harmony Books, 1989.

PANTOMNESIA

Pantomnesia is the experience of the unfamiliar as familiar, such as feeling, upon entering a new place, that one has been there before. It is an alternative term for the much more commonly used *déjà vu.* The French expression *déjà vu* literally means "already seen," and therefore properly refers specifically to visual experiences. It has been extended by popular usage, however, to cover other experiences—dreams, thoughts, statements, emotions, meetings, sounds, conversations, and so forth. *Pantomnesia,* on the other hand, is a term with Greek roots meaning "all" or "universal" (*panto-*) and "mind" or "memory" (*-mnesia*), and hence is technically a better general term. For a more extended discussion of this phenomenon, refer to the entry on déjà vu.

Sources:

Bletzer, June G. *The Donning International Encyclopedic Psychic Dictionary.* Norfolk, VA: Donning, 1986.

Neppe, Vernon M. *The Psychology of Déjà Vu.* Johannesburg, South Africa: Witwatersrand University Press, 1983.

PARADISE

The Persian word for garden, *pairidaeza,* was adopted in the Hebrew, Aramaic, and Greek languages to indicate the Garden of Eden. The earliest image of a garden of delights appeared in the Sumerian (ancient **Mesopotamian**) civilization. Called Dilmun, it was described as a place of abundant vegetation, set aside for the joy and pleasure of the gods. The Garden of Eden is referred to in the holy scriptures of Judaism, Christianity, and Islam. In Genesis, the plants that grew in the garden constituted the only sources of nutrition for humans. It was only after the flood that humankind began to eat flesh. The notion of a gardenlike paradise seems to reflect the idea of an oasis of refreshing waters and abundant foods that contrasts sharply with the deserts of the Middle East, cradle of the three monotheisms, and has helped to shape these religions' views of the afterlife realm.

Adam's loneliness in the Garden of Eden was relieved by the introduction of all kinds of animals and by the creation of woman. Eve was then tempted and convinced by the serpent to eat fruit from the only tree that had been forbidden by God, the Tree of the Knowledge of Good and Evil. This act of disobedience, the original sin, cost man and woman the pain and suffering to which humankind is subject and expulsion from the Garden of Eden. Afterward, Adam and Eve were driven out of the garden, so that they would not discover the Tree of Life, which gives **immortality.** An **angel** with a flaming sword was placed at the entrance to guard the garden.

At one time, Paradise was believed, particularly in the Judeo-Christian tradition, to exist in a particular geographical location, such as Central America or around the Arctic pole. In the three monotheisms the lost paradise is not completely lost, however, for those who believe in the spiritual message of their prophets. With the introduction of the idea of **resurrection** of the dead in all three religions, the promise of a return to paradise is guaranteed to religious martyrs and the righteous—those who have been loyal to the religious message. The images of primordial paradises contrast sharply with the evil and suffering of humankind's earthly existence. In

15TH CENTURY PAINTING IN WHICH HEAVEN IS PICTURED AS A GARDEN.

contrast to this world, paradise is characterized by material abundance, wealth, and spiritual and psychological happiness.

Whereas the Middle Eastern monotheistic idea of an original paradise is linked to a linear view of history, in the Hindu tradition the idea of recurring ages of the world reflects a cyclical vision of history. Four ages continuously follow one another, beginning with an age of perfect plenitude and justice (a paradise) and going on through a gradual decline that ends in the fourth, darkest age. The idea of cyclical history was transmitted from Hinduism to the Buddhist tradition, which envisions an age in which the appearance of the final Buddha, Maitreya, will signal a new paradisiacal age in which no evil will occur.

In the ancient world, a similar notion of cyclical history was found in ancient Greece. The poet Hesiod believed that the world was passing through five ages, corresponding to four metals—gold, silver, bronze and iron—and with the latter being preceded by the age of the heroes. Here the original paradisiacal golden age, undergoing a gradual increase in evil forces, is followed by a declining age that ends in the present iron age. A few centuries later Plato spoke of the opposite process, of a regenerating time during which ordinary processes would be inverted and humankind would grow younger instead of older. A new race would be born, and a new age of peace and abundance would ensue.

Besides the idea of a garden, paradise has also been depicted in certain civilizations as an island or a mountain—remote places inaccessible to humans. The ancient Greeks envisioned the remote Isles of the Blessed as an abode for their glorious gods. The Hindus pictured their gods as dwelling on the utopian mountain Mount Meru. In the Middle Ages, Dante Alighieri's *Paradiso* posited a kingdom of the afterlife arranged in concentric circles, at the center of which God resides. A different idea of paradise is also found in what are called the "cargo cults" of Melanesia and Micronesia: One day the ancestors will return with a ship loaded with a cargo that will overcome poverty and evil and invert the old world system.

Sources:

Eliade, Mircea, ed. *The Encyclopedia of Religion.* 16 vols. New York: Macmillan, 1987.
Smart, Ninian. *The Religious Experience of Mankind.* 3d ed. New York: Charles Scribner's Sons, 1984.

PARAPSYCHOLOGY AND SURVIVAL RESEARCH

The term *parapsychology,* which was coined in 1889 by German psychologist Max Dessoir, refers to the scientific study of paranormal and mediumistic phenomena. These phenomena include practically everything beyond those normally understood in terms of physical cause and effect, such as telepathy, clairvoyance, precognition, psychokinesis, and so on. One subject of investigation is the problem of survival—the continued possession of personality after death. Major efforts have been made in this area, which, during the first half of parapsychology's history, was given more attention by investigators than any other issue.

Interest in spirit communication has always been part of popular culture. In the nineteenth century, the practice of mesmerism had popularized the trance state, encouraging the idea of a psychical ability to communicate with deceased spirits during such altered states. Thought transference, hypnosis, and experiments in telepathy provided the first scientific support of the contention that mind can exist independently of brain.

Most of the early researchers of survival after death, such as **William James,** Oliver Lodge, and **F. W. H. Myers,** belonged to the **Society of Psychical Research,** founded in Britain to investigate mesmerist, psychical, and **Spiritualist** claims. They were convinced that the statements of many mediums were accurate and that the mediums gave correct information that could not be obtained in any normal sensory way. Trance communications, such as those received by one Mrs. Piper, and **cross-correspondences** were often regarded as proof that the communicators survived death. However, the investigators of the Society for Psychical Research were never able to state whether the information was definitely coming from the world of the dead or was obtained through the medium's abilities to pick up relevant facts through telepathy or clairvoyance.

Other important experimental studies on mediumship and telepathy were undertaken during the first quarter of this century in many university departments of psychology, particularly at Harvard and Stanford Universities in the United States and the University of Groningen in Holland. Laboratory research on parapsychology was launched in 1927 at Duke University, and parapsychology was established as a reputable field for scientific studies with the publication of J. B. Rhine's report *Extrasensory Perception* (1934). Emphasis on mediumistic studies decreased when Professor McDougall reached the conclusion that the mediumistic approach to the problem of survival after death could never result in a definitive solution.

Apparitions and hallucinations, the occurrence of which has been considered an alternative proof of survival after death, have been extensively investigated over the years and found to be connected with telepathy. None of these investigations brought scientific validation to the idea of the immortality of the soul or to the possibility of communication between the living and the dead. Newer developments in survival research, such as investigations of poltergeists, out-of-body experiences, psychokinesis, and reincarnation have as yet not provided unassailable proof of life after death.

Sources:

Cavendish, Richard, ed. *Encyclopedia of the Unexplained: Magic, Occultism and Parapsychology.* London: Arkana Penguin Books, 1989.

Pratt, J. Gaither. *ESP Research Today: A Study of Developments in Parapsychology Since 1960.* Metuchen, NJ: The Scarecrow Press, 1973.

Shepard, Leslie A., ed. *Encyclopedia of Occultism & Parapsychology.* Detroit, MI: Gale Research, 1991.

PAST-LIFE THERAPY

Past-life therapy consists of treating patients affected by various emotional and physical symptoms by guiding them through memories about their previous lives (thus presupposing the doctrine of **reincarnation**). The most common symptoms treated through past-life therapy include phobias, anxieties, fears, and panic attacks, as well as obesity, insomnia, acrophobia, allergies, and the like. Past-life therapists assert that most of these symptons are carryovers from other lifetimes, and that even certain physical disorders are manifestations of wounds or other accidents from previous lifetimes.

Past-life therapy differs from conventional therapies in that it is conducted while the patient is in an altered state of consciousness, that is, a state of mind resulting from restricting and intensifying the focus of attention through particular techniques of induction. Among the most common techniques are hypnosis, relaxation, breathing exercises, and visualizations. Visualizations usually suggest the transition from one level or state of consciousness to another state where the earlier experience can be contacted. The transition is visualized by imagining a stairway, an elevator, a tunnel, or some other passageway that finally leads to a past lifetime, or to a prenatal or birth state.

Retrieving memories of past lives involves a three-step process: (1) identification of a figure perceived as a personal projection or subpersonality; (2) disidentification, through which one realizes one's true nature as being distinct from that of the perceived figure; and (3) transformation, by which the individual begins to change attitudes and perceptions regarding past traumas and events, psychological patterns, or particular individuals.

It has been argued that simply living out a regression with its physical and emotional aspects leads to the remission of the troubling symptom. The remission of symptoms by such processes as cathartic abreaction (partial reliving of a repressed trauma) of a related traumatic situation was the principal focus of past-life therapy through the 1970s. This focus continued through the 1980s, but increasing emphasis was placed on the concept of the soul's journey and on the meaning of life.

The basis of present-day past-life therapy can be found in Freud's idea that what individuals experienced earlier determines their current behavior, and that making the unconscious conscious would induce healing. Jung's use of active imagination influenced the emergence, in the 1970s, of imagery techniques, which were considered particularly useful for reporting past-life memories.

There were few reports of people remembering past lives, except under hypnosis, prior to the 1960s, and it was not until the 1970s that the concepts of prenatal memory and pastlife recall were seriously explored. However, some authors, such as Stanislav Grof, found that deep breathing and imaging could facilitate recall of birth memories. Paul Brunton, in his *Hermit in the Himalayas* (1927), explored the techniques used by the yogis to access past lives, and in the late 1950s the movement called **Dianetics** proposed a therapeutic approach that sometimes involved past-life recall.

During the 1960s, improved hypnotic techniques and applications led to attempts to retrieve past lives, as in the famous **Bridey Murphey** case, and by the early 1970s the use of age regression—the process of moving chronologically backward under hypnosis to access early childhood memories—became generally acceptable. Past-life therapy began to gain approval when the British psychiatrist Denys Kelsey postulated the existence in human beings of an element that is capable of recording events even in the absence of a physical body. This hypothesis was strengthened by reports of Joan Grant, who recorded her own past-life memories in the book *Far Memory and Pharaoh.* Kelsey and Grant's joint book *Many Lifetimes* (1967) was one of the first accounts of responsible (professional) regression therapy.

Many experiments in retrieving past-life memories were conducted during the 1970s, such as those reported in G. M. Glaskin's *Windows of the Mind* (1974), and Marcia Moore's *Hypersentience* (1976). Especially important were four innovative books published in 1978 in which symptom remission was considered the principal goal of past-life therapy. The best known is Helen Wambach's *Reliving Past Lives,* in which the author summarizes the results of various small hypnosis workshops during which participants were asked about their previous lives in one of 10 specified past time periods. Wambach gathered data about artifacts, customs, and clothing of the various periods. Another important—and popular—book published in 1978 is Edith Fiore's *You Have Been Here Before,* an account of past-life memories through the process of age regression. The other two important books about past-life therapy published in 1978 are Morris Netherton's *Past Lives Therapy* and Thorwald Dethlefsen's *Voices from Other Lives,* which had a strong impact on European psychologists.

In the next decade the emphasis shifted from relieving symptoms to examining spiritual implications and understanding the meaning of life. This shift was facilitated by increasing interest in ancient Eastern philosophical theories, encouraged by authors such as Paul Brunton and L. Adams Beck. New theorizing in modern physics and biology that referred to consciousness as a fundamental aspect of existence had considerable impact on this shift of emphasis. In addition, Larry Dossey's *Recovery of the Soul* (1989), Bernie Siegel's *Love, Medicine, and Miracles* (1988), and Deepak Chopra's *Quantum Healing* (1989) contributed to the revision of the medical model in the late 1980s, when modern medicine started to refer to the physical body as an energy field and to healing as a transformation of energy. These changes helped to provide a theoretical grounding for therapy involving past-life memories, as Marilyn Ferguson's *The Aquarian Conspiracy* (1980) documents.

The **Association for Past-Life Research and Therapy** was established in 1980 to organize seminars and establish criteria for the practice of past-life therapy. Its *Journal of Regression Therapy*, started in 1986, is a forum for examining therapeutic procedures, case histories, and research.

Recent contributions to the field of past-life therapy include Joel Whitton's *Life Between Life* (1986) and Brian Weiss's *Many Lives, Many Masters* (1989), both dealing with the experience between lives; Roger Woolger's *Other Lives, Other Selves* (1987); Raymond Moody's *Coming Back: A Psychiatrist Explores Past-Life Journeys* (1990); and Garret Oppenheim's *Who Were You Before You Were You?* (1990).

Sources:

Diamond, Nina L. "Dr. Brian Weiss. Interview." *Omni* 16, no. 7, (April 1994).

Lucas, Winafred B. *Regression Therapy: A Handbook for Professionals.* Vol. 3, *Past-Life Therapy.* Crest Park, CA: Deep Forest Press, 1993.

PERSEPHONE

In classical Greek mythology, Persephone was the wife of **Hades,** ruler of the underworld. The offspring of Demeter and Zeus, Persephone was unusually beautiful. Demeter kept Persephone isolated on the island of Sicily for protection. With the consent of his brother, Zeus, Hades kidnapped Persephone while she was picking flowers and took her off to the underworld. When Demeter discovered her daughter's whereabouts, she demanded that Persephone be returned to the surface. Persephone had eaten underworld food (pomegranate seeds) however, preventing her from ever being entirely free of Hades' realm. Distraught over the loss of her daughter, Demeter, who was a goddess of fertility, grain, and the harvest, neglected to perform her divine tasks, and the earth became barren. The dispute between Hades and Demeter was finally resolved when they agreed that Persephone would spend half of the year with her mother and half with her husband. This arrangement was said to explain the seasons; fall and winter occur when Persephone is with her husband (and Demeter mourns), and spring and summer when she is reunited with her mother.

Because of her association with the seasons, Persephone became a symbol of the springtime, renewal, and rebirth. Like **Orpheus,** Persephone was one of the few mythological figures to enter the realm of the dead and return. This characteristic of returning from the dead seems to have been the primary reason Persephone and Demeter her mother, as well as Orpheus, became the central figures in mystery religions (so called because certain secrets were given to the individual aspirant at the moment of initiation)—Orphism in the case of Orpheus, and the Eleusinian mysteries in the case of Persephone.

Sources:

Grant, Michael and John Hazel. *Who's Who in Classical Mythology.* New York: Oxford University Press, 1993.

Tripp, Edward. *The Meridian Handbook of Classical Mythology.* New York: New American Library, 1970.

PHONE CALLS FROM THE DEPARTED

In the field of investigating communications with the dead, the phenomenon of receiving phone calls from the departed—usually someone with whom the recipient has had a close relationship—is regularly reported. In such calls, the telephone may sound flat and abnormal or it may ring normally. The connection usually seems to be bad, and the voice often fades. One can recognize the voice, however. In many cases the communication is abruptly terminated when the ghost hangs up or the line goes dead.

In cases where phone call recipients are aware that the people on the other end are deceased, they may be too surprised to say anything, so that the conversation ends before it can begin. In cases where the callee is unaware that the caller is among the departed, the person may converse for the length of time she or he normally spends on a typical phone conversation. For the most part, these telephone calls take place within a day of the death of the caller, although there have been reports of such conversations up to a couple of years after death.

There often seems to be a clear intention behind many of these calls, such as to say good-bye, to warn about some danger, or to convey some important information (e.g., the whereabouts of the will). At other times, this phenomenon occurs during anniversaries, birthdays, and so on. There are also a few reported instances of people placing calls, conducting an unexceptional conversation, and later finding that the person called had died before the conversation.

In an effort to explain this phenomenon, it has been theorized that the spirit of the departed is somehow able to influence telephone circuitry to bear their messages. Other types of explanations rely upon notions of psychokinesis, subconsciously projecting unconscious wishes into the telephone. Skeptics, of course, dismiss the phenomenon as complete fantasy. Even parapsychologists rarely take the phenomenon seriously. At the beginning of the present century, researchers worked on both the telegraph and the wireless hoping to be able to receive messages from the deceased. Thomas Edison, for example, who was the son of **Spiritualists,** attempted to build a phone that he anticipated would bear messages back and forth across the veil.

Sources:

Harlow, Ralph, S. *A Life after Death.* Garden City, NY: Doubleday, 1961.
McAdams, Elizabeth, and Raymond Bayless. *The Case for Life after Death.* Chicago: Nelson-Hall, 1981.
Rogo, D. Scott, and Raymond Bayless. *Phone Calls from the Dead.* Englewood Cliffs, NJ: Prentice-Hall, 1979.

PIKE, BISHOP JAMES ALBERT

The Episcopal bishop of California James Albert Pike (1913–1969), well known for his unorthodox theological views, became a **Spiritualist** when his son Jim killed himself in 1966 after experimenting with hallucinogenic drugs. Pike began his journey toward Spiritualism as a result of poltergeist phenomena that occurred in at least two different places, in Christ Church rectory in Poughkeepsie, New York, where he heard books being moved and found candles mysteriously extinguished, and in the library of the Cathedral of St. John the Divine in New York City, where he heard shuffling feet and footsteps on the floor and stairs.

Beginning February 20, 1966, Bishop Pike felt that his son might be trying to communicate with him when other poltergeist phenomena occurred in his apartment. He sat in **séances** with a London medium, Mrs. Ena Twigg, who, after examining a passport belonging to his son, became very distressed and reported that he was trying to get through to his father in order to ask forgiveness for the suicide and to express his love. During another séance, Twigg went into trance, allowing the son to speak through her and to prophesy that his father would leave his post very soon and go to Virginia. Both events happened.

In the United States, Pike sat with mediums **Arthur Ford** and George Daisley, through whom he received detailed messages from his son about standing fast against the charges of doctrinal heresy, which Pike countered with the publication of *If This Be Heresy.* Pike published his communications with his son in *The Other Side* in 1968. He died in the Israeli desert in 1969, during a trip to the Holy Land that he took with his wife, Diane Kennedy. Three days before his body was discovered, he communicated with Mrs. Twigg. In a long and painful message, Pike told her what had happened, how he had struggled against death and the transition to "the other side," and that his body would be found on a cliff in the Judaean desert near the Dead Sea (which it was).

Sources:

Guiley, Rosemary. *The Encyclopedia of Ghosts and Spirits.* New York: Facts on File, 1992.
Pike, Diane Kennedy. *Search: The Personal Story of a Wilderness Journey.* Garden City, NY: Doubleday, 1970.
Pike, James A., and Diane Kennedy. *The Other Side.* New York: Doubleday, 1968.
Twigg, Ena, with Ruth Hagy Brod. *Ena Twigg: Medium.* London: W. H. Allen, 1973.

PLATO

Plato (ca. 428–347 B.C.) was a Greek thinker who has been widely acknowledged as the greatest philosopher of Western history. A student of Socrates, Plato was also the teacher of Aristotle. The particular manner in which he posed key philosophical questions, from the issue of knowledge (How do we know what we know?) to the issue of ethics (How do we determine right action?), set the agenda for the ongoing discussion and debate that we refer to as Western philosophy. He also had a major impact on the development of Western religious thought.

Plato was born in Athens in about 428 B.C. to a family of stature. He lived during a time of turmoil and transition, when the city-states of classical Greece were crumbling. (Aristotle's pupil Alexander the Great would conquer all of Greece.) After the city of Athens put on trial and ordered the death of his teacher Socrates in 399 B.C., Plato left his native city and traveled widely through Greece, Egypt, and Italy. During his travels, he met a Pythagorean mathematician, Archytas of Tarentum, and became convinced of the value of mathematics. Later occultists would assert that he was initiated into the mysteries of Egypt in the Great Pyramid during his travels.

Plato returned to Athens and founded his school, the Academy, in 387 B.C. In Plato's day, the various fields of knowledge were not so distinct as they are today, and the Academy pursued knowledge of all subjects. Plato died in Athens around age 80. His students went off in two different directions. While the Academics continued to meet at the Academy and followed Plato's thinking without much deviation, another group—the Peripatetics—followed Aristotle, who introduced fundamental changes into Plato's system.

The surviving works of Plato are his semipopular works, which are cast in the form of dialogues. The spokesperson for Plato's views in these writings is his friend and tutor Socrates. The earliest dialogues appear to reflect the personality and views of Socrates, whereas the ideas expressed in the later dialogues are Plato's own. In the middle group of dialogues, it is difficult to tell where Socrates's ideas end and Plato's begin.

Plato is best remembered for his theory of forms, also called the theory of ideas. In brief, Plato believed that the patterns (the "forms") for all identifiable objects exist separately from these objects, at a deeper level of reality than we normally perceive. The key ingredients, the essences, of all objects we might name are their eternally unchanging patterns, which are more real than any particular object. Thus there exists in this other realm the essences of everything from tables to horses. Plato was particularly concerned with the essences of such notions as goodness, justice, and beauty.

According to Plato's student Aristotle, Plato derived his notion of the forms more or less directly from the Pythagorean notion of numbers. The abstract notion of, let us say, the number *three* can be considered independently of any given collection of three birds, three chariots, three stones, and so forth. Because numbers like three can be understood and reflected upon independently of any particular set of three objects, Pythagoras believed that such numbers must exist independently of the ordinary world. Plato merely extended Pythagoras's notion of number to other things.

This other world, the world of ideas, was far more real for Plato than the world we experience through our bodily senses, which is a watered-down copy of the realm of essences. The world of everyday experience Plato likened to a group of people who had been chained in a cave from birth so that they were able to perceive only the shadows cast by models of objects that were passed in front of a fire. He further held out the possibility that the aspiring soul could escape the thralldom of this world of shadows and seek the realm of pure ideas.

It is natural to see from this image how it was possible for succeeding generations of thinkers to interpret Plato's theorizing about the realm of the forms as theorizing about religious truths, and adherents to a major strand of Neoplatonism viewed his ideas mystically. Mystical Neoplatonism takes a step beyond Plato by viewing the universe as fundamentally united, so that even individuals are ultimately parts of the One. Although the One is regarded as divine, it is not a personal god. Plotinus (ca. 205–270 A.D.) was probably the greatest mystical Neoplatonist who aspired for a vision of the One.

Plato's criticisms of this world led to a philosophy in which withdrawal from everything that is worldly is seen as necessary in order to concentrate on higher, spiritual truths. Plotinus further taught that individual souls descend from the World Soul (where they are in unity with the One), incarnate in this finite world, and lose all memory of their spiritual origins. In this way, they became trapped in the cycle of death and rebirth, a portrayal of the human situation that suggests these ideas were ultimately derived from India. Souls can become untrapped by detaching themselves from the physical world, purifying themselves, and contemplating the One. Minus the theory of reincarnation, mystical Neoplatonism was incorporated into early Christian mysticism.

Although Plato did not devote much of his thinking or writing to the idea of an afterlife, he clearly believed in the immortality of the soul, and probably also in reincarnation. In one of his dialogues, for example, Plato, through his spokesperson Socrates, demonstrates to a skeptical group of friends that an uneducated servant already knows the answer to a geometric problem, even though the servant has never thought about the problem before. How can the servant know this? Socrates asserts that, *before it was incarnated,* the soul of the servant saw the forms (the patterns for all identifiable objects, which exist separately from these objects) relevant to the geometric problem and has them deeply planted in his mind (in what we today might call the subconscious). Even though the servant has completely forgotten seeing the forms in his disembodied state, his soul still contains a memory, a memory that Socrates' method of dialogue is able to draw out of him.

The most extended discussion of the immortality of the soul in the Platonic corpus is contained, as one might anticipate, in the *Phaedo,* the dialogue in which Plato recounts what is portrayed as the last conversation with Socrates before his execution. (Condemned to death by the city of Athens, Socrates was executed by being forced to drink hemlock.) In that conversation, Socrates advances various arguments for the existence of an afterlife.

For instance, referring to his proof of the proposition that all knowledge is a memory of what we saw before entering the body, Socrates asks, if the soul existed independently of the body prior to birth, then should it not also exist independently of the body after death? Also, referring to the existence of the realm of eternal essences, he asks if it does not seem that the human soul, which is able to comprehend the forms and abstract patterns of things, is more like these eternal forms than like the external world? For these reasons, we can conjecture that the soul is also eternal.

Sources:

Grube, G.M.A. *Plato's Thought.* 1935. Reprint. Boston: Beacon Press, 1958.

Happold, F. C. *Mysticism: A Study and an Anthology.* 1963. Rev. ed. Harmondsworth, Middlesex, England: Penguin Books, 1970.

Jowett, B., trans. *The Dialogues of Plato.* 1982. Reprint. New York: Random House, 1936.

PLURALITY OF EXISTENCES

The dominant understanding of life after death within the contemporary metaphysical subculture is that of **reincarnation,** the notion that the **soul** enters into a new body after death and lives a series of successive lifetimes in different physical embodiments. This has sometimes been referred to as a plurality of existences. The notion of a plurality of existences has also been used to refer to a related but somewhat different idea—namely, that the same soul *simultaneously* incarnates in different bodies, sometimes at great distances from each other, as when one claims to be in both a terrestrial and an **extraterrestrial incarnation** simultaneously.

Sources:

Bletzer, June G. *The Donning International Encyclopedic Psychic Dictionary.* Norfolk, VA: Donning, 1986.

Head, Joseph, and S. L. Cranston. *Reincarnation: The Phoenix Fire Mystery.* New York: Julian Press/ Crown, 1977.

POSSESSION

Enthusiasmós (from Greek *en theos,* "to be in God") and ecstasy characterized the initiation and purification process of the cult of Dionysus in ancient Greece. Women, and to a lesser extent men, who were possessed by the god and surrendered to a state of

A POSSESSED WOMAN IS REDEEMED FROM THE DEMONS OF THE SEVEN DEADLY SINS. (DERIVED FROM A 13TH CENTURY ENGLISH MANUSCRIPT.)

wild madness (induced by wine and sexual rites) could become free forever. This wild ritual was quite widespread in the ancient Greek world and became so popular that in ancient Rome it was legally suppressed in 186 B.C. because of excesses.

This type of phenomenon, known as possession, was not limited to the Mediterranean world. Spirit possession is found in different forms throughout history and across the world, with somewhat more emphasis in traditional Pacific and indigenous American cultures. But it was also widespread in the Western world (and made famous in medieval, and later, reports by the Church on possessed women), the Mediterranean region, and Africa. The different social and cultural background of civilizations determined the variations from one version to another in rituals and the values attributed to such an experience.

Possession by a god, spirit, or demon is related to dissociation, ritual trance, and similar altered states of consciousness and has drawn much attention from anthropologists, psychologists, and religious authorities. Typically, spirit possession involves a dramatic change in the physiognomy and behavior of the host, and historically it has been found to occur more among women and the lower classes. It was and still is widespread among southern Asian women (who tend to explain their problems as a result of evil spirits) and in the ancestor worship of voodoo and Santeria and certain African religions. In shamanic cultures, possession is viewed as an integral part of the healing power of the shaman: When somebody's sickness is diagnosed to be caused by the loss of their soul in the netherworld, the shaman performs a ritual and enters a trance state in order to seek out the lost soul, which has frequently wandered off to the realm of the dead (often an underworld). If the rite is successful, the wandering spirit is persuaded to return and the ill person recovers.

The ritual trance that leads to spirit possession can be induced through various techniques, such as inhaling the fumes of certain substances (e.g., the oracle of Delphi), taking drugs (e.g., peyote by certain native American groups and alcohol by Dionysus cults), performing rituals (e.g., animal sacrifices in India), using certain body techniques (such as hyperventilation, monotonous drumming, dancing, or chanting), and fasting. Once this altered state of consciousness is created, the host is no longer in a regular state of wakefulness and may, at times not even remember the experience of possession.

Where possession is viewed as an evil phenomenon, the practice of exorcism has been developed to expel the spirit from the host. The Roman Catholic church is one of the few Christian denominations to formally develop a practice of exorcism aimed at liberating the host from the destructive power of the evil spirit. Outside the Christian tradition, the possessing spirit is viewed as a neutral entity that can be transformed into a benign one through specific rituals and religious practices.

A mid-nineteenth-century movement known as spiritism was based on consulting spirits of the dead through séances and mediums. Spiritualism became the true scientific religion to some, including the reflective Sir Arthur Conan Doyle (creator of the Sherlock Holmes mysteries). Spiritism, which was developed in France by Allan Kardec, also emphasized invoking spirit guides that could help heal diseases that originated from a spiritual need.

In more recent times, especially in the New Age milieu, mediums have become channels. Several religious movements are based on the authority of channeled messages, such as the I AM Religious Activity and the Church Universal and Triumphant (however, they would not call their mediumship ''channeling''). Since the 1970s, a variety of literature has been produced that is believed to be directly inspired by spirits, such as Emmanuel and Bartholomew, which present their perspective on the afterlife and the future of humankind.

Within Christianity, the ecstatic experience of being possessed by the Holy Spirit (which began with the descent of the Holy Spirit in the form of flames on the day of Pentecost) has been reinstituted by the Pentecostal movement, which recognizes as a gift of the Holy Spirit such phenomena as the ability to speak in tongues (glossolalia).

In psychology and psychiatry, spirit possession has been explained in terms of multiple personality disorders or related disturbances, such as schizophrenia, paranoia, hysteria, and compulsive behaviors. But medicine has not been able to demonstrate psychological problems in all cases of multiple personalities. In fact, in some cases doctors have actually asserted that spirit possession may be responsible for the disturbance.

Sources:

Bletzer, June G. *The Donning International Encyclopedic Psychic Dictionary.* Norfolk, VA: Donning, 1986.
Guiley, Rosemary Ellen. *The Encyclopedia of Ghost and Spirits.* New York: Facts on File, 1992.
Shepard, Leslie A., ed. *Encyclopedia of Occultism & Parapsychology.* Detroit, MI: Gale Research, 1991.

PREEXISTENCE

Preexistence refers to the notion that the essence of the individual existed prior to its union with the body. Traditionally, this concept has been restricted to forms of preexistence other than **reincarnation.** In esoteric spiritual schools that reject reincarnation, preexistence is sometimes conceived of as a spark of the divine descending into matter from a pure spiritual realm in order to partake of the lessons offered in the sphere of ordinary human life.

Preexistence solves a speculative problem for traditions that accept the idea of an immortal soul but do not accept reincarnation: If the individual soul is an incorruptible, immortal spirit, how can that soul come into existence at the moment of ordinary physical conception? Serious reflection on this issue has led many thinkers to postulate that the creation of the soul takes place independently of the conception of the body. Further reflection on independent creation of the soul and the body in turn led to the idea that perhaps souls were created prior to conception and resided in a spirit realm before birth.

Sources:

Eliade, Mircea, ed. *The Encyclopedia of Religion.* 16 vols. New York: Macmillan, 1987.
Shepherd, Leslie A. *Encyclopedia of Occultism and Parapsychology.* Detroit, MI: Gale Research, 1985.

PSYCHOMANTEUM

Psychomanteums were ancient Greek oracles of the dead, where seekers could come to consult spirits of the deceased. After fasting and certain other preparatory exercises, the seekers could evoke a vision of the departed by staring into a pool or pan of water. At other psychomanteums, seekers attempted to contact the dead through dreams. Previously unknown to most people who were not scholars of antiquity, this ancient practice has begun to receive attention as a result of the efforts of **Raymond Moody** to establish a modern psychomanteum at his research facility in rural Alabama, the **Theater of the Mind.**

Sources:

Moody, Raymond A. "Family Reunions: Visionary Encounters with the Departed in a Modern-Day Psychomanteum." *Journal of Near-Death Studies* 11, no. 2 (Winter 1992): 83–121.
———. *Reunions.* New York: Villard Books, 1993.

PURGATORY

In religious traditions that postulate a heaven and a hell as the final abode of the soul, serious thinkers have grappled with the fate of those who, although not ethical exemplars, have been more-or-less good, and not guilty of truly evil actions. This has led to the development of ideas of intermediate afterlife abodes in which ''mixed'' souls are purified and made fit for paradise. Such an intermediate realm is referred to as purgatory, alluding to the purification (*purgation*) that souls in purgatory undergo. The basic idea seems to have first appeared in later **Zoroastrianism,** which postulates that, after the final battle between good and evil, there will be a general judgment in which everyone will be put through an ordeal of fire—a river of molten metal in which morally mixed individuals will have their dross burned away rather than be consumed in hell.

The Zoroastrian purgatory, which is more of an event than a realm, appears to have influenced the traditional Catholic notion of purgatory (easily the most well known of such ''mixed'' realms), especially in the particular of a purifying fire. Officially, however, the Catholic acceptance of purgatory did not begin until a papal letter of 1253, and the dogma was not canonized until the Council of Trent, which issued the following proclamation: ''[T]here is a purgatorial fire in which the souls of the pious are purifed by a temporary punishment so that an entrance may be opened for them into the eternal country in which nothing stained can enter.''

Purgatory, which in this view is a kind of **Limbo,** provided explanations for such questions as the eternal fate of babies who died in infancy; unbaptized babies entered heaven after a *brief* sojourn in purgatory. It also helped to explain ghosts, which were viewed as souls undergoing purgatorial cleansing.

The Catholic church also cautiously embraced the notion that the prayers and other actions of the living could shorten the time the deceased spent in purgatory. As a merciful intercessor, the Virgin Mary became Queen of Purgatory, to whom prayers for the deceased were addressed. As is well known to those familiar with the history, it was the doctrine of the role the living could play to rescue souls from purgatory that set the stage for the Protestant Reformation.

To raise money for the facade of Saint Peter's in Rome, certain officials of the church sold indulgences, which, it was advertised, could free souls from purgatory. Although the actual nature of what was being promised was more complex than this, some less-than-scrupulous indulgence salesmen presented the arrangement in an oversimplified manner: In the words of the jingle that so offended Martin Luther, ''As soon as the money in the coffer rings, the soul from purgatory springs.'' The Reformation began as a protest against such a simplified view of release from purgatory.

Because purgatory had been the bone of contention, Protestants rejected the doctrine and everything connected with it. The veneration of the Virgin Mary, for example, was eschewed. The doctrine of purgatory was even one of the reasons Protestants rejected certain books of the Bible (the Old Testament Apocrypha)—

RAEL. COURTESY OF THE RAELIAN MOVEMENT.

RAELIAN MOVEMENT

The Raelian movement is a flying saucer religion founded by French racing car driver and journalist Claude Vorihon (Rael to his followers) in 1973 as a result of an alleged encounter with space aliens (referred to as Elohim by Raelians). Denying the existence of God or the **soul,** Rael presents as the only hope for **immortality** a regeneration through science, and to this end members participate in four annual festivals so that the Elohim can fly overhead and register the Raelians' DNA codes on their machines. This initiation ritual, "the transmission of the cellular plan," promises a kind of immortality through cloning. New initiates sign a contract that permits a mortician to cut out a piece of bone in their forehead (the "third eye") and mail it packed in ice to Rael, who in turn reputedly relays it to the Elohim.

Sources:

Palmer, Susan J. "Woman as Playmate in the Raelian Movement." *Syzygy: Journal of Alternative Religion and Culture* 1, no. 3 (1992): 227–45.

Raelian Movement. *An Embassy for Extra-Terrestrials.* Geneva: International Raelian Movement, n.d.

RAM DASS, BABA

Baba Ram Dass, born Richard Alpert, is a popular spiritual teacher and author well known in New Age circles. One of the more interesting phases of his "ministry" has been his work with dying people. A colleague of **Stephen Levine,** he has helped to develop the contemporary field of **conscious dying.**

Ram Dass was born in Boston on April 6, 1931, to Gertrude Levin and George Alpert, a lawyer and one of the founders of Brandeis University. He pursued a career in psychology, attending Tufts University (B.A., 1952), Wesleyan University (M.A., 1954), and Stanford University (Ph.D., 1957). He was appointed assistant professor at Harvard in 1958. Timothy Leary came to Harvard the next year, and the two became friends. Ram Dass subsequently became involved in experimentation with psychedelic drugs, for which both he and Leary were eventually dismissed. For the next four years, he was a major spokesman for psychedelic drugs. With Leary and Ralph Metzner he wrote *The Psychedelic Experience* (1964).

By 1967 Ram Dass had become severely depressed and traveled to India to seek deeper answers about drugs and the altered states of consciousness available through them. While in India, he met Neem Karoli Baba, who became his guru. Adopting the spiritual name Ram Dass, he returned to the United States the next year, eventually lecturing about his experiences and becoming a spiritual teacher in his own right. He told the story of his experiences and presented a westernized Hinduism in his popular *Be Here Now* (1972). The publication of *Be Here Now* has been viewed as a key event in the emergence of the New Age movement. The book was also instrumental in contributing to the widespread acceptance of the notion of **reincarnation** within this emerging spiritual subculture.

In 1974 his continued spiritual seeking led Ram Dass to a metaphysical teacher in New York City, Joya Santanya (Joyce Green). For the next two years Ram Dass was her disciple. This period ended in a dramatic break, at which time he denounced Joya and began a period of withdrawal from public activity. He eventually resumed his career as a writer and lecturer. His popular books include *The Only Dance There Is* (1976), *Grist for the Mill* (1977), *Journey of Awakening* (1978), and *Miracle of Love* (1979). During the 1980s Ram Dass was involved with the Seva Foundation, a charitable enterprise founded with the ambitious objective of ending blindness in Nepal. Subsequently, his public speaking has been on the foundation's behalf.

Sources:

Dowling, Colette. "Confessions of an American Guru." *The New York Times Magazine* (December 4, 1977): 41–43, 136–49.

Fentress, Calvin. "Ram Dass, Nobody Special." *New Times* (September 4, 1978): 37–47.

Leary, Timothy, Ralph Metzner, and Richard Alpert. *The Psychedelic Experience.* New Hyde Park, NY: University Books, 1964.

Ram Dass, Baba [Alpert, Richard]. *Be Here Now.* Christobal, NM: Lama Foundation, 1972.

RAPPING

In the context of afterlife beliefs, rapping refers to knocking noises that are attributed to disembodied spirits. Rapping can refer to any variety of thumping, tapping, or knocking noises conveying messages from the beyond. With agreed-upon guidelines between those in a **séance** (or less formal setting) and the spirits—such as one knock means yes, two knocks mean no—this relatively simple manifestation of the other side can be an effective method of communication.

There are many precedents for the contemporary phenomenon of rapping. In the ninth century, the chronicle *Rudolf of Fulda* mentions communications from an invisible rapper. The great Swiss alchemist Paracelsus referred to raps and *pulsatio mortuorum,* omens of death. In the medieval period, rapping entities under the designation *spiritus percutiens* were dismissed from the premises during benedictions of churches. Melanchthon, an important figure in the Reformation, mentioned that the phenomenon occurred at Oppenheim, Germany, in 1520. In his *Sadiucismus Triumphatus,* Joseph Glanvil wrote at length about another occurrence at Tedworth, England, in 1661. Also, Samuel Wesley—father of John Wesley, Methodism's founder—and his family reported rapping at his Epworth Vicarage in 1716. And there are yet other cases that are too numerous to mention here.

Rapping acquired fame as the method by which the **Fox sisters** communicated with the dead in 1848 in Hydesville, New York. Bothered by extensive rapping noises, Maggie and Kate Fox requested Mr. Splitfoot (a reference to the cloven foot of the Devil) to respond to questions with his raps. While such phenomena are not particularly unusual, the Foxes attracted a great deal of public attention, and people from miles around would stop by to observe the phenomenon of spirit communication. Initially, the spirit knocked two times for yes and made no noise for no. After a while, however, David Fox, an older brother, developed a complex code of knocks for the alphabet with which the ghost was able to communicate more complex messages.

Not long afterward, Leah Fish, the two girls' older sister, brought their mother and Kate to Rochester, and the phenomena followed Kate. Around the time of the move, news of the rappings was beginning to create national interest, and other people in the Rochester area discovered that they had abilities as mediums. Spirit knockings were everywhere, and the ''Rochester knockings'' generated tremendous coverage by the press. The denominational family that we know as **Spiritualism** grew directly out of this ''craze'' initiated by the Fox sisters, despite the fact that they later claimed to have faked the original rapping noises.

Sources:

Brandon, Ruth. *The Spiritualists*, New York: Alfred A. Knopf, 1983.

Doyle, Sir Arthur Conan. *The History of Spiritualism.* 2 vols. New York: Arno Press, 1975.

RECALL OF PAST INCARNATIONS

The publication of Morey Bernstein's *The Search of Bridey Murphy* (1956), about a Colorado housewife who claimed to have relived memories of a previous life as the nineteenth-century Irish girl Bridey Murphy, gave great impetus to a series of studies about the phenomenon of past-life regression. Some investigators believe that past-life regression, also known as recall of past incarnations, provides evidence for reincarnation.

Among the most recent studies on this phenomenon are the works of **Ian Stevenson** and Helen Wambach. Stevenson, professor and chair of the Department of Psychiatry at the University of Virginia, has documented cases in India, Africa, the Near East, the Far East, Britain, and the United States in which young children exhibited xenoglossy, the ability to speak a foreign language to which they had no previous exposure. They also knew details about places they had never seen. Some of these children recognized former homes and neighborhoods, as well as still-living friends or relatives. Among the events of their purported previous incarnations, they usually recalled violent deaths. Their birthmarks or congenital malformations often resembled scars compatible with the wounds they claimed led to their death. The results of these studies are contained in the books *Twenty Cases Suggestive of Reincarnation,* (1974) *Cases of the Reincarnation Type, Unlearned Language: New Studies in Xenoglossy,* (1984) and *Telepathic Impressions: A Review and Report of Thirty-five New Cases.* (1970)

Psychologist Helen Wambach, in her books *Reliving Past Lives: The Evidence Under Hypnosis, (1978)* and *Life Before Life, (1979)* examines the results of data about subjects who participated in small hypnosis workshops. During each workshop the subjects were allowed to choose one of 10 specified past time periods and were asked about their lives during the period chosen. They were asked about their gender, appearance, clothing, diet, occupation, and similar matters. In other cases the subjects were invited to concentrate on their return to life and were asked such questions as whether they had chosen to be born, whether they had chosen their sex, when their soul had entered their physical body, and so forth. Although interesting, the results of Wambach's studies have not been considered as providing significant evidence of reincarnation because of the vagueness and lack of specificity with regard to historical facts in the recollections reported in her studies.

Sources:

Lucas, Winafred Blake. *Regression Therapy: A Handbook for Professionals,* 2 vols. Crest Park, CA: Deep Forest Press, 1993.

Moore, Brooke Noel. *The Philosophical Possibilities Beyond Death.* Springfield, IL: Charles C Thomas, 1981.

Stevenson, Ian. *Twenty Cases Suggestive of Reincarnation.* 2d ed. Charlottesville: University Press of Virginia, 1974.

Wambach, Helen. Reliving Past Lives. New York: HarperCollins, 1978.

REGRESSION (HYPNOTIC REGRESSION)

As a psychoanalytic term, *regression* traditionally refers either to a defense mechanism (as when an adult under extreme stress "regresses" to childhood patterns of coping with anxiety) or to the therapeutic movement backward into a client's often repressed memories of unpleasant prior experiences. With respect to the latter meaning, the understanding is that current problems are based on earlier traumas and that recalling and facing the original trauma will release the patient from the current psychological problem. Such therapeutic regression is sometimes accomplished with the aid of hypnosis.

The same basic theoretical orientation underlies the contemporary practice of **past-life therapy,** in which the client is regressed to memories from prior lifetimes, often with the aid of hypnosis. (An alternative name for past-life therapy is regression therapy.) As in classical psychoanalysis, once the trauma from the past is faced, the client is cured of the current problem. The association of hypnosis with earlier lifetimes goes back at least as far as **Allan Kardec,** founder of spiritism. However, hypnosis need not always be the key to past lives, as memories from earlier incarnations can emerge in dreams and even through conscious recall.

Regression to past lives is not always carried out for therapeutic purposes. In **parapsychological** research, for example, tapping memories of earlier lifetimes and then seeking verification of the information revealed in such memories is one method for demonstrating the reality of **reincarnation.** Also, in contemporary metaphysical circles people sometimes wish to be hypnotically regressed to past incarnations merely out of a sense of curiosity about who they were in earlier lifetimes.

Sources:

Gauld, Alan. *Mediumship and Survival: A Century of Investigations.* London: Heinemann, 1982.

Grof, Stanislav. *The Adventure of Self-Discovery.* Albany, NY: State University of New York Press, 1988.

Netherton, Morris, and Nancy Shiffrin. *Past Lives Therapy.* New York: Morrow, 1978.

REINCARNATION

Reincarnation is the rebirth of the soul after the body's death into a new physical body, which may be human or animal as well as divine, angelic, demonic, vegetative, or celestial. Reincarnationists usually believe that the goal of reincarnation is to stop being reborn, and to go on to some other state of existence, although sometimes reincarnation is regarded as an unending process. In some traditions reincarnation is supposed to happen immediately after death; in others only after a certain period of time has passed, during which the soul dwells in some other plane of existence.

Many efforts to validate claims of past lives have been made, including the notable research of **Ian Stevenson,** professor of psychiatry at the University of Virginia, who began investigating spontaneous reincarnational memories among children around the world in the 1960s. However, reincarnation has yet to be proved to the satisfaction of mainstream science.

The notion of reincarnation is very ancient and is still widely prevalent in every part of the world, especially in parts of Asia and in the native societies of Africa and Australia. In many tribes in West Africa (such as the Ewe, Edo, Igbo, and Yoruba) and in southern Africa (for example, the Bantu-speaking groups and the Zulu), human beings are believed to reincarnate. Failure to be reborn and childlessness are regarded as evil, so considerable emphasis is placed upon fertility rites. Rebirth and the veneration of ancestors are considered fundamental, for their spirits are viewed as returning in one or another life form connected to the various totemic groups characterizing the organizational structure of the society.

In central Australia aboriginal tribes believe that the spirits of human beings periodically reincarnate in nonhuman or even in inanimate entities, and that the soul is separable from the body and from any other physical object. The departed souls of the ancestors are believed to return to earthly life by entering the body of a mother at the moment of conception, which occurs when she comes into the proximity of a local totem center, where the soul of a deceased ancestor is waiting to be reborn.

The most elaborate doctrines of rebirth and reincarnation belong to the ancient Greek and Indian traditions. In ancient Greece, where the idea of metempsychosis (reincarnation) was imported from the East, the concept of reincarnation was associated principally with the philosophy of Pythagoras, Empedocles, and **Plato.** Reincarnation and the idea that human beings can incarnate in animal forms were among the main insights of Pythagoras, who avowed that he had formerly been Aethalides. He also claimed that he had received the memory of his soul's transmigrations as well as the memories of what his own soul and the souls of others had experienced between death and rebirth, as gifts from the god Mercury.

According to Empedocles, nothing in the cosmos is either created or destroyed, and all living things achieve transmutation on the basis of the relations among the four basic elements. Plato, on the other hand, synthesized the beliefs of the philosophers who preceded him, believing that the immortal soul is attached to objects of material and transitory desire and is therefore a prisoner of the physical body. The only way for the soul to achieve a state of eternal bliss is by detaching itself completely from the pleasures of the material world—into which it descends periodically in all creatures—and attaining a pure contemplation of the Absolute.

In India belief in reincarnation is best known in connection with the teachings and practices of Hinduism and Buddhism, although all traditions native to southern Asia (e.g., Sikhism and Jainism) accept reincarnation as one of their tenets. Hinduism regards present life as preparation for life after death. According to the law of **karma,** the results of good and evil actions in previous existences determine the circumstances of this lifetime. A person can escape rebirth only by suppressing all desires except the desire for perfect unification with the universal self or with the divine.

Buddhism, which derives its doctrine of rebirth from Hinduism, propagates the doctrine of ''no self'' (**anatta**), according to which the human being has no immortal soul. Rather, the self is nothing more than the manifestation of a complex succession of psychosomatic moments propelled along the temporal continuum according to the law of karma. This self can experience suffering, however, and the goal of Buddhism is to end the cycle of rebirth, dissolve the illusory self, and thus put an end to the process of suffering. Buddhism also holds that every human being may be reborn successively into any one of five classes of living beings: gods, human beings, animals, hungry ghosts, or denizens of hell.

The doctrine of reincarnation can also be found in certain ancient Near Eastern religions, such as the royal cult of the pharaohs in ancient **Egypt** and the mystery cult of **Orpheus** in second-century Greece. It is also a tenet of certain modern schools of thought, such as **Theosophy,** and the philosophy of thinkers like **Carl Gustav Jung** and Aldous Huxley.

In Western countries, belief in reincarnation vanished in the early Middle Ages, being incompatible with Christian orthodoxy, although it was periodically revived by such heretical groups as the **Cathars** and Albigenses, by groups such as the Knights Templars, Rosicrucians, and Freemasons, and by alchemists, Cabalists, and others. Belief in reincarnation has grown in the modern West as a result of the impact of Eastern religions. Reincarnation is a fundamental element of New Age and more generally of metaphysical philosophy, providing an alternative to traditional Christian belief in bodily **resurrection** and future existence in heaven.

Sources:

Banerjee, H. N., and W. C. Oursler. *Lives Unlimited: Reincarnation East and West.* New York: Doubleday, 1974.

Evans-Wentz, W. Y., ed. *The Tibetan Book of the Dead.* 3d ed. London: Oxford University Press, 1960.

Hall, Manly Palmer. *Reincarnation: The Cycle of Necessity.* Los Angeles: The Philosophical Research Society, 1956.

Head, Joseph, and S. L. Cranston, eds. *Reincarnation in World Thought.* New York: Crown, 1967.

Stevenson, Ian. *Twenty Cases Suggestive of Reincarnation.* 2d ed. Charlottesville: University Press of Virginia, 1974.

Reincarnation Report

The *Reincarnation Report* is a publication of Reincarnationists, Inc., an organization established in 1984 by the American seminar trainer and hypnotist **Richard Sutphen** in Malibu, California, to sponsor and conduct seminars on **reincarnation** and past-life regression.

Sources:

Guiley, Rosemary Ellen. *Harper's Encyclopedia of Mystical & Paranormal Experience.* San Francisco: HarperCollins, 1991.

Reincarnationists, Inc.

The organization Reincarnationists, Inc., was established in 1984 by the American seminar trainer and hypnotist **Richard Sutphen** in Malibu, California, to conduct and sponsor seminars on reincarnation and past-life regression. The organization was directed by Sutphen's third wife, Tara. It became inactive by 1987 after an attempt to establish a new center for the group in Sedona, Arizona, was abandoned because of lack of public interest and financial support.

Sources:

Guiley, Rosemary Ellen. *Harper's Encyclopedia of Mystical & Paranormal Experience.* San Francisco: HarperCollins, 1991.

RESURRECTION

Resurrection (from Latin *resurgere,* to rise again) is a religious notion that implies the resurgence or revival to life of the bodies of the dead. In polytheistic religions, resurrection is experienced only by certain gods, and often is linked to fertility and to the seasonal cycle of the death and rebirth of nature. In the Canaanite religion, Aliyan Baal, god of fertility, is killed by his enemy Mot (''death''), but returns to life upon the intervention of his sister Anat. Similarly, in ancient Egypt the god Osiris, whose body had been killed and dismembered by his brother Set, is brought back to life by his wife, the goddess Isis. In the monotheistic religions resurrection from death has often been attributed to human beings. Human resurrection is found for the first time in Zoroastrianism, and was later developed in the principal monotheistic religions (Judaism, Christianity, and Islam).

The concept of resurrection as formulated in Zoroastrianism represents one of the earliest efforts to conceive of immortality. It is part of an optimistic vision of the end of the world, in which the forces of light overcome darkness, sinners are purified, and all humankind rejoices with the renewal of creation. An entire section of the *Avesta* (Zoroastrian scriptures) explains how the body is returned to the soul at the moment of reunion and resurrection.

There are few references to resurrection in Judaism. The earliest explicit mention of the belief is in the Jewish apocalyptic literature of second century B.C., where it is viewed as the revival of bodies—to a fate of eternal bliss for the righteous and eternal shame for sinners. At the end of the first century B.C., resurrection is mentioned as the restoration, and sometimes the transfiguration, of the body, and in different sources is conceived of as a renewal of righteous people in a new earth, or their transformation into angelic form, or the reunification of their body and soul. In rabbinic Judaism, the belief in resurrection is completely accepted as reunion of body and soul, using images drawn from nature, such as sprouting forth from the earth.

THE RESURRECTION OF CHRIST. (FROM *LEIDEN CHRISTI* [THE PASSION OF CHRIST], PRINTED BY ALBRECHT PFISTER, BAMBERG, 1470.)

In Christianity the idea of resurrection is derived from the Jewish tradition, and is considered to be one of the most important beliefs for salvation. Christian resurrection refers both to the resurrection of Jesus Christ (after the Crucifixion) and to the resurrection of the righteous (during the Last Judgment). The early church developed the belief that the immortal soul will reunite with the body at the moment of resurrection. Modern twentieth-century theology presents resurrection as a moment of re-creation of the whole being, which was dissolved with death.

In Islam the final day of resurrection is considered an extremely important moment. In the early tradition resurrection is related to the omnipotence of God as creator, who could accomplish whatever he willed, even restoring the dead to life. Later doctrines developed the notion of the immortality of the soul and its reunion with the body.

Sources:

Eliade, Mircea. *Encyclopedia of Religion.* 16 vols. New York: Macmillan, 1987.
Frazer, James George. *The Golden Bough: A Study in Magic and Religion.* New York: Macmillan, 1922.

REYES, BENITO

Benito F. Reyes, author of more than 20 books about philosophy, psychology, religious studies, and Oriental culture, graduated from the University of the Philippines. Before founding the University of the City of Manila in 1967, he was professor at the Far Eastern University in Manila, taught at the State University of New York as a Fulbright-Hays philosophy professor, and also taught at Boston University as a Fulbright-Smith-Mundt professor. In 1975 he and his wife, Dominga, founded the World University of America in Ojai, California. The university is dedicated to promoting world peace through education and to enhancing human consciousness.

Reyes's interest in **out-of-body experiences** and the nature of consciousness after life began at age 16, when he first consciously traveled out of his body. At age 12, he had begun accompanying his mother, a *pho-O* (one who helps people to die by enabling the spirit to release the body and rejoices with it at its conscious departure). He maintained that he had out-of-body experiences every night, consciously and with full control, and sometimes without having to first allow his body to sleep.

In his *Scientific Evidence of the Existence of the Soul (1949),* Reyes postulates that the soul exists and that it constitutes a nonphysical element in the human being. This postulate explains a multitude of phenomena concerning human consciousness, its metaphysical character, its indestructibility and permanency, and its complete inaccessibility to physical and chemical laws. Reyes analyzes various facets of consciousness—memory, sleep, dreams, death, psychical research, and parapsychology—and concludes that they are explicable empirically, consistently, coherently,

DR. BENITO F. REYES, FOUNDER AND TEACHER-IN-RESIDENCE, INTERNATIONAL ASSOCIATION FOR CONSCIOUS DYING (IACD). COURTESY OF THE INTERNATIONAL ASSOCIATION FOR CONSCIOUS DYING (IACD).

and comprehensively only when the human being is viewed as essentially a nonphysical being in possession of will, thought, and action. This nonphysical human reality is the **soul.**

In the works *Conscious Dying,* (1986) and *The Practice of Conscious Dying,* (1990), Reyes deals with the psychology of dying based from the phenomenological perspective of near-death experiences. Reyes claims that conscious dying, (which is also one of the themes of the Bardo Thodol, the Tibetan Book of the Dead) is the key that will unlock the door to immortality, which is achieved by going through death consciously, through birth consciously, and between death and rebirth consciously. Thus, the broken strand of consciousness is reconstituted through all major alterations, and the integrity of one's true being is restored. Reyes also presents a set of guidelines that must be followed in this process and a set of prayers and formulas that must be heard, repeated, and internalized with total acceptance.

Sources:

Reyes, Benito. *Conscious Dying: Psychology of Death and Guidebook to Liberation.* Ojai, CA: World University of America, 1986.

———. *The Practice of Conscious Dying: Off-Ramp and Freeway to Conscious Immortality.* Ojai, CA: World University of America, 1990.

———. *Scientific Evidence of the Existence of the Soul.* Wheaton, IL: Theosophical Publishing House, 1970.

RING, KENNETH

Kenneth Ring (1935–), professor of psychology at the University of Connecticut and president of the International Association for Near-Death Studies, is concerned with the analysis of the **near-death experience** (NDE) from a scientific point of view.

In his *Life at Death: A Scientific Investigation of the Near-Death Experience* (1980), Ring examined the findings of **Raymond Moody** on NDEs in *Life After Life* and focused on what were considered the core components of near-death experiences, including hearing oneself pronounced dead, and feeling great peace. Most of the core phenomena reported in Moody's account, such as a feeling of loneliness, sensing a second body, traveling through a tunnel, approaching a border, appeared to occur infrequently in Ring's research.

Ring's aim was also to answer some of the questions that Moody's work had not answered. For example, he found that prior religiousness is not related to the occurrence or quality of an NDE, and that the onset of an NDE is independent of its cause, such as an illness, accident, or suicide attempt. Like Moody, he found no hellish experiences. Although people sometimes reported feeling scared or confused near the beginning of their experience, none felt that they were on their way to hell, even in attempted suicide cases. On the contrary, both the affective tone and the visionary aspects of the near-death experiences tended to be highly positive. Also, the aftereffects of the near-death experiences are uniformly described as profoundly transforming, particularly in regard to the loss of the fear of death, to the belief in life after death, and to the increase in religiousness.

In another study of NDEs, *Heading Toward Omega: In Search of the Meaning of the Near-Death Experience* (1984), Ring focused on the changed values and changed attitudes toward life, resulting from near-death experiences. He asserted that NDEs can be essentially perceived as spiritual experiences that serve as a catalyst for spiritual development. Moreover, near-death experiencers usually manifest a variety of psychic abilities, which are signs of a transformation in their attitude toward life.

Sources:

Berger, Arthur S., and Joice Berger. *The Encyclopedia of Parapsychology and Psychical Research.* New York: Paragon House, 1991.

Ring, Kenneth. *Life at Death: A Scientific Investigation of the Near-Death Experience.* New York: Quill, 1982.

Wilson, Ian. *The After Death Experience. The Physics of the Non-Physical.* New York: William Morrow, 1987.

River Symbols

In most cultures, the postmortem passage from this world to the afterlife is not envisioned as a quick, easy process that takes place immediately upon death. Instead, after dying one often undertakes a journey to "the other side." This trip is symbolized in many different ways, often by crossing a river, either in a boat or across a **bridge.** The most well known afterlife bridge is the Chinvat Bridge of the Zoroastrian tradition, although it spans **hell** rather than a river. The most well known boat is that of the Greek figure **Charon,** who ferries the souls of the dead across the river Styx to **Hades.**

In southern Asian regions (particularly the **Hindu** and **Buddhist** traditions) the symbol of stream-crossing is carried over to the process of seeking liberation from the cycle of death and rebirth (**reincarnation**). In mainstream southern Asian thought this cycle is not viewed as attractive. Rather, reincarnation is viewed negatively, as a process that keeps the individual bound to suffering. When liberation from the wheel of death and rebirth is the goal, crossing the stream no longer symbolizes the transition from life to death. Rather, ferrying over to the other side represents leaving the realm of countless deaths and rebirths to a state of existence in which one need never again reincarnate.

Sources:

Biedermann, Hans. *Dictionary of Symbolism: Cultural Icons and the Meanings Behind Them.* New York: Meridian, 1994.

Feuerstein, Georg. *Encyclopedic Dictionary of Yoga.* New York: Paragon House, 1990.

Roman Catholic

Christian concern about death and the afterlife has always been a significant aspect of that faith's outlook on life. There are some differences with respect to views of death and afterlife among the various Christian churches, but most have more in common than not.

Like other branches of the Christian faith, Roman Catholicism accepts the vision of death as the inevitable end of life postulated in the Scriptures, according to which everyone will be raised to an everlasting renewal of life, following the model of Jesus Christ. The soul is considered immortal and survives the death of the body, which is subject to the limitations of its physical nature. Faith in Christ and defeat of sin are fundamental in order to achieve eternal life and to avoid the possibility of eternal punishment.

Besides heaven and hell, the Roman Catholic church specifies an intermediate condition—purgatory—which is usually not accepted by other Christian bodies. In this place the souls that have succumbed to temptation have the possibility of being purged and ascending on to heaven. The doctrine of purgatory was established in the thirteenth century, and since then numerous versions of it have been adopted according to the beliefs and cultural and political developments of the time.

Sources:

Johnson, Christopher Jay, and Marsha G. McGee. *Encounters with Eternity: Religious Views of Death and Life After-Death.* New York: Philosophical Library, 1986.

Kastenbaum, Robert, and Beatrice Kastenbaum, eds. *Encyclopedia of Death.* Phoenix, AZ: Oryx Press, 1989.

S

Sacrifice

From the Latin *sacrificium,* the term *sacrifice* refers to a religious act in the highest sense, as well as to the act of sanctifying or consecrating an object to a supernatural being with whom the giver wants to be in communion. Originally, the object of the sacrifice was something living or a symbol of life, including even inanimate things. The material for sacrifice and its characteristics varied according to the recipient. For instance, brightly colored animals were offered to the heavenly divinities, whereas black animals were addressed to the dead and to the demonic beings of the underworld.

The recipients of a sacrifice may be any beings that humans venerate or fear. They may thus be spirits, demonic beings, or human beings (e.g., ancestors) thought to possess a superhuman power after their death and to have a considerable influence on living people. The most common reasons for sacrifices, are supplication and expiation. The purposes of sacrifices of supplication usually range from simple material goods to more complex spiritual blessings, such as forgiveness (expiation) of sins and divine grace.

Expiatory sacrifices, on the other hand, are attempts to atone for a moral fault that is supposed to be punished by a higher being, or, in a broader sense, they aim to prevent or to remove every kind of evil. Expiation and redemption are the intentions of what in the Roman Catholic church is considered the definitive and perfect sacrifice, that is, the self-giving of Jesus in his death on the Cross. This act—which in Christian understanding makes all of the sacrifices described in the Old Testament superfluous—is symbolized by the celebration of the Eucharist, which is regarded as a rendering of Jesus' sacrifice itself.

Sources:

Eliade, Mircea, ed. *The Encyclopedia of Religion.* 16 vols. New York: Macmillan, 1987.

Sadducees

As anyone passingly familiar with the New Testament knows, biblical lands were under the control of the Romans during the lifetime of Jesus. The new social situation resulting from this foreign occupation led to the development of competing factions within the Jewish community. Although all parties agreed on the authority of the Torah, they disagreed on certain interpretations. One powerful faction was the Sadducees, a group of long-time landowners that included many priests. The name of this party may have come from Sadoq, the priest of David.

The Sadducees emphasized the authority of the first five books of Hebrew Scriptures (the books of Moses) and dismissed most later interpretation—particularly the oral laws articulated by the Pharisees—as human invention. Consequently, they also rejected the influx of new ideas that was reshaping popular Judaism, such as beliefs in a **final judgment** and belief in **resurrection.** As both the historian Josephus and the New Testament witness, the Sadducees emphatically rejected the notion of an afterlife; like the ancient Hebrews, they emphasized the present. As the aristocracy, the Sadducees were comfortable with the ancient Hebrew idea that God's rewards and punishments were meted out in the present life.

Sources:

Nielsen, Niels C., Jr., *et al. Religions of the World.* New York: St. Martin's Press, 1983.

Tyson, Joseph B. *The New Testament and Early Christianity.* New York: Macmillan, 1984.

Samsara

Samsara, (literally, ''passing through'') is an Indic term denoting the world we experience in our everyday lives. This constantly changing, unstable world is contrasted with the spiritual realm, which is stable and unchanging. Samsara also involves the process of death and rebirth (reincarnation) through which we are ''trapped'' in this world. Unlike many Western treatments of reincarnation, which make the idea of coming back into body after body seem exotic, desirable, and even romantic, Hinduism, Buddhism, and other Asian religions portray the samsaric process as unhappy: Life in this world is suffering; hence, we should strive to break out of samsara.

Sources:

Feuerstein, Georg. *Encyclopedic Dictionary of Yoga.* New York: Paragon House, 1990.
Zimmer, Heinrich. *Philosophies of India.* New York: Bollingen, 1951.

SAMSKARA

Samskara, not to be confused with **samsara,** roughly means ''ritual'' and is often used to refer to certain traditional rites of passage. However, in southern Asian thought—and, particularly, in yogic psychology—samskara usually refers to the subconscious habit patterns that result from our experiences in the world. In yoga psychology samskaras are seen as the subconscious motivators of the impulse to action. Such actions produce karma, which further serves to bind one to the process of death and rebirth (reincarnation). Because of this, one of the goals of classical yoga is to free the self from the power of these subconscious motivations. Various yoga practices, particularly certain meditative practices, are said to be effective for this purpose.

Sources:

Feuerstein, Georg. *Encyclopedic Dictionary of Yoga.* New York: Paragon House, 1990.
Eliade, Mircea. *Patanjali and Yoga.* New York: Shocken, 1975.

SÉANCE

A séance is a meeting convened to either communicate with discarnate spirits or produce and witness paranormal phenomena. A professional **medium** is usually present. References to séance-type communications date back as far as the third century, to the Neoplatonist Porphyry. A candidate for the earliest recorded séance may be Meric Casaubon's *A True and Faithful Relation of What Passed Between Dr. Dee and Some Spirits* (1659). Little was written on this topic until the time of the **Fox sisters** and early **Spiritualism** in the mid-nineteenth century, when the popularity of such gatherings boomed.

The **home circle** was a type of séance popular in the late 1800s and early 1900s, oftentimes not involving a professional medium, that helped make Spiritualism a popular movement extending well beyond Spiritualist denominational boundaries. Early practitioners claimed that low lighting was necessary for spirit communications. Skeptics naturally felt that this particular condition served only to help the medium fake phenomena. In the nineteenth century, when the fantastic phenomena associated with physical mediumship characterized séances, drafts of cool air, rapping noises, and strange lights signaled the arrival of discarnate entities. Contemporary mental mediums have dispensed with such dramatic manifestations.

Séances usually take place in the home of one of the participants (one of the "sitters"), often in the house of the medium if a professional psychic is involved. Certain guidelines for conducting séances have been developed that, it is claimed, increase the probability of successful communications. As much as possible, sitters should be an even admixture of males and females and should sit in a circle. A regularly meeting circle should be cautious about admitting new people. To avoid becoming too obsessed with spirit contact, meetings should be restricted to two or three per week and, under normal circumstances, for periods of two hours or less. Sitters must also respect the medium by not grabbing or jarring the person. Such gatherings often begin with prayers and hymns to set the proper "mood."

Sources:

Chaney, Rev. Robert G. *Mediums and the Development of Mediumship.* Freeport, NY: Books for Libraries Press, 1972.

Fodor, Nandor. *An Encyclopaedia of Psychic Science.* Secaucus, NJ: The Citadel Press, 1966. (Originally published 1933.)

Pearsall, Ronald. *The Table-Rappers.* New York: St. Martin's Press, 1973.

SHAMANISM

Although the terms *shaman* and *shamanism* have come to be used quite loosely, in the disciplines of anthropology and comparative religion shamanism refers to a fairly specific set of ideas and practices that can be found in many world cultures. Characteristically, the shaman is a healer, a psychopomp (someone who guides the souls of the dead to their home in the afterlife), and more generally a mediator between her or his community and the world of spirits (most often animal spirits and the spirits of the forces of nature).

For smaller-scale societies, especially for hunter-gatherer groups, shamans perform all of the functions that doctors, priests, and therapists (and sometimes mystics and artists as well) perform in contemporary Western societies. The religious specialists of traditional American Indian societies that people sometimes refer to as "medicine men" are examples of shamans. True shamans are more characteristic of hunting societies than pastoral or farming societies, although one can often find segments of the shamanic pattern in nonhunting cultures. Shamanism in the strict sense is not found in certain culture areas, such as in Africa, although there are religious specialists that fill the same "slot" in traditional African societies.

As a system, shamanism frequently emphasizes contact and communication with spirits in the otherworld, healing practices in which the shamans search for lost souls of the living, and rituals in which shamans guide the spirits of the deceased to the realm of the dead. Shamanism thus has certain parallels with **Spiritualism.** The word *shaman* comes from the Tungusic term for this religious specialist, *saman.* The term was originally coined by an earlier generation of scholars who were studying societies in Siberia and central Asia, and was later extended to similar religious complexes found elsewhere in the world. Depending on how one interprets the archaeological evidence, shamanism is many thousands of years old.

There are various traditional ways in which one becomes a shaman. Often the role is simply inherited. At other times, the person to become a shaman is chosen by spiritual forces. This supernatural election frequently involves a serious illness, in which the chosen person comes close to death, making this part of the process a kind of **initiatory death** in which the old person ''dies'' to her or his former self. The death theme is emphasized in certain traditions in which the chosen individual has a vision of being slain, dismembered, reconstructed, and revived. In other traditions, the initiate is swallowed alive and regurgitated (e.g., the story of Jonah and the whale, which has shamanic overtones).

Sometimes it is during the course of the initiatory sickness that the shaman-to-be learns how to enter supernatural realms and meets the spirits that will be central in the initiate's shamanic career. It is easy to see the parallels between this initiation and the **near-death experience.** After healing, shamans usually complete their training under the guidance of an experienced shaman.

Depending on the specific culture, the shaman's helping spirits may take a number of different forms, from animals to personified forces of nature to the spirits of the dead. These spirits often have very specific functions and help the shaman in specific tasks.

When performing their spiritual role, shamans enter an altered state of consciousness in order to contact supernormal reality. This altered state can be brought on by diverse techniques, from drumming and chanting to fasting and sweat baths. Shamans sometimes make use of mind-altering drugs. Once in their altered frame of mind, shamans can see or sense normally invisible realms, and are also able to serve as mediums. In this transformed state, they can travel to the realm of the gods—usually conceived of as in the heavens—and serve as intermediary between their community and divine beings. They can also descend to the underworld.

The motif of a human being descending to the underworld while yet alive is widespread in world culture. In certain kinds of shamanic healing, the sick person is diagnosed as having lost his or her soul. The attending shaman then performs a ritual and enters a trance state in order to seek out the lost soul, which has often wandered off

LAPP SHAMAN IN A TRANCE. COURTESY OF THE ARC.

to the realm of the dead (often an underworld). If the rite is successful, the wandering spirit is persuaded to return and the ill person recovers.

Shamans also function as *psychopomps,* guides who accompany the souls of the dead to the otherworld. In most of the world's religions, the transition from this world to the otherworld is not thought of as a smooth, immediate step that one takes immediately upon death. Rather, after death one must frequently undertake a journey (or at least a short trip) to the otherworld. In many cases the soul, which either cannot find the way to the realm of the dead or wants to linger around the family for whatever reasons, does not even begin the journey. When the spirit's presence begins to bother the living, the shaman is called in. Entering a trance state, the shaman convinces the deceased to leave the living alone, and is then conducted to the city of the dead.

These rituals have often been compared with Western **séances** at which mediums demonstrate their powers. Spiritualistic phenomena may indeed occur, and those assembled to witness the rite may hear spirit voices, rappings, and other noises. In more dramatic ceremonies, one may experience poltergeist effects, such as shaking of the house, movement of objects independent of human touch, levitation, and howling animals, which are sometimes interpreted as representing the "voices" of spirits.

Within the past decade or so, shamanism has become a hot topic in the West's occult/metaphysical subculture (the subculture that gave birth to the so-called New Age movement) owing to recent interest in American Indian religions. Although there is a long tradition romanticizing native Americans and their spiritual traditions, Anglos have rarely been prompted to engage in actual Indian religious practices. This changed in the 1960s when certain groups of counterculturists made an effort to adopt what they conceived of as "tribal" life-styles. Of particular note in this regard is the Bear Tribe, a nontraditional "tribe" composed of young Anglos that was founded by a Chippewa Indian, Sun Bear. Although claiming to retrieve and revive an authentic tradition, Sun Bear and people like him have clearly adapted Indian traditions to the needs of contemporary Euroamericans. Thus, despite claims of traditionalism, Indian spirituality that has been repackaged so as to appeal to modern-day sensibilities constitutes yet another "new religion."

The revival of interest in Indian spirituality did not become a major phenomenon, however, until the advent of the New Age movement of the late 1980s. The New Age, which in some ways represents a successor movement to the counterculture, did not turn its attention to native American religion until shamanism— and, more particularly, the phenomenon that has come to be known as neo-shamanism— became a popular topic within the movement.

New Agers have been attracted to shamanism for a variety of reasons. One reason is that the shaman's mysticism is one of attunement to the forces of nature, rather than an otherworldly mysticism. Shamans may go off in the wilderness to seek a vision, but they return to society and to ordinary human life. Also, traditional shamanism's stress on healing is very much in line with the New Age tendency to combine health-seeking, both physical and psychological, with spiritual pursuits. Yet other factors in Shamanism's appeal are the association of shamanism with mind-altering drugs and its association with romanticized images of nature.

Many contemporary New Agers have thus come to adopt some of the trappings and selected aspects of American Indian shamanism. The popularity of native spirituality has evoked hostility from certain Indian groups, however. These critics, many associated with the American Indian Movement, have asserted that New Agers are engaged in a kind of cultural imperialism; whereas the older Euroamerican invaders stole the land, the new invaders are trying to steal the religions of native peoples. The New Age movement has, of course, commercialized many of the other spiritual traditions of the world, but few of the world's peoples feel themselves as directly oppressed and exploited by Euroamericans as do the aboriginal people of this continent. It is thus natural that native Americans should be more hostile to anything that they feel exploits their culture.

Sources:

Barnouw, Victor. "Siberian Shamanism and Western Spiritualism." *Journal of the Society of Psychical Research* 36 (1942):140–68.

Eliade, Mircea. *Shamanism: Archaic Techniques of Ecstasy.* Princeton, NJ: Princeton University Press, 1964.

Grim, John A. *The Shaman: Patterns of Siberian and Ojibway Healing.* Norman, OK: University of Oklahoma Press, 1983.

Harner, Michael. *The Way of the Shaman.* New York: Bantam Books, 1986.

Hultkrantz, Ake. "A Definition of Shamanism." *Temenos* 9 (1973):25–37.

Melton, J. Gordon, et al. *New Age Encyclopedia.* Detroit, MI: Gale Research, 1990.

SHE'OL

The **Christian** tradition regards the Hebrew Scriptures, designated within Christianity as the Old Testament, as composing the larger part of its own Scriptures. This is a surprising viewpoint because, on many points, Old Testament notions contrast markedly with New Testament teachings. Nowhere is this more striking than in the area of afterlife ideas.

Whereas Christianity emphasizes the importance of the afterlife, the ancient Hebrews emphasized the present life. As with both the ancient Greeks and the Mesopotamians, the Hebrews, if they thought of it at all, conceived of the afterworld as a pale shadow of earthly life, much like the Greeks did **Hades.** Similarly also to the way the Greeks viewed Hades—and again in sharp contrast to the Christian picture of the afterworld—the Hebrews made no distinction between the treatment of the just and the unjust after death. Instead, rewards and punishments were very much part of the present life.

The ancient Hebrews, like many of the other traditional peoples of the world, imagined the universe as a three-tiered cosmos of heaven, earth, and underworld. Heaven was reserved for God and the angels; living human beings occupied the middle world; and the spirits of the dead resided beneath the earth in She'ol. As in other cultures, imagining the realm of the dead to be located beneath the earth's surface probably derived from the custom of burying the dead underground. Again similar to the Mesopotamian underworld, She'ol was not much more than a gloomy pit.

Sources:

Nielsen, Niels C. Jr., et al. *Religions of the World.* New York: St. Martin's Press, 1983.
West, James King. *Introduction to the Old Testament.* New York: Macmillan, 1981.

SIDGWICK, HENRY

The philosopher Henry Sidgwick (1838–1900) was a founding member and first president of the **Society for Psychical Research (SPR).** He was born in Skipton, Yorkshire, England, and raised by his mother after his father, Rev. William Sidgwick, died when he was three years old. His interest in psychical research began when he was an undergraduate student in classics and mathematics at Trinity College, where he graduated in 1859. In 1883 he became Knightbridge professor of moral philoso-

HENRY SIDGWICK. COURTESY OF THE ARC.

phy, and among his students were SPR members Arthur Balfour, Edmund Gurney, and **Frederic W. H. Myers.**

On a starlight walk in the summer of 1871, Sidgwick had a conversation with Myers about the possibility of achieving some form of knowledge of the unseen world by observing psychical phenomena. In 1874 they both joined a group formed by Balfour, Gurney, and others, whose purpose was the study of **mediumship.** He attended numerous séances, most of which had discouraging results because of detected or strongly suspected trickery. However, his interest in psychical research continued to occupy a central role in his life, especially after Sir William Barrett's successful experiments on telepathy.

In 1882 Sidgwick was elected president of the Society for Psychical Research, which he established with Myers and Gurney, as well as other members of the group that had been formed in 1874 to study psychical phenomena. Among his most important investigations were the cases of **Helena P. Blavatsky,** founder of the **Theosophical Society,** and the medium Eusapia Palladino. This last case and the sittings he had at the end of his life with the medium Leonora Piper confirmed his earlier distrust of mediumship.

Sidgwick played a major part in the organization of the Census of Hallucinations, conducted between 1889 and 1894. His works include *The Methods of Ethics* (1874), *Principles of Political Economy* (1883), *Phantasms of the Living* (1886), written with other members of the Theosophical Society, and *Practical Ethics* (1898).

Sources:

Berger, Arthur S. *Aristocracy of the Dead.* Jefferson, NC: McFarland, 1987.
Gauld, Alan. *The Founders of Psychical Research.* London: Routledge & Kegan Paul, 1968.
Guiley, Rosemary Ellen. *The Encyclopedia of Ghosts and Spirits.* New York: Facts on File, 1992.
Haynes, Renee. *The Society for Psychical Research, 1882–1892: A History.* London: Heinemann, 1982.

SKANDHAS

In Buddhist thought, skandhas are the five components of each individual that delude us into thinking we have a stable, unitary self. Against the grain of ordinary thinking as well as that of most prior religiophilosophical thought, Buddha asserted that we have no permanent self or soul (the doctrine of *anatta*). To support this contention, he pointed out that with a little reflection we can see that we are composed of a physical body, memories, perceptions, feelings, and consciousness (the five skandhas). None of these components exhibits the stable, ongoing nature that we normally associate with the notion of a permanent soul, and thus none of the skandhas is the soul. On the other hand, when we imaginarily remove these five aspects, we find that we have nothing left. Hence, we have no permanent, eternal soul.

The skandhas hang together in a ''bundle,'' however, in such a way as to delude us into thinking that we consist of a stable, lasting self, one that even reincarnates in body after body. Because Buddhism views life in our everyday world negatively, it seeks to persuade human beings to turn their attention away from the attractions of the world and work on liberating the self from the cycle of death and rebirth. Understanding that it is not self-evident that life is really all that bad, however, Buddha—to convince people that they should turn away from worldly pursuits and seek liberation—analyzed life in terms of suffering, according to what are referred to as the three marks of being.

First, Buddha points out, we have to contend with the experiences everyone recognizes as painful—illness, accidents, disappointments, and so forth. Second, the world is in a constant state of change, so even the things we experience as pleasurable do not last and ultimately lead to pain. (Romantic relationships, for example, initially bring us great happiness, but usually end in greater suffering.) And third, because we ourselves are in a continuous process of change (because of the continuously changing skandhas), we ultimately lose everything we have gained, particularly in the transition we call death.

Sources:

Conze, Edward. *Buddhist Thought in India.* 1962. Reprint. Ann Arbor: University of Michigan Press, 1967.
Zimmer, Heinrich. *Philosophies of India.* New York: Bollingen, 1951.

SLATE WRITING

Slate writing, also called psychography, is the mediumistic phenomenon in which, through the intervention of the spirits, the appearance of writing occurs on a blank slate.

Although they often employed trickery, many early Spiritualists considered slate writing an irrefutable proof of spirit presence during **séances,** when sitters usually brought their own slates, a common tool for schoolwork in the nineteenth century. Kate Fox (one of the **Fox Sisters**) showed a variation of slate writing called mirror-writing, in which the medium wrote on the back of a slate to be read through a mirror. Sometimes pictures were produced, instead of words. Among the most famous slate writers was "Dr." Henry Slade, who after many years of activity was destroyed when convicted of fraud. He thus lost his place of supremacy to William Eglington, Dr. Francis Ward Monck, and later to a member of the **Society for Psychical Research,** S. J. Davey.

Some of the most common tricks of slate writing were explained by magicians, such as J. N. Maskelyne and **Harry Houdini.** They showed how it was possible to write under the table through a tiny bit of slate pencil attached to a ring on one of the fingers. Other methods involved switching slates while the sitters' attention was diverted by various elements, like a knock at the door, or implied that writing was produced on the inside surfaces of a locked double slate. Sometimes chalk, magnets, and mirrors were used, and when the slate writer needed more help, firms such as the

Ralph E. Sylvestre Co. in Chicago offered trick slates of various types, which were mail-ordered through catalogues like *Gambols with the Ghosts*.

Sources:

Bletzer, June G. *The Donning International Encyclopedic Psychic Dictionary*. Norfolk, VA: Donning, 1986.
Cavendish, Richard. *The Encyclopedia of the Unexplained*. New York: McGraw-Hill, 1967.
Doyle, Sir Arthur Conan. *The History of Spiritualism, Vol. I and II*. New York: Arno Press, 1975.
Fodor, Nandor. *An Encyclopaedia of Psychic Science*. Secaucus, NJ: The Citadel Press, 1966. (Originally published 1933.)

SLEEP

A natural association between sleep and death has often been noted in different cultures and time periods. A person in a state of sleep appears to be dead, and vice versa. Some contemporary metaphorical expressions even convey a sense of this ancient association, as when a sleeping person is described as being "dead to the world," or when a deceased individual is referred to as having gone to her or his "eternal rest."

Beyond external appearances, the inner experience of dreaming is often that of entering another world. In this other, seemingly more spiritual world, one can sometimes meet deceased individuals, and can even receive specific information from departed friends and relatives. In such dreams (as well as in **out of body experiences**) one has the subjective sense that the soul can be at least partially separated from the physical body, thus constituting yet another way in which sleep is similar to death.

Sources:

Bletzer, June G. *The Donning International Encyclopedic Psychic Dictionary*. Norfolk, VA: Donning, 1986.
Head, Joseph, and S. L. Cranston. *Reincarnation: The Phoenix Fire Mystery*. New York: Julian Press/Crown, 1977.

SNAKE SYMBOLS

Snake symbols are universal. There are numerous reasons these reptiles have exercised a fascination over the human imagination, including their limblessness as well as the deadliness of certain poisonous snakes. The principal reason snakes have been employed as religious symbols, however, is their trait of periodically shedding their skins. That this characteristic should be given much significance seems rather surprising to us moderns; scales and other components of snakes' outer layers cannot grow and must periodically be shed. Why should this trait be invested with such importance? The reason is that in this process snakes appear to be shedding an old

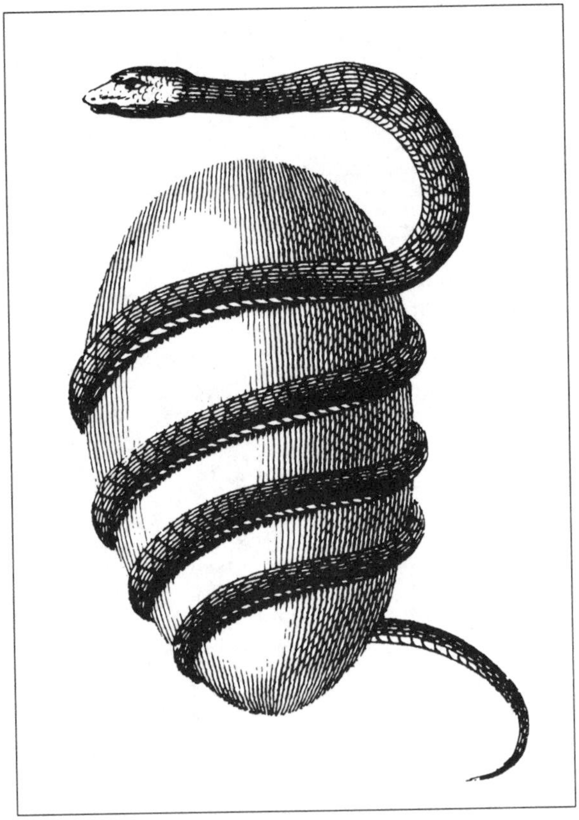

THE EGG AND THE SERPENT: A GREEK MYTHOLOGICAL SYMBOL

body for a renewed, more youthful one and thus appear to know the secret of immortality—or at least the secret of rejuvenation. They were thus regarded as wise and became symbols of both immortality and wisdom.

These two traits are reflected in the biblical story of the Garden of Eden. Eden contains two trees. Eating the fruit of the first gives one knowledge; eating the second grants immortality. The snake, as the most clever of God's creatures, knows this and, for reasons that are unclear in the original story (it is only later that the snake was viewed as an agent of Satan), makes a point of informing Eve. When God discovers what happens, he ejects Adam and Eve from the garden, explicitly stating that he wishes to prevent them from also eating from the tree of life and thus living forever.

One of the consequences of this story is that snakes have acquired extremely negative associations in societies influenced by the Judeo-Christian religious tradition. In other societies, snakes have more positive connotations. One usage in which the ancient meaning of the snake as a symbol of rejuvenation has survived is in the medical caduceus. The familiar image of two snakes entwined around a staff goes back to the ancient **Mesopotamian** deity Ningizzida, a god of healing. The same symbol carried forward to the legendary **Greek** healer Aesculapius, who carried a serpent-entwined staff and from whom our contemporary medical doctors inherited the caduceus. The association here is clearly that healing is in some sense a process of rejuvenation, in which patients are restored to their original condition.

Sources:

Biedermann, Hans. *Dictionary of Symbolism: Cultural Icons and the Meanings Behind Them.*New York: Meridian, 1994.

Cirlot, J. E. *A Dictionary of Symbols.* 1971. Reprint, New York: Doreset Press, 1991.

SOCIETY FOR PSYCHICAL RESEARCH

The Society for Psychical Research (SPR), founded in 1882 in London, is one of the most important organizations for scientific research into the paranormal. Its activities are directed toward research and validation of Spiritualist phenomena, and its fields of study include the nature of all forms of paranormal cognition (such as telepathy, clairvoyance, and precognition), and paranormal action (for example, poltergeist phenomena, teleportation, and human levitation). Other subjects studied include altered states of consciousness in connection with hypnotic trance, dreams, out-of-body and near-death experiences and sensory deprivation, as well as phenomena associated with psychic sensitivity or mediumship, such as automatic writing and physical manifestations of spirits. The SPR also deals with evidence suggesting survival after death, or reincarnation, and other relevant phenomena that appear to contravene accepted scientific principles, as well as the social and psychological aspects of such phenomena.

The SPR was established by Henry Sidgwick—who was the first president—along with Frederic W. H. Myers, and Edmund Gurney, to develop their interest in Spiritualist phenomena and to investigate fraudulent mediums. The society, which established research committees on mesmerism, hypnotism, clairvoyance, and related phenomena; sensitives (a person having occult or psychical abilities); apparitions and hauntings; and physical phenomena associated with Spiritualist mediums, failed to scientifically validate survival after death. It did expose many mediums, however, contributing to a decline of interest in mediumship. In the late 1940s, the SPR began to devote more attention to laboratory experiments.

The society's numerous research articles are also concerned with the development of new conceptual models and new ways to apply accepted scientific theories to the findings of psychical research. Among its major publications are *Phantasms of the Living* (1886) and *Human Personality and Its Survival of Bodily Death* (1903).

Sources:

Cavendish, Richard. *The Encyclopedia of the Unexplained.* New York: McGraw-Hill, 1967.

Gurney, Edmund, F. W. H. Myers, and Frank Podmore. *Phantasms of the Living.* 1886. Reprint, London: Kegan Paul, Trench, Trubner & Co., 1918.

WEIGHING THE SOUL IN THE AFTERLIFE: A SCENE FROM THE *EGYPTIAN BOOK OF THE DEAD* (EGYPT, 14TH CENTURY B.C.)

In ancient **Egypt** individuals were given multiple souls:

1. The *ka,* which generally corresponded to a vital force, supplied the ability to do things divine, royal, or human, depending on one's state.
2. The *ba,* usually depicted as a bird with a human head, symbolized a vitalizing force that enabled a deceased person to move in the heavens or locate food.
3. The *akh,* represented as a crested ibis, symbolized a glorious status of the deceased in the state of death.
4. The *ab,* the conscience or center of ethical values and moral judgment, typically depicted as a human heart weighed against a feather in one's postmortem judgment, either made union with Osiris if pure or was punished if tainted.

Funerary rites and ancestor cults were never an important component of ancient Greek religion. In the early stages of Greek civilization, at the time of the Homeric poems, the souls of the individual represented various human faculties. The *thymos* was considered the seat of emotions, the *nous* was the intellect, and the *psyche* (from which the English words psychology and psychiatry developed) was the center of consciousness. Upon death, the *thymos* and the *nous* were believed to cease to exist, but the *psyche* wandered around (if the corpse had not been buried) or went to the netherworld called Hades. Mythic heroes, however, ended up in the Isles of the Blessed or in the Elysian Fields in different late-Greek traditions.

By way of contrast, in Pythagoreanism the soul—in the form of the psyche—was believed to wander from existence to existence—not only in human form, but also in the form of any living being, even animals—in the process of metempsychosis (**reincarnation**). In the Hellenistic period, which was a time of marked religious syncretism, the idea of the hereafter was more fully developed in the mystery religions—religions that combined elements from the cults of Isis, and Dionysos and Sabazios, as well as from Orphism and Mithraism. The psyche, used in the philosophical speculations of various Greek philosophers to denote the eternal soul, was ultimately replaced in Hellenistic Judaism and early Christianity by *pneuma,* a word originally meaning breath, to describe an eschatological soul.

In early Judaism there were various words for soul: *nefesh,* which indicates life and breath (like the Hellenistic pneuma), *neshamah* (consciousness), and *ruah* (spirit in the form of a divine wind). Upon one's death, the soul was believed to go with the body into **She'ol,** a place at times identified with the grave itself. The ideas of **resurrection** and a **final judgment,** which became very influential in the elaboration of the Christian doctrine, were a later development. The three early ideas of soul were elaborated by the Cabalistic system (Jewish mysticism) as an innate soul (the nefesh is present at birth) and two others built through spiritual self-discipline (the neshamah, a divine spark), and the ruah.

In Christianity the Greek word *psyche* and the Hebrew *nefesh* have been used to indicate the soul; and similarly, the Greek word *pneuma* and the Hebrew *ruah* were used to indicate spirit. The two concepts have been used interchangeably in the scriptures. The origin of the soul in Christian theology has been conceived in terms of (1) the creation of individual souls by God at the moment of conception, (2) traducianism, the notion that the soul is transmitted to the newborn by the parents, and (3) reincarnation, implying the preexistence of the soul in a process of embodiments that determine its spiritual growth. Depending on one's merits, the soul is destined to different locations: **hell,** where the soul is punished for an eternity; **purgatory,** where impure souls can purify and ultimately reach paradise; and paradise, conceived of in terms of eternal union with God and the saints.

In Islam the notion of the soul varies greatly in different mystical, theological, and philosophical traditions. The Arabic words *ruh* (spirit) and *nafs* (self)—etymologically corresponding to the Hebrew *ruah* and *nefesh*—in pre-Islamic Arabic corresponded respectively to breath and blood, two basic vital forces. The two words are both found in the *Koran* to indicate the human soul, which upon death separates from the body to rejoin it on Judgment Day. In Sufism the mystic experience of union of the human soul with God was conceived of in different traditions as annihilation of the soul (annihilation of the ego self, or the I), closeness of the soul to God (which is the more traditional approach of the Islamic mainstream), or as a reflection of the perfect essence of God.

Although there are regional and historical variants with respect to the ontological status of the soul, in general it is broadly believed in Asian religions that there is something uncreated and unchangeable that survives one's physical death and reincarnates afterward. In ancient Vedic religion the soul is conceived of as an immaterial spirit that, when departing from the body (upon death, or in trance or dreams), leaves it lifeless and inert. An idea of the soul was introduced by the authors of the Upanishads that emphasized the importance of going beyond one's personal individuality—the I—to reach the unchanging eternal self. A further distinction was made between **Atman,** the individual soul, and Brahma, the cosmic godhead, which are ultimately the same immutable reality.

Buddhism adopted the Vedic word *Atman* to refer to the existence of an individual functional self that lives in an impermanent reality as a combination of physical body, sensations and perceptions, and habits and consciousness. The soul itself, as a permanent, ongoing reality, is illusory (the Buddhist doctrine of **anatta**). Because consciousness is self-reflective, enlightenment is achieved by progressive development of insight into the true nature of the self.

In ancient Chinese thought a nourishing cosmic spirit animates the two souls that inhabit the human being: the *hun,* the vital force that determines one's intellectual activities and at death goes to heaven, and the *p'o,* which determines the physical functions and which at death goes to the earth. The two souls are complementary entities that embody the ideas of *yin* (expansive force) and *yang* (contractive force), the two primordial cosmic forces. The interaction of these two opposing forces causes the continuously changing process that is at the core of reality. The Chinese idea of soul *(ling),* is as an intermediary between the human dimension and the spiritual world, thus emphasizing the distinguishing role of humans as co-creators of the universe and harmonizers of nature on behalf of heaven and earth.

Sources:

Badham, Paul, and Linda Bodham, eds. *Death and Immortality in the Religions of the World.* New York: Paragon House, 1987.

Eliade, Mircea. *The Encyclopedia of Religion.* 16 vols. New York: Macmillan, 1987.

Obayshi, Hiroshi, ed. *Death and Afterlife: Perspectives of World Religions.* Westport, CT: Greenwood Press, 1992.

Nielsen, Niels C., Jr., et al. *Religions of the World.* New York: St. Martin's Press, 1983.

SOUL VS. BODY

Many traditional cultures distinguish between one's spiritual essence, or **soul,** and the physical body, which is often seen as simply a vehicle for the soul. Among world religions, the chief exceptions to this pattern are **Judaism,** in which the essential self is bound up with the body (which will be **resurrected** in the end time), and **Buddhism,** which explicitly rejects the soul notion. In traditions that accept such a dichotomy, the relationship between body and soul need not be conceived of antagonistically, although it frequently is. This conflict can range from a fairly mild one in which worldly concerns—including bodily matters—are seen as simple hindrances to spiritual interests, to outright war, in which the body and physical desires are mortified at the expense of the spirit.

Western religions, especially **Christianity,** were influenced by **Gnosticism,** a movement that emphasized the conflict between soul and body. This school of thought, which was prominent in the Mediterranean world during the early Christian centuries, taught that this world and, especially, the human body, are the products of an evil deity—the demiurge—who had trapped human souls in the physical world. The human soul's true home is the absolute spirit, and hence we should reject the pleasures of the flesh as a way of escaping this prison. Although many mystery religions (so called because certain secrets were given to the individual aspirant at the moment of initiation) and other religious movements in antiquity emphasized a dualism between the body and the soul, none went to the extreme of Gnosticism.

Although the Church fathers rejected Gnostic Christianity as heresy, Gnosticism nevertheless left its imprint on the Christian tradition. For example, Paul portrays the antagonism between body and soul quite explicitly in Romans 7:22–25:

> In my inmost self I delight in the law of God, but I perceive that there is in my bodily members a different law, fighting against the law that my reason approves and making me a prisoner under the law that is in my members, the law of sin. Miserable creature that I am, who is there to rescue me out of this body doomed to death?

This statement, the spirit of which is familiar to most people raised in the Christian tradition, is profoundly Gnostic. In contrast to Judaism, which views the self as a psycho-spiritual-physical unity, Gnosticism, as seen in Paul's lament, separates the self into warring factions, attributing noble motivations to the soul and ignoble desires to the body. For Paul, the grace of Christ was important because it allowed him (the soul) to conquer the physical body.

Sources:

Eliade, Mircea. *The Encyclopedia of Religion.* 16 vols. New York: Macmillan, 1987.
The New English Bible. New York: Oxford University Press, 1976.
Turner, Alice K. *The History of Hell.* New York: Harcourt Brace, 1993.

SOUL MATE

The notion of a soul mate, another person who is one's ideal partner and with whom one has a preexisting spiritual bond, is a distinctly contemporary, Western notion shaped by Western romanticism. The soul mate idea, in other words, is part of no traditional religion, but is a new idea that arose from the West's occult/metaphysical subculture and was adopted by that subculture's offspring, the **New Age** movement. The soul mate idea became particularly popular in the 1970s and 1980s. Part of the notion is the idea that one usually seeks one's soul mate across many **reincarnations.** Beyond these basics, there are many variations in the soul mate idea.

Some conceptualizations of soul mates postulate that they are two halves of one **soul** that have been split apart to speed up the process of spiritual evolution by taking in earth-plane experiences twice as fast. From this perspective, finding one's soul mate is quite literally finding one's other half. Although in some ways a significantly different idea, a similar notion is advanced in Plato's *Symposium.* In the distant past, according to this scenario, humanity was composed of self-sufficient beings who had two heads, four arms, and four legs. Humanity had the audacity to challenge the gods, however, and as punishment the people were severed in half. Thenceforth, rather than seeking to overthrow the gods, humanity was preoccupied with the pursuits of love and sex, caused by the craving to reunite with one's other half. This story may have shaped the notion of soul mates.

Another, more modest theory is that a soul mate is not one's missing half, but rather someone whom one has been with for many different lifetimes and with whom one thus has an exceptionally strong link. These pairs of soul mates are reunited in lifetime after lifetime to continue their relationship, and to help each other out. They are so attuned to each other that they can often communicate without words. Over the course of many lifetimes, they sometimes exchange sex roles. (The possibility of a homosexual romance is rarely considered in existing literature on soul mates.)

Yet another, less popular, conceptualization postulates that a wide variety of different people are our soul mates and we are reunited with them in a wide diversity of roles—as lovers, spouses, siblings, parents/children, and so forth.

Some people have taken the notion of soul mates quite seriously, devoting a good deal of time and effort to the task of finding their own soul mate. Richard Bach, author of the popular book *Jonathan Livingston Seagull* (1970), described his three-year search in *The Bridge Across Forever* (1984). He found that his soul mate was actress Leslie Parrish. Others seek out astrologers, psychics, and past-life regressions in the quest for their perfect partner. There are even visualization and ''dream programming'' methods that supposedly allow one to find or to attract a soul mate.

Sources:

Bach, Richard. *The Bridge Across Forever.* New York: Dell, 1984.
Steam, Jess. *Soul Mates.* New York: Bantam Books, 1984.
Sutphen, Dick. *You Were Born Again to Be Together.* New York: Pocket Books, 1976.
Van Auken, John. *Past Lives and Present Relationships.* Virginia Beach, VA: Inner Vision, 1984.

SPIRIT PHOTOGRAPHY

Spirit photographs, which purportedly show **ghosts** and spirits of the dead, have been controversial since their first appearance in 1861 and have often been interpreted as tricks of light, oras flaws on the film or in developing. They have not been considered reliable proof of survival after death.

William Mumler, a Boston jewelry engraver, is considered the first spirit photographer. In 1861, after developing a self-portrait, he noticed the image of a ghost next to him, and his discovery became very famous in a period during which the popularity of **Spiritualism** and communication with the spirit world was increasing. As a result, many individuals attempted to prove the existence of life after death by capturing the images of spirits, which usually appeared above or alongside portraits of living subjects. The most famous example of spirit photography declared real by scientists is a photograph of the Brown Lady of Raynham Hall.

Many "spirit" photographers began creating special effects through double exposure and sometimes by superimposing famous faces. Some of the fraudulent photographs were accepted as real. Fraud led to the decline of both spirit photography and physical mediumship (e.g., levitation, table-tilting). Psychic photography is still practiced, however, although for a different purpose. It is usually employed by investigators of hauntings, who sometimes obtain unexplainable streaks of light and white shapes.

Simulacra (1979) is a book written by John Michell about false effects, called simulacra, which are usually due to random patterns like those created by ground cover, foliage, shadows, grains in paneling, and building facades. Most of the spirit photographs collected and analyzed by the Ghost Research Society (GRS) of Oak Lawn, Illinois, can be explained naturally. Only 10 percent remain unexplained and are considered paranormal, showing what is called paranormal fog, which is a mysterious blue-gray color difficult to duplicate. There are about five photographs that seem to show what could be actual spirits, characterized by semitransparent human shapes with distinct facial features.

Some spirit images are purportedly created on film by psychokinesis on the part of the photographer or subject. This phenomenon, which was called thoughtography by Tomokichi Fukarai in the early 1900s, is studied by parapsychologists and is sometimes considered an explanation of some of the GRS photographs. *Scotographs* are images that appear on film that has not been exposed, and the term *psychograph* is used to describe direct spirit writing occurring on film and containing messages from the deceased.

Sources:

Carrington, Hereward. "Experiences in Psychic Photography." *Journal of the American Society for Psychical Research*, 19 (1925): 258-67.

Fukarai, T. *Clairvoyance & Thoughtography*. New York: Arno Press, 1975. (Originally published 1931.)

Guiley, Rosemary Ellen. *The Encyclopedia of Ghosts and Spirits*. New York: Facts on File, 1992.

Holzer, Hans. *Psychic Photography: Threshold of a New Science?* New York: McGraw-Hill, 1970.

Perlmutt, Cyril. *Photographing the Spirit World: Images from Beyond the Spectrum*. Willingborough, Northamptonshire, England: Aquarian Press, 1988.

SPIRITISM

Spiritualist religious bodies are divided over several issues, including the idea of **reincarnation,** which is generally accepted by a related group referred to as spiritists, whose doctrine goes beyond proof of survival after death to include the notion of rebirth. Their origins lie in the philosophy of **Allan Kardec,** a French writer and physician who believed that spiritual progress is possible only by compulsory reincarnation to correct past mistakes, and that each rebirth enables the soul to improve (to ''evolve'') and attain a higher plane of existence. Although it enjoyed brief popularity in Europe, Kardec's spiritism, also known as Kardecism, is today well established in South America, especially Brazil. Spiritist belief in reincarnation is related to the reincarnation theories of **Theosophy,** which can be considered a blending of Spiritualism with Oriental religions.

Sources:

Cavendish, Richard, ed. *Encyclopedia of the Unexplained: Magic, Occultism and Parapsychology.* London: Arkana Penguin Books, 1989.

Shepard, Leslie A., ed. *Encyclopedia of Occultism & Parapsychology.* Detroit, MI: Gale Research, 1991.

SPIRITUALISM

Spiritualism is a religious movement emphasizing the belief in survival after death, a belief Spiritualists claim is based upon scientific proof and communication with the surviving personalities of deceased human beings by means of **mediumship.** Spiritualism is regarded by its adherents as a religion based on science, combining elements from other religions and creeds. Sir Arthur Conan Doyle wrote, ''Spiritualism is a religion for those who find themselves outside all religions; while on the contrary it greatly strenghtens the faith of those who already possess religious beliefs.''

The continuity of the personality after death through a new birth into a spiritual body (not a new physical body) is a central tenet of Spiritualism. According to Spiritualists, at death the soul, which is composed of a sort of subtle matter, withdraws itself and remains near the earth plane for a period of time. After this, it advances in knowledge and moral qualities and proceeds to higher planes, until it eventually reaches the sphere of pure spirit. The rapidity at which the soul advances is in direct proportion to the mental and moral faculties acquired in earth life. Spiritualists originally conceived of planes as spheres encircling the earth, one above the other, whereas now they are more commonly supposed to interpenetrate each other and to coexist at different rates of vibration. Bliss, hell, and eternal damnation are not part of Spiritualist belief, nor are a last judgment and the resurrection of the physical body. Communication with the dead, through the agency of mediums, is the second central belief of Spiritualism.

The phenomena advanced by Spiritualism fall into three main groups: physical mediumship, spiritual healing, and mental mediumship. The physical phenomena include acoustic incidents, such as raps and blows; apports (materializations), passing of matter through matter, spiritual transport of the human body; chemical phenomena, such as psychic photography; electric and magnetic phenomena; fire immunity; levitation of the human body and materialization; telekinesis (moving objects without touching them); psycho-physiological phenomena, such as elongation, transfiguration, stigmata, trance, ectoplasm, aura, and emanations; and thermodynamic effects, such as psychic winds (breeze with no physical cause).

Spiritual healing includes contact healing, which is laying on of hands, and absent healing, in which the medium, working with spirit doctors, has no direct contact with the patient and effects healing at a distance. Mental mediumship phenomena include clairvoyance, clairaudience, crystal gazing, divination, premonition, monition, dowsing, healing, personation, psychometry, trance-speaking, telepathy, and xenoglossis. Many of these phenomena have been explained as the result of unknown mental processes of the medium, although the more common interpretation involves the role of an extraneous factor, which can be the will of another living person, a disembodied human consciousness (a spirit), or something unknown of nonhuman origin. The most obvious explanation and the one with the greatest appeal is the spirit hypothesis. This theory has been adopted by many well-known, non-Spiritualist psychical researchers, according to whom a human spirit that has survived death can cause such phenomena. Both Spiritualist and alternative explanations must deal with the validation of paranormal phenomena, as the history of mediumship has too often been plagued by fraud and tricks by fake mediums.

The belief in the possibility of communication with the spirit world has been held in most of the societies of which we have records. Spiritualism has many parallels and predecessors among so-called primitive people, in the miracles of world religions, and in the phenomena associated with witchcraft, poltergeist activity, and possession. These manifestations were not always associated with the spirits of deceased people, but they were traditionally associated with angelic or diabolic possession, most frequently with the latter.

The significance of the doctrine of animal magnetism, described in Franz Antoine Mesmer's *De Planetarum Influxu* (Of Planetary Influence) in 1766, was very considerable from the Spiritualist point of view. Mesmerism (along with Swedenbörgianism) began in Europe in the late eighteenth century and was later exported to the United States. Its transition to Spiritualism was effected by Andrew Jackson Davis, a student of Swedenbörg who practiced the psychic diagnosis of illness. Davis wrote several books on harmonial philosophy, dealing with the origins and nature of the universe and with the afterlife.

What is generally regarded as the origin of modern Spiritualism, however, took place in America in 1848, when sisters Maggie and Katie **Fox** started communicating with spirits through rappings in their house at Hydesville, New York. The Fox sisters discovered that if they clapped their hands, they received a response from a spirit who claimed to have been killed by a former occupant of the house. Their older sister Leah took charge of them, and eventually took them on tour, during which they made money with their increasingly elaborate **séances,** despite accusations of fraud. At the same time other mediums appeared, inspired by the success of the Fox sisters, and by about the mid-1850s Spiritualism had achieved considerable popularity.

Among the most common physical phenomena reported by mediums were cases of telekinesis, such as those that allegedly occurred in the presence of the famous medium D. D. Home. One of the most common mental phenomena, which had already attained some prominence in the mesmeric movement of the preceding half-century, was clairvoyance. Trance mediums, such as Gladys Osborne Leonard and Leonora E. Piper, sometimes asserted having been in the otherworld and having spoken with its inhabitants. In other cases the medium's body was purportedly controlled by spirits that, through automatic writing and automatic speaking, gave information about their earthly lives and transmitted detailed and often lengthy accounts of the next world and its inhabitants. Sometimes they communicated ethical and theological teachings, like those of British clergyman Rev. W. Stainton Moses, whose *Spirit Teachings* (1883) is considered the Bible of Anglo-American Spiritualism.

Although a considerable number of people began to discover and practice mediumistic powers, the Spiritualist movement soon began to come under attack. It was condemned by official religions and suffered negative publicity as a result of the many investigations of mediums that exposed frauds. After enjoying a resurgence of popularity during and after World War I, the heyday of mediumship was over by 1920, although interest in Spiritualism continued in various parts of the world, including the United States, Britain, and Brazil, countries where Spiritualist churches continue to exist.

In Britain Spiritualism enjoys a larger following than in the United States, even though its growth was difficult because habit and tradition were more firmly settled, especially owing to the great influence of the well-established Church of England. Efforts to organize Spiritualist groups began in 1865, and one of the key figures in British Spiritualism was the medium Maurice Barbanell, who founded *Psychic News,* a leading Spiritualist newspaper. The British National Association of Spiritualists was founded in 1884, and in 1890 Emma Hardinge Britten, founder of the Spiritualist journal *Two Worlds,* established the National Federation of Spiritualist Churches, which reorganized in 1901 as the Spiritualist National Union in order to unite Spiritualist churches and promote research on mediumship and healing.

In the United States, in response to fraud and other issues within the movement, the **National Spiritualist Association of Churches** (NSAC) was established in Chicago in 1893. A presbyterial structure was established, with state associations of member congregations and an annual national convention.

The NSAC immediately set about establishing standards for Spiritualist ministry and investigating reports of fraud. Even today, with several other Spiritualist organizations in existence, the NSAC maintains the highest standards for ordination. The NSAC has also spent a great deal of time and energy on establishing a common statement of Spiritualist beliefs. In 1899 it adopted a Declaration of Principles with six articles; three other articles were added at a later time. The full nine articles are as follows:

(1) We believe in Infinite Intelligence.
(2) We believe that the phenomena of Nature, both physical and spiritual, are the expression of Infinite Intelligence.

(3) We affirm that a correct understanding of such expression and living in accordance therewith constitute true religion.
(4) We affirm that the existence and personal identity of the individual continue after the change called death.
(5) We affirm that communication with the so-called dead is a fact, scientifically proven by the phenomena of Spiritualism.
(6) We believe that the highest morality is contained in the Golden Rule: "Whatsoever ye would that others should do unto you, do ye also unto them."
(7) We affirm the moral responsibility of the individual, and that he makes his own happiness or unhappiness as he obeys or disobeys Nature's physical and spiritual laws.
(8) We affirm that the doorway to reformation is never closed against any human soul here or hereafter.
(9) We affirm that the precept of Prophecy and Healing contained in the Bible is a divine attribute proven through Mediumship.

The last three articles, added later, reflect a move away from emphasizing remarkable phenomena and toward an emphasis on philosophical development. Besides these nine articles, the NSAC has also established common definitions of Spiritualist terms and practices. The two major controversies of the twentieth century for Spiritualists have centered on the questions of whether Spiritualists are also Christians and whether Spiritualists believe in reincarnation. In 1930 the NSAC explicitly condemned belief in reincarnation, but not without repercussions in the form of lost memberships. The controversy over Christian identity has not been as clear-cut. Spiritualism in general has historically drawn most of its membership from the Christian denominations, and most Spiritualists identify with some form of Christian practice in the sense that they may believe that Jesus was a master medium and Spiritualist healer. If, however, they are asked to identify themselves as Christians in a more traditional sense, in the context of denominations and historic creeds, most are reluctant to do so. The NSAC has generally taken the position that Spiritualists are not also Christians. Those who wish to identify as Christians have tended to gravitate to other Spiritualist organizations.

Sources:

Cavendish, Richard, ed. *Encyclopedia of the Unexplained: Magic, Occultism and Parapsychology.* London: Arkana Penguin Books, 1989.
Doyle, Arthur Conan. *The History of Spiritualism.* New York: Arno Press, 1975.
Melton, J. Gordon. *The Encyclopedia of American Religions.* 4th ed. Detroit, MI: Gale Research, 1993.
Shepard, Leslie A., ed. *Encyclopedia of Occultism & Parapsychology.* Detroit, MI: Gale Research, 1991.
Ward, Gary L., ed. *Spiritualism I: Spiritualist Thought.* New York: Garland Publishing, 1990.

Spiritualist Episcopal Church

The Spiritualist Episcopal Church has been an important organization in Spiritualist circles. From its history and membership have come several other groups, including

St. Paul's Church of Aquarian Science, Universal Spiritualist Association, and the Church of Metaphysical Christianity. The Spiritualist Episcopal Church was founded in 1941 by Revs. Clifford Bias, John Bunker, and Robert Chaney, all Spiritualist ministers/mediums at Camp Chesterfield, a popular Spiritualist training center in Indiana.

Bias, Bunker, and Chaney all desired to create an organization more focused on philosophy and theology than on physical séance phenomena such as rappings and materializations. Bias and Bunker had been members of the Independent Spiritualist Association, and Chaney had been a member of the National Spiritualist Association of Churches (NSAC). Camp Chesterfield, up to that point a fairly independent setting, became more identified with the Spiritualist Episcopal Church, which conducted the camp's important summer training institutes.

The beliefs of the Spiritualist Episcopal Church are similar to those of the NSAC, in that communication with disembodied spirits is considered proof of life after death. Various other precepts and practices are drawn from Christianity and Buddhism and in smaller portions from Theosophy and Rosicrucianism. Reincarnation is rejected. True morality is considered living according to the Golden Rule (Do unto others as you would have them do unto you) and in accordance with the universal laws of nature, both physical and spiritual.

In 1956 controversy over morals charges brought against a prominent medium led to a split in the church. Ultimately, the church moved its headquarters to Lansing, Michigan, and Camp Chesterfield became the headquarters of a splinter group, the Universal Spiritualist Association. It is unclear to what degree the Spiritualist Episcopal Church remains active.

Sources:

Chaney, Robert G. "Hear My Prayer." Eaton Rapids, MI: Spiritualist Episcopal Church, 1942.
Melton, J. Gordon. *The Encyclopedia of American Religions.* 4th ed. Detroit, MI: Gale Research, 1993.

STEINER, RUDOLF

Rudolf Steiner (1861–1925), the founder of the Anthroposophical Society (anthroposophy is a blend of Rosicrucian, theosophical, and Christian traditions), was born in Kraljevic, Austro-Hungary.

When the Steiner family moved to Vienna, Rudolf met the rustic herbalist Felix Kotgutski, who taught him the occult lore of plants. In 1879 he went to the College of Technology in Vienna to study mathematics and science. He also studied the philosophies of Kant, Fichte, and Hegel and the natural science writings of Goethe. He earned his doctorate in 1891, with a thesis on the scientific teaching of the German philosopher Johann Gottlieb Fichte, which was followed in 1894 by his major philosophical work, *The Philosophy of Freedom* (1894).

By age 40 Steiner had accumulated various experiences in metaphysical realms. He conceived humankind as a microcosm of the universe, whose secrets could be revealed by exploring the true nature and the true history of humankind, which Steiner claimed to be able to discover through access to the **Akashic records.** According to his interpretation of human evolution, humankind lost its original spiritual and supersensible capabilities in its descent to the material plane. Steiner believed in the ideas of **reincarnation** and **karma** and developed his own philosophy about them, according to which some spiritual beings, who exist in higher planes, interact constantly with human beings and encourage their advancement toward spiritual consciousness, while others, who are the personification of evil, wish people to remain anchored to a materialistic world.

In his lectures Steiner found an enthusiastic audience in the **Theosophical Society,** with which, however, he eventually became disillusioned because he believed that it was not possible to build a spiritual science on Eastern mysticism. In 1913 he left the society, formed the Anthroposophical Society, and established the Goetheanum, a school for esoteric research, at Dornach, near Basel.

During his last 25 years, Steiner traveled around Europe and gave more than six thousand lectures on spiritual science, the arts, social sciences, religion, education, agriculture, and health. His published works include more than 350 books, articles, reviews, and dramas. His key publications illustrating his occult philosophy are *Knowledge of the Higher Worlds and its Attainment* (1904–1905), *Theosophy: An Introduction to the Supersensible Knowledge of the World and the Destination of Man* (1904), and *An Outline of Occult Science* (1909).

Sources:

Berger, Arthur S., and Joice Berger. *The Encyclopedia of Parapsychology and Psychical Research.* New York: Paragon House, 1991.

Cavendish, Richard, ed. *Encyclopedia of the Unexplained. Magic, Occultism and Parapsychology.* New York: McGraw-Hill, 1974.

Guiley, Rosemary Ellen. *Harper's Encyclopedia of Mystical & Paranormal Experience.* San Francisco: HarperCollins, 1991.

STEVENSON, IAN

Ian Stevenson is a medical doctor and psychiatrist who has acquired fame for his careful case studies of people—mostly children—who claim to recall previous lifetimes. Stevenson is also a psychic researcher whose interests encompass apparitions, mediumship, and poltergeists. One of the most academically credentialed and respected psychical researchers in the contemporary world, he has contributed theoretically and methodologically to many areas, especially to the field of postmortem survival.

STEVENSON, IAN

Born in Montreal on Halloween 1918, Stevenson went to school at the University of St. Andrews in Scotland and McGill University in Montreal, where he earned an M.D. degree in 1943. He took specialized training in psychosomatic medicine and psychiatry, eventually teaching psychiatry at the Louisiana State University Medical School. He did not become involved in psychic research until after becoming professor of psychiatry at the University of Virginia in 1957. He acquired interests in ESP (extrasensory perception) and survival after death and researched instances of apparent past-life memory. He is best known for his careful research on the latter topic. In 1960 he published a two-part article, ''The Evidence for Survival from Claimed Memories of Former Incarnations,'' in the *Journal of the American Society for Psychical Research,* for which it won a prize in an essay contest honoring **William James.**

Before this article, reincarnation had received comparatively little attention among psychical researchers, who had examined mediumistic and related phenomena as survival evidence. After a systematic search, Stevenson had gathered 44 published cases of individuals claiming to be the reembodiment of people who could be shown to have actually existed. Following this preliminary research into existing cases, he initiated his own investigation of similar cases. By the early part of this decade, he had gathered information on 2,500 cases.

Stevenson chaired the University of Virginia's psychiatry department in 1967, when the inventor of the Xerox machine, Chester Carlson, endowed a special faculty chair. Becoming Carlson Professor of Psychiatry, Stevenson was able to invest all of his energies into research. His study of mediums has focused on what he terms ''drop-in communicators,'' discarnate spirits unrelated to any of the sitters in a **séance** that simply drop by to communicate. Stevenson regards drop-in communicators as especially valuable for survival research because the information they relay is unlikely to be provided or influenced by telepathic input from any of those present.

Stevenson's credentials and careful research methods have led to acceptance of his work by colleagues who would dismiss other psychic researchers out of hand. He was president of the international Parapsychological Association in both 1968 and 1980, and served as president of the Society for Psychical Research in 1988–89. His publications include *Telepathic Impressions* (1970), *Twenty Cases Suggestive of Reincarnation* (1974), *Cases of the Reincarnation Type* (in four volumes, 1975–1983), and *Children Who Remember Previous Lives: A Question of Reincarnation* (1987).

Sources:

Berger, Arthur S. *Lives and Letters in American Parapsychology: A Biographical History, 1950–1987.* Jefferson, NC: McFarland, 1988.

Pleasants, Helene, ed. *Biographical Dictionary of Parapsychology.* New York: Helix Press, 1964.

Stevenson, Ian. "Are Poltergeists Living or Are They Dead?" *Journal of the American Society for Psychical Research* 366 (1966): 233–52.

———. *Cases of the Reincarnation Type.* Vols. 1–4. Charlottesville: University Press of Virginia, 1975–83.

———. *Twenty Cases Suggestive of Reincarnation.* 2d ed. Charlottesville: University Press of Virginia, 1974.

SUFFERING AND THE AFTERLIFE

The cultures of the ancient world from which the modern West descends did not imagine human beings as having an immortal soul, although a dim and devitalized "shade" or "ghost" of each individual continued to exist in a dull, cheerless afterlife world. These ancient afterlives, confined to such realms as the Jewish **She'ol** and the Greek **Hades,** were pale shadows of earthly life, making death a thing to be dreaded rather than looked forward to. The Mesopotamian afterlife—described in an oft-cited passage from *The Epic of Gilgamesh* in which Enkidu, **Gilgamesh's** servant and companion, relates a dream of the otherworld—is fairly typical:

> There is the house whose people sit in darkness; dust is their food and clay their meat. They are clothed like birds with wings for covering, they see no light, they sit in darkness. I entered the house of dust and I saw the kings of the earth, their crowns put away forever. . . . (Sandars 1972, 92)

The underworld of the ancients was dark, dusty, and unpleasant. The deceased wandered aimlessly about, with nothing but dirt to eat. In these afterlife realms, no distinction was made between the treatment of the just and the unjust. What was differentiated was the state of those who had received proper burial and memorial services and those who had not. When these matters were attended to properly, the soul rested easily. When neglected, the dead became agitated ghosts and haunted the living.

Most of the traditional cultures of the world visualized the universe as a three-tiered cosmos of heaven, earth, and underworld. Heaven was reserved for deities, most of whom resided there. Living human beings occupied the middle world. The spirits of the dead resided beneath the earth, perhaps as a result of the custom of burying corpses in the ground.

The notion of a heaven world where the righteous dead reside after death seems to be rooted in ancient Greek tales about heroes who were so admired by the gods that they made them immortal by inducting them as citizens of heaven, rather than allowing them to suffer the common fate of humanity, which was to reside beneath the earth in Hades after death. It is not difficult to see how this basic notion might have developed, by the time of early, Hellenistic **Christianity,** into the idea that the souls of Christian dead would be immortalized in heaven, and the souls of non-Christians condemned to Hades. (Contemporaneous Jewish ideas of the afterlife clustered around the notion of **resurrection,** rather than heaven and hell.)

However, it did not seem to be enough to simply condemn non-Christians—and particularly active, persecuting enemies of Christianity—to a bland, boring afterlife. Thus, the ancient underworld, which originally was the common fate of humanity, became a realm of torture in which unbelievers were tormented for eternity. The result

INFERNAL PUNISHMENT FOR THE SEVEN DEADLY SINS. THE ANGRY ARE DISMEMBERED ALIVE. (FROM *LE GRANT KALENDRIER ET COMPOST DES BERGIERS*, PRINTED BY NICOLAS LE ROUGE, TROYES, 1496.)

was a bifurcated afterlife that provided a realm in which the righteous were rewarded and another in which the wicked were punished. In the Christian tradition in particular, underworld devils acquired employment tormenting the souls of the damned, although the earliest Christian idea was that stern, righteous angels tormented the damned. The basic schema of heaven for believers and hell for unbelievers carried over into **Islamic** conceptualizations of the afterlife.

Sources:

Cooper, Jerrold S. "The Fate of Mankind: Death and Afterlife in Ancient Mesopotamia." In Hiroshi Obabyashi, ed., *Death and Afterlife: Perspectives of World Religions.* New York: Greenwood Press, 1992.

Eliade, Mircea, ed. *The Encyclopedia of Religion.* 16 vols. New York: Macmillan, 1987.

McDannell, Colleen, and Bernhard Lang. *Heaven: A History.* Reprint, New York: Vintage, 1990.

Sandars, N. K., trans. *The Epic of Gilgamesh.* Rev. ed. New York: Penguin, 1972.

Turner, Alice K. *The History of Hell.* New York: Harcourt Brace, 1993.

Zimmer, Heinrich. *Philosophies of India.* New York: Bollingen, 1951.

SUICIDE

Suicide has always been present in most human societies, as many myths, fairy tales, sagas, and historical documents demonstrate. Although it has been found in numerous tribal societies, it appears to have been unknown in a few isolated groups, such as the Andaman Islanders, the Yahgans of Tierra del Fuego, and some aborigine tribes.

In ancient Egypt suicide was regarded as a neutral method to go from one form of existence to another. By way of contrast, it was relatively infrequent among ancient Hebrews because it was clearly prohibited and considered an affront to normal death. However, suicide is not actually condemned in either the Old Testament or the New Testament as it is reported in various accounts. Among the Greeks, Plato and Aristotle condemned suicide, whereas the Epicureans and Stoics regarded it as an appropriate escape from suffering. Socrates himself committed suicide, although he disapproved of it. The Romans generally held a permissive attitude toward suicide, and in the early Christian era it was even approved of by the Church, which, nevertheless, decided to condemn suicide in the fourth century, following St. Augustine's position in *The City of God.* In the following centuries the penalties against suicide increased and the position of the Church was summarized by Thomas Aquinas in his *Summa Theologica,* in which suicide was viewed as contrary to man's natural inclinations.

Attitudes toward suicide vary considerably in other world cultures and religions. The practice of *hara kiri* was very popular in Japanese tradition, while Hinduism approves of suicide only in special cases, such as in the self-immolation of a widow after the death of her husband. Islam condemns suicide severely, considering it an attempt to escape Allah's will.

With the industrial revolution, death started to be seen as an escape from suffering, and suicide has been more often viewed as acceptable behavior since then, although only under specific conditions. In the eighteenth and nineteenth centuries, the degree of individualism and urbanization increased as a result of the spread of capitalism, which was accompanied by a rise in suicide, as is reported in numerous sociological studies. Among the most important studies of suicide are Emile Durkheim's

Le Suicide (1897), in which the author argues that suicide results from the characteristics of social organization, and the works of Sigmund Freud about personality and the unconscious, which led to an understanding of the psychological dynamics contributing to suicide.

Sources:

Kastenbaum, Robert, and Beatrice Kastenbaum. *Encyclopedia of Death.* New York: Avon, 1989.

SUMMERLAND

Summerland is a **Spiritualist** name for the realm in which the **souls** of the departed reside. Less frequently used than such expressions as "the other side," it was said to have been coined in 1845 by **Andrew Jackson Davis,** "the American Swedenbörg." The pleasant name reflects the Spiritualist image of the afterlife as a radiant, harmonious home for the departed. Current Spiritualists rarely, if ever, use the names. Summerland is also the name of a town that was once a Spiritualist colony in southern California, just south of Santa Barbara.

Sources:

Berger, Arthur S., and Joyce Berger. *The Encyclopedia of Parapsychology and Psychical Research.* New York: Paragon House, 1991.

Cavendish, Richard, ed. *Encyclopedia of the Unexplained: Magic, Occultism and Parapsychology.* London: Arkana Penguin Books, 1989.

SURVIVAL PACT

A survival pact is a method of providing evidence for the existence of an afterlife. As the name suggests, a survival pact is an agreement between two individuals that the first to die will attempt communication with the survivor. Sometimes the agreement is to communicate some very specific item of information.

Before his death, Harry Houdini made such a pact with his wife, with the understanding that he would attempt to communicate with her by a series of coded messages. She attended various séances in order to receive messages from him, but, after years of trying to communicate with him through Spiritualist mediums, she declared the experiment a failure.

Sources:

Ernst, Bernard M. L., and Hereward Carrington. *Houdini and Conan Doyle: The Story of a Strange Friendship.* London: Hutchinson & Co., 1933.

Shepard, Leslie A., ed. *Encyclopedia of Occultism & Parapsychology.* Detroit, MI: Gale Research, 1991.

SUTPHEN, RICHARD

The American author and hypnotist Richard Sutphen (1937-) has become a popular figure in **New Age** circles through his lectures about metaphysics, **reincarnation,** and human potential. He is especially well known for his study of past-life regression, developed during group hypnosis sessions (of which he was a pioneer).

After the breakup of his first marriage, Sutphen moved to Arizona, living in Prescott and Scottsdale. He worked as an advertising free-lancer and continued to research paranormal phenomena and past-life regression. In Arizona, Sutphen's interest in the "power point" (if the planet were a person, a power point would be similar to a chakra or an acupuncture point) near Sedona induced him to visit one of the power vortices, where he had strong psychic experiences.

During some experiments with a **Ouija board,** Sutphen experienced images from one of his past lives, when he was a Maya killed by Spanish invaders. In hypnotic regressions, he also discovered that he and his second wife shared previous past lives, including one as American Indians and one as poor peasants in Marseilles, France, in the early 1700s.

Sutphen founded the Hypnosis Center in 1973 in Scottsdale, where he conducted regression research for six months, until the center was closed. He continued to conduct lectures, however, and he published his first book, *You Were Born Again to Be Together,* in 1976.

In 1980 Sutphen moved to California, where he established the Sutphen Corporation, dedicated to organizing seminars and publishing books, audiotapes, and videotapes. He also established Reincarnationists, an organization with the same purpose and directed by his third wife. Sutphen is the author of more than 35 books, including *Past Lives, Future Loves* (1978), *Unseen Influences* (1982), *Predestined Love* (1988), and *Finding Your Answers Within* (1989).

Sources:

Guiley, Rosemary Ellen. *Harper's Encyclopedia of Mystical & Paranormal Experience.* San Francisco: HarperCollins, 1991.

Melton, J. Gordon, Jerome Clark, and Aidan A. Kelly. *New Age Encyclopedia.* Detroit, MI: Gale Research, 1990.

SWEDENBÖRG, EMANUEL

Emanuel Swedenbörg (1688–1772) was a Swedish mystic who became famous for his visions of higher spiritual realms and for his supposed travels to these realms. His voluminous writings record, among other topics, the state of spirits in the afterlife.

EMANUEL SWEDENBÖRG. (FROM AN ENGRAVING BY BATTERSBY IN "THE EUROPEAN MAGAZINE," 1787.) COURTESY OF THE ARC.

Swedenbörg did not begin to have visions until later in life, after a modest career as a scientist with the Royal College of Mines. He had little interest in religious matters until 1743, when at age 56 he had a remarkable dream about the spiritual realm. Then followed a whole series of visions and dreams in which he met Jesus, God, and some of the great figures of history, visited the spirit realms, and conversed with the dead (whom he referred to as angels). He was instructed in the true nature of the universe. He also had clairvoyant experiences, including, in 1759, an incident in which he was able to perceive a fire in Stockholm (three hundred miles away).

Swedenbörg began to think of himself as a divinely appointed messenger and started communicating the information he was receiving to other people. Letting go of his career, he shut himself away from other people so that he could work on receiving and recording information from paranormal sources. Many of his friends feared that he had gone crazy, and religious leaders opposed him. He learned how to self-induce his ecstatic states, as well as how to become a **medium** for communication in the form of **automatic writing**. He died at age 84 in London in 1774. A Swedenbörgian church was formed in England in 1778, and in the United States in 1792. In 1810 the Swedenbörg Society was founded for the purpose of publishing and disseminating

Swedenbörg's works. His most popular book, *Heaven and Hell,* offers a description of the afterlife. The **Spiritualist** movement of the nineteenth century adopted certain Swedenbörgian notions, especially as reformulated and expressed in the writings of **Andrew Jackson Davis.**

Swedenbörg pictured the human being as existing simultaneously in the spiritual realm and the realm of everyday experience. The spiritual realm, he thought, has a powerful influence over human life, although people are, for the most part, unaware of the spirit. After dropping the physical body, souls transit into an intermediate, earthlike realm where they meet deceased friends and relatives. Following a period of self-examination, the dead are compelled to go to a particular afterlife world (a "heaven" or a "hell"). These realms were created by the mind during the deceased's embodiment in the physical world. For the most part, hell is an unpleasant place, containing spirits with frightening faces ("demons"), but no chief devil or Satan. Heaven is a more pleasant copy of physical life, containing good souls ("angels"). In heaven as well as hell, people engage in work, play, marriage, and even war and crime. Both realms also have governments and social structures. One may progress though various afterlife realms, or levels of heaven and hell with the exception that one is never able to leave heaven or hell.

Sources:

Brown, Slater. *The Heyday of Spiritualism.* New York: Hawthorn Books, 1970.

Douglas, Alfred. *Extrasensory Powers: A Century of Psychical Research.* London: Victor Gollancz, 1976.

Guiley, Rosemary Ellen. *The Encyclopedia of Ghosts and Spirits.* New York: Facts on File, 1992.

Swedenbörg, Emanuel. *Divine Love and Wisdom.* New York: American Swedenbörg Printing and Publishing Society, 1904. (Originally published 1763.)

———. *Divine Providence.* New York: The Swedenbörg Foundation, 1972. (Originally published 1764.)

T

THEATER OF THE MIND

The Theater of the Mind is **Raymond Moody's** research center in rural Alabama. After formulating the field of near-death studies and investigating such phenomena for many years, Moody became interested in communication between the living and the so-called dead. The Theater of the Mind represents an attempt to establish a modern psychomanteum, inspired by the ancient Greek oracles of the dead, where seekers could consult spirits of the deceased.

The core of the facility is a mirror into which the individual stares in an effort to contact the dead. Almost half of the people who have participated in the structured exercise have reported success. Although Moody himself has not conduced systematic research involving his psychomanteum, he is optimistic that he has discovered a context in which communication with the so-called dead can be scientifically investigated. Perhaps more important, Moody reports that the individuals who have been successful at contacting a departed relative have had experiences that permitted them to resolve relationship issues that still existed when the relative died.

Sources:

Moody, Raymond A. "Family Reunions: Visionary Encounters with the Departed in a Modern-Day Psychomanteum." *Journal of Near-Death Studies* 11, no. 2 (Winter 1992): 83–121.

———. *Reunions.* New York: Villard Books, 1993.

THEOSOPHY

The name Theosophy originated in Alexandria, Egypt, in the third century A.D. in connection with the Greek mysteries and referred to the divine wisdom believed to

DR. RAYMOND MOODY'S OLD GRIST MILL IN ALABAMA, WHICH IS NOT ONLY HIS PRIVATE RESIDENCE BUT THE SITE OF HIS RESEARCH FACILITY, THE THEATER OF THE MIND.

underlie the teachings of all religions. In contemporary usage, Theosophy refers to the particular synthesis of ideas from the philosophical systems of China and India and from the works of the Gnostics, the Neoplatonists, and the Cabalists, manifested in the Theosophical Society, which was founded in New York in 1875 by **Helena Blavatsky**.

As a part of the religious phenomenon known as esotericism, Theosophy concerns a gnosis (intellectual insight) offering enlightment to the individual through knowledge of what is believed to unite that person to the world of the divine and to its hidden mysteries. Although Theosophists might reject the characterization of the society as a religion (the Theosophical Society and its offshoots claim to have no dogma, creed, or ritual), Theosophy, as do other religions, shows its followers a way to salvation, a way to guarantee their soul a more favorable destiny.

Theosophy postulates a rather complex view of the universe within which humanity's origins, evolution, and destiny after death are delineated. According to its principles, the visible world arises from an omnipresent and immutable Source, an

LONNETTE BRAWNER, ADMINISTRATOR OF THE THEATER OF THE MIND, STANDS INSIDE THE PSYCHOMANTEUM—A CHAMBER DEVELOPED BY DR. RAYMOND MOODY TO EVOKE APPARITIONS OF THE DEPARTED. COURTESY OF THEATER OF THE MIND.

immaterial reality of which, as in Hindu philosophy, the universe is the manifestation and from within it is worked and guided.

The process of cosmic manifestation is characterized by two phases, the first being *involution,* during which a multitude of spiritual units emerge from the Source and, after becoming more and more involved in matter, finally achieve self-consciousness in the physical world. Thus, the individual spiritual units (*the monads*) reach the causal body (a spiritual body containing the seeds of karma that "cause" everything else) by descending through various grades of being. During the second phase, *evolution,* the human monads—which possess the triple functions of will, wisdom, and activity, like the ultimate Being from which they come—develop their inner potentials, free themselves from matter and return to the Source, with an increased consciousness.

The spirit, which can never be lost (it is intrinsically eternal), attains mastery through cycles of **reincarnation,** in accordance with the inexorable law of cause and effect called **karma**. In each incarnation new experiences are attained, leading to development of the soul to a degree that is proportionate to the use that is made of each experience. According to Theosophy, a long series of reincarnations is required for the soul to achieve its supreme aim, which is rising to its original Source, and the duration of the period spent on each plane before another incarnation depends upon good and evil deeds done in the body.

Sources:

Eliade, Mircea, ed. *The Encyclopedia of Religion.* 16 vols. New York: Macmillan, 1987.
Hastings, James, ed. *Encyclopedia of Religion and Ethics.* Edinburgh: T. & T. Clark, 1980.
Shepard, Leslie A., ed. *Encyclopedia of Occultism & Parapsychology.* Detroit, MI: Gale Research, 1991.

TIME BETWEEN INCARNATIONS

Various theories of **reincarnation** speculate about the determinants of the period of time between death and the **soul's** next lifetime. Some cultures, most notably traditional Tibetan, postulate a specific period of time between incarnations. In most other traditions this period is not specified and is viewed instead as a variable function of the individual's **karma.**

A matter that is usually not addressed in most reincarnationist traditions is what the soul "does" between lifetimes. When the question is addressed, this period is conceived of in vague terms, as a cycle of residence in a spirit realm of some sort, sometimes even in a temporary heaven or hell world. In more recent, "metaphysical" thought, the soul between lifetimes is sometimes pictured as undertaking a course of study in an otherworldly "school" of some sort.

Sources:

Bletzer, June G. *The Donning International Encyclopedic Psychic Dictionary.* Norfolk, VA: Donning, 1986.
Head, Joseph, and S. L. Cranston. *Reincarnation: The Phoenix Fire Mystery.* New York: Julian Press/ Crown, 1977.

TIME TRAVEL

In certain **out-of-body experiences** (OBEs), people sometimes seem to be able to travel backward or forward in time. In **past-life therapy** individuals also experience a sense of moving back in time, especially when they vividly relive certain portions of a previous lifetime. Past-life therapists further report that, when prompted, some people appear to be able to tap "memories" of *future* lifetimes, thus constituting a kind of time travel into the future.

Sources:

Bletzer, June G. *The Donning International Encyclopedic Psychic Dictionary.* Norfolk, VA: Donning, 1986.

Head, Joseph, and S. L. Cranston. *Reincarnation: The Phoenix Fire Mystery.* New York: Julian Press/Crown, 1977.

TOMBS

Tombs, probably the most common means of disposing of the dead, have since recorded history, reflected human belief in the religious significance of death. During the Paleolithic era, graves usually were located in natural caves. Bodies were buried in accord with certain conventions (e.g., in a fetal position) and were accompanied by items that had played an important role in life, such as the person's weapons or implements. Burying the dead with their possessions indicates that humanity has held some kind of belief in a life after death from very early in its history.

As a parallel development to the emergence of agriculture in the Neolithic Near East, tombs were built in the shape of *tumuli* (mounds). Whereas the dead had been buried in or near settlements during the Paleolithic period, Neolithic peoples seemed to have a need for a separate abode for the dead. The prehistoric tumulus can be interpreted as an embodiment of the archetypal cosmic mountain where earth, heaven, and underworld meet, and hence where the departed can more readily find their way to the otherworld. This same archetype was copied in ancient Mycenaean and Greek civilization in Egyptian pyramids, in some tombs during the Roman and Byzantine periods, and in Buddhist *stupas* (shrines) and *pagodas.*

Ancient tombs were created in the form of temples, chamber tombs cut in hard rock (found in ancient Semitic settlements in the Near East), cremation urns (by the Etrurians), and sarcophagi (mostly a Phoenician tradition). The tombs were also decorated with religious symbols that bear witness to sundry spiritual beliefs about the dead. Ancient nonmonotheistic religions used their symbologies to represent life beyond death and immortality (e.g., the cornucopia), and also employed zodiacal signs; Christianity used the symbol of the cross, Judaism the menorah (a seven-branched candelabrum) or the shofar (a ceremonial horn).

Sources:

Eliade, Mircea. *Encyclopedia of Religion.* 16 vols. New York: Macmillan, 1987.
Van Der Leeuw, G., trans. *Religion in Essence and Manifestaton.* Vol. I. Gloucester, MA: Peter Smith, 1967. (Originally published 1933.)

TRANSCENDENTALISM

Transcendentalism, which has its origins in literature, philosophy, and religion, is a form of idealism that views the foundation for absolute truths—for ''reality''—as being immanent in the human mind or soul. This foundation, variously called reason, the ego, or the absolute spirit, is often identified with God.

In modern philosophy the term was adopted by Immanuel Kant (1724–1804) in an attempt to establish a philosophical foundation for universal and necessary truths.

At the same time, he accepted the premise, put forward in both his *Critique of Pure Reason* and his *Critique of Practical Reason,* that human cognitive powers are incapable of grasping nonempirical objects that transcend human cognition, which are accessible to autonomous practical reason only through an act of faith. Among these objects are the existence of God, the freedom of will, and the immortality of the soul, which represent the central doctrines of many religions. They cannot be proved and have to be accepted as necessary truths of the supersensible reality, and, as such, they can be accepted in faith. The notion of immortality of the soul, in particular, is required for moral perfection. Because of the natural propensity of humanity to go against the moral dictates of pure reason, moral perfection can be reached only through the transformation of this inclination into acquiescent obedience to the moral law, and, since this process requires an infinite period of time, moral perfection can be achieved only if the soul continues to live after the death of its body.

The ideas of Kant and his successors were picked up by the transcendentalists of New England, who did not, however, preserve the epistemological rigor of the European idealists, although they adopted some of their notions. American transcendentalism, which flourished from the mid-1830s until the mid-1840s, supported the intuitive idea of an organic universe permeated by an immanent God and stressed the importance of the individual's own moral experience.

According to the transcendentalists, human ideas are the result of direct revelation and inspiration from God. In addition to the body of flesh there exists a spiritual body, which is variously named the oversoul, conscience, or inner light. It cannot be annihilated and continues to live after death and, eventually, to reach its Source.

The most important members of the Transcendental Club, founded in Boston in 1836, were Ralph Waldo Emerson (1803–1882) and Henry David Thoreau (1817–1862). Emerson's publications concerning transcendentalism include: *Nature* (1836), about the basic principles of transcendentalism; the *American Scholar Address* (1837), about the necessity of an original American literature; the *Divinity School Address* (1838), which called for a religion of inspiration to replace the formalism of the day; *Essays* (1841); and *Essays: Second Series* (1844). Thoreau's works include *Walden* (1854), *A Week on the Concord and Merrimack Rivers* (1849), "Civil Disobedience" (1849), and "Life Without Principle" (1863).

The permanent traits of an intuitive religion, similar to the philosophy of Transcendentalism, as opposed to the doctrines of the existing religions, are illustrated in Theodore Parker's (1810–1860) "A Discourse on the Transient and Permanent in Christianity" (1841) and *A Discourse of Matters Pertaining to Religion* (1842). Although other transcendentalists were involved with other areas within the large eclectic framework that Emerson had established, the movement had a relatively short life.

Sources:

Christy, Arthur. *The Orient in American Transcendentalism.* New York: Octagon Books, 1963.
Hastings, James A., ed. *Encyclopedia of Religion and Ethics.* Edinburgh: T. & T. Clark, 1980.
Neville, Robert Cummings. *Eternity and Time's Flow.* Albany: State University of New York Press, 1993.

HIERONYMUS BOSCH'S *THE ASCENT INTO THE EMPYREAN,* SHOWING ANGELS TAKING DEPARTED SOULS UP TO HEAVEN.

TUNNEL, VISION OF

The passage from this world to the next is only infrequently viewed as a quick transition that occurs immediately after death. Instead, most traditional cultures conceive of the soul as undertaking a postmortem journey to the afterlife. This trip may be represented in many ways. Often the departed soul crosses a **river,** either across a **bridge** or on a **boat.**

In contemporary reports of **near-death experiences** (NDEs), this journey is often expressed in terms of a transition through a ''tunnel.'' Typically, people who have experienced an NDE do not realize that they have died and attempt to communicate with others at the scene of death. If in a hospital, they frequently experience watching their body from the outside as medical personnel attempt to resuscitate them.

TUNNEL, VISION OF

In **Raymond Moody's** outline of NDEs he refers to a fourth stage as the tunnel experience—the experience of being drawn into darkness through a tunnel (or going up a stairway or some other symbol of crossing a threshold) until the person emerges into a realm of light. Some critics of assigning metaphysical significance to NDEs have speculated that this tunnel is actually a deeply buried memory of the birth canal to which people regress in reponse to the overwhelming experience of death.

Sources:

Biedermann, Hans. *Dictionary of Symbolism: Cultural Icons and the Meanings Behind Them.* New York: Meridian, 1994.

Moody, Raymond A., Jr. *The Light Beyond.* Rev. ed. New York: Bantam, 1989.

populated by those who consciously committed evil, mythical characters included. The idea of hell subsequently developed as a philosophical concept of total annihilation. Although several traditional stories depict hell as a place of suffering and pain, in general the Hindu religion places more emphasis on the cycle of **reincarnation.**

In the contemporary world, the underworld has come to be viewed psychologically rather than literally, as a symbol for the subconscious. Particularly among thinkers influenced by **Jung** and by the Jungian tradition, various portrayals of the underworld have come to be interpreted as reflecting the subconscious of a society.

Sources:

Eliade, Mircea, ed. *The Encyclopedia of Religion.* 16 vols. New York: Macmillan, 1987.
Turner, Alice K. *The History of Hell.* New York: Harcourt Brace, 1993.

UNITED METHODIST

United Methodist belief in life after death, which is very similar to that of most mainline Protestant churches, is concerned with the Resurrection of Jesus Christ and his promise of eternal life to those who accept him. According to Methodist doctrine, eternal life after death is symbolized by baptism, through which the believer becomes a part of the Church on earth, and after death becomes a part of the same in heaven.

Among the most important practices is the funeral service, in which death is acknowledged as real and the concepts of resurrection and immortality are emphasized, by pointing to the triumph of Jesus Christ over death, considered the enemy. God's everlasting love and care are proclaimed at the end of the service, when the mourners are reminded of the transience of temporal life, after which the whole person—body, mind, spirit—rises to eternal life.

The body that rises is spiritual and differs from the earthly one, even though it is the same recognizable person, whose life after death has continuity with the one on earth, fulfilling the deepest relationships. The ideas of **purgatory** and **reincarnation** are rejected by United Methodists, who also are not particularly dogmatic regarding the nature of heaven and the day of the final judgment.

Sources:

Johnson, Christopher Jay, and Marsha G. McGee. *Encounters with Eternity: Religious Views of Death and Life After-Death.* New York: Philosophical Library, 1986.
Kastenbaum, Robert, and Beatrice Kastenbaum, eds. *Encyclopedia of Death.* Phoenix, AZ: Oryx Press, 1989.

UNITED SPIRITUALIST CHURCH

The United Spiritualist Church, based in Gardena, California, was founded in 1967 by Edwin Potter, Howard Mangen, and an independent Spiritualist minister, Floyd Humble. The beliefs of the church typify the norm of Spiritualist tradition. Jesus is considered the master teacher, and members seek to follow him in preaching, healing, and prophecy. Followers find the proof of human immortality in both mental and physical mediumship, and communication with souls in the next world is a prime means of advancing humanity toward the kingdom of God.

Sources:

Humble, Floyd. *Bible Lessons.* Gardena, CA: United Spiritualist Church, 1969.
Melton, J. Gordon. *The Encyclopedia of American Religions.* 4th ed. Detroit, MI: Gale Research, 1993.

UNIVERSAL CHURCH OF THE MASTER

The Universal Church of the Master is one of the larger Spiritualist organizations in the United States, reporting about 300 congregations, 1,300 ministers, and 10,000 members. It was founded in 1908 in Los Angeles and has remained in California, moving its headquarters at various times to Oakland, San Jose, and (currently) Santa Clara.

The church understands itself to be following the master Jesus, and an important teaching source is a book produced in the late nineteenth century by Levi Dowling, *The Aquarian Gospel of Jesus the Christ.* The beliefs of the church are set down in *A New Text of Spiritual Philosophy and Religion,* by Dr. B. J. Fitzgerald, the major leader of the church until his death about 1960. The foundation of the church's faith is a liberal Christianity, but the basic doctrine allows a wide range of interpretation and belief. The church places importance on having a philosophy that is not parochial, but universal and eclectic. Its 10-point statement of belief affirms: (1) the fatherhood of God, (2) the family of all humans, (3) the need to live in accordance with the laws of nature, (4) the continuance of life after the death of the body, (5) the ability to communicate with spirits of the deceased, (6) morality as centered on the Golden Rule, (7) individual responsibility, (8) the continual option for improvement—there is no utter damnation, (9) prophecy, and (10) the soul's eternal progress in the next life.

Sources:

Fitzgerald, B. J. *A New Text of Spiritual Philosophy and Religion.* San Jose, CA: Universal Church of the Master, 1954.
Melton, J. Gordon. *The Encyclopedia of American Religions.* 4th ed. Detroit, MI: Gale Research, 1993.

UNIVERSAL SPIRITUALIST ASSOCIATION

The Universal Spiritualist Association was founded in 1956 after Camp Chesterfield, a popular Spiritualist camp in Indiana, severed ties with the Spiritualist Episcopal Church, which had long been in charge of its summer training institutes. Charter members of the Universal Spiritualist Association were largely former members of the **Spiritualist Episcopal Church** and included Mabel Riffle, well known both as a medium and as secretary of Camp Chesterfield. For a long time Camp Chesterfield was the heart of the association, but in 1985 headquarters for the group was moved to Maple Grove in Anderson, Indiana.

The association believes itself to be led by Christ and defines Spiritualism as the "Science, Philosophy, and Religion of continuous life, based upon the demonstrated fact of communication, by means of mediumship, with those who live in the spirit world." To demonstrate more completely this immortal life and communication with the spirit world, the association uses the full range of physical phenomena during mediumship sessions, including spirit photography, materializations, direct writing, and **rappings.**

The Ancient and Mystical Order of Seekers, patterned after the Ancient and Mystical Order of the Rosae Crucis (AMORC) is a fraternity within the association for serious students wishing to delve into areas of study rather unusual for Spiritualists, particularly the occult sciences, ranging from yoga to ritual magic. The order uses texts written by Clifford Bias, who was president of the Universal Spiritualist Association until his death in 1987.

Sources:

Melton, J. Gordon. *The Encyclopedia of American Religions.* 4th ed. Detroit, MI: Gale Research, 1993.

Universal Spiritual Church. Universal Spiritualist Manual. N.p.: Universal Spiritual Church, n.d.

V

VIRGIL

The Roman poet Virgil (70–19 B.C.) was born Publius Vergilius Maro to a humble family in Andes, a village near Mantua in northern Italy. He attended school at Cremona and Milan, and then he went to Rome to study medicine, mathematics, and rhetoric. Later he moved to Naples, where he studied philosophy under Siron the Epicurean. Lucretius's naturalistic philosophy of *De rerum natura* and Catullus's poetry were the two major influences on Virgil during his formative years. His earliest certain work was the *Bucolica* or *Eclogae,* 10 poems modeled on the Greek pastorals of Theocritus. The *Georgica,* his next work, is a didactic poem on farming describing the country life with which Virgil was personally familiar and dealing with all aspects of universal life, as the themes of the four books—war, peace, death, and rebirth—suggest.

Virgil's last years were devoted to the *Aeneid,* left unfinished at his death, telling about the wanderings of Aeneas after the fall of Troy, similar to the wanderings of Odysseus, and his final settlement in Latium. The poem is an epic about the founding of Rome and the great role the Roman people played in the history of the world according to a divine decree. The agency of fate is predominant in the poem, even though in some parts a spiritual dispensation is awarded to virtuous men, according to their actions.

This image of fate is particularly easy to perceive in the sixth book of the *Aeneid* (which can be considered the jumping-off point for **Dante's** *Inferno*). In this part of the poem, Virgil offers his concept of individual destiny after life, describing the descent of Aeneas into **Hades,** the underworld, escorted by the Sibyl, to reach his father, from whom he will receive a mystic revelation and a prophecy before returning to the upper world.

Virgil's world of the dead is described as a place below the earth, which can be entered by a cave near Lake Avernus. It is thus very different from Homer's underworld, located in the far northwest, but still apparently on the earth. Virgil's underworld is populated by the shades (ghosts), with full personality, of great personages of legend and of ordinary men. The righteous souls are allocated to the right region, called Elysium, and the sinners are punished in the left one, called Tartarus. The souls of those who died in infancy and of those who died a violent death inhabit **Limbo** and the region next to it.

Anchises, Aeneas's father, leads his son on to a third division of the underworld, the banks of Lethe, where the souls destined to return for another life to the upper world are gathered. Here Aeneas receives the famous philosophical account of life in the underworld, in which **reincarnation** and the Stoic doctrine of the *anima mundi,* the world-spirit running through every part of the universe (refined through purification after being corrupted during man's life on earth), play an important part. Through the words of Anchises, Virgil presents his own vision of the afterlife, of the fate of the individual soul and the cycle of its existence, reflecting the images of the "pagan theology" that lay behind his philosophy. These ideas had an important influence on the medieval concept of hell, purgatory, and heaven, as seen in Dante's *The Divine Comedy,* in which Virgil himself is the guide to the lower world.

Sources:

Academic American Encyclopedia. Danbury, CT: Grolier, 1993.
Bailey, Cyril. *Religion in Virgil.* Oxford: Oxford University Press, 1935.
Quinn, Kenneth. *Virgil's Aeneid. A Critical Description.* Ann Arbor: University of Michigan Press, 1968.

VOODOO (VODOUN)

Voodoo is a Caribbean religion blended from traditional African religions and Catholic Christianity. Originally a slave religion, it is especially associated with the island of Haiti, although identifiably voodoo forms of spiritual expression are also present in Jamaica and Santo Domingo. *Vodoun* is a derivative of the Nigerian word *vodu,* which means divinity or spirit or deity in the Fon language of Dahomey. The term has been variously spelled *voudou, voudoun, vodoun, voodoo,* and *hoodoo.* Partly because of sensationalistic portrayals in the entertainment media, voodoo has come to be regarded pejoratively.

Voodoo postulates a complex and extensive pantheon of divinities, referred to as *loas* or *mystères.* A supreme being who created the world, Gran Met, is acknowledged, although he is too distant from the world to be worshiped. Voodoo focuses instead on the more immediate divinities, serving the loas in return for favors. In line with African tradition, ancestors are revered.

Within Voodoo, the human being is pictured as being composed of five ingredients: *n'âme, z'étoile,* corps *cadavre, gros bon ange,* and *ti bon ange. Corps cadavre* refers to the physical flesh. *N'âme* is the vital energy that allows the body to function during life. *Z'étoile* refers to the star of destiny of the particular human being.

Gros bon ange (literally, ''big good angel'') and *ti bon ange* (literally, ''little good angel'') constitute one's soul. The gros bon ange enters humans during conception. It is a portion of the universal life energy, the life force that all living things share. The ti bon ange, by contrast, is one's individual soul or essence. This ''small soul'' journeys out of the body when one dreams, as well as when the body is being possessed by the loa. It is the ti bon ange that is attacked by sorcerers.

When one dies, according to voodoo belief, the soul remains near the corpse for a week. During this seven-day period, the ti bon ange is vulnerable and may be captured and made into a ''spiritual zombie'' by a sorcerer. Assuming the soul has escaped this fate, the priest ritually severs it from the body so that the soul many live in the dark waters for a year and a day. At that point, relatives ritually raise the soul, and put it in the *govi* now referred to as *esprit* (spirit). These spirits are fed, clothed, and treated like divinities. Later they are set free and abide among the rocks and trees until rebirth. Sixteen embodiments later, spirits merge into the cosmic energy.

Communion with a god or goddess occurs in the context of **possession,** referred to as ''the hand of divine grace.'' The gods sometimes work through a govi, and sometimes take over a living person, referred to as ''mounting a horse.'' The person loses consciousness, the body becoming completely the instrument of a loa. Gestures and facial expressions become that of the possessing loa. A special priest (*houngan*) or priestess (*mambo*) assists both in summoning the divinities and in helping them to leave at the termination of the possession. These priests and priestesses are also diviners, healers, and religious leaders.

Sources:

Davis, Wade. *The Serpent and the Rainbow.* New York: Warner Books, 1985.

Denning, Melita, and Osborne Phillips. *Voudou Fire: The Living Reality of Mystical Religion.* St. Paul, MN: Llewellyn Publishing, 1979.

Devillers, Carole. "Of Spirits and Saints: Haiti's Voodoo Pilgrimages." *National Geographic* (March 1985).

Rigaud, Milo. *Secrets of Voodoo.* San Francisco: City Lights Books, 1969.

W

Walk-ins

A walk-in is an entity that occupies a body that has been vacated by its original soul. The situation is somewhat similar to "**possession,**" although in possession the original soul is merely overshadowed— rather than completely supplanted— by the possessing entity. The walk-in concept seems to be related to certain traditional Indian tales about aging yoga masters taking over the bodies of young people who died prematurely.

Another possible source for the contemporary walk-in notion is the well-known (in theosophical circles) teaching that Jesus and Christ were separate souls. According to this teaching, Jesus prepared his physical body to receive Christ and, at a certain point in his career, vacated his body so as to allow Christ to take it over and preach to the world. An underlying notion here is that Christ was such a highly evolved soul that it would have been difficult if not impossible for him to have incarnated as a baby, and that even if he could have done so, it would have been a waste of precious time for such a highly developed soul to have to go through childhood.

The contemporary notion of walk-ins was popularized by Ruth Montgomery in *Strangers Among Us* (1979, 11–12), in which she describes the walk-in phenomenon rather dramatically:

> There are Walk-ins on this planet. Tens of thousands of them. Enlightened beings, who, after successfully completing numerous incarnations, have attained sufficient awareness of the meaning of life that they can forego the time-consuming process of birth and childhood, returning directly to adult bodies. A Walk-in is a high-minded entity who is permitted to take over the body of another human being who wishes to depart. . . . The motivation of a Walk-in is humanitarian. He returns to physical being in order to help others

> help themselves, planting seed-concepts that will grow and flourish for the benefit of mankind.

Montgomery's *Threshold to Tomorrow,* containing case histories of 17 walk-ins, was published in 1983. According to Montgomery, history is full of walk-ins, including such famous historical figures as Moses, Jesus, Muhammad, Christopher Columbus, Abraham Lincoln, Mary Baker Eddy, Gandhi, George Washington, Benjamin Franklin, Thomas Jefferson, Alexander Hamilton, and James Madison. In fact, it seems that Montgomery would identify as a walk-in almost everyone manifesting exceptional creativity and leadership. In her words, "Some of the world's greatest spiritual and political leaders, scientists, and philosophers in ages past are said to have been Walk-ins" (1983, 12).

In a later book, *Aliens Among Us* (1985), Montgomery developed the notion of extraterrestrial walk-ins—the idea that souls from other planets have come to earth to take over the bodies of human beings. These ideas became extremely popular in New Age circles, and for a while it seemed that almost every hard-core New Ager was claiming to be some kind of walk-in. Some New Age magazines even carried articles that asked the question, "Are you a Walk-in?" Such articles utterly trivialized the notion by presenting criteria for determining whether or not one had "walked in," criteria that were often so general that almost anyone could imagine being an exotic walk-in.

According to Montgomery, walk-ins are frequently people who have gone through an exceptionally traumatic experience, most often a life-threatening one, after which they feel they are different individuals. Sometimes this event is an actual death/revival (near-death) experience. At other times it is an emotional trauma that leads one to question the value of living itself (a condition that enables the disembodied entity to convince the original soul to abandon its body). In most cases, the walk-in inherits the memory patterns of the former inhabitant of the body.

The prominent near-death researcher Kenneth Ring has compared the walk-in experience with the near-death experience, noting that parallel transformations occur in individual's lives after both such experiences. The walk-in notion has been enthusiastically accepted by some and summarily rejected by others. This divergence is reflected in the reactions of Carol W. Parrish-Harra and Dick Sutphen, prominent New Age figures named by Montgomery as walk-ins.

Parrish-Harra, minister of the Light of Christ Community Church in Oklahoma, has accepted the idea of herself as a walk-in, although she thinks the term *messenger* is more accurate. She believes that she "walked in" during a near-death experience resulting from the birth of her daughter in 1958. She even wrote an autobiography built around the "messenger" experience, *Messengers of Hope* (1983). Dick Sutphen, in contrast, has rejected the walk-in notion. Montgomery had asserted that Sutphen's walk-in occurred around the time of the breakup of his first marriage. Sutphen, however, does not accept the assertion that he has a different soul from the one that inhabited his body in his earlier years.

Sources:

Montgomery, Ruth. *Aliens Among Us.* New York: Putnam's, 1985.

———. *Strangers Among Us: Enlightened Beings from a World to Come.* New York: Coward, McCann & Geoghegan, 1979.

———. *Threshold to Tomorrow.* New York: Putnam, 1983.

Parrish-Harra, Carol W. *Messengers of Hope.* Marina Del Ray, CA: DeVorss, 1983.

Ring, Kenneth. *Heading Toward Omega.* New York: Morrow, 1984.

WICKLAND, CARL A.

Dr. Carl A. Wickland (1861–1945), in cooperation with his wife, Anna, a medium, practiced a mild form of **exorcism** that relied heavily upon simply persuading possessing spirits to exit their victims. The Wicklands also utilized mild electric shocks, which they asserted forced discarnate entities to leave the bodies of the possessed. Their procedure was to persuade or force the possessing spirit to let go of its victim, move into Anna's body, and, finally, leave forever.

Wickland moved to the United States in 1881 from his native Sweden. Marrying Anna in 1896, he studied at Durham Medical College in Chicago, graduating with his medical degree in 1900. He worked in private practice, eventually becoming interested in psychiatry. He came to believe that possessing spirits were often involved in mental illness.

After researching the matter, Wickland concluded that the bothersome discarnates were frequently not even aware that they were no longer disconnected from their physical form. Exorcism involved informing the spirit and simply persuading it to leave. In the case of uncooperative discarnates, he called in helper spirits, who were able to place the offending entity in a spiritual "dungeon," outside the **aura** of the possessed, until such time as the discarnate abandoned its uncooperative attitude and left. To speed up the process, he constructed a static electricity device that, according to Wickland, made the discarnate quite uncomfortable when low-voltage shocks were administered to the victim.

Unlike psychic researchers, Wickland was uninterested in demonstrating the discarnates' identities, partly because he thought their confused mental states were too disordered to give verifiable data. In part because of his negative attitude toward such research, his work did not attract the attention of established parapsychologists. The Wicklands moved to Los Angeles in 1918, where they established the National Psychological Institute for the treatment of obsession. Wickland wrote several books in which he described his work, including *Thirty Years Among the Dead* (1924) and *The Gateway of Understanding* (1934).

Sources:

Guiley, Rosemary Ellen. *The Encyclopedia of Ghosts and Spirits.* New York: Facts on File, 1992.

Rogo, D. Scott. *The Infinite Boundary.* New York: Dodd, Mead, 1987.

Wickland, Carl. *Thirty Years Among the Dead.* N. Hollywood, CA: Newcastle Publishing, 1974. (Originally published 1924.)

Y

Yama

Yama is the Hindu god of the dead. In the earliest Hindu texts Yama was a hero king, ruler of the afterlife realm. For the Vedic Aryans of the time, this afterlife was a kind of Indian Valhalla, in which the deceased enjoyed carnal pleasures. As Hinduism was transformed in the post-Vedic period, Yama, along with the rest of the chief deities of the Vedic pantheon, was demoted in the divine hierarchy. Yama became a rather grim demigod who snared the souls of the departed and conducted them to the otherworld.

Sources:

Eliade, Mircea, ed. *The Encyclopedia of Religion.* 16 vols. New York: Macmillan, 1987.
Sykes, Egerton. *Who's Who: Non-Classical Mythology.* New York: Oxford University Press, 1993.

Yoga

Yoga, a Sanskrit term meaning ''union'' that is related to the English word *yoke,* refers to a complex variety of practices, all of which ''unite'' the individual with the godhead. In the industrialized West, the widespread popularity of hatha yoga has caused the term to be associated with an exotic set of physical exercises. However, in its original south Asian setting, *yoga* referred to everything from devotional love of the divine (bhakti yoga) to the study of metaphysical ideas (jnana yoga).

In common with other forms of South Asian spirituality, the ultimate goal of yoga is **moksha,** release from the endless chain of deaths and rebirths (*samsara*). To effectively realize this aim, traditional yogic authorities agree that how one dies is of extreme importance: ''Only complete control of the death process, as effected by full awareness during and after the dropping of the body, guarantees a benign postmortem existence'' (Feuerstein, 1990, 88).

An esoteric yoga focused on the dying process is alluded to in many classical Hindu texts, which indicates that the "conscious dying" practices developed in Tibet (see **Buddhism**) have an Indian origin. For example, in the **Bhagavad Gita** Krishna informs his friend Arjuna that "[He who] at the time of his departure is in union of love and the power of Yoga and, with a mind that wanders not, keeps the power of his life between his eye-brows, he goes to that Spirit Supreme, the Supreme Spirit of Light" (Gita 8:10).

The yoga of conscious dying teaches that different "apertures" exist through which the soul can depart. Focusing one's attention between the eye-brows enables one to leave the body through the top of the head, a "gate" out of the physical form that presumably allows one to escape the wheel of rebirth.

Sources:

Bhagavad Gita. Juan Mascaro, trans. Baltimore, MD: Penguin, 1970.
Feuerstein, Georg. *Encyclopedic Dictionary of Yoga.* New York: Paragon House, 1990.
Zimmer, Heinrich. *Philosophies of India.* New York: Bollingen, 1951.

YAMA, THE HINDU GOD OF DEATH. COURTESY OF THE ARC.

YOGI IN SIDDHASANA.
COURTESY OF THE ARC.

Z

Zombie

A zombie is a dead person—or, more precisely, the soulless body of a dead person—that has been artificially brought back to life, usually through magic. Lacking the ingredient of consciousness, the zombie's motions are undirected, mechanical, and robotlike. By extension, living people who behave like unconscious automatons are sometimes referred to as zombies.

Other than in the movies, the best-known zombies are the dead people who appear to have been brought back to life by a **voodoo** magician. (The term *zombie* seems to be derived from the African word *nzambi,* meaning spirit of the dead.) Seemingly supernatural, voodoo "zombification" has a natural explanation. Wade Davis, an ethnobiologist, studied Haitian zombies and found that they were actually individuals who were given drugs that made them *appear* dead and then buried alive. The victim is given a strong poison, either through an open wound or in food. The potion, usually a powder, contains various toxic animal and plant products—including such natural poisons as bufotoxin and tetrodotoxin—that induce a deathlike state. The sorcerer later uses other substances that revitalize the victim.

A victim who has received the potion experiences malaise, dizziness, and a tingling that soon becomes a total numbness. The person then suffers excessive salivating, sweating, headaches, and general weakness. Both blood pressure and body temperature drop, and the pulse is quick and weak. This is followed by diarrhea and regurgitation. The victim then undergoes respiratory distress, until the entire body turns blue. Sometimes the body goes into wild twitches, after which it is totally paralyzed, and the person falls into a coma in which he or she appears to be dead.

The sorcerer retrieves the victim from the grave and revives the person with a potion referred to as "zombie's cucumber." Disoriented, afraid, and psychologically or physically abused, the revived victim is given a new name and becomes the de facto slave of the sorcerer. Zombies are traditionally put to work in the fields, although some are said to do other kinds of work. They need minimal nourishment. It is said, however, that they cannot be fed salt, which activates their speaking ability as well as an instinct that takes them back to their tombs.

There is also a tradition of what we might term "spiritual zombiism," in which a sorcerer catches souls of the departed. This *zombie astral,* like his physical counterpart, is bound to obey the magician.

Sources:

Cohen, Daniel. *Voodoo, Devils and the New Invisible World.* New York: Dodd, Mead, 1972.
Davis, Wade. *The Serpent and the Rainbow.* New York: Simon & Schuster/Warner Books, 1985.
Eliade, Mircea, ed. *The Encyclopedia of Religion.* 16 vols. New York: Macmillan, 1987.
Gibson, Walter B. *Witchcraft.* New York: Grosset & Dunlap, 1973.

ZOROASTRIANISM

Zoroastrianism has been an unusually fruitful faith, exercising an influence on the doctrines of other religions disproportionate to its size. It was founded in ancient Persia (modern-day Iran) in about 1000 B.C. (some sources say much earlier) by the prophet Zoroaster and was the official religion of the area until the Muslims took over the region. A relatively small body of Zoroastrians, called Parsis, survive in contemporary India.

The religion of Zoroaster is best known for its good versus evil dualism. The god of light and the upper world, Ohrmazd or Ahura Mazda ("wise lord"), and his angels are locked in a cosmic struggle with the god of darkness and the lower world, Angra Mainyu or Ahriman ("evil spirit"), and his demons. Unlike Christianity, in which the outcome of the war between god and the Devil has already been decided, Zoroastrianism portrays the struggle as a more or less even match. Individual human beings are urged to align themselves with the forces of light and are judged according to the predominance of their good or evil deeds.

As for the afterlife, Zoroastrianism teaches that for three days after death the soul remains at the head of its former body. All of the individual's good and bad deeds are entered in a sort of accountant's ledger, recording evil actions as debits and good actions as credits. The soul then embarks on a journey to judgment, walking out onto the Chinvat ("accountant's") Bridge. In the middle of the bridge, according to the Pahlevi (Pahlevi is the ancient language of Persia) text, the Bundahishn.

> There is a sharp edge which stands like a sword; and Hell is below the Bridge. Then the soul is carried to where stands a sword. If the soul is righteous, the sword presents its broad side. If the soul be wicked, that sword continues to stand edgewise, and does not give passage. With three steps which the soul takes forward—which are the evil thoughts, words, and deeds that it has performed—it is cut down from the head of the Bridge, and falls headlong to Hell. (Pavry 1926, 92–93)

If, when bad deeds are weighed against good ones, debits outweigh credits, "even if the difference is only three tiny acts of wrongdoing," the sinner falls off the bridge and into hell. Hell is a dismal realm of torment, where the damned can consume only the foulest food for nourishment. If debits and credits cancel each other out, the soul is placed in Hammistagan ("region of the mixed"), a transitional realm in which souls are neither happy nor sorrowful and in which they will abide until the final **apocalypse.** In latter texts, a person's deeds greet him on the bridge in personified form—a beautiful maiden for a good person; an ugly hag for a bad person—who either leads the soul to paradise ("the luminous mansions of the sky") or embraces the soul and falls into hell, according to whether the person has been good or evil.

After the final battle between good and evil, there will be a general judgment in which everyone will be put through an ordeal of fire (a river of molten metal); good individuals will have their dross burned away and evil people will be consumed. Thus, the souls of the damned will trade their ongoing torment in hell for a painful annihilation. The souls of the blessed, on the other hand, will be resurrected in physical bodies, which Ahura Mazda will make both immortal and eternally youthful. (In a later modification of tradition, both good and evil souls have their dross burned away, so that everyone shares the postresurrection paradise.)

The concept of resurrection as formulated in Zoroastrianism represents one of the earliest efforts to conceive of immortality. It is part of an optimistic vision of the end of the world, in which the forces of light overcome darkness and all humankind rejoices with the renewal of creation. An entire section of the Avesta explains how the body is returned to the soul upon the moment of reunion and resurrection.

The final great transformation, called the "making wonderful," is described by scholar Norman Cohn (1993, 98–99) as follows:

> The earth will be flattened by the fiery flood, so that its surface will be a single level plain: the snow-covered mountains of Iran—first thrown up as a result of Angra Mainyu's onslaught—will be no more. In this perfect environment the surviving human beings will live in the most perfect harmony with one another. Husbands and wives and children, including of course the resurrected dead, will be re-united and will live together as they do in this present world—except that there will be no more begetting of children. All mankind will form a single community of devout Zoroastrians, all united in adoration of Ahura Mazda and the Holy Immortals, and all at one in thought word and deed.

Many of the components of this vision of the end times—a final battle between good and evil, judgment of the wicked, resurrection of the dead—were adopted by Jewish apocalyptic thinkers. From texts composed by these apocalypticists, such notions were adopted by Christianity and Islam.

Sources:

Biedermann, Hans. *Dictionary of Symbolism: Cultural Icons and the Meanings Behind Them.* New York: Meridian, 1994.

ZOROASTRIANISM

Cohn, Norman. *Cosmos, Chaos and the World to Come: The Ancient Roots of Apocalyptic Faith.* New Haven, CT: Yale University Press, 1993.

Eliade, Mircea. *The Encyclopedia of Religion.* 16 vols. New York: Macmillan, 1987.

Pavry, Jal Dastur Cursetji. *The Zoroastrian Doctrine of a Future Life.* New York: Columbia University Press, 1926.

Turner, Alice K. *The History of Hell.* New York: Harcourt Brace, 1993.

List of Illustrations

p. 14 A ghost dancer who has passed out, and who is presumably communicating with departed relatives and friends. (From James Mooney, *The Ghost-Dance Religion and Wounded Knee.* [1896]) Courtesy of the American Religions Collection.

p. 18 Ancestor mask, Western Sudan. Courtesy of Dover.

p. 20 *Death and the Gravedigger* by Belgian painter Carlos Schwabe (1866–1926).

p. 21 Angel from *The Fall of the Rebel Angels* by Peter Brueghel the Younger, ca. 1600. Courtesy of Dover.

p. 22 Botticini's *Tobias and the Angels* (15th century).

p. 24 The opening of the sixth seal. Courtesy of Dover.

p. 31 Babylon at the time of Nebuchadrezzar II. The great Ziggurat stands at the left. Courtesy of the American Religions Collection.

p. 32 The ascension of Christ. Courtesy of Dover.

p. 36 The constellations and the stars. Courtesy of Dover.

p. 41 Aztec god of death. Courtesy of Dover.

p. 49 Bai, or soul-bird, from a wall painting, 13th century B.C. Courtesy of Dover.

p. 51 Helena Petrovna Blavatsky and American Co-Founder of the Theosophical Society, Henry Steele Olcott. Courtesy of the American Religions Collection.

p. 54 *The Last Judgment* by Hieronymus Bosch.

p. 56 Souls crossing the bridge to the otherworld. Fresco in the Church of Santa Maria, Loretto Aprutino, Italy, 13th century.

p. 57 Mara, the Buddhist tempter and arch fiend. Courtesy of Dover.

p. 58 Citipati, bronze figurine, Tibet, 19th century. Courtesy of Dover.

Related Organizations Appendix

ACADEMY OF PSYCHIC ARTS AND SCIENCES
100 Turtle Creek Village, Ste. 363
PO Box 191129
Dallas, TX 75219
Publishes *The Timothy Letter.*

ACADEMY OF RELIGION AND PSYCHICAL RESEARCH (ARPR)
PO Box 614
Bloomfield, CT 06002
Publishes *The Journal of Religion and Psychical Research.*

AMERICAN ASSOCIATION—ELECTRONIC VOICE PHENOMENA
726 Dill Rd.
Severna Park, MD 21146
Individuals interested in researching evidence of post-mortem survival, especially as evidenced in verbal communication via tape recorders, television, or other electronic equipment. Publishes *AA-EVP News.*

AMERICAN ASSOCIATION FOR PARAPSYCHOLOGY (AAP)
PO Box 225
Canoga Park, CA 91305
Formerly, American Parapsychological Research Association.

AMERICAN SOCIETY FOR PSYCHICAL RESEARCH (ASPR)
5 W. 73rd St.
New York, NY 10023
Publishes the *ASPR Newsletter* and *The Journal of the American Society for Psychical Research.*

ASSOCIATION FOR RESEARCH AND ENLIGHTENMENT (ARE)
PO Box 595, Atlantic Ave.
Virginia Beach, VA 23451
Affiliated with the Edgar Cayce Foundation. Publishes *Perspective on Consciousness and Psi Research* and *Venture Inward.*

ASSOCIATION FOR THE STUDY OF KARMA
23 S. Knoxville
Tulsa, OK 74112
Publishes *The Inner "I."*

Appendix of Related Organizations

AWARENESS RESEARCH FOUNDATION (ARF)
c/o Jewell Pallant, Msc.D
PO Box 218
Brasstown, NC 28902
Publications include *Meet the Lords* and *My Visits to Other Planets, Technique of Past Lives Recall.*

CHURCH OF SCIENTOLOGY INTERNATIONAL
6331 Hollywood Blvd.
Los Angeles, CA 90028
Headquarters of Scientology movement and overall organizing body for Dianetic therapy.

GHOST RESEARCH SOCIETY
PO Box 205
Oak Lawn, IL 60454
Publications include the *Astrology Directory* and the *International Directory of Psychic Sciences.*

HAUNT HUNTERS (HH)
2188 Sycamore Hill Ct.
Chesterfield, MO 63017
Publications include *Haunt Hunters Handbook for the Psychic Investigator* and *To Catch a Ghost: A New Approach to the Ancient Art of Exorcism.*

IMMORTALIST SOCIETY (IS)
c/o Mae Junod
24443 Roanoke
Oak Park, MI 48237
Promotes research and education in life extension sciences, particularly cryobiology, cryogenics, and cryonics. Publishes *The Immortalist* in conjunction with the American Cryonics Society.

INTERNATIONAL ASSOCIATION FOR CONSCIOUS DYING
PO Box 1359
Ojai, CA 93024-1359
Conducts seminars and publishes *The Clear Light* newsletter.

INTERNATIONAL ASSOCIATION FOR NEAR-DEATH STUDIES
PO Box 7767
Philadelphia, PA 19101-7767
Publishes the *Journal of Near-Death Studies* and *Revitalized Signs.*

LAST WORD: THERAPIES, INC.
PO Box 20151
Riverside, CA 92516
Formerly, Association for Past-Life Research and Therapies (APRT).

NATIONAL PSYCHIC SCIENCE ASSOCIATION
c/o Rev. Richard Breitbarth
17 Baird Pl.
Whippany, NJ 07981

NATIONAL SPIRITUAL SCIENCE CENTER
409 Butternut St., NW, Ste. 1
Washington, DC 20012
Publishes *In Spirit Newsletter* quarterly.

NATIONAL SPIRITUALIST ASSOCIATION OF CHURCHES
PO Box 217
Lily Dale, NY 14752-0217
Publishes the *National Spiritualist.*

PARAPSYCHOLOGY ASSOCIATION (PA)
PO Box 12236
Research Triangle Park, NC 27709
Publishes *Research in Parapsychology.*

PARAPSYCHOLOGY SERVICES INSTITUTE
5575 B Chamblee-Dunwoody Rd., Ste. 323
Atlanta, GA 30338
Absorbed the Psychical Research Foundation. Publishes *The InPSIder.*

PSYCHIC SCIENCE INTERNATIONAL SPECIAL INTEREST GROUP
7514 Belleplain Dr.
Huber Heights, OH 45424-3229
Publications include the *PSI-M.*

REINCARNATIONISTS, INC.
Malibu, CA
Sponsors and conducts seminars on reincarnation and past-life regression.

SURVIVAL RESEARCH FOUNDATION (SRF)
PO Box 63-0026
Miami, FL 33163-0026
Maintains Institute for the Interdisciplinary Study of Death.

THEATER OF THE MIND
PO Box 417
Anniston, AL 36202

UNIVERSAL SPIRITUALIST ASSOCIATION
c/o Maple Grove Spiritual Retreat
PO Box 379
Pendleton, IN 46064-0379

INDEX

C

D

E

F

G

H

I

J

K

L

N

P

S

U

V

W

X

Y

Z